UNDERSTANDING AND USING LOTUS® 1-2-3®

Release 2.2

Steven C. Ross
College of Business and Economics
Western Washington University

West Publishing Company
St. Paul ▪ New York ▪ Los Angeles ▪ San Francisco

Cover Design: Bob Anderson, Computer Arts, Inc.

CREDITS:

• Certain screen displays Copyright© Lotus Development Corporation. Reprint by permission

50 West Kellogg Boulevard
P.O. Box 64526
St. Paul, MN 55164-1003

Printed in the United States of America

97 96 95 94 93 92 91 8 7 6 5 4 3 2 1

Library of Congress Cataloging-in-Publication Data

Ross, Steven C.
Understanding and using Lotus 1-2-3, release 2.2

1. Lotus 1-2-3 (Computer program) 2. Business Data processing.
I. Title. II. Title: Understanding and using Lotus one-two-three.
HF 5548.4.L67 1986 650'.028'55369 85-26505
ISBN 0-314-70104-4

CONTENTS

PUBLISHER'S NOTE

This book is part of THE MICROCOMPUTING SERIES. We are proud to announce that this unique series is now entering its fifth year, and currently includes four different types of books:

1. A core concepts book, now in its second edition, teaches basic hardware and software applications concepts. This text is titled UNDERSTANDING AND USING MICROCOMPUTERS.

2. A series on introductory level, hands-on workbooks covering a wide variety of specific software packages. These provide both self-paced tutorials and complete reference guides. Each book's title begins with UNDERSTANDING AND USING . . . .

3. Several larger volumes combine DOS with popular software packages. Several of these volumes are called UNDERSTANDING AND USING APPLICATION SOFTWARE, while one is titled UNDERSTANDING AND USING SHAREWARE APPLICATION SOFTWARE. These versions condense components of the individual workbooks while increasing the coverage of DOS and the integration of different application packages.

4. An advanced level of hands-on workbooks provides a strong project/systems orientation. These titles all begin with DEVELOPING AND USING . . . .

Our goal has always been to provide maximum flexibility in meeting the changing needs of microcomputing courses through this "mix and match" approach. We remain committed to offering the widest variety of current software packages.

We now offer these books in THE MICROCOMPUTING SERIES:

Understanding and Using Microcomputers, 2nd Edition
by Steven M. Zimmerman and Leo M. Conrad

(continued)

OPERATING SYSTEMS

Understanding and Using MS-DOS/PC DOS: The First Steps, 2nd Edition
by Laura B. Ruff and Mary K. Weitzer

Understanding and Using MS-DOS/PC DOS 4.0
by Jonathan P. Bacon

Understanding and Using MS-DOS/PC DOS: A Complete Guide
by Cody T. Copeland and Jonathan P. Bacon

Understanding and Using MS-DOS/PC DOS: Hard Disk Edition
by Cody T. Copeland and Jonathan P. Bacon

PROGRAMMING LANGUAGES

Understanding and Using Microsoft BASIC/IBM-PC BASIC
by Mary L. Howard

WORD PROCESSORS

Understanding and Using DisplayWrite 4
by Patsy H. Lund and Barbara A. Hayden

Understanding and Using Microsoft Word
by Jonathan P. Bacon

Understanding and Using MultiMate
by Mary K. Weitzer and Laura B. Ruff

Understanding and Using PC-Write
by Victor P. Maiorana

Understanding and Using WordStar 4.0
by Patsy H. Lund and Barbara A. Hayden

Understanding and Using pfs:WRITE
by Mary K. Weitzer and Laura B. Ruff

Understanding and Using WordPerfect
by Patsy H. Lund and Barbara A. Hayden

Understanding and Using WordPerfect 5.0
by Patsy H. Lund

Understanding and Using WordStar
by Steven C. Ross

SPREADSHEET PACKAGES

Understanding and Using Lotus 1-2-3
by Steven C. Ross

Understanding and Using Lotus 1-2-3 Release 2
by Steven C. Ross

Understanding and Using Lotus 1-2-3 Release 2.2
by Steven C. Ross

Understanding and Using SuperCalc 3
by Steven C. Ross and Judy A. Reinders

Understanding and Using SuperCalc 4
by Judy A. Reinders and Steven C. Ross

Understanding and Using VP-Planner Plus
by Steven C. Ross

DATABASE PACKAGES

Understanding and Using dBASE III (Including dBASE II)
by Steven C. Ross

Understanding and Using dBASE III PLUS
by Steven C. Ross

Understanding and Using dBASE IV
by Steven C. Ross

Understanding and Using pfs:FILE/REPORT
by Laura B. Ruff and Mary K. Weitzer

Understanding and Using R:BASE 5000 (Including R:BASE System V)
by Karen L. Watterson

INTEGRATED SOFTWARE

Understanding and Using Appleworks (Including Appleworks 2.0)
by Frank Short

Understanding and Using Educate-Ability
by Victor P. Maiorana and Arthur A. Strunk

Understanding and Using FRAMEWORK
by Karen L. Watterson

Understanding and Using Symphony
by Enzo V. Allegretti

Understanding and Using pfs:First Choice
by Seth A. Hock

COMBINATION VOLUMES

Understanding and Using Application Software, V. 1: WordStar 4.0, DOS, Lotus 1-2-3 Release 2, and dBASE III PLUS
by Steven Ross, Patsy Lund and Barbara Hayden

Understanding and Using Application Software, V. 2: DOS, WordPerfect 4.2, Lotus 1-2-3 Release 2, and dBASE III PLUS
by Steven Ross, Patsy Lund and Barbara Hayden

Understanding and Using Application Software, V.4: DOS, WordPerfect 5.0, Lotus 1-2-3 Release 2, and dBASE III PLUS
by Patsy Lund, Jonathan Bacon and Steve Ross

Understanding and Using SHAREWARE Application Software: DOS, PC-Write, ExpressCalc, and PC-FILE
by Victor P. Maiorana

Understanding and Using Application Software, Volume 3: DOS, WordPerfect 4.2, VP-Planner Plus, and dBASE III PLUS
by Steven C. Ross and Patsy H. Lund

ADVANCED BOOKS

Developing and Using Decision Support Applications
by Steven C. Ross, Richard J. Penlesky and Lloyd D. Doney

Developing and Using Office Applications with AppleWorks
by M. S. Varnon

Developing and Using Microcomputer Business Systems
by Kathryn W. Huff

We are delighted by the popularity of THE MICROCOMPUTING SERIES. We appreciate your support, and look forward to your suggestions and comments. Please write to us at this address:

West Publishing Company,
College Division
50 West Kellogg Blvd.,
P.O. Box 64526, St. Paul, MN 55102

ABOUT THE AUTHOR

Steven C. Ross holds a B.S. degree in History from Oregon State University and M.S. and Ph.D. degrees in Business Administration from The University of Utah. He is an Associate Professor of Management Information Systems at Western Washington University, Bellingham. His previous positions were as Associate Professor of Information Systems at Montana State University, Bozeman, and Assistant Professor of Management at Marquette University in Milwaukee, Wisconsin. His responsibilities include the introduction of microcomputers into the primary computer courses and the integration of computer applications throughout the curriculum.

Dr. Ross is author or co-author of a dozen articles dealing with information management and education, and this is one of fifteen books in microcomputing that he has written or edited. Two of his books in this series have been translated into French. He also consults with businesses of all sizes to integrate microcomputers into the managerial operations of those organizations. His teaching and consulting experiences have provided ample material for this book.

PREFACE

. . . if you had no power of calculation you would not be able to calculate on future pleasure, and your life would be the life, not of a man, but of an oyster.

Socrates

Understanding and Using Lotus 1-2-3 Release 2.2 is about calculating using personal computers — specifically, the use of the popular program Lotus 1-2-3. Calculation is a fundamental aspect of the analysis of data, and the business student and professional must be a skillful analyst if he or she is to be a successful manager. Not only is the Lotus 1-2-3 package a powerful analysis tool in its own right, it is also a good tool for learning about data analysis in general.

WHY THIS BOOK?

There are many books available that discuss Lotus 1-2-3 Release 2.2. Why then would anyone write another book? I decided to do so because both my students and my colleagues at several universities desired a book tailored to the way personal computing is taught at the college and professional level. We felt that there was no book designed for use in academic or workshop settings. We felt a need for a book that would present concepts and skills as well as provide activities, applications, and questions for practice and teaching purposes. *Understanding and Using Lotus 1-2-3 Release 2.2* is such a book.

This book is designed to support the efforts of the instructor by providing the essential facets of the software combined with activities and exercises to reinforce and evaluate the student's learning experience. Examples are drawn from the fields of business administration and economics to illustrate how the software may be used in other course work and in the daily tasks performed by business professionals. The instructor's manual provides supplementary materials and suggestions for integrating this book with other course materials.

This book serves a different role than the reference manuals furnished with the Lotus 1-2-3 Release 2.2 software. These manuals are quite comprehensive, but often are difficult to read and fail to provide adequate examples. This book is designed for instruction in fundamental, intermediate, and advanced operations, supported with substantial reference material. When more detailed information is required, the user will have a significant foundation.

Finally, *Understanding and Using Lotus 1-2-3 Release 2.2* serves as a member of THE MICROCOMPUTING SERIES published by West Publishing Company. It may be used alone, in combination with other books in the series (listed in the Publisher's Note starting on page xiii), or to supplement any other book in a course where a knowledge of Lotus 1-2-3 Release 2.2 is required.

HOW TO USE THIS BOOK

You should complete the first four units in the order presented. With that background, the material in the remainder of the book may be covered in the order that suits you best — although several units do assume that you have completed earlier units and build upon that knowledge base. The more work you do on the computer, the better you will learn the topics. As a minimum, you should complete the Guided Activities with each unit. I strongly encourage you to work through the Exercises and Applications also. Each activity and exercise is designed to illustrate points made in the previous units, and many contain additional material that is best presented during a computer session.

Each unit includes the following features:

Learning Objectives: the knowledge and skills addressed in the unit.

Important Commands: the commands to be covered, which will later serve as a quick reference to the contents of the unit.

Computer Screens: figures depicting the steps and results of most commands.

Guided Activities: step-by-step, hands-on illustrations of the operations discussed in the unit. The activities contain Checkpoints, which ask you questions as you work to further develop your knowledge and skill level. The answers to the Checkpoints are found in Appendix B.

Exercises: additional computer work designed to challenge your knowledge of the material presented in the unit. Some of these have specific instructions, others provide less guidance.

Review Questions: questions designed to test your understanding of the material presented. The answers to selected review questions are contained in Appendix B.

Documentation Research: exercises that require you to use the software publisher's documentation to learn more about the commands and functions discussed in the unit.

Additional features of *Understanding and Using Lotus 1-2-3 Release 2.2* are as follows:

Applications: nine exercises spread throughout the book that provide additional practice using the material presented. These are designed to be more challenging than the Guided Activities and Exercises.

Getting Started on Your Microcomputer: this appendix is provided as a quick reference for those who need a refresher or minimal reference for the computer hardware and the disk operating system.

Lotus 1-2-3 Release 2.2 Functions: this appendix contains a list and short discussion of each Lotus 1-2-3 Release 2.2 function.

Lotus 1-2-3 Release 2.2 Commands: this appendix contains a list and short discussion of each Lotus 1-2-3 Release 2.2 command.

Indexes: several indexes cover commands, functions, symbols, and other topics. These are designed to allow you to quickly locate the relevant information.

Keyboard Diagram and **Quick Reference**: these references are placed at the back of the book, where you can easily refer to them.

The West Student Data Disk: the data disk, included in this manual, contains the files needed as input for the Guided Activities, Exercises, and Applications.

A NOTE OF THANKS . . .

to my mother and father, who are still encouraging my analytical interests;

to the students and faculty at the many universities and colleges who have used the earlier editions of this book;

to Rick Leyh, Susan Smart, and Connie Austin of West Publishing, and copy editor Sheryl Rose, who guided me in the development of a presentable manuscript;

to the reviewers of this manuscript, Barbarann Beckett, Jefferson State Community College; Paul Chase, Becker Junior College; Maria A. Fine, Lakehead University; Eleanor J. Flanigan, Montclair State College; Donald J. Huffman, Lorain County Community College; Thomas Lightner, University of Colorado; Joseph C. Otto, California State University, Los Angeles; Cheryl Rumler, Monroe County Community College; Jerry Sands, Indian Hills Community College; and Robert E. Schubert, Johnson County Community College; whose comments have enhanced the accuracy and readability of this work;

to the reviewers of earlier versions of the Lotus 1-2-3 books, Bill Cummings, Northern Illinois University; Mary Joan Draxler, Madison Area Technical College; Gary Gora, Northern Alberta Institute of Technology; Leonard Presby, William Paterson State College; Ralph Shafer, George Washington University; David Cooper, University of Connecticut; Eileen Bechtold Dlugoss, Cuyahoga Community College; Arthur Strunk, Queensborough Community College; and Kathleen Tesker, St. Louis Community College; whose efforts laid a strong foundation for this edition; and

to Meredith, Kelly, and Shannon: nobody said this was going to be easy.

I hope each of you is pleased with the final product.

S.C.R.
Bellingham
New Year's Eve, 1989

PART I

FUNDAMENTAL SPREADSHEET OPERATIONS

This is the first of three parts in this manual. In this part, we cover fundamental information that you must know to use Lotus 1-2-3 and to construct useful spreadsheets. We discuss how Lotus 1-2-3 uses the keyboard, the screen display, and the spreadsheet concept.

With that background, we address the types of cell entries, how to enter and edit information in cells, and how to save worksheets to and retrieve worksheets from disk storage. Then we learn how to use Lotus 1-2-3 arithmetic and functions to enter information into a spreadsheet. This part includes an introduction to some of the more commonly used worksheet and range commands. The final topic concerns printing the worksheet.

The application exercise at the end of this part guides you through the development of a simple spreadsheet. At the conclusion of the application exercise, you will have a good introduction to working with Lotus 1-2-3. The remainder of this manual prepares you to accomplish more sophisticated tasks.

Which Release of Lotus 1-2-3 are you using? This book was written specifically for Release 2.2 of Lotus 1-2-3, and separate books are available for other releases. If you will be using one of the other releases (1A, 2, or 3) exclusively, you should obtain the version of *Understanding and Using Lotus 1-2-3* written specifically for that release. Many of the features of Lotus have not changed from one version to the next, however, so the knowledge you gain from this book is generally applicable to all versions of Lotus 1-2-3.

The West Student Data Disk. A disk containing five files is supplied with this lab manual. This disk is called the *West Student Data Disk to Accompany Understanding and Using Lotus 1-2-3 Release 2.2*. In Unit 2, we make a backup copy of the West Student Data Disk, but the files on the disk are not needed until you start to work on assignments in Part 3 of this manual.

UNIT 1

THE LOTUS ENVIRONMENT

Before the fun of spreadsheeting can begin, we must know how to load Lotus 1-2-3 into the computer and how Lotus uses the keyboard.

LEARNING OBJECTIVES

1. At the completion of this unit, you should know
   a. how Lotus uses the keyboard keys,
   b. what the 1-2-3 Access System is.
2. At the completion of this unit, you should be able to
   a. load the 1-2-3 Access System,
   b. enter Lotus 1-2-3 spreadsheet mode.

IMPORTANT COMMANDS

LOTUS
123

THE LOTUS DISKETTES

The Lotus 1-2-3 software package is supplied on several diskettes. If you are using a hard disk or networked computer system in a school or other organization, you might never see the diskettes. But, if you own your own copy of Lotus 1-2-3 or are using a floppy disk system, you will need to use one or more of the diskettes to load the program. The most important disk is the **System Disk**, which contains the 1-2-3 program. In some cases, this disk also has a copy of PC-DOS on it so that the system can be turned on or reset using the Lotus 1-2-3 System Disk (therefore eliminating the need for a separate DOS disk).

The 1-2-3 program contained on the System Disk is used for all spreadsheet, data, and on-screen graphics operations. To obtain graphics output on paper, the PrintGraph program is used; it is contained on the Lotus 1-2-3 **PrintGraph Disk**.

Lotus tells you when to insert the PrintGraph Disk into the disk drive.

Additional disks are labeled with names like **Help Disk**, **Translate Disk**, **Install Disk**, **Install Library Disk**, and several **Allways** disks. (The names differ slightly between 5¼" and 3½" disk sets.) Lotus prompts you when you need to insert a disk other than the disk currently in the disk drive.

THE LOTUS 1-2-3 KEYBOARD

In this section we describe typical personal computer keyboards, illustrated in the back of this manual. Other keyboards are similar, although placement and color of specific keys and the text or characters used to identify the key might vary slightly. The IBM and other personal computers have over eighty keys, about forty more than most typewriters. Many of the "extra" keys have symbols or mnemonics rather than characters. To minimize confusion, we use the following conventions in this manual to refer to specific keys.

The names of keys with multiple character names or symbols[1] are enclosed in < > (less-than and greater-than signs) and spelled out, usually followed by the word *key* (e.g., <F1> key, <Home> key, <Shift> key). The following keys are identified only by symbols on some keyboards — make sure you know where they are on *your* keyboard.

<Tab>	A gray key, usually to the left of the Q key, with two arrows pointing in opposite directions on it.
<Shift>	Two gray keys, usually to the left and right of the bottom row of letter keys, with open arrows that point up.
<Backspace>	A gray key at the top of the keyboard, with an arrow pointing left.
<Enter>	A gray key with a "bent" arrow pointing down and left. This key is sometimes called "the return key."
<Arrow> keys	A set of white keys on the right of the keyboard, also called <Up>, <Left>, <Down>, and <Right>. Note that <Left> and <Backspace> are two different keys and that they do different things. Some keyboards have a separate keypad containing only the <Arrow> keys.

MULTIPLE KEY COMBINATIONS

Most people know how to use the <Shift> key on a typewriter to produce a capital letter: hold down the <Shift> while pressing the letter key. On a computer, the <Ctrl> and <Alt> keys work like the <Shift> key. To type <Alt-M>, hold down the <Alt> key, press **M**, then release both keys.

1. On some keyboards, the <Tab>, <Shift>, <Backspace>, and <Enter> keys have words and symbols; on other keyboards they contain only symbols.

FUNCTION KEYS

These are the gray keys across the top or on the left of the keyboard. Lotus names all the function keys and furnishes a template that identifies the names of the keys. (Your organization might attach the template, or a copy, to the keyboard; if not, mark the location of Table 1-1 so you can quickly refer to it as you use this book.) We follow the Lotus convention of naming keys; for instance, the <F1> key is called HELP and it is listed in this book as <HELP (F1)>. The names apply to function keys <F1> through <F10>, and also to <Alt-F1> through <Alt-F5> and <Alt-F7> through <Alt-F10>.

Four of the keys are immediately useful:

<HELP (F1)> Starts you through a series of Help menus. When you have had enough help, press the <Esc> key to get back to the spreadsheet.

<EDIT (F2)> Allows you to edit the contents of the cell under the cursor. Press the <Enter> key when finished editing.

<GOTO (F5)> Takes you to a specific spreadsheet cell or named range.

<UNDO (Alt-F4)> Allows you to reverse the most recent change to the worksheet. Usually used when you make an entry in the wrong cell: press <UNDO (Alt-F4)> and the wrong entry is replaced by the original entry.

The others are discussed as needed in later units. See Table 1-1 for a complete list.

Table 1-1 Lotus 1-2-3 Function Key Names

HELP (F1)	COMPOSE (Alt-F1)
EDIT (F2)	STEP (Alt-F2)
NAME (F3)	RUN (Alt-F3)
ABS (F4)	UNDO (Alt-F4)
GOTO (F5)	LEARN (Alt-F5)
WINDOW (F6)	
QUERY (F7)	APP1 (Alt-F7)
TABLE (F8)	APP2 (Alt-F8)
CALC (F9)	APP3 (Alt-F9)
GRAPH (F10)	APP4 (Alt-F10)

NUMERIC KEYPAD KEYS

These are the white keys on the right side of the keyboard. On some keyboards, these keys appear in two places, both by themselves and also combined with the numeric keypad.

<Arrow> keys	These keys move the cell pointer one cell up, left, right, or down. If you try to move beyond the edge of the screen, the screen will shift so the cell can be viewed. You cannot move <Up> from row 1, <Left> from column A, <Down> from row 8192, or <Right> from column IV.
<Home>	Moves the cell pointer to Cell A1: upper left corner of spreadsheet.
<PgUp>	Moves the cell pointer up one screen, usually 20 rows.
<PgDn>	Moves the cell pointer down one screen, usually 20 rows.
<End>	Used with other cell pointer movement keys: press <End>, then press one of the <Arrow> keys or the <Home> key. (Do not hold down <End> while pressing the other key; release it first.) <End> + <Home> moves to the lower right cell of the active area. <End> + <Arrow> key moves to the last occupied cell in the direction of the arrow. Experiment with this key to learn what it does.
<Del>	Used to delete the character under the cursor.

OTHER KEYS

Several other keys are assigned special functions in Lotus 1-2-3:

<Num Lock>	Puts keypad in numeric mode. To use the <Arrow> keys, you must hold down the <Shift> key.
<Backspace>	Erases the character to the left of the cursor in either input or edit mode.
<Scroll Lock>	When engaged, the <Arrow> keys move the spreadsheet instead of the cell pointer; try it!
<Esc>	Use the <Esc> key to **undo** or **back up** as you move through command menus. Also cancels the cell entry if pressed before you press <Enter>.
<Tab> and <Ctrl-Right>	Move the cell pointer to the right one full screen.
<Shift-Tab> and <Ctrl-Left>	Move the cell pointer left one full screen.
<Break>	The combination of <Ctrl> and <Scroll Lock> keys: hold down <Ctrl> and press <Scroll Lock>. This stops most printing and calculating processes.
<PrtSc>	The combination of <Shift-PrtSc> sends a snapshot of the screen to the printer. This capability is especially useful when you are having problems and no one is available to help you. Make a screen print and take that print to your instructor or friend.

GUIDED ACTIVITY: STARTUP PROCEDURE

The procedure for starting Lotus 1-2-3 varies from place to place, and perhaps from computer to computer.[1] In this Guided Activity, we discuss two typical procedures with floppy disk and hard disk and network systems; if necessary your instructor will describe any differences for your particular organization. To start Lotus 1-2-3, you need a configured copy of Lotus 1-2-3[2] and a formatted disk to hold the files you create.

FLOPPY DISK SYSTEMS

If the computer you are using has Lotus 1-2-3 installed on a hard disk or network, you should skip this section and follow the instructions under "Hard Disk and Network Systems."

1. Insert a disk with the Disk Operating System (DOS) in Drive A. Your instructor will tell you how to locate a DOS disk. Place a formatted disk in Drive B. This disk is for the worksheet files that you create. Note: *Do not* use the West Student Data Disk supplied with this manual. That disk is write-protected and you cannot save files on it. The West Student Data Disk is not used until you start Part 3 of this manual.
2. Reset or turn on the machine, as appropriate. Remember to enter the date and time as prompted. Once you have the command prompt (A>_), remove the DOS disk and insert the Lotus System Disk.
3. Enter the command **B:** <Enter> to make Drive B the default disk drive.
4. Enter the command **LOTUS**<Enter> and the disk will load the 1-2-3 Access System.
5. You should now see the 1-2-3 Access System Menu (Figure 1-1). `1-2-3` is highlighted; press the <Enter> key to initiate the 1-2-3 session.
6. After the program is loaded, you see the copyright screen (Figure 1-2). This screen clears after a short time and you see an empty Lotus 1-2-3 spreadsheet (Figure 1-3). Cell A1 is highlighted. In Lotus there are two cursors: one in the second line that shows where you are as you make an entry, and another in the bottom 20 lines that shows which cell is active. The latter cursor is also called the **cell pointer.**
7. The next Guided Activity takes you on a short tour of the spreadsheet using many of the keys discussed earlier in this unit.

---

1. If this is your first encounter with a personal computer, you should read Appendix A, *Getting Started on Your Microcomputer*, before proceeding.

2. If your copy of Lotus 1-2-3 has not been configured, read the *Setting Up 1-2-3* pamphlet that is in the Lotus package. Configuration is normally performed by the person who owns or is responsible for the software. The instructions that follow assume that a DOS PATH statement is included in the AUTOEXEC.BAT file pointing to A: (floppy disk systems) or C:\123 (or other appropriate directory in hard disk/network systems).

```
1-2-3  PrintGraph  Translate  Install  Exit
Use 1-2-3

                       1-2-3 Access System
                      Copyright  1986, 1989
                  Lotus Development Corporation
                       All Rights Reserved
                           Release 2.2

The Access system lets you choose 1-2-3, PrintGraph, the Translate utility,
and the Install program, from the menu at the top of this screen.  If
you're using a two-diskette system, the Access system may prompt you to
change disks.  Follow the instructions below to start a program.

o  Use → or ← to move the menu pointer (the highlighted rectangle
   at the top of the screen) to the program you want to use.

o  Press ENTER to start the program.

You can also start a program by typing the first character of its name.

Press HELP (F1) for more information.
```

Figure 1-1 The 1-2-3 Access System Menu

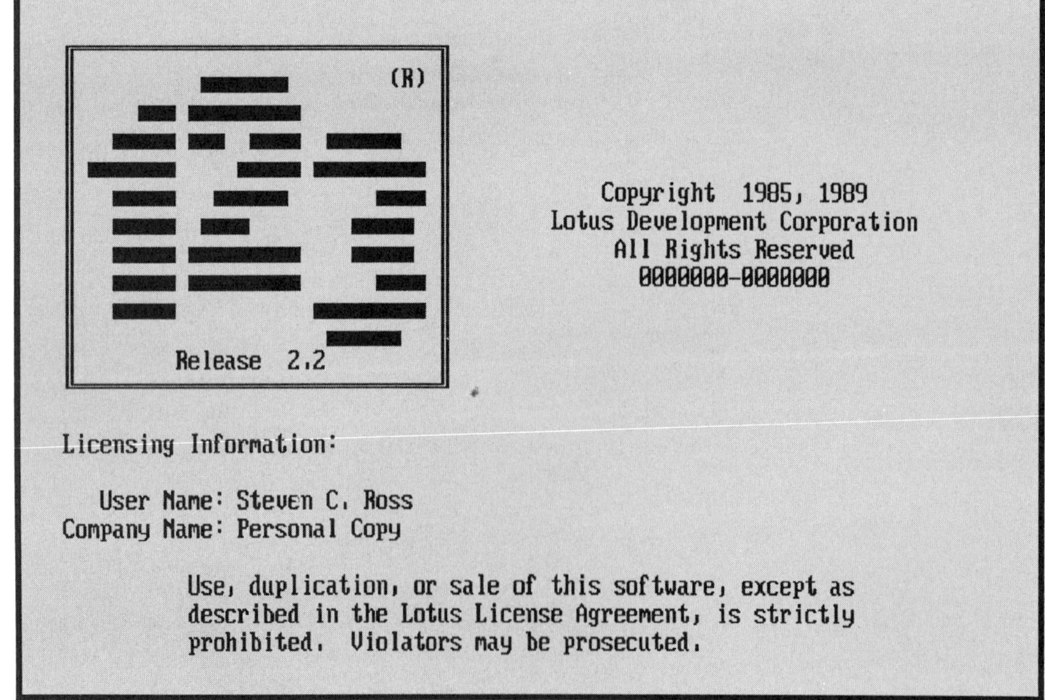

Figure 1-2 The Lotus Copyright Screen

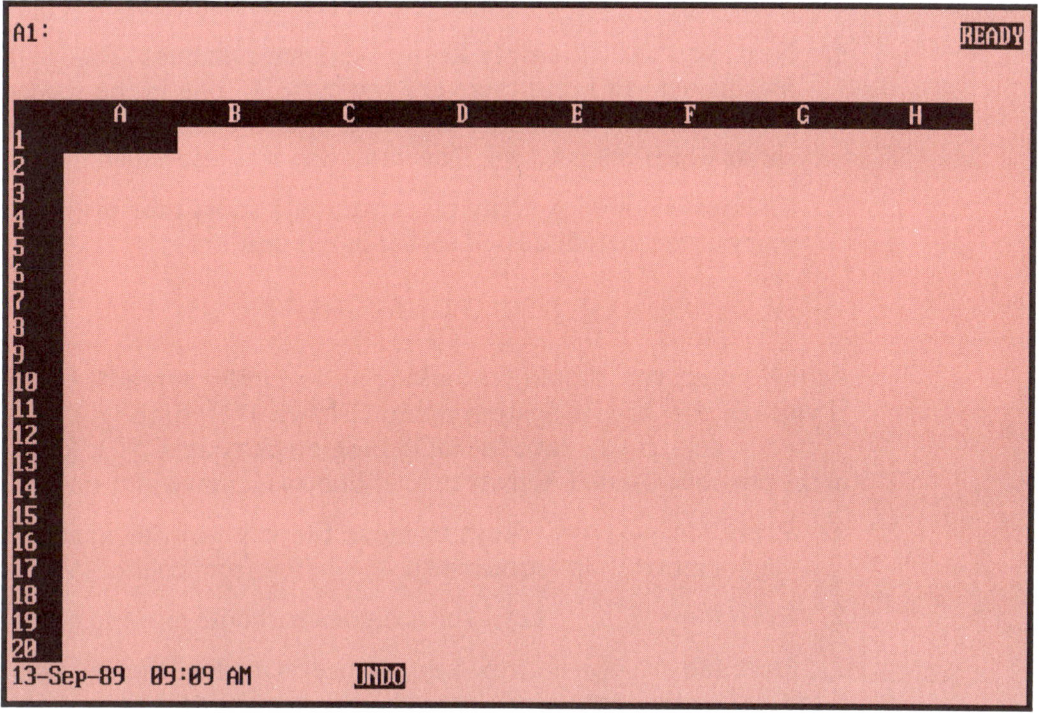

Figure 1-3 An Empty Lotus Spreadsheet

HARD DISK AND NETWORK SYSTEMS

Most hard disk and network systems have the Lotus 1-2-3 program installed on the hard disk and you do not need to use the Lotus System Disk. The command prompt for most hard disk and network systems is C>_ , indicating that the hard disk is the default disk drive.

1. Reset or turn on the machine, as appropriate. Remember to enter the date and time as prompted.

2. Put a formatted disk in the floppy disk drive. This disk is for the worksheet files that you create. Enter the command **A:** <Enter> to make Drive A the default disk drive.[1] Note: *Do not* use the West Student Data Disk supplied with this manual. That disk is write-protected and you cannot save files on it. The West Student Data Disk is not used until you start Part 3 of this manual.

3. Type **LOTUS**<Enter>, which loads the access system and presents you with the 1-2-3 Access System menu (Figure 1-1).

4. You should now see the 1-2-3 Access System Menu (Figure 1-1). `1-2-3` is highlighted; press the <Enter> key to initiate the 1-2-3 session.

---

1. If you are storing your data files in a hard disk directory, enter the command `CD\GEORGE`<Enter> (substituting the name of your directory for GEORGE) instead of changing the default disk drive.

5. After the program is loaded, you see the copyright screen (Figure 1-2).
6. Next, you see an empty Lotus 1-2-3 spreadsheet (Figure 1-3). Cell A1 is highlighted. In Lotus there are two cursors: one in the second line that shows where you are in making an entry, and another in the bottom 20 lines that shows which cell is active. The latter cursor is also called the **cell pointer.**
7. The next Guided Activity takes you on a short tour of the spreadsheet using many of the keys discussed earlier in this unit.

GUIDED ACTIVITY: A TOUR OF THE SPREADSHEET

At this point, you should be looking at an empty spreadsheet (like Figure 1-3). If you see the Access System menu (Figure 1-2), highlight 1-2-3 and press the <Enter> key. If you have the DOS prompt (A>_ or C>_), follow the instructions in the previous Guided Activity to load Lotus and move into spreadsheet mode.

1. Press the <Arrow> keys to move the cell pointer around. Note that you cannot move <Up> from row 1 or <Left> from column A.
2. Press the <Home> key. The cell pointer should move to cell A1.
3. Hold the <Down> arrow key. Notice that when the cell pointer moves below row 20, other rows scroll into view. Note which is the lowest row displayed (e.g., in Figure 1-3, row 20 is the lowest row).
4. Press the <PgDn> key. This should cause the display to jump down twenty rows.[1]
5. Press the <End> key, then press the <Right> arrow key. The cell pointer should stay in the same row, but move all the way to column IV.
6. Press the <End> key, then press the <Down> arrow key. The cell pointer should stay in column IV, but move all the way to row 8192. You are at the extreme lower right corner of the spreadsheet.
7. Press the <Arrow> keys to move the cell pointer around. Note that you cannot move <Down> from row 8192, or <Right> from column IV.
8. Move the cell pointer back to cell A1.

   CHECKPOINT

   1a. What key do you press to move quickly to cell A1?

   The answers to Checkpoint questions are contained in Appendix B.

9. We discuss how to use the spreadsheet in the next unit. At this time, exit to the 1-2-3 Access System by pressing the following sequence of keys: **/QY** (*Note*: You might have inadvertently made entries in the spreadsheet. If Lotus beeps and displays the message `WORKSHEET CHANGES NOT SAVED! End 1-2-3 anyway?`, press **Y** again.) Then exit the 1-2-3 Access System menu by pressing **E**.

---

1. Some computer systems display more than twenty rows at a time. The <PgDn> key should take you down a full page.

DIRECT ENTRY INTO 1-2-3

It is possible to bypass the 1-2-3 Access System and enter the spreadsheet mode directly. Instead of entering the command **`LOTUS`**<Enter>, enter the command **`123`**<Enter> (note: no hyphens). This displays the copyright screen (Figure 1-2), then moves directly into the 1-2-3 worksheet (Figure 1-3). This works with either floppy or hard disk systems, and is slightly quicker than going through the 1-2-3 Access System.

THE 1-2-3 ACCESS SYSTEM

MAKING CHOICES FROM LOTUS MENUS

All Lotus 1-2-3 menus work in the same manner. A number of options are listed across one row of the screen, and a detailed description of the highlighted option is listed in the next row. Use the <Left> and <Right> arrow keys to move the menu pointer, the highlighted block, from one option to another. (You can also use the <Space> bar to move the menu pointer to the right, making selection of menu choices slightly easier.) As you move the detailed description changes to correspond with the highlighted option. For instance, in Figure 1-1, the cursor is on `1-2-3` and the description below tells you that this choice allows you to `Use 1-2-3.`

Once you have highlighted the choice you want, press the <Enter> key and Lotus will execute that choice. To save time, you can press the first letter of your choice instead of using the <Arrow> and <Enter> keys.

1-2-3 ACCESS SYSTEM MENU CHOICES

You can choose among the major features of Lotus 1-2-3 with these Access System selections:

1-2-3	Enters 1-2-3; the most common choice.
PrintGraph	Used for printing graphs; we use this later.
Translate	Converts files used by other programs to and from Lotus 1-2-3 format.
Install	Used to customize Lotus; normally accomplished by the person who owns or is responsible for the software.
Exit	Returns you to the operating system command prompt (A>_ or C>_).

As discussed above, use the <Arrow> keys to highlight your choice, then press the <Enter> key. When you choose `1-2-3` the next screen is a copyright screen (see Figure 1-2). Make sure that your data disk is in Drive B (or the only drive on a hard disk or network system) and the door is closed. The screen clears again and you are presented with a blank spreadsheet (see Figure 1-3). The next unit discusses how to enter data and perform calculations on the spreadsheet.

REVIEW QUESTIONS

The answers to questions marked by an asterisk are in Appendix B.

1. List the Lotus diskettes and describe the purpose of each.
2. Describe how Lotus uses the following keyboard keys:
   a.* <HELP (F1)>
   b. <EDIT (F2)>
   c. <GOTO (F5)>
   d.* <Home>
   e. <PgUp>
   f.* <Esc>
   g. <Del>
   h.* <Backspace>
3. What are the options offered by the 1-2-3 Access System, and what do they do?
4. How do you load the 1-2-3 Access System into the computer?
5.* Once the 1-2-3 Access System is loaded, how do you enter Lotus 1-2-3 spreadsheet mode?
6. How can you bypass the Access System and directly load 1-2-3?

UNIT 2

THE LOTUS WORKSHEET

This unit takes you into the worksheet, where the value of Lotus 1-2-3 is realized. The major topics include an introduction to the spreadsheet concept, a discussion of entering and editing information in the worksheet, and an introduction to Lotus commands. Also, the very important concept of file backup is introduced.

LEARNING OBJECTIVES

1. At the completion of this unit, you should know
   a. what a cell is,
   b. the difference between label and value cell entries,
   c. how to determine a cell's address,
   d. the dimensions of the Lotus 1-2-3 worksheet,
   e. what is meant by **control panel area**,
   f. what the **pointing method** is.
2. At the completion of this unit, you should be able to
   a. determine whether or not any of the <Lock> keys are engaged,
   b. enter a label into a worksheet cell,
   c. enter a constant value into a worksheet cell,
   d. enter a formula into a worksheet cell,
   e. edit the contents of a worksheet cell,
   f. save a file to disk,
   g. retrieve a file from disk,
   h. back up the files on a data disk,
   i. exit to the 1-2-3 Access System.

IMPORTANT COMMANDS

/File Save
/File Retrieve
/System
/Quit

THE SPREADSHEET CONCEPT

WORKSHEET OR SPREADSHEET?

To differentiate its product, Lotus Development Corporation uses the term **worksheet** where the rest of the world would use the term **spreadsheet**. In this book, the two terms are used interchangeably when referring to the row and column matrix. **Worksheet file** refers to the disk file that is used to save data and other information about the worksheet.

CELLS

The **spreadsheet cell** is the building block of Lotus 1-2-3 or any other spreadsheet program. Cells can contain either numeric or text data. Text data in Lotus 1-2-3 are called **labels**, while numeric data are called **values**.

Labels. Label entries are used to explain the contents of the worksheet. Labels are primarily for user information, although they can be used in some formulas.

Values. Value entries can be one of two types, either **constant values** or **formulas**. The value of a formula changes when the arguments of the formula change, while the value of a constant value does not change unless you put a new value into that cell. The great appeal of spreadsheet programs is the ability to change one value and watch all other values that depend on the first value (via formulas) automatically change when the spreadsheet is recalculated.

ROWS

The Lotus 1-2-3 Release 2.2 worksheet contains 8192 rows, numbered 1 through 8192.

COLUMNS

The Lotus 1-2-3 worksheet contains 256 columns, lettered A through Z, AA through AZ, BA . . . IV.

CELL ADDRESSES

Cell addresses are the combination of column letter and row number. The upper left address is A1, while the extreme lower right cell address is IV8192. Notice how cell D5 is related to D4, D6, C5, and E5:

C4 D4 E4
C5 D5 E5
C6 D6 E6

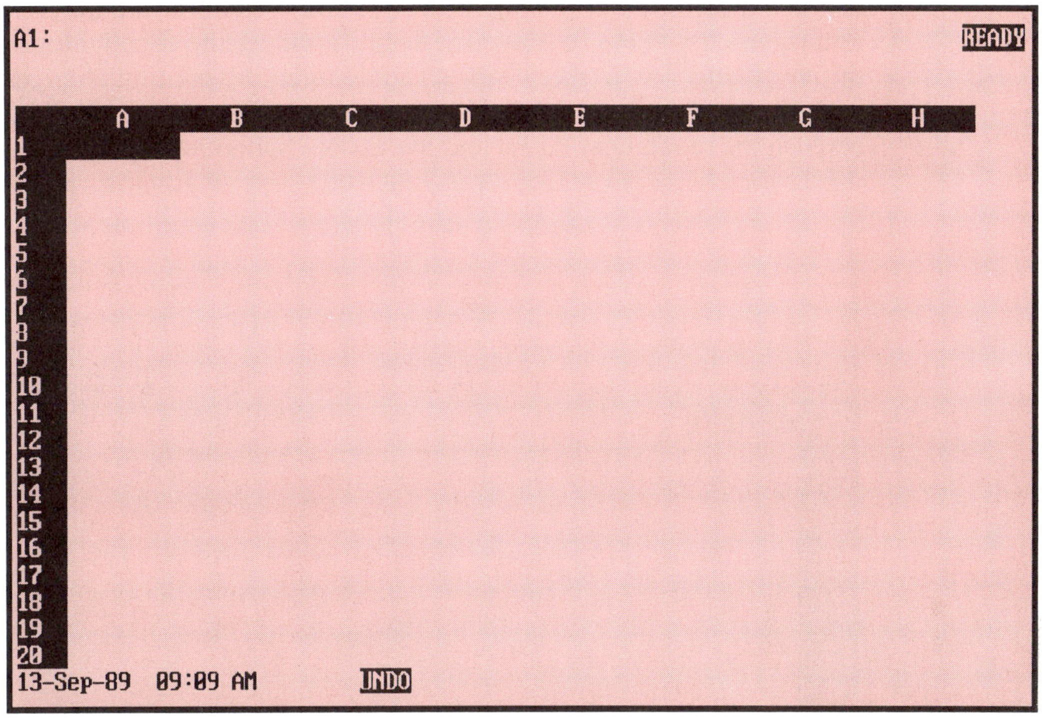

Figure 2-1 An Empty Lotus 1-2-3 Spreadsheet

THE LOTUS 1-2-3 SCREEN

Most of the screen is devoted to the display of the spreadsheet (see Figure 2-1). Typically, 20 rows and 8 columns are displayed.

The three rows on the screen above the spreadsheet are known as the **control panel** area. The left portion of the top line shows the address of the cell to which the cell pointer is pointing, the contents of the cell (formula, value, or label), and other information about the cell. In the upper right corner is the **program mode indicator**. This changes to `READY, VALUE, LABEL, EDIT, HELP,` or others as appropriate. The second and third rows are used for input and menu selections.

The bottom line of the screen contains the current system date and time and also **status indicators** that light when <Caps Lock>, <Num Lock>, or <Scroll Lock> keys are engaged: `CAPS, NUM,` and `SCROLL`. Other indicators are used to inform you of other program conditions, especially whether the Undo feature is active.

LOTUS 1-2-3 COMMANDS

Press the / (**slash** or **frontslash**) key and Lotus presents you with the top level of the command hierarchy. Remember that all Lotus 1-2-3 menus work in the same manner. A number of options are listed across the second row of the screen, and a detailed description of the highlighted option is listed in the third row. Use the left and right arrow keys to move the **menu pointer**, the highlighted block, from one option to another. As you move, the detailed description changes to correspond with the highlighted option. For instance, in Figure 2-2, the highlighted cursor rests on the menu item `File` and the various suboptions for `File` are listed on the third row.

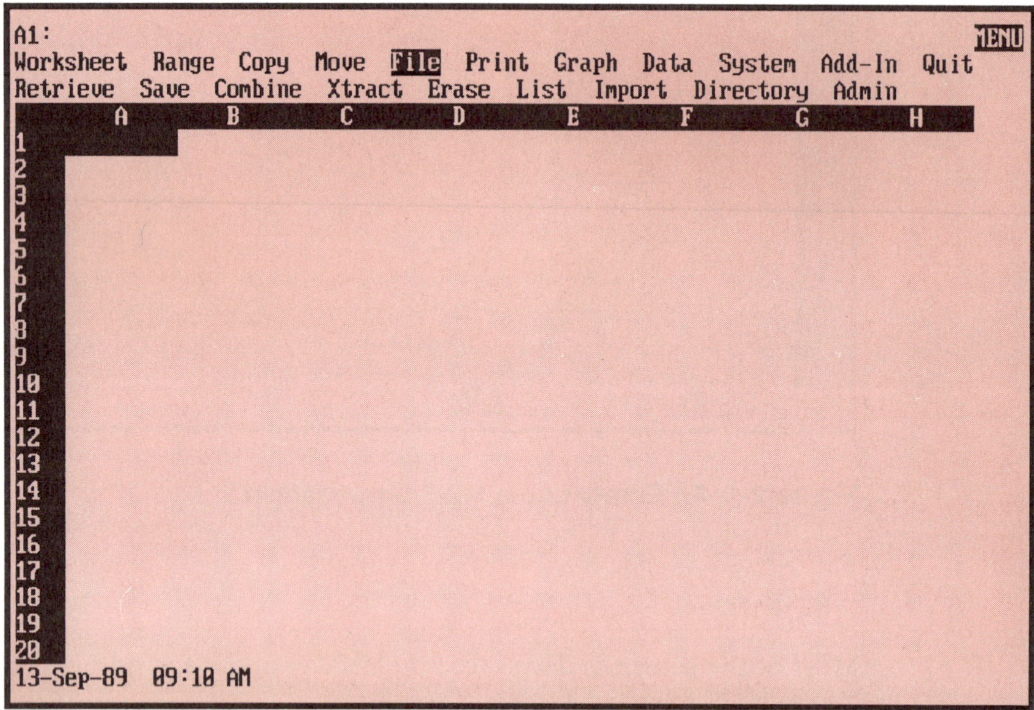

Figure 2-2 The Lotus Command Menu with /File Selected

Once you have highlighted the choice you want, press the <Enter> key and Lotus will execute that choice. To save time, you can press the first letter of your choice instead of using the <Arrow> and <Enter> keys. At the top level of the command hierarchy, the choices are

Worksheet	Operations affecting the entire worksheet.
Range	Operations affecting a selected part of the worksheet.
Copy	Operation that makes a copy of a range in a new location.
Move	Operation that moves a range to a new location.
File	Operations that move worksheet data to and from disk storage.

Print	Operations that print all or part of the worksheet; can be directed to either printer or disk file.
Graph	Operations to draw graphs on the screen and to prepare graphs for later printing.
Data	Operations that rearrange or summarize worksheet data.
System	Allows you to issue DOS commands while keeping Lotus and your current worksheet active in memory.
Add-In	Manages additional "add-in" programs designed to enhance 1-2-3.
Quit	Ends 1-2-3 program, returns to 1-2-3 Access System menu.

There are two standard methods for referring to Lotus commands. One spells out the command words, while the other shows just the initial letters (the way you would type the command). For instance, **/File Save** and **/FS** are the same command. (Uppercase letters are used in this book for command instructions, but you can use lowercase letters as well, e.g., **/fs** yields the same result as **/FS**.)

Recall that the <Esc> key can be used to **undo** or **back up** as you move through command menus. For instance, if you wished to type **/FS** but typed **/FR** instead, pressing <Esc> one or more times takes you back to **/F**. Then you can complete the command. If you press <Esc> again instead of completing the command, you will return to the main command menu, where you could choose another major command (e.g., **/R**ange). Another press of <Esc> would take you to the READY mode.

HEADS-UP COMPUTING

The Lotus 1-2-3 program is designed to provide hints and helpful information on the screen as you progress through menus and data entry. Learn to practice "Heads-Up Computing" — watch the screen as you do your work.[1] Commands do not always work the way you think they will; if you watch the screen you will be able to avoid many mistakes.

/FILE COMMANDS

The two commands discussed below are the first you should learn. They make it possible to save your worksheet on a diskette and to retrieve it for later use.

/File **S**ave writes the entire worksheet onto the disk in the disk drive. Lotus asks you for the file name, and presents you with the name most recently used in a **/F**ile **S**ave or **/F**ile **R**etrieve operation (if you have done either). Either enter a new name or press <Enter> to accept the previous name. (See section below concerning legitimate file names.) A .WK1 extension is appended automatically to the file

1. The term "heads-up" comes from military fighter aircraft, which project information on the pilot's windshield so he does not have to continually watch his instruments.

name to identify it as a worksheet file in the file directory.[1]

If a file with the same name already appears on the disk, Lotus informs you of that fact and asks if you wish to cancel the save operation, replace the file on the disk with the current version, or back up the file on the disk. You usually tell Lotus to Replace, because you have made changes that you wish to save. If you wish to have two versions of the file, one being current and the other being the worksheet prior to the most recent changes, then select **B**ackup. The previous version will have the same file name, but the extension will be .BAK instead of .WK1.

/**F**ile **R**etrieve loads a previously saved file from disk into the computer. The loaded file replaces any worksheet you might have had active at the time, so remember to /**F**ile **S**ave the current worksheet before you /**F**ile **R**etrieve a new worksheet.

NAMING FILES

Worksheet files are saved on the disk with an eight-character name (usually called the **file name**) and a .WK1 extension. The name can consist of the following characters:

```
A...Z 0...9 _ -
```

The last two characters are the underscore and the hyphen. Alphabetic characters can be in upper or lower case. Lotus tells you if you try to enter an illegal file name. If the file is not on the default disk drive, include the drive designation (e.g., B:\BALANCE). If you are using a tree-structured hard or floppy disk, you can also include a DOS subdirectory specification as part of the name of the file to be saved or retrieved (e.g., B:\FINANCE\BALANCE).

/SYSTEM COMMAND

This command allows you to move to the operating system level while the Lotus program and worksheet remain in the computer's internal memory. You can now perform DOS commands such as COPY, FORMAT, and DIR without losing your worksheet. Among other uses, this enables you to obtain and format a disk if you are trying to /**F**ile **S**ave a large file for which you do not have room on your current data disk. You can also use other applications software, such as a word processor, before re-entering Lotus. The primary constraint is the amount of memory in your computer. When you are finished with DOS, type **EXIT**<Enter> to return to Lotus.

/QUIT COMMAND

/**Q**uit exits the Lotus 1-2-3 worksheet mode and returns to the 1-2-3 Access System Menu, where `Exit` can be selected to return to the DOS command level. *Very important:* /**Q**uit *does not automatically save the most recent version of your work.*

---

1. When entering the file name as part of a /**F**ile **S**ave or /**F**ile **R**etrieve command, *do not* enter a period or the file extension. If you enter a period (and no extension), then the file is saved without an extension and Lotus will not recognize it as a worksheet file in the disk directory. Entering the extension is permissible, but duplicates what Lotus does automatically.

Make sure you do a **/File Save** *(discussed above) immediately before you* **/Quit**. Usually, Lotus warns you that you have not saved the latest changes before it executes the **/Quit** command.

ENTERING INFORMATION INTO A SPREADSHEET

In a new spreadsheet, all the cells are empty. When you point the cell pointer to a cell, that cell lights up on the monitor. If you enter information (label or value), that information is stored in the cell to which the cell pointer points. The first character entered in a cell determines how 1-2-3 treats that entry:

- A number or the characters `( @ + - . # $` start a value.
- A letter or any other characters, including <Space> start a label.

ENTERING LABELS

Pressing any letter alerts Lotus 1-2-3 that you wish to enter a label. The mode indicator in the upper right corner of the screen changes to `LABEL`. The label is left-justified (aligned with the left side of the cell) unless you press one of the following special characters:

- ' *Left-justified label* (the default).
- ^ *Label centered* in cell.
- " *Right-justified label.*
- \ *Repeating text* (`\-` yields `---------` across the full width of the cell).

The default label alignment can be changed; see the discussion of the **/Worksheet Global Label-Prefix** command later in this book.

Because Lotus automatically right justifies numeric entries and drops leading zeros, you must enter numbers as labels if you wish to achieve any special format (e.g., the year centered over a column, identification numbers with leading zeros). Numbers entered as labels are not normally available for calculation. If you wish to enter a number into a cell as a label, you must press one of the following before you type the number: <Space> `'` `^` or `"`

Label entries can be up to 240 characters in length. Even if the label is wider than the column, the remainder of the label is displayed across the row except where it would conflict with another entry in that row.

When you have typed the full text of the label, press the <Enter> key or one of the <Arrow> keys to enter the label into the cell.

ENTERING CONSTANT VALUES

Pressing any number or the symbols `( @ + - . # $` alerts Lotus 1-2-3 that you wish to enter either a constant value or a formula. The mode indicator in the upper right corner of the screen changes to `VALUE`. *Note*: Two common mistakes are often made by beginning spreadsheet users when entering values:

- Do not type commas when entering numbers, even though the example on the screen display might show commas.

- Do not press the <Space> bar to attempt to right justify numbers; Lotus automatically places value entries on the right side of the cell. If you press the <Space> bar, you are creating a label entry instead of a value entry.

When you have typed the value, press the <Enter> key or one of the <Arrow> keys to enter the value into the cell. If the value is too large to be displayed in the column, Lotus displays ********* across the cell. You must change the column width using either the /Worksheet Global Column-Width or the /Worksheet Column commands, which are discussed in a later unit.

FORMULAS

When a formula is entered into a cell, the formula itself is displayed in the control panel area when that cell is pointed to, and the result of the formula is (usually) displayed in the cell in the worksheet area. Formulas contain constant values, cell addresses, ranges, and functions connected by arithmetic and logical operators. (These elements of formulas are discussed later in this book.) Formulas can be up to 240 characters in length.

Formulas can be entered by typing or by using a combination of typing and pointing. Regardless of what you type or where you point, the formula is entered into the cell where the cell pointer was when you started typing. A formula begins with a number or one of the following characters: `( @ + - . # $`

For example, assume that you want to sum the values in A2 and B2 and store the result in cell A1. Using the <Arrows> or <GOTO (F5)> key, move the cell pointer to A1, then type:

+a2+b2 <Enter>

which would do the job quite nicely. The preferred alternative is pointing. To achieve the same result as above, do the following:

Move to cell A1

Press	**+**	*Lotus is ready for a formula,*
	<Down>	*move to A2,*
	+	*begin next address; cell pointer returns to A1,*
	<Down> <Right>	*move to B2,*
	<Enter>	*enters formula and calculates result in A1.*

This is about as fast and has the advantage of displaying what you are including in your formula. Pointing is recommended, especially when your worksheet is larger than the visible area of the screen. *Note*: Do not type spaces when you are entering formulas; spaces are permitted only in label entries.

When you have typed the full text of the formula, press the <Enter> key or one of the <Arrow> keys to enter the formula into the cell. (When using the pointing method, you usually must press the <Enter> key to enter the formula; Lotus would interpret an <Arrow> key as another pointing instruction.) If the entry is not correct, for example, mismatched parentheses, the computer beeps and you are in EDIT mode (see the section below titled "Editing Cell Entries"). If the formula is acceptable, a result is displayed. If the resulting value is too large to be displayed in the column, Lotus displays ********* across the cell. You must change the column width using either the /Worksheet Global Column-Width or the /Worksheet

Column commands.

The result of the formula is calculated immediately and displayed in the cell. Whenever you make a change or enter a new value in the worksheet, all formulas that are affected by that change are recalculated. (An exception to this statement is discussed in Part 2, but automatic recalculation is the normal state.) Lotus displays ERR in the cell if the formula is correct but the result cannot be computed. For example, the formula might be attempting to divide by 0 (zero) because the cell referred to in the denominator is currently empty. ERR means that the formula is correct, but the result is an error. The ERR is replaced by a result when whatever caused the incorrect result is changed (e.g., placing a value in the cell that caused the division by zero error).

Formulas can also use label-type data. We discuss that feature of Lotus in the next unit.

EDITING CELL ENTRIES

There are two ways to edit cell entries. If the label, constant, or formula is short, then the easiest method is to move the cell pointer to the cell and retype the entire entry. When you press <Enter>, the previous entry is replaced by what you have just typed.

The second method, EDIT mode, is better for correcting minor errors in long entries. Move the cell pointer to the cell and then press the <EDIT (F2)> key. (If you enter a formula that it cannot accept, Lotus automatically brings you to this point.) The cell contents are displayed in the second row of the control panel area. Use the <Left> and <Right> arrows to move to the point to be corrected. The <Backspace> key deletes one character to the left of the cursor and the <Del> key deletes the character at the cursor. Any character typed is inserted into the line to the left of the character at the cursor. Tell Lotus that you are finished editing by pressing the <Enter> key.

GUIDED ACTIVITY: ENTERING LABELS AND CONSTANT VALUES

An old Spanish proverb proclaims that

> *It is not the same to speak of bulls*
> *as to be in the bull ring.*

Let us therefore speak no more, but proceed to the ring, or rather, the sheet.

1. Follow the startup procedure outlined in Unit 1 to load Lotus and enter the 1-2-3 program.

2. For our first worksheet, we count the bulls on our ranch. We have four kinds of bull:

```
Type      Count
Brahma       10
Hereford      5
Elephant      1
Chicago      12
```

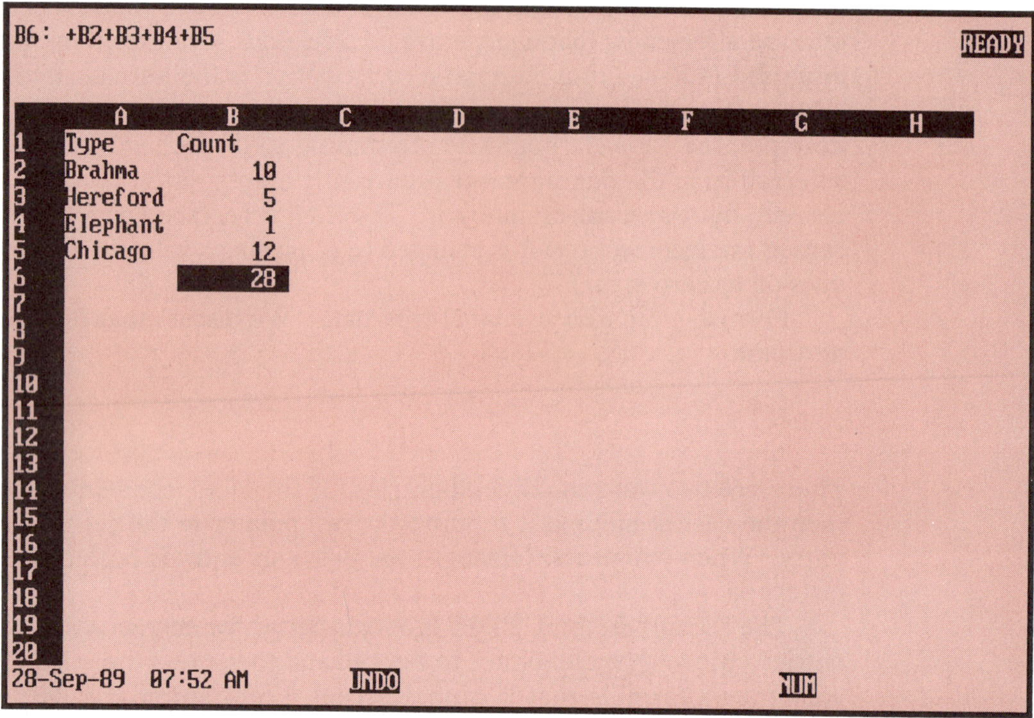

Figure 2-3 The Finished Worksheet

3. The first task is to enter the labels in Column A. (As you work, refer to Figure 2-3, which illustrates the finished spreadsheet.)

    a. Move the cell pointer to cell A1.

    b. Type the word **Type**. Lotus changes the mode indicator to LABEL and repeats what you type in the control panel:

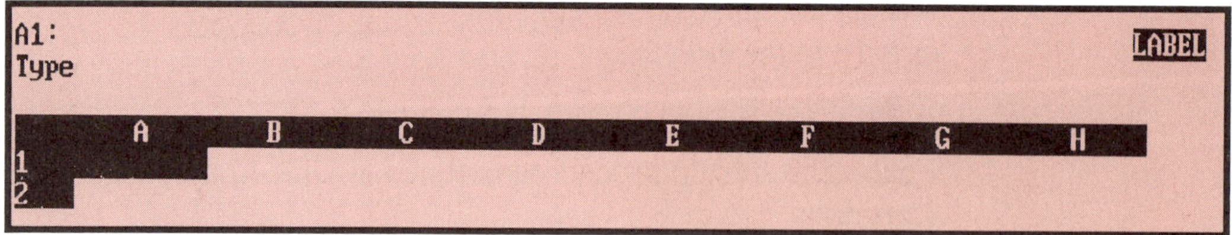

    c. Press the <Enter> key to enter the word into the cell. When the cell pointer is on cell A1, you see the entry in both the control panel and on the worksheet. Notice the ' (single quotation mark) before the word Type in the control panel. This mark was added automatically by Lotus and indicates that the label is to be left-justified.

```
A1: 'Type                                                        READY

         A         B         C         D         E         F         G         H
1    Type
2
```

d. Press the <Down> arrow key to move to cell A2.

e. Enter the labels **Brahma . . . Chicago** down column A.

f. Notice that each label is left-justified, that is, aligned with the left edge of the column.

4. Use the <Arrow> keys to move to cell B1. Enter the label **Count** in that cell.

5. Use the <Down> arrow key to move the cell pointer to cell B2.

   a. Type **10** — Lotus changes the mode indicator to VALUE and repeats the entry in the control panel:

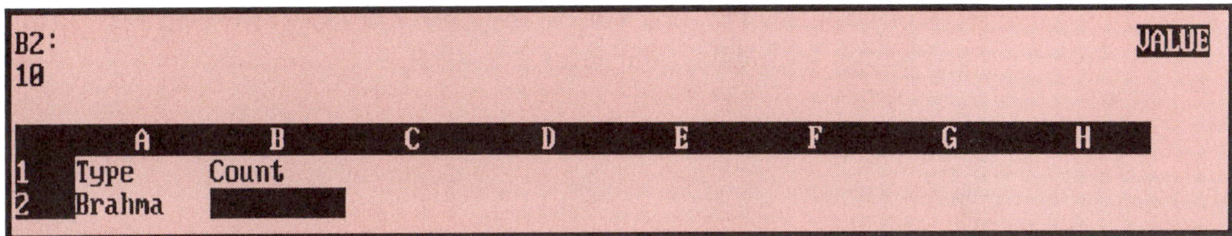

   b. Press the <Down> arrow key. Note that the <Down> arrow enters the value into the cell (just like the <Enter> key) and then moves the cell pointer down one row, to cell B3.

6. Enter the remainder of the counts down column B. (*Remember*: Do not press the <Space> bar to align the number; Lotus aligns it automatically.) Do not enter the value **28** in cell B6; we create a formula in the next Guided Activity that computes the sum of the counts.

7. Before proceeding, save your work. Enter the following; notice how the control panel changes with each character pressed.

   a. Press **/F** (*or*, **/f**). The control panel will appear like this:

```
Retrieve  Save  Combine  Xtract  Erase  List  Import  Directory  Admin
Erase the current worksheet from memory and display the selected worksheet
```

   b. Press **S**

```
Enter name of file to save:
```

c. Type **bull**

```
Enter name of file to save: bull
```

d. Press the <Enter> key.

You now have a worksheet named BULL.WK1 on your disk.

8. In the next Guided Activity you enter the formula that computes the sum of bulls. If you must leave the computer, enter the command **/Q**uit to exit to the 1-2-3 Access System. Exit to the operating system.

GUIDED ACTIVITY: ENTERING A FORMULA

1. If you are not continuing from the previous Guided Activity, load Lotus and **/F**ile **R**etrieve BULL (the command is **/FRbull**<Enter>.)

2. Next, compute the sum of bulls (the formula is +B2+B3+B4+B5). Arrow to cell B6. Enter the following; notice how the control panel and worksheet change with each character pressed:

a. Press **+**

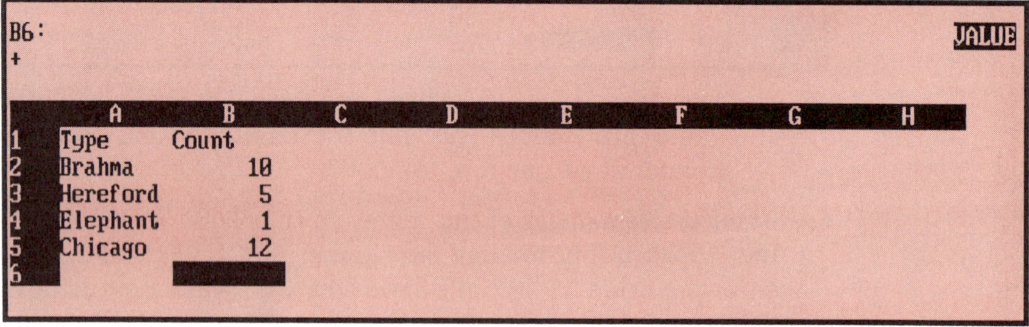

b. Press the <Up> arrow key four times, highlighting cell B2:

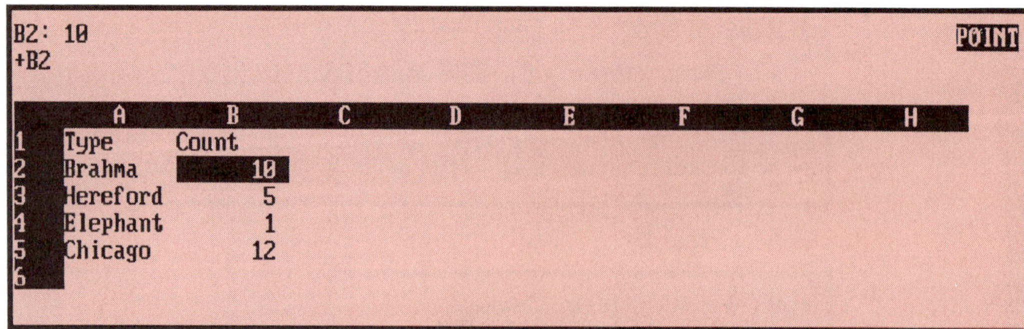

c. Press **+**

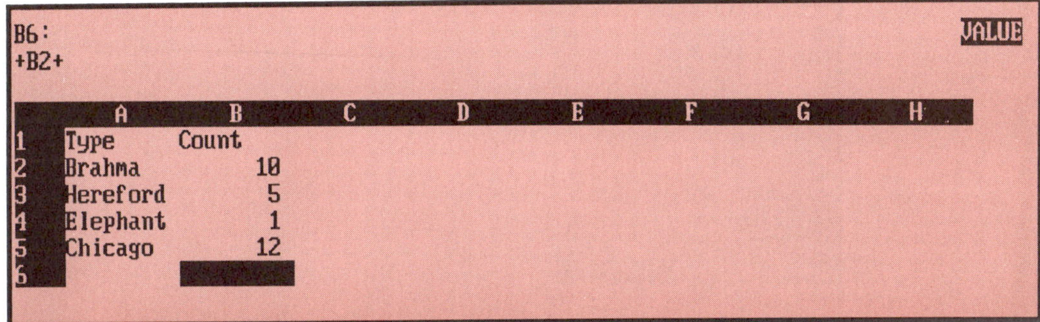

d. Press the <Up> arrow three times:

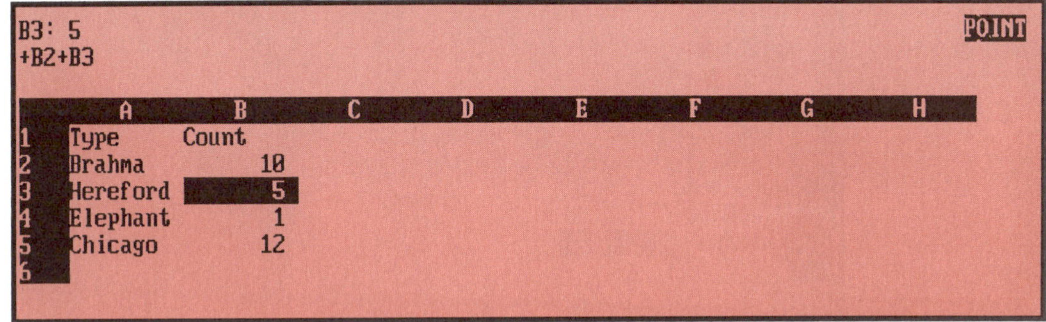

e. Press **+**

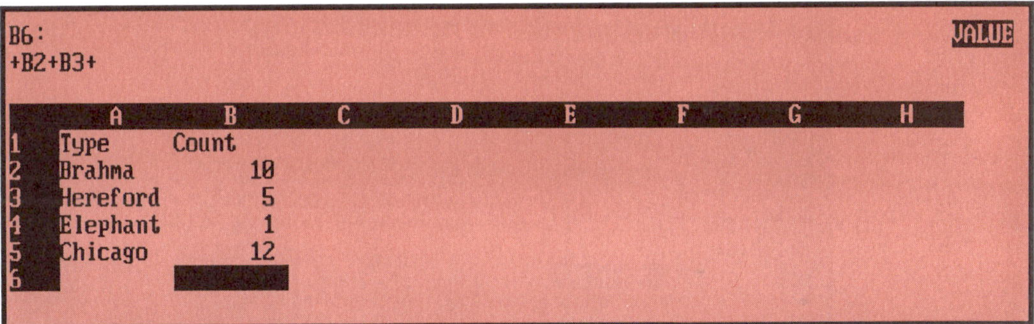

f. Press the <Up> arrow twice:

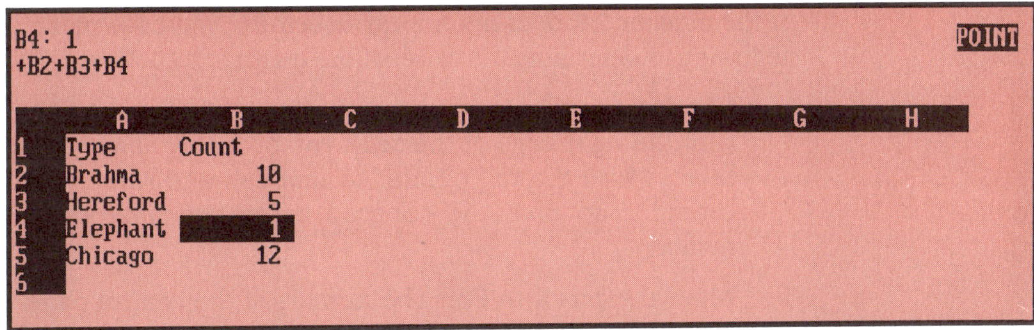

g. Press +

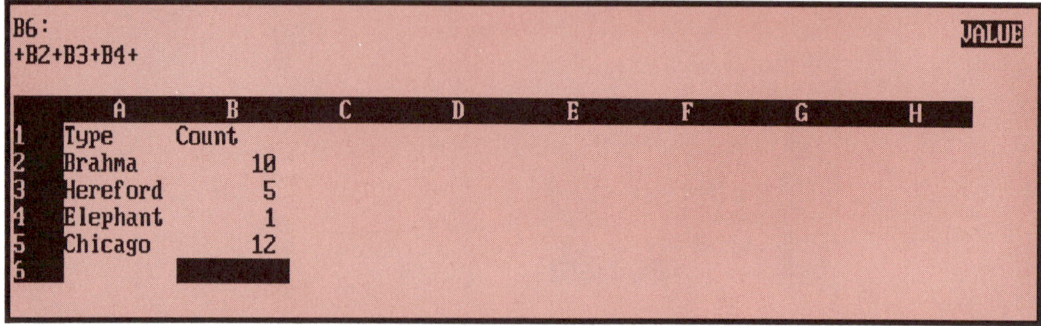

h. Press the <Up> arrow once:

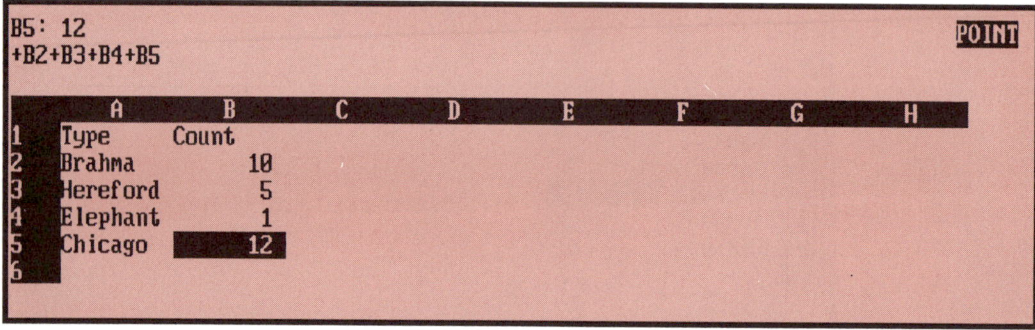

i. Press <Enter>

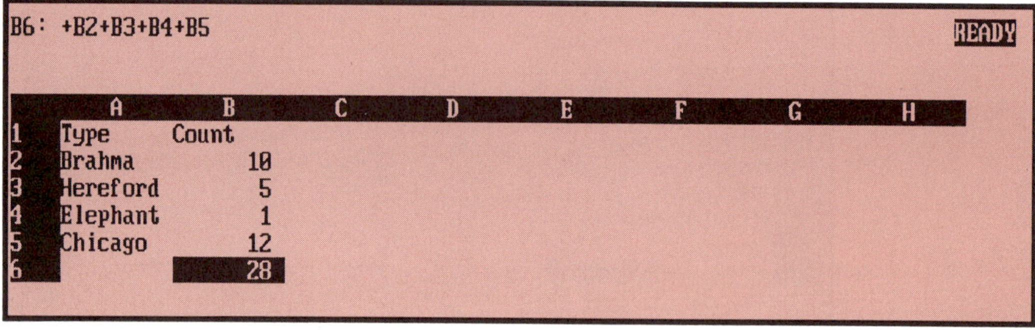

3. Your worksheet should now look like Figure 2-3.

4. If the number `28` does not appear in cell B6, you have made an error. Do the following to determine the cause of the error:

   a. Check the numbers in column B. If a number is not right justified (aligned with the right edge of the cell), you probably entered it as a label by mistake. Move the cell pointer to that cell and re-enter the number, being careful to not press the <Space> bar or any other key before entering the number.

   b. Move the cursor to B6. The formula in the control panel area should now read `+B2+B3+B4+B5`. If you have made an error, either re-enter the formula or press the <EDIT (F2)> key to edit the entry.

5. The advantage of using a formula to calculate the total number of bulls is illustrated by the following example. Assume that one of the Chicago Bulls was sold to a Dallas ranch; change the number in cell B5 to `11` (eleven) and note that the total is immediately recalculated. If we had entered the constant `28` in cell B6, the total would no longer be correct.

6. In this step we experiment with the Undo feature. (If `UNDO` does not appear at the bottom of the screen, Undo is not available to you and you should skip this step.)

   a. Enter `12` in B5. The total in B6 should change back to `28`.

   b. Press <UNDO (Alt-F4)> (that means, press and hold the <Alt> key, then press the <F4> key, then release both keys).

   c. Notice that the previous value in B5 — 11 — reappears and the total in B6 reverts to `27`. Pressing <UNDO (Alt-F4)> immediately after making an entry has removed the new entry and restored the previous contents of the cell.

   d. Press <UNDO (Alt-F4)> again. This has the effect of "undoing the undo" with the result that `12` reappears in B5. You can continue to cycle between the two entries in B5 as long as you wish.

7. Save your work again by pressing

   /FS

   Notice that the old file name (BULL.WK1) is presented by Lotus after you enter **/**File **S**ave:

```
B6: +B2+B3+B4+B5                                          EDIT
Enter name of file to save: A:\BULL.WK1
```

   Press the <Enter> key (accepting BULL.WK1 as the file name). Lotus asks if you want to **C**ancel, **R**eplace, or **B**ackup:

```
B6: +B2+B3+B4+B5                                          MENU
Cancel  Replace  Backup
Cancel command -- Leave existing file on disk intact
```

   You usually replace the old version of the file (on the disk) with your current version (on the screen); do so by pressing **R**.

8. **/Q**uit to exit to the 1-2-3 Access System. Exit to the operating system.

BACKUP

Backup is one of those computer terms that is a noun, an adjective, and a verb. A backup is a copy of the original file, usually stored in a safe place in case something happens to the original to render it unusable. Backup disks contain backups. To back up is to make backup copies.

There are a multitude of gremlins lurking out there that can ruin your day if you are not prepared. You might inadvertently ruin a file by making the wrong changes and saving it. Disks occasionally develop bad spots that make previously saved files unreadable. Spills (coffee, soda) and ashes can ruin a disk. Someone might steal your briefcase (backpack) or you might misplace your box of disks. Unexpected electromagnetic radiation can erase disks. (Telephones, magnetic paper clip holders, and library security systems all look innocent; but any of these might damage your disks). Disks left in cars can freeze or boil (not really, but excessive heat or cold might physically damage the disks).

You should become obsessive about making backup copies of your work. I recommend that you make a backup every time you finish a session at the computer. There are several levels of backup:

- Same disk, different file name.
- Different disk, same location.
- Different disk, different location.

SAME DISK, DIFFERENT FILE NAME

This method saves the file under two different names. If something goes wrong with one version of the file, the other might be OK. To implement, **/F**ile **S**ave the file with two different names. (Choosing the Backup option when saving the file saves an *earlier* version of the file under a different name, not the most recent version.)

This provides a minimal level of protection. It does protect you from random glitches that affect single data files, and might provide you a previous version if you later make unwanted changes. It does not help, however, if something (like a spilled cup of coffee) destroys the entire disk.

DIFFERENT DISK, SAME LOCATION

This method saves the file on two different disks, under the same file name. If one disk is destroyed, the other is available. To implement, either **/Q**uit from the worksheet and Exit from the 1-2-3 Access System, or use the **/S**ystem command. When you have the PC-DOS command prompt (A>_), put the backup disk in Drive A, leaving your data disk in Drive B. (The backup disk must have been formatted previously, and can contain other files.) Type the command

```
copy b:*.* a:
```

which copies all files from the B: disk to the A: disk. *Be careful*: If you type the command incorrectly, or put the disks in the wrong drives, you can copy old versions of files over new versions. I recommend putting a tab over the write-protect notch of the disk you wish to copy from (new versions of the files) to prevent wrong-way copying.[1]

To use this backup method on a hard-disk system with only one floppy disk drive, you can use the same command as above. DOS can treat one physical disk drive as two logical disk drives, and instructs you to change disks as necessary to accomplish the copy. Again, be careful and use a write-protect tab on the disk you

---

1. After completing the copying, remove the tab so you will be able to store files on the disk in the future.

are copying from to prevent wrong-way copying.

To use this backup method on a hard-disk or network system where you have been storing your data files on the hard disk, place your backup (floppy) disk in the disk drive and use the COPY command to copy the files. Because the hard disk can hold many more files than your floppy disk, you must specify each file, or each type of file, with a series of commands such as the following:

`copy c:bull.wk1 a:`	*copies one file.*
`copy c:*.wk1 a:`	*copies all worksheet files.*

and so on. Your instructor might suggest additional methods available in your particular organization.

This backup method provides additional protection. Keep the backup disk in the box except when you are using it, so that most local disasters (such as the spilled coffee) do not affect it. You are still at risk, however, for disasters such as theft of your backpack, fire, or electromagnetic fields.

DIFFERENT DISK, DIFFERENT LOCATION

This method saves the file on two different disks, under the same file name. The disks are stored in separate locations, so that if the disk box is destroyed, the backup is available. This is implemented in the same manner as version 2, except that you have to find a place to store the backup. If you have a desk or locker at work/school, you could leave a copy there and take the other copy home. You might ask a friend to take your backup disk. Some computer areas have a place to store disks, and you could leave the backup there. This provides the greatest protection. It is very unlikely that the same disaster would destroy both of your disks.

GUIDED ACTIVITY: FILE RETRIEVAL AND BACKUP

This Activity is designed to explore the two most common methods of backing up your work. Your organization might have developed different procedures.

1. Before starting, you should have your data disk (the one with BULL.WK1 on it), the West Student Data Disk supplied with this manual, and *two* other formatted disks. If you are using a hard disk or network to store your data, then your "data disk" is the hard disk or network server.

2. Enter Lotus spreadsheet mode.

3. /**F**ile **R**etrieve BULL. Notice that Lotus presents a list of worksheet files on the disk:

```
A1:                                                          FILES
Name of file to retrieve: A:\*.wk?
BULL.WK1
```

   The easiest way to retrieve a file is to highlight its name and then press the <Enter> key. (If you have several files on the disk, press the <Right> or <Down> arrows until the one you seek comes into view.)

4. The first backup method is **Same Disk, Different File Name**. Save the file under the name BULL2.WK1 with the command

   /FSbull2 <Enter>

5. Use the **/Q**uit command to exit to the 1-2-3 Access System. Then Exit to the operating system.

6. Next, we want to copy files from the West Student Data Disk to our data disk (or hard disk directory). Do one of the following:

- If you are keeping your data on a floppy disk and the computer you are using has two disk drives, place your data disk in Drive A and the West Student Data Disk in Drive B. Issue the command

  copy b:*.* a: <Enter>

- If you are keeping your data on a floppy disk and the computer you are using has one disk drive, place the West Student Data Disk in the disk drive. Issue the command

  copy a:*.* b: <Enter>

  The computer will instruct you to change disks as necessary.

- If you are keeping your data on a hard disk or network file server, place the West Student Data Disk in the disk drive. Issue the command

  copy a:*.* c: <Enter>

  Your instructor might tell you to use a different drive or path for this command.

7. The effect of the previous step is to copy files to your data disk, just as if you had created them yourself. You can now put the West Student Data Disk in a safe place.

8. The next step is to back up all the files on your data disk, creating a *backup data disk*. Again, the precise method depends on what you are using as your data disk and the type of computer system. Do one of the following:

- If you are keeping your data on a floppy disk and the computer you are using has two disk drives, place your data disk in Drive A and your backup data disk in Drive B. Issue the command

  copy a:*.* b: <Enter>

- If you are keeping your data on a floppy disk and the computer you are using has one disk drive, place your data disk in the disk drive. Issue the command

  copy a:*.* b: <Enter>

  The computer will instruct you to change disks as necessary.

- If you are keeping your data on a hard disk or network file server, place your backup data disk in the disk drive. Issue the command

  copy c:*.* a: <Enter>

  Your instructor might tell you to use a different drive or path for this command.

9. Remove your disks, place them in their protective jackets, and put them in a secure place. A plastic disk box is best if you will be carrying your disks around. If possible, store your backup disks in a different location.

10. Your instructor might request that you prepare a disk for handing in your homework. Generally, the procedures followed in Step 8 to make a backup disk are the same ones to be used to make a *homework* disk.

11. Use labels to clearly mark all your disks. At a minimum, you will have the original West Student Data Disk, a *working data disk*, and a *backup data disk*.

EXERCISE: HAROLD'S G.P.A.

Besides the Guided Activities, which are step-by-step discussions of the techniques discussed in a unit, this manual also includes Exercises at the end of most units. These challenge your understanding of the material presented and do not include as many specific instructions as the Guided Activities.

1. Create a worksheet that contains the following information from Harold's last report card. Start the worksheet in cell A1. You need columns for the courses he has taken, the credit hours, and the grade received for the course (in numeric form, e.g., an A grade is recorded as a **4** — *do not enter the letters*). Put each course on a different row, each type of information in a column.

Course	Hours	Grade
English	3	B
History	3	A
Psychology	3	A
Chemistry	4	C
Accounting	3	B
Statistics	4	B

Note: Convert letter grades to numbers before entering in spreadsheet!

2. Note that some of the course names are shortened to nine characters after you enter data in the hours column. If you feel adventuresome, try using the /Worksheet Column command to change the width of the column containing the course names (put the cell pointer in that column before giving the command). If you do not feel adventuresome, leave things the way they are until after you have read Unit 4.

3. Next, put the product of hours times grades (this product is called **grade points**) in another column. For example, to compute the product of cells B2 and C2, place a formula such as the following in D2: **+B2*C2** (The asterisk means multiply.) If your worksheet does not begin in cell A1, you will need to determine a different formula.

4. Finally, sum the hours and grade points columns, putting the sums in the row below the last class (as you summed the bulls, putting the sum below Chicago). Then divide the sum of grade points by the sum of hours to determine Harold's G.P.A., putting this formula in the next row down. To divide D8 by B8, place the following formula in D9: **+D8/B8** (The slash means divide.) You should get `3.1` as the answer.

5. Save your work with the file name HAROLD.

EXERCISE: THE PERFECT JOB (I)

In this exercise we begin the development of a spreadsheet that we use to keep track of our numerous job offers. The spreadsheet developed here is quite simple, but we will expand on it in later units.

1. Start with a clear worksheet. (If you have another worksheet on the screen, save it; then use the command **/W**orksheet **E**rase **Y**es to erase the worksheet on the screen.)

2. Starting in A1, build a table like the following. Put each column of data in a separate worksheet column; for instance, put the salary data in column D. Use label prefix characters to make your work easier. For instance, enter **\=** in cells A2, B2, C2, and D2. The backslash instructs Lotus to repeat the character across the width of each column. Also, the entry in D3 should be **"Salary**. The double quotation mark causes the entry to be right-justified.

```
My Job Prospects
====================================
Company  City     Title        Salary
------------------------------------
Arthur's Chicago  Manager       25000
Freddy's Seattle  Buyer         26300
Mack's   Bangor   Associate     22135
Mickey's L.A.     Partner       24900
Al's     Memphis  Executive     21467
```

3. Save the worksheet with the name JOBS.

REVIEW QUESTIONS

1.* What is a cell?

2. What is the difference between label and value cell entries?

3. How do you determine a cell's address?

4.* What are the dimensions of the Lotus 1-2-3 worksheet?

5.* What is meant by **control panel area**?

6. What is the **pointing method**?

7.* Look at Figure 2-1. Are any of the <Lock> keys engaged?

8. How would you enter the label **General Generators** into a worksheet cell?

9.* How would you enter the constant value **98.6** into a worksheet cell?

10. How would you enter the formula **+A6-B7** into the worksheet cell B6?

11. How would you save the file ASSETS to disk?

12. How would you retrieve ASSETS from disk?
13. Why should you back up your data?
14. Develop a backup system that will work for you. Consider the most likely hazards to your data, organization policies about using data, and access to computers. Describe the system.
15. How do you exit to the 1-2-3 Access System?

DOCUMENTATION RESEARCH

The Lotus 1-2-3 Release 2.2 documentation is contained in two major books and several smaller books. One of the books is entitled *Reference* and contains a list of all Lotus commands and functions. One of the most useful skills you can develop in this course is the ability to use the documentation supplied by the software manufacturer. If your school or organization makes that documentation available for your use, then use the documentation to determine the answers to the following questions. Documentation Research sections are at the end of most units.

1. **/F**ile **S**ave — is the current position of the cell pointer saved?
2. **/F**ile **R**etrieve — what happens if there is a file named AUTO123.WK1 on the disk?
3. **/Q**uit — what should you do before ending a session?
4. The Undo Feature — what operations can't you Undo?

UNIT 3

OPERATORS AND FUNCTIONS

Recall that *formulas contain constant values, cell addresses, ranges, and functions connected by arithmetic and logical operators.* We used constant values and simple addition of cells in the preceding unit. This unit introduces the remaining elements of formulas: arithmetic and logical operators, and mathematical, logical, special, financial, date, and statistical functions. This unit presents those functions that are most useful to the business student and professional; discussion of several of the functions is deferred to Part 3.

Do not try to memorize this material. Skim the unit to see how the material is arranged, look at the Function Index (at the end of the manual) and Appendix C, "Lotus 1-2-3 Release 2.2 Functions," and work the review problems at the end of the unit. You will need to refer back to this unit often, but you do not need to memorize everything that follows.

LEARNING OBJECTIVES

1. At the completion of this unit, you should know
   a. what **order of precedence** means,
   b. how each of the numeric operators is used in formulas,
   c. what the various categories of functions are.
2. At the completion of this unit, you should be able to
   a. write formulas using arithmetic operators,
   b. write formulas using functions.

ARITHMETIC AND LOGICAL OPERATORS

Operators are the glue that binds elements of formulas, the **operands**, together. Most of us are familiar with operators such as the + (plus) sign:

    2 + 2

In Lotus 1-2-3, the operands can be constant values (e.g., `25`), references to other cells (e.g., `A8`), or functions [e.g., `@MAX(17,A9)`, which determines the maximum (largest) of a list of values]. Thus we might enter the following in a cell:

```
@MAX(17,A9)-25*A8
```

We must know the order in which the expression will be calculated to ensure we achieve the proper result. Will Lotus determine the maximum of 17 or the value contained in A9, then subtract 25, then multiply the result by the value in A8? Or, will Lotus subtract the product of 25 and the value of A8 from the maximum of 17 and the value of A9?

ORDER OF PRECEDENCE

Order of precedence refers to the sequence of calculation. (Another term for this concept is **hierarchy of operations.**) Formulas are evaluated from left to right, with expressions enclosed by parentheses ( ) evaluated first, and those operators with higher precedence evaluated before operators with lower precedence. For instance, from algebra we remember that

$$\frac{6^2}{12} = \frac{36}{12} = 3$$

and not

$$\frac{6^2}{12} = \frac{1^2}{2} = \frac{1}{4}$$

The same situation occurs in Lotus, where the cell entry

```
6^2/12
```

yields the result 3.

ARITHMETIC OPERATORS IN ORDER OF PRECEDENCE

Expressions containing arithmetic operators are computed in the following order, that is, exponentiation is done before multiplication.

^	*Exponentiation.*
+ -	The *sign* (positive or negative) of a numeric expression; primarily used to begin entry of formulas.
* /	*Multiplication* and *division.*
+ -	*Addition* and *subtraction.*

Now we know how to evaluate the formula

```
@MAX(17,A9)-25*A8
```

Lotus will first determine the product of 25 and the value of A8, then subtract that from the maximum of 17 and the value of A9. More examples are in the following section.

USING ARITHMETIC OPERATORS IN FORMULAS

Arithmetic operators are used to tie together constants, cell references, and functions into formulas. In the following examples, assume that cells A5 through A10 contain the following values:

A5: 3
A6: 4
A7: 2
A8: 2
A9: 7
A10: 5

The following are entered in various cells, yielding the indicated results:

+A5+A6	*Value of cell A5 is added to value of cell A6*: 7
+A5*A7	*The product of the values of cells A5 and A7*: 6
+A5^A8	*Value of A5 to the value of A8th power*: 9
(A5+A6+A7)/A9	*Sum of cells A5, A6 and A7, divided by A9*: 1.285714
+A8/A9+A10	*A8 divided by A9, plus A10*: 5.285714
+A8/(A9+A10)	*A8 divided by sum of A9 and A10*: 0.166666

LOGICAL OPERATORS

The logical operators are as follows. There are three levels of precedence, with the top group (=, <, etc.) having the highest precedence.

Highest Precedence

=	*Equal to.*
<	*Less than.*
<=	*Less than or equal to.*
>	*Greater than.*
>=	*Greater than or equal to.*
<>	*Not equal to.*

Middle Precedence

#NOT#	*Logical not* (inverse).

Lowest Precedence

#AND#	*Logical and* (both of).
#OR#	*Logical or* (either of).

The use of logical operators in formulas is discussed in Part 3.

STRING REFERENCE AND MANIPULATION

Lotus 1-2-3 gives you the ability to refer to and manipulate labels (or **strings**). The label contents of a cell can be referred to by another cell. Labels can be entered as usual in cells, but labels used in formulas must be enclosed in " (double quote marks). A label used in a formula is called a **literal string**. Labels and literal strings can be combined in formulas using the & (**concatenation**) operator. For instance, if cell A1 contains the label `'United Consolidated Industries` and cell F9 contains the label `' Overdrawn,` then

The cell entry **+A1**	displays the contents of cell A1 — United Consolidated Industries — in the current cell.
The cell entry **+A1&F9**	yields United Consolidated Industries Overdrawn
The cell entry **+A1&" Ltd."**	yields United Consolidated Industries Ltd.

The virtue of all this is that the same worksheet can be used to analyze a different company by simply changing the contents of A1, which then changes the result displayed by all cells that reference A1. Several functions are provided to further enhance use of string data. These are discussed in Unit 16, Advanced Functions.

GUIDED ACTIVITY: OPERATORS

This activity provides experience in entering formulas that contain arithmetic and string operators. You will enter the formulas presented as examples in the preceding section.

1. Follow the startup procedure outlined in Unit 1 to load Lotus and enter the 1-2-3 program. If you are continuing from a previous activity or exercise and already have a worksheet on the screen, use the command **/W**orksheet **E**rase **Y**es to clear the screen. (*Remember*: Save it before erasing it.)

2. Enter the following values and labels in the cells indicated. Remember, to enter a value or label, move the cell pointer to the cell that is to contain the value or label, type the number (for a value) or words (for a label), then press the <Enter> key or one of the <Arrow> keys. The completed worksheet should look like Figure 3-1; refer to that figure to see how the values and labels are arranged.

Cell	Value or Label
A1	United Consolidated Industries
A5	3
A6	4
A7	2
A8	2
A9	7
A10	5
F9	Overdrawn *(there is a <Space> before the word)*

3. Move the cell pointer to cell C5. Enter the formula **+A5+A6**. You can use either pointing or typing methods (I recommend pointing). The result, 7, should appear. Notice that the result of the formula appears on the worksheet. When the cell pointer is on the cell, the formula appears in the control panel area (this is illustrated in Figure 3-1).

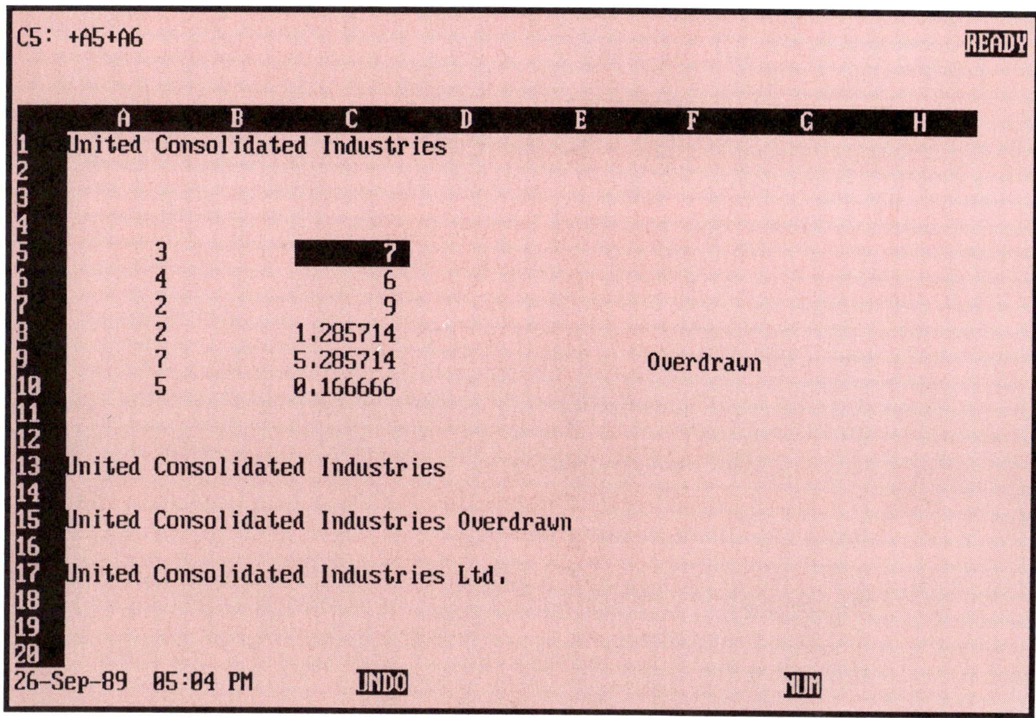

Figure 3-1 The Finished Worksheet

4. Enter the following formulas in the indicated cells. Use either pointing or typing methods. As you enter the formulas, the results illustrated in Figure 3-1 should appear on the worksheet.

Cell	Formula
C6	**+A5*A7**
C7	**+A5^A8**
C8	**(A5+A6+A7)/A9**
C9	**+A8/A9+A10**
C10	**+A8/(A9+A10)**

5. Move the cell pointer to cell A13.
6. Enter **+A1** in A13. Note that the contents of the label are displayed in A13.
7. Enter **+A1&F9** in A15. This formula concatenates the contents of two label cells.
8. Enter **+A1&" Ltd."** in A17. This formula concatenates the contents of a label cell and a literal string.
9. At this point the spreadsheet should appear as Figure 3-1.
10. Change the entry in cell A1 to **General Industries** Note the effect in the cells that reference this label.

11. Change the entry in cell A5 to **2**. Notice that the values displayed by several of the formulas change.
12. Use the **/**File **S**ave command to save the file with the file name OPERATOR.
13. The next Guided Activity deals with functions. If you must leave the computer, use **/Q**uit to exit to the 1-2-3 Access System. Exit to the operating system. Remember to back up your work.

FUNCTIONS

Functions are used to form all or part of a formula. Lotus functions always begin with the @ (**at** or **apiece**) sign. Below is a partial list; see the remainder of this book and the Lotus manual for discussions of the other functions. The index lists all functions discussed in this book.

The terms in parentheses that follow a function are called **arguments** of the function. In the examples below, *x* can be a cell, a constant value, a formula, or another function. For instance, @ABS(x) could be either **@ABS(A10)**, **@ABS(5029)**, **@ABS(A10-B12)**, or **@ABS(@MIN(G9,H9))**. Some functions accept a range of cells as an argument (the concept of a range of cells is discussed in the next unit).

MATHEMATICAL FUNCTIONS

Lotus provides two general types of mathematical functions: those that are of use to business applications, and those that are more oriented to engineering and higher mathematics. The discussion that follows is limited to those mathematical functions that are of use in business applications. The remainder of the mathematical functions are presented in Part 3 as an advanced topic.

@ABS(x) *Absolute value* of *x*. If cell J5 contains the value -2.95, the cell entry **@ABS(J5)** yields the result 2.95, a negative number is changed to a positive value.

@INT(x) *Integer part* of *x*. If cell J5 contains the value -2.95 and cell K5 contains the value 2.95, the cell entry **@INT(K5)** yields the result 2 and the cell entry **@INT(J5)** yields the result -2, everything beyond the decimal point is eliminated.

@MOD(x,y) *Modular part* (remainder) of *x* divided by *y*: *x mod y*. If cell J6 contains the value 6 and cell K6 contains the value 4, the cell entry **@MOD(J6,K6)** yields the result 2. (Remember: "Four goes into six one time, with a remainder of two.")

@ROUND(x,n) *Round number x* to *n* decimal places. If cell J6 contains the value 6 and cell K6 contains the value 4, the cell entry **@ROUND(K6/J6,2)** yields the result 0.67.

SPECIAL FUNCTIONS

Lotus provides several special functions that are used in advanced operations. These are discussed in Part 3.

LOGICAL FUNCTIONS

Lotus also provides logical functions which, in conjunction with logical operators, allow a great deal of flexibility and sophistication. We discuss Lotus logic in Part 3.

FINANCIAL FUNCTIONS

These are especially useful in finance and accounting applications. The financial function used most often in the remainder of this book is @PMT; the others are listed for future reference. Where the argument is a percentage, it can be entered either as a decimal number, e.g., **.139**, or with a percent sign, e.g., **13.9%**. Lotus determines what you mean.

Cash Flows. The following functions are used by financial analysts to determine how attractive an investment is over a period of time. In these functions, you must either estimate the interest rate you will receive, or the amount of money you will receive, and Lotus computes the other. The first two functions, @IRR and @NPV, deal with a series of numbers that must be put into a row or column of the worksheet. This series of numbers is the anticipated net return (e.g., *revenue-cost*) an investment generates.

@IRR(guess,range) *Internal rate of return* of the series of cash flows in the *range*. The *guess* is necessary because some income streams have more than one IRR. It is generally safe to use 0.10 as the guess. An example of the use of this function is contained in Exercise: The Lottery Winner at the end of this unit.

@NPV(x,range) *Net present value* of the series of cash flows in the *range*, discounted at *x* interest rate. An example of the use of this function is contained in Exercise: The Lottery Winner at the end of this unit.

Annuities. The functions @FV, @PV, @TERM, and @PMT deal with a fixed payment (an **annuity**) over a period of time. @FV is used to determine *how much you will have in the future*. @PV is used to determine *the current value of a set of payments* (e.g., "would you rather have $20,000 now or $100 a month for life?"). @TERM is used to determine *how long you must save to accumulate a specific amount*. @PMT is used to determine *the periodic payment level necessary to pay back a loan*.

@FV(pmt,int,term) *Future value of an ordinary annuity* with payments of *pmt* at the end of each period, at a per-period interest rate of *int*, for *term* periods. (See note below concerning monthly and annual data.) For instance, if cell M1 contains 100 (the payment), M2 contains .12 (the annual interest rate), and M3 contains 5 (the number of years), then the cell entry **@FV(M1,M2/12,M3*12)** would be used to determine how much would accumulate with *monthly* payments of $100, invested at 12% interest, over a period of five years. (The result is 8166.97.)

@PV(pmt,int,term) *Present value of an ordinary annuity* with payments of *pmt* at the end of each period, at a per-period interest rate of *int*, for *term* periods. (See note below concerning monthly and annual data.) For instance, if cell M1 contains 100 (the payment), M2 contains .12 (the

stance, if cell M1 contains `100` (the payment), M2 contains `.12` (the annual interest rate), and M3 contains `5` (the number of years), then the cell entry **`@PV(M1,M2/12,M3*12)`** would be used to determine the current dollar equivalent of *monthly* receipts of $100, invested at 12% interest, over a period of five years. (The result is `4495.50`.)

@TERM(pmt,int,fv) *Number of periods*, the number of end-of-period payments necessary to achieve the future value *fv*, given the payment *pmt* and interest *int*. (See note below concerning monthly and annual data.) For instance, if cell M1 contains `100` (the payment), M2 contains `.12` (the annual interest rate), and M4 contains `10000` (the desired future value), then the cell entry **`@TERM(M1,M2/12,M4)`** would be used to determine the number of months necessary for a $100 monthly payment to grow into $10,000 at 12% annual interest. (The result is `69.7` months.)

@PMT(prn,int,term) *Payment* on a loan of principal *prn* at a per-period interest rate of *int*, for *term* periods. (See note below concerning monthly and annual data.) For instance, if cell M2 contains `.12` (the annual interest rate), M3 contains `5` (the number of years to repay the loan), and M4 contains `10000` (the amount borrowed), then the cell entry **`@PMT(M4,M2/12,M3*12)`** would be used to determine the monthly payment on a $10,000 loan at 12% annual interest. (The result is `222.44`.)

Monthly Payments Based on Annual Interest and Term. Typically, interest rates and term are expressed in annual figures, e.g., 11.9% annual interest and 3 years to repay. Payments are usually made monthly, however, so many of the formulas for annuities (above) and compounding (below) must be adjusted. To convert annual interest rates to monthly interest rates, divide by 12. To convert number of years to number of months, multiply by 12. For example, the monthly payment on $1000 for 2 years at 18% is calculated by the cell entry **`@PMT(1000,0.18/12,2*12)`**.

Compounding. The functions @CTERM and @RATE are used to determine the amount of time or the necessary interest rate for a current amount to grow to some desired future amount with compound interest. Unlike the annuity functions, there are no periodic payments, only the initial investment.

@CTERM(int,fv,pv) *Compounding periods*, number of periods required for present value *pv* to increase to desired future value *fv* at stated interest rate *int*. (See note above concerning monthly and annual data.) For instance, if cell N1 contains `.12` (the annual interest rate), N2 contains `2000` (the future value), and N3 contains `1000` (the current value), then the cell entry **`@CTERM(N1/12,N2,N3)`** would be used to determine how many months it would take for $1000 to double in value if invested at 12%, compounded monthly. (The result is `69.66` months.)

@RATE(fv,pv,term) *Periodic interest*, the rate necessary for the present value *pv* to grow into the future value *fv* over the number of periods in the *term*. (See note above concerning monthly and annual data.) For instance, if cell

N4 contains 5 (the number of years), N2 contains 2000 (the future value), and N3 contains 1000 (the current value), then the cell entry **@RATE(N2,N3,N4*12)** would be used to determine the investment rate necessary for $1000 to double in value over a period of five years, compounded monthly. (The result is .011619, which, multiplied by 12, is 13.94% per annum.)

Depreciation. The practice of reducing the value of an asset as it becomes older is called **depreciation**. There are several methods for determining the amount of depreciation which can be charged in a given year, three of which are available in Lotus 1-2-3 Release 2.2. Each of the methods requires that you state the original cost of the item, the useful life of the item (how long it will last), and the salvage (resale or scrap) value at the end of that life.

@DDB(cost,salvage,life,period) *Double declining balance depreciation*, the depreciation amount in a specific *period*, given the initial *cost*, *salvage* value, and *life* of the item.

@SLN(cost,salvage,life) *Straight-line depreciation*, which is the same amount for each period, given the initial *cost*, *salvage* value, and *life* of the item.

@SYD(cost,salvage,life,period) *Sum-of-the-years' digits depreciation*, for a specified *period*, given the initial *cost*, *salvage* value, and *life* of the item.

DATE AND TIME FUNCTIONS

Lotus date functions provide a method for doing arithmetic using dates (e.g., *how many days have elapsed since July 4, 1976?*) and for displaying those dates in an orderly manner. Lotus calculates dates by counting the number of days that have elapsed between the date in question and January 1, 1900. To Lotus, year 00 is 1900, year 85 is 1985, and year 150 is 2050. The following three functions yield a **serial date number**:

@DATE(year,month,day) *Serial number of a given date*, where **@DATE(00,01,01)** [January 1, 1900] is number 1 and **@DATE(199,12,31)** [December 31, 2099] is number 73050. *Note*: Do not enter the year 1990 as 1990, enter it as 90; enter 2001 as 101.

@NOW *Current date and time*, assuming you set the proper date when you started or reset the system. This returns both date (integer) and time (fractional) components. To see both current date and time, have two **@NOW** entries; one formatted as date and the other as time. I like to include these in my worksheets so I can see exactly when a given printout was produced. @NOW is updated whenever the worksheet is recalculated.

@DATEVALUE(date string) *String to date*, converts a string to a serial date number, for example **@DATEVALUE("16-Feb-87")** yields 31824.

The results of @DATE, @NOW, and @DATEVALUE must be formatted using the /Range Format command (see Unit 4) before they are meaningful. You can use these functions in formulas, e.g., **@NOW+7** is one week from today.

Lotus 1-2-3 Release 2.2 also gives you the ability to calculate time as a fractional serial number, with midnight being 0 (zero) and noon being 0.5. One way to enter exact hours is to use fractions (e.g., 16/24 is 4:00 PM), and to use the **/R**ange **F**ormat command to format the result as time. If the @NOW function is formatted to Time, then the current time is displayed. You can also use either of the following two functions:

@TIME(hr,min,sec) *Serial time number*, computes the time number of the arguments.

@TIMEVALUE(time string) *String to time*, converts a string to a serial time number, for example **@TIMEVALUE("6:06 PM")** yields 0.754166.

The other date and time functions yield a number:

@DAY(date) *Day of the month* of the given date. If today is May 21, 1989, then **@DAY(@NOW)** yields 21.

@MONTH(date) *Month number* of the given date. If today is May 21, 1989, then **@MONTH(@NOW)** yields 5.

@YEAR(date) *Year number* of the given date. If today is May 21, 1989, then **@YEAR(@NOW)** yields 89.

@HOUR(time number) *Hour value of time number.* If the time is now 8:08:25, then **@HOUR(@NOW)** yields 8.

@MINUTE(time number) *Minute value of time number.* If the time is now 8:08:25, then **@MINUTE(@NOW)** yields 8.

@SECOND(time number) *Second value of time number.* If the time is now 8:08:25, then **@SECOND(@NOW)** yields 25.

STATISTICAL FUNCTIONS

These are very useful for business calculations. For instance, we can use @MIN to discover the minimum value in a list of sales figures, and @AVG to determine the average sales. In the examples below, *list* can be any number of arguments (up to the 240 character limit), separated by commas. The arguments can be any combination of numbers, formulas, cell addresses, range specifications, or range names. For instance, @AVG(list) could be **@AVG(A1..A25)** or a more complex list, such as **@AVG(A1,A9,25,B6..B32,@SUM(D3..D18))**.

@AVG(list) The *average value* of the items in the list. If the list contains @NA or @ERR, then the average is @NA or @ERR. (@NA and @ERR are special functions discussed with Lotus logic in Part 3.) The cell entry **@AVG(-5,8,3/12,(-6-2))** yields the result -1.1875, which is the average of the values. **@AVG(A1,B5,C8)** would compute the average of the current values of those three cells.

@COUNT(list) The *number of items* in the list. Every non-blank cell in a range counts, whether it contains a value or a label.

@MIN(list) The *minimum value* in the list. The cell entry **@MIN(-5,8,3/12,(-6-2))** yields the result -8, which is the smallest of the values. **@MIN(A1,B5,C8)** would display the smallest of the current values of those three cells.

@MAX(list) The *maximum value* in the list. The cell entry **@MAX(-5,8,3/12,(-6-2))** yields the result 8, which is the largest of the values. **@MAX(A1,B5,C8)** would display the largest of the current values of those three cells.

@STD(list) The *standard deviation* of the items in the list (N weighted).

@SUM(list) The *sum* of the items in the list. If the list contains @NA or @ERR, then the sum is @NA or @ERR. **@SUM(A1,B5,C8)** would display the sum of the current values of those three cells.

@VAR(list) The *variance* of the items in the list (N weighted).

If you have not taken a course in statistics, the terms **standard deviation** and **variance** might be new to you. There are also **database statistical functions** that operate on a subset of the data in a range. See Part 3 for more detail.

GUIDED ACTIVITY: FUNCTIONS

This activity requires you to use the formulas in a worksheet.

1. If you are not continuing from the previous Guided Activity, follow the startup procedure outlined in Unit 1 to load Lotus and enter the 1-2-3 program. If you are continuing from a previous activity or exercise and already have a worksheet on the screen, use the command /Worksheet Erase Yes to clear the screen. (*Remember*: Save it before erasing it.)
2. In cells D5 and D6, enter the numbers **18** and **7**, as shown in Figure 3-2.
3. Move the cell pointer to D7. In D7, enter a formula that computes the sum of the numbers in D5 and D6. Use the @SUM function; do not enter the result that is visible in Figure 3-2. To enter the function using the pointing method:

   a. Type **@SUM(** [*or*, **@sum(**]:

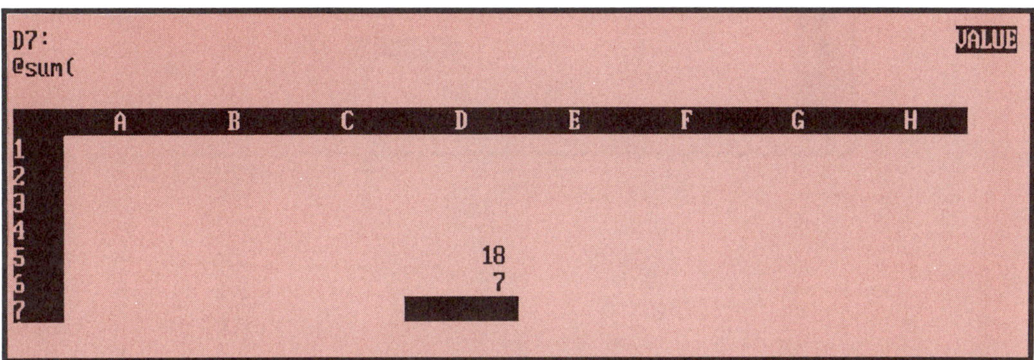

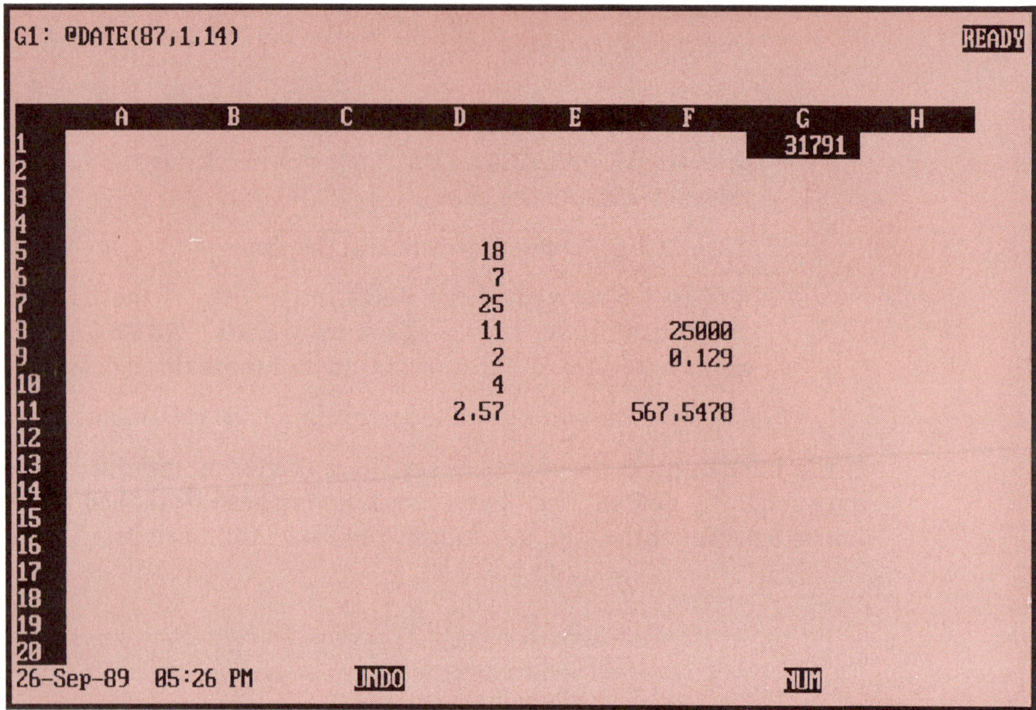

Figure 3-2 The Finished Worksheet

b. Press the <Up> arrow key twice:

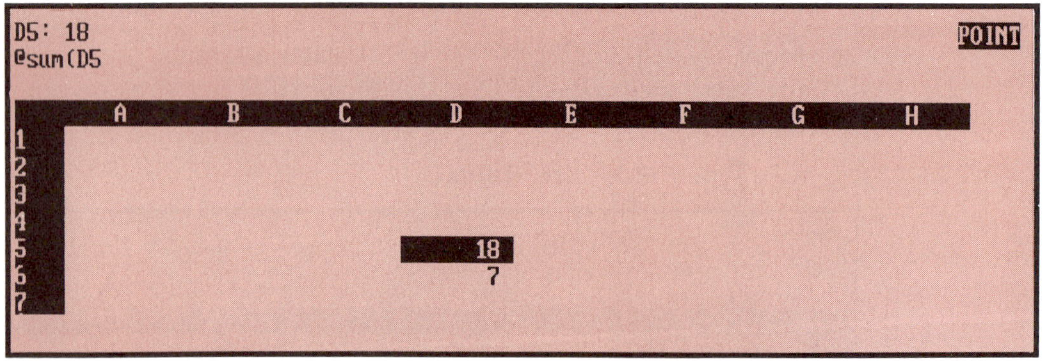

c. Press **.** (a period):

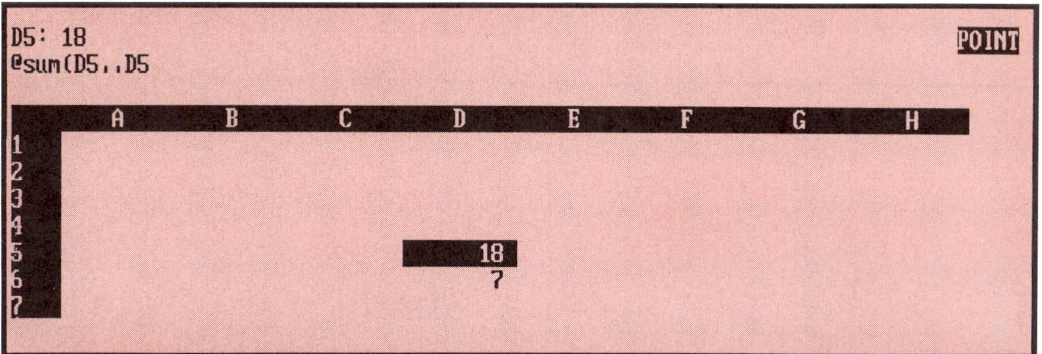

d. Press the <Down> arrow key:

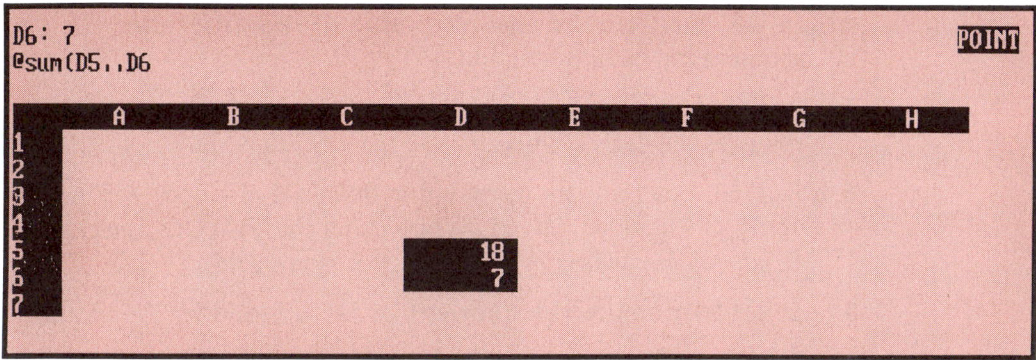

e. Press **)** (a right parenthesis):

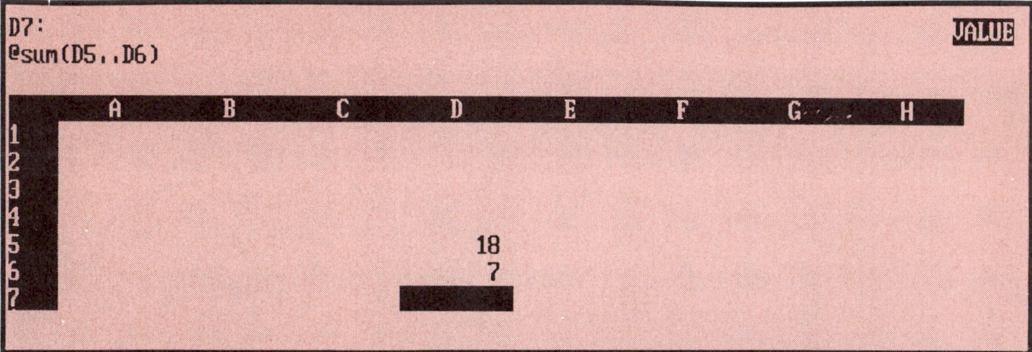

f. Press the <Enter> key:

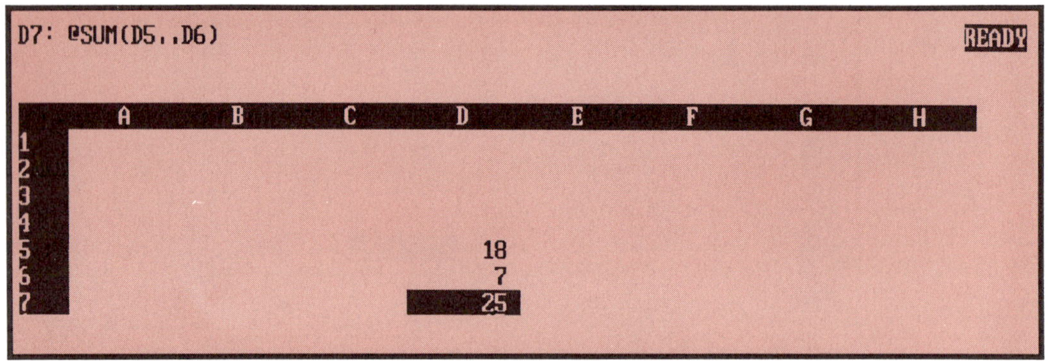

When the formula is entered properly, the sum appears as illustrated.

4. In D8, compute the absolute value of the difference (i.e., +D5-D6). This requires the @ABS function.

5. In D9, compute the integer part of D5 divided by D6 (i.e., +D5/D6). This requires the @INT function.

6. In D10, compute the remainder from D5 divided by D6. This requires the @MOD function. (*Note*: When using the @MOD function, separate the dividend and the divisor by a comma, not by a slash.)

7. In D11, compute the quotient of D5 divided by D6, rounded to 2 decimal places. This requires the @ROUND function.

8. In cell F8, enter the amount **25000** (the amount you need to borrow to buy your BMW). In cell F9 enter the annual interest rate: **12.9%**. You plan to pay back the amount in 5 years (payments will be made monthly). In cell F11, write a formula that computes the monthly payment. This requires the @PMT function.

9. In cell G1, enter the formula to calculate the serial number of the date January 14, 1987. This requires the @DATE function. The result is a number. We learn how to format the number so it appears as a date in Unit 4.

10. The completed worksheet should look like Figure 3-2. Save your work with the file name FUNCTION.

CHECKPOINT

3a. What command do you use to save the file?

11. /Quit to exit to the 1-2-3 Access System. Exit to the operating system. Remember to back up your work.

EXERCISE: MORE FUN WITH FUNCTIONS

1. If you are not continuing from the previous Guided Activity, follow the startup procedure outlined in Unit 1 to load Lotus and enter the 1-2-3 program. If you are continuing from a previous activity or exercise and already have a worksheet on the screen, use the command /**W**orksheet **E**rase **Y**es to clear the

screen. (*Remember*: Save it before erasing it.)

2. Put your name in cell A1. Put the name of your boy/girl/dog/cat/hamster friend in A2. In A3, enter **+A1&"<Space>loves<Space>"&A2**. Cute. Now, change the name in A2 and notice the result in A3. (You could use the pointing method to enter this formula, but this is one case where typing is probably easier.)

3. In A5, put the number **123.456789**. In A6, round the number in A5 to 3 decimal places. In A7, place a formula that computes (integer (A5 multiplied by 1000) divided by 1000). You should see 123.457 in A6 and 123.456 in A7. Why are the numbers different?

4. You want to accumulate a million dollars. Put **1000000** in D1. You have a thousand dollars. Put **1000** in D2. If you can earn 15% per year on your money, how long will it take for you to have a million dollars? (49.4 years.) What rate would you have to earn for you to have a million dollars after 50 years? (14.8%.) If you invest $1000 each year at 15% per year, how long will it take for you to accumulate a million dollars? (35.9 years.)

5. With A12 as the upper left corner, build the following table:

```
Cost        23,450
Salvage        950
Life            10
Period           1
```

   Remember that you do not enter commas as part of a value. In C12 through C14, compute the depreciation for each of the following methods: double declining balance, straight-line, and sum-of-the-years' digits. Note which yields a higher depreciation in period 1, then change the period to 2, 3, . . . 10 and notice how the amount of depreciation changes. (For period 1, you should obtain these results: DDB yields 4690, SLN yields 2250, and SYD yields 4090.91.)

6. /**F**ile **S**ave your work with the file name MOREFUNC.

7. /**Q**uit to exit to the 1-2-3 Access System. Exit to the operating system. Remember to back up your work.

EXERCISE: THE LOTTERY WINNER

1. If you are not continuing from the previous Exercise or Guided Activity, follow the startup procedure outlined in Unit 1 to load Lotus and enter the 1-2-3 program. If you are continuing from a previous activity or exercise and already have a worksheet on the screen, use the command /**W**orksheet **E**rase **Y**es to clear the screen. (*Remember*: Save it before erasing it.)

2. Your friend Troy has just won the state lottery. He has been given the choice of receiving his $1,000,000 prize immediately, or $80,000 per year for the next 20 years. Since $80,000 for 20 years is $1,600,000, he thinks that he should take the money over time. He would like you to use your Lotus expertise to deter-

mine the internal rate of return implied in this choice, that is, by spreading the receipt of $1.6 million over 20 years, what rate of interest is he earning?

3. To analyze this problem, start by putting the label **Prize** in cell A1. Enter the amount of money that Troy is giving up, **-1000000** (negative one million) in cell B1. Enter his receipts in the cells below B1, that is, enter **80000** in *every cell* in the range B2 through B21.

4. In cell C1, enter the label **IRR**. In D1, enter the function **@IRR(10%,B1..B21)**. You should get the result 0.049643, which means that Troy is earning less than 5% per year on his prize.

5. Another way to analyze this problem is to determine the *net present value*, how much the stream of income is worth if it were to be paid today, assuming that you could earn a certain percentage (called the *discount rate*) on the money. Troy figures he could earn 10% on the money if he had it available now. To determine the net present value, enter the label **NPV** in C2 and the formula **@NPV(10%,B2..B21)** in cell D2. You should get the answer 681085, which means that the million dollar prize is really worth less than $700,000 *if paid at $60,000 for each of 20 years* ***and*** *he could earn 10% on the money if he had it available now.*

6. Save this worksheet with the name LOTTERY. If you would like to know more about how @IRR and @NPV formulas are used to analyze the time value of money, consult with a Finance or Accounting professor.

REVIEW QUESTIONS

1. What is meant by the **order of precedence**?

2. Cells D5 and D6 contain two numbers. What is the formula to compute
   a.* the sum of the numbers?
   b.* the absolute value of the difference?
   c.* the integer part of D5 divided by D6?
   d.* the remainder from D5 divided by D6?
   e.* the quotient of D5 divided by D6, rounded to 2 decimal places?

3.* F8 contains the amount you need to borrow to buy your BMW. Cell F9 contains the annual interest rate. You plan to pay back the amount in 60 equal monthly payments. Write the formula that computes the monthly payment.

4.* What formula calculates the serial number of the date January 14, 1987?

DOCUMENTATION RESEARCH

Using the reference manual, find and record the page number of each of the functions discussed in this unit. Write the page number by the discussion of the function, above. What formula does Lotus use for each of the following functions?

1. @AVG(list)

2. @FV(pmt,int,term)

3. @NPV(x,range)
4. @PMT(prn,int,term)
5. @PV(pmt,int,term)
6. @STD(list)
7. @VAR(list)

APPLICATION A

POOR RICHARD'S (I)

In this exercise you build a simple worksheet, utilizing a good sample of the material presented in the previous units. You start a Lotus 1-2-3 session; enter labels, constant values, and formulas; use a function; and save your work. Read the following instructions carefully: every word is important.

1. Follow the startup procedure outlined in Unit 1 to load Lotus and enter the 1-2-3 program.
2. Enter the following label into A1:

   `Poor Richard's Automotive Company`

3. Use the following information to complete the worksheet so that it looks like Figure A-1.

   a. Enter the labels shown into column A and column E. Note that most of the labels in column A extend into column B, and also from column E into column F.

   b. Enter the numbers shown into cells C4, C5, C6, C8, C9, G4, G5, G6.

   c. In cell C12, enter the formula for Net Cost, which is Dealer Cost less Trade in Value (i.e., **`+C5-C8`**).

   d. The formula for Net Price is List Price less Trade in Allowance. Note that this is a formula: do not enter the value `10100`.

   e. The formula for Percent Profit is

   $$\frac{\text{Net Price - Net Cost}}{\text{Net Cost}}$$

   Remember the rules of order of precedence as you compose this formula.

   f. In cell C18, enter the function that computes payments based on principal, interest, and term:

@PMT(C13,G5/12,G6)

Recall the discussion in Unit 3 concerning the conversion of annual data for monthly payments. Why is the interest rate divided by 12, but the term not multiplied by 12?

4. Periodically, **/F**ile **S**ave your work under the name AUTO. After the first **/F**ile **S**ave, Lotus presents the previously used file name AUTO and you can press <Enter> to accept that name. If a worksheet file with that name (i.e., AUTO.WK1) already exists on the disk, Lotus informs you of that fact and asks if you want to Cancel the operation or Replace the file on the disk with your current version. You almost always want to Replace.
5. When you are satisfied with your worksheet, press <Shift-PrtSc> to print a copy.
6. Now enter the number **2500** as the Trade in Allowance. Notice what happens to the Net Price, Percent Profit, and Monthly Payment. If these numbers did not change, you probably entered constant values instead of formulas into cells C13, C15, and/or C18. If you have a mistake, correct it. Print the worksheet again.
7. When you are finished, save your work one last time, then **/Q** to exit to the 1-2-3 Access System. Exit to the operating system. Remember to back up your work.

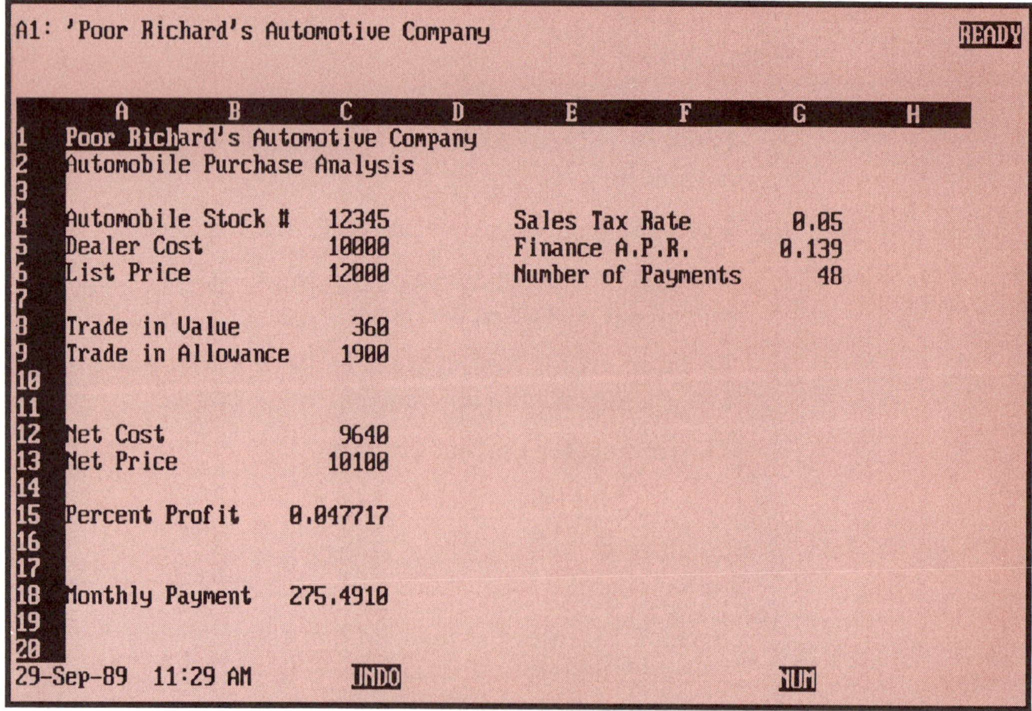

Figure A-1 The Finished Worksheet

UNIT 4

CHANGING THE APPEARANCE OF THE WORKSHEET

In this unit we introduce commands that affect the appearance of the worksheet: the /**W**orksheet and /**R**ange Commands. Here we discuss only a subset of the commands, with more complete descriptions in later units.

LEARNING OBJECTIVES

1. At the completion of this unit, you should know
   a. the characteristics of general, fixed, currency, percent, and date formats,
   b. what a range is.
2. At the completion of this unit, you should be able to
   a. change the global numeric display format to any of the five formats noted above,
   b. insert and delete rows and columns in a worksheet,
   c. specify a range using the pointing method,
   d. erase a specific area of the worksheet,
   e. erase the entire worksheet,
   f. reformat values within a specified range,
   g. realign labels within a specified range.

IMPORTANT COMMANDS

/**W**orksheet **G**lobal **F**ormat
/**W**orksheet **G**lobal **C**olumn-Width
/**W**orksheet **I**nsert
/**W**orksheet **D**elete
/**W**orksheet **C**olumn
/**W**orksheet **E**rase
/**W**orksheet **S**tatus

IMPORTANT COMMANDS

/**R**ange **F**ormat
/**R**ange **E**rase
/**R**ange **L**abel
/**R**ange **N**ame
/**R**ange **J**ustify

/WORKSHEET COMMANDS

Worksheet commands affect the entire worksheet. They are used to set **global** formats, to insert and remove rows and columns, to display information about the worksheet, and to erase the worksheet. This unit treats the most common uses of worksheet commands. More sophisticated worksheet commands are discussed in later units. Remember that you enter commands by either (1) pressing the letters (e.g., **/WGF**) or (2) moving the menu pointer with the <Arrow> keys, then pressing the <Enter> key to select an option.

/**W**orksheet **G**lobal commands are primarily used to change the display format for the entire worksheet and the width of all worksheet columns. The two most commonly used /**W**orksheet **G**lobal commands are the /**W**orksheet **G**lobal **F**ormat and /**W**orksheet **G**lobal **C**olumn-Width commands.

/**W**orksheet **G**lobal **F**ormat allows you to specify the format for all numbers not specifically formatted by a /**R**ange **F**ormat operation. Some of the formats available are

- *General format*, which displays as many decimal places as fit or as are needed (the default). With general format, a number entered as **1.234** is displayed as 1.234.
- *Fixed format*, which displays numbers with a fixed number of decimal places. Set to 0 (zero) decimal places for integers. With fixed format and 2 decimal places, a number entered as **1.234** is displayed as 1.23.
- *Currency format*, which puts dollar signs in front, negative values in parentheses, and as many decimal places as you specify. With currency format and 2 decimal places, a number entered as **1.234** is displayed as $1.23.
- *Percent format*, which converts real numbers to percentages and puts a percent sign after the right digit. Again, you specify the number of decimal places. With percent format and 2 decimal places, a number entered as **1.234** is displayed as 123.40%.
- *Date formats*, which convert the result of the @NOW and @DATE(. . .) functions to a readable format, such as 01-Jan-87, 01-Jan, or Jan-87. There are also *DateTime formats* that allow the display of time in several formats. Time is generated with the @NOW and @TIME(. . .) functions.

/**W**orksheet **G**lobal **C**olumn-Width is used to change the width of all columns not specifically set by the /**W**orksheet **C**olumn **S**et-Width command. When you are asked for the width, you can either enter a number or use the <Left> and <Right>

arrow keys to adjust the width (and see what the effect is). The <Enter> key is pressed in either case to complete the command. Column width can vary from 1 to 240 characters; the default column width is nine characters.

Several other /**W**orksheet commands are handy as you develop the worksheet. These are discussed in the remainder of this section.

/**W**orksheet **C**olumn **S**et-Width is used to Set the width of one column at a time (**/WCS**). The cell pointer must be in the column prior to issuing the command. When you are asked for the width, you can either enter a number or you can use the <Left> and <Right> arrow keys to adjust the width (and see what the effect is). The <Enter> key is pressed in either case to complete the command. Column width can vary from 1 to 240 characters. To change the width of several columns at once, use the command /**W**orksheet **C**olumn **C**olumn-Range **S**et-Width. To change the width back to the default width (set by the /**W**orksheet **G**lobal **C**olumn-Width command), use either /**W**orksheet **C**olumn **R**eset-Width or /**W**orksheet **C**olumn **C**olumn-Range **R**eset-Width.

/**W**orksheet **I**nsert is used to insert one or more Rows (**/WIR**) or Columns (**/WIC**) in the worksheet, adjusting formulas as necessary. Prior to issuing this command, the cell pointer should be at the point where you wish to insert the row or column.[1]

/**W**orksheet **D**elete is used to delete one or more Rows (**/WDR**) or Columns (**/WDC**) in the worksheet, adjusting formulas as necessary. Prior to issuing this command, the cell pointer should be at the point where you wish to delete the row or column.

/**W**orksheet **E**rase erases the worksheet and all settings, returning you to the initial blank screen. *CAUTION: Once you erase, there is no way to recover, except by* /**F**ile **R**etrieve – assuming that you have a copy to retrieve. Generally, you should do a /**F**ile **S**ave prior to using /**W**orksheet **E**rase. As a safety measure, Lotus asks you to confirm your desire to erase before it executes the **/WE** command.

/**W**orksheet **S**tatus gives you useful information about the worksheet, especially how much memory is available. After checking the status, press <Enter> to resume work.

Remember, when dealing with /**W**orksheet or any other commands, to practice "Heads-Up" computing. In many cases, you might not remember the exact sequence of a command but Lotus will guide you through the menus to achieve the result you seek. Lotus can only provide that guidance if you look at the screen.

/RANGE COMMANDS AND SPREADSHEET RANGES

Range commands affect a specific portion of the worksheet. They are used to set formats for specific cells, to realign labels, to name a specific portion of the worksheet, and to erase a specific area of the worksheet. This unit treats the most common uses of range commands. More sophisticated range commands are discussed in later units.

---

1. When you insert one or more rows, the row containing the cell pointer is "pushed down"; when you insert one or more columns, the column containing the cell pointer is "pushed right."

RANGES AS A CONCEPT

A range is a rectangular block of cells (see Figure 4-1):

One row by one column, a single cell (e.g., cell A1 in Figure 4-1).

One row by many columns, a partial row.

Many rows by one column, a partial column.

Many rows by many columns, a block.

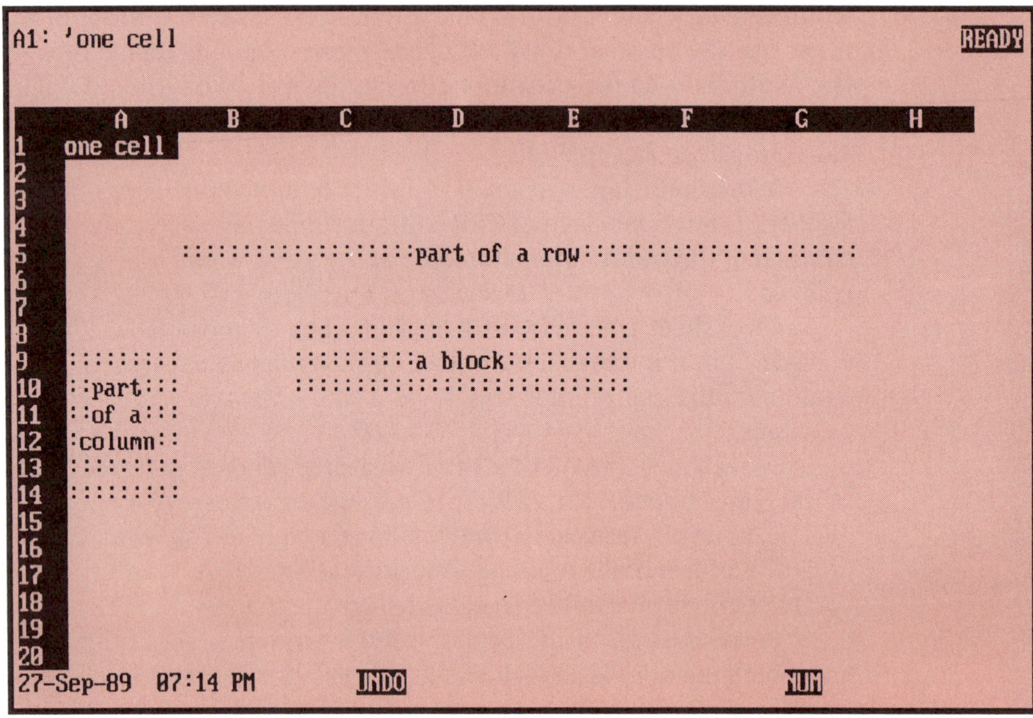

Figure 4-1 Types of Ranges

Ranges are specified by listing the upper left and lower right corners, separated by two periods. The following are legitimate range specifications (see Figure 4-1):

A1..A1 *a single cell.*

A9..A14 *part of a column.*

B5..G5 *part of a row.*

C8..E10 *a block.*

Many things are accomplished using ranges. For instance, the format used to display values can be changed for an entire range. All the values in a range can be referred to when writing a formula. A range of cells can be protected, which means that the contents of those cells cannot be altered. Data input can be set to proceed through a specific sequence.

Ranges can have permanent names assigned or they can be indicated as required by commands or in formulas. **Named ranges** are created using the /**R**ange **N**ame **C**reate command. Once named, the range can be referred to by either entering the range name or using the <NAME (F3)> key and pointing. (Named ranges are discussed in detail in Unit 13.)

Ranges can be used to simplify input of data from other worksheets and to specify the portion of a spreadsheet to be printed. You can also **goto** a named range using the <GOTO (F5)> and then the <NAME (F3)> keys.

We discuss advanced range topics in later units. This unit is devoted to the most commonly used /**R**ange commands.

/RANGE COMMANDS

Some of the /**R**ange commands are similar to the /**W**orksheet commands discussed earlier in this unit. The difference is that /**R**ange commands affect only a portion of the worksheet, while /**W**orksheet commands affect the entire worksheet (or an entire row or column). The following are the most commonly used /**R**ange commands.

/**R**ange **F**ormat allows specification of a format for a specified range of cells. See the discussion of /**W**orksheet **G**lobal **F**ormat, above, for a list of the commonly used formats.

/**R**ange **E**rase erases a specified area of the worksheet.

/**R**ange **L**abel allows you to change the alignment of labels in a specified range of the worksheet. Labels can be left-justified, centered, or right-justified.

/**R**ange **N**ame provides for the creation (/**RNC**) of named ranges.

/**R**ange **J**ustify allows a modest amount of word processing within a worksheet. See the Reference Manual for several good illustrations.

SPECIFYING RANGES IN COMMANDS

All range commands, and many other commands, require that you specify the range to be affected by the command. When Lotus prompts you for the range, you have four options: type the range, point to the range, type the range name, or select the range from the range name list. The latter two work only if you have previously named the range, a topic to be covered in detail in Part 3 of this manual.

In most cases, you are dealing with an unnamed range. Unnamed ranges are indicated by either typing or pointing:

- **Type** one corner of the range, then a period, then the diagonal corner, and finally, press the <Enter> key: **a9.c12**<Enter>
- **Point** to one corner of the range, press a period to anchor the range, point to the diagonal corner, finally press the <Enter> key. The range is highlighted as you move the cell pointer to the diagonal corner.

In either case, when you press one period, Lotus supplies a second period automatically.

Although the *normal* procedure is to specify the upper left corner first, and then the lower right corner, most Lotus procedures allow you to specify the corners of a range in any order. Thus, each of the following refers to the same range:

A1..D6 **A6..D1** **D1..A6** **D6..A1**

Some Lotus commands remember the most recently specified range (this feature is called a **remembered range**) and offer that to you when you are prompted for a range. *If you do not like the range offered, press the <Esc> key to unanchor, then proceed as above.* Pressing the <Esc> key has the effect of backing up to the point prior to pressing the period and thus allows you to move the upper left corner of the range. If the upper left corner is acceptable and you wish to move only the lower right corner, you need not press <Esc>. Simply use the <Arrow> keys to reposition the lower right corner.

GUIDED ACTIVITY: NUMERIC AND DATE FORMATS

This activity requires you to use several of the formatting commands in a worksheet.

1. Follow the startup procedure outlined in Unit 1 to load Lotus and enter the 1-2-3 program.

2. Enter formulas, numbers, and labels in the cells indicated:

Cell	Formula or Number	Cell	Label
A1	**186000**	B1	**speed of light**
A2	**1/3**	B2	**one third**
A3	**.0525**	B3	**interest**
A4	**21000**	B4	**salary**
A5	**@NOW**	B5	**today**

After you enter these data, your worksheet should look like Figure 4-2, except that the (date) entry in A5 should be different.

4a. Why is the date different?

3. Set the global format to fixed, 0 (zero) decimal places using the /Worksheet Global Format command. As you give the command, watch the control panel as Lotus presents successive menus:

   a. Press **/W** and Lotus will present the following submenu:

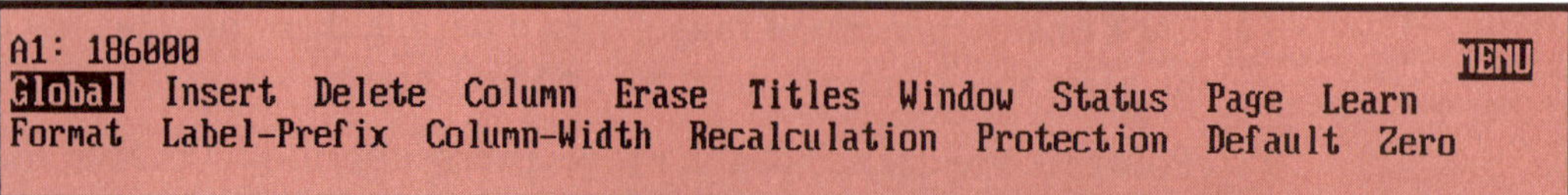

b. Press **G** to call the global settings screen (only the top of which is shown here):

```
A1: 186000                                                                MENU
Format  Label-Prefix  Column-Width  Recalculation  Protection  Default  Zero
Fixed  Sci  Currency  ,  General  +/-  Percent  Date  Text  Hidden
```

c. Press **F** and Lotus will present the following set of format options:

```
A1: 186000                                                                MENU
Fixed  Sci  Currency  ,  General  +/-  Percent  Date  Text  Hidden
Fixed number of decimal places (x.xx)
```

d. Press **F** to indicate fixed format, and Lotus will ask for the number of decimal places:

```
A1: 186000                                                                EDIT
Enter number of decimal places (0..15): 2
```

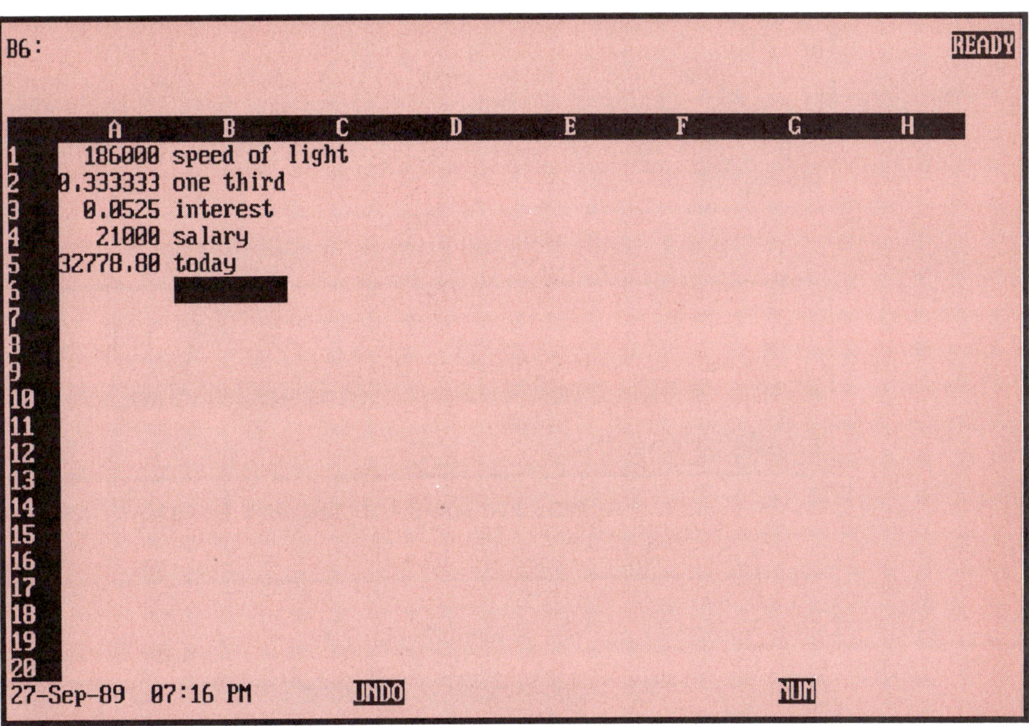

Figure 4-2 The Worksheet before Formatting

e. Enter **0** (zero):

```
A1: 186000                                                   EDIT
Enter number of decimal places (0..15): 0
```

f. Press the <Enter> key to conclude the command.

After giving this command, some of your entries will change to 0 (zero). Do not be concerned. The entries in cells A2 and A3 round to zero, but the original values are still in the cells as we shall see when we format those cells in the next step.

4. Using the /**R**ange **F**ormat command, format the following cells as indicated.

Cell	Format
A2	Fixed, 3 decimal places
A3	Percent, 1 decimal place
A4	Currency, 0 decimal places
A5	Date, 1 (DD-MMM-YY)

a. To format cell A2, move the cell pointer to that cell.

b. Press **/R** and Lotus will present the following submenu:

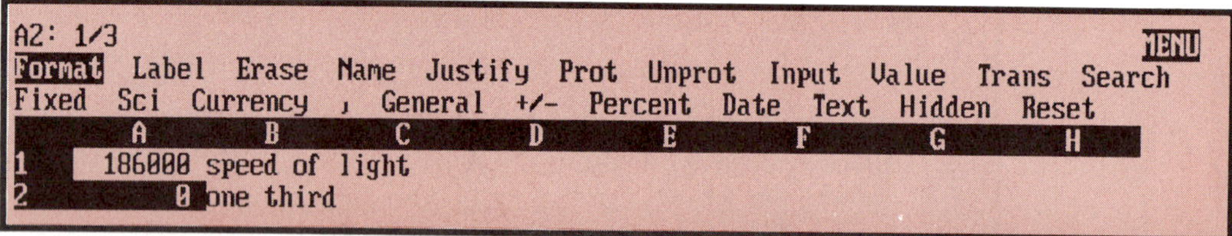

c. Press **F** and Lotus will present the following set of format options:

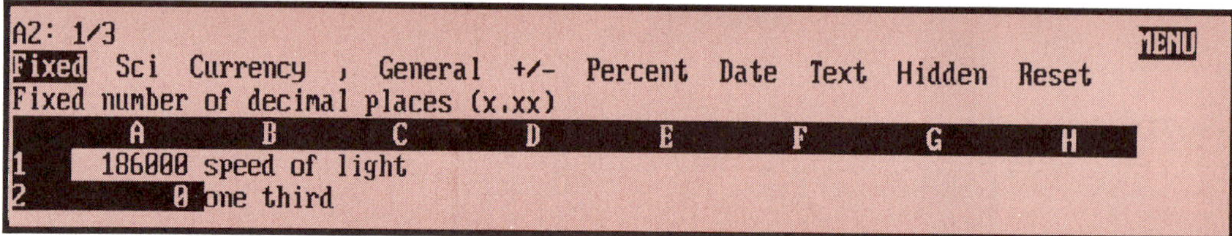

d. Press **F** to indicate fixed format, and Lotus will ask for the number of decimal places:

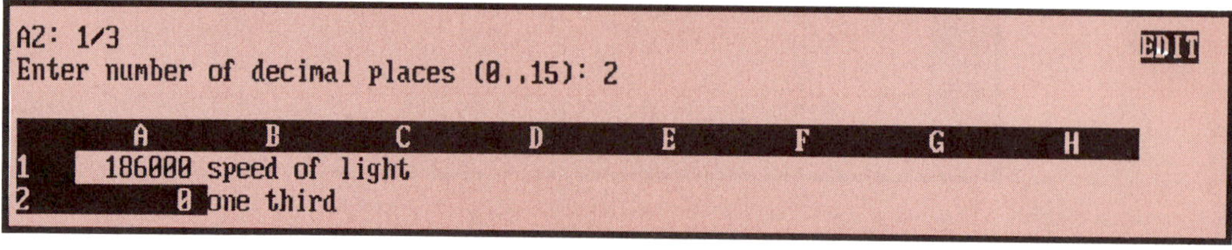

e. Enter **3** (three):

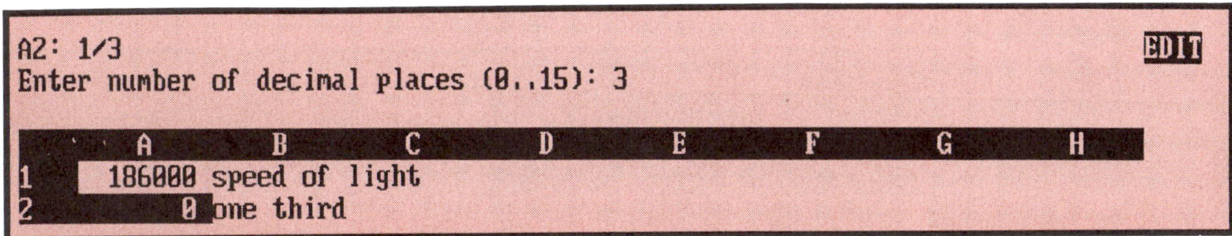

```
A2: 1/3                                                          EDIT
Enter number of decimal places (0..15): 3

       A         B         C         D         E         F         G         H
1    186000 speed of light
2         0 one third
```

f. Press the <Enter> key. Then Lotus asks you to enter the range to format:

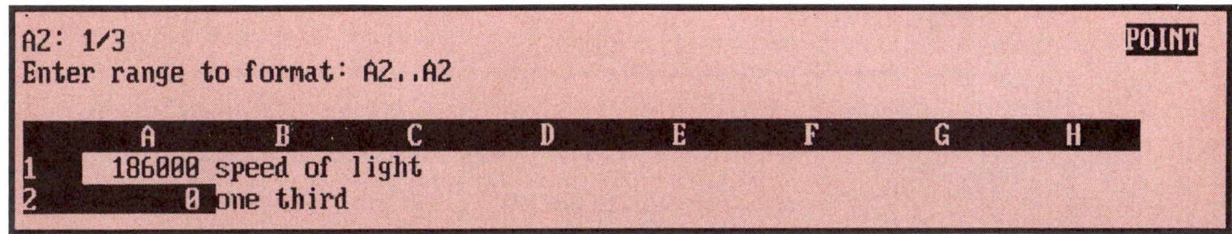

```
A2: 1/3                                                          POINT
Enter range to format: A2..A2

       A         B         C         D         E         F         G         H
1    186000 speed of light
2         0 one third
```

g. Since you want to format *only* A2, press the <Enter> key to accept this single cell range.

h. Use the same sequence to format the other cells. Cell A5 appears as a row of ********* because the date format is too wide for the column. We change the column width in step 6.

5. Using the **/R**ange **L**abel command, change the alignment of cells B2..B5 to centered.

a. Move the cell pointer to B2.

b. Press **/R** and Lotus will present the following submenu:

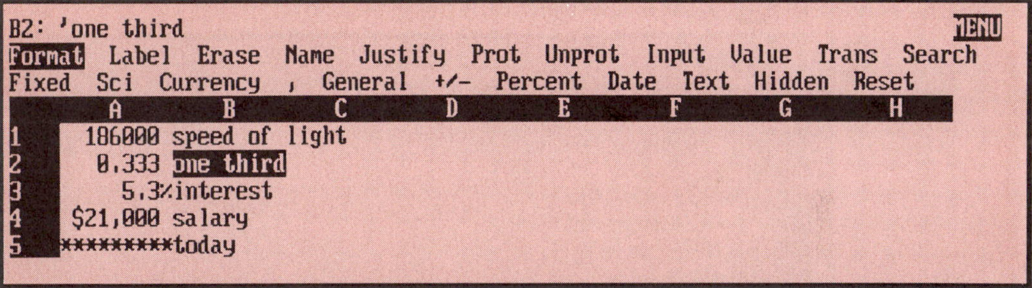

```
B2: 'one third                                                   MENU
Format  Label  Erase  Name  Justify  Prot  Unprot  Input  Value  Trans  Search
Fixed  Sci  Currency  ,  General  +/-  Percent  Date  Text  Hidden  Reset
       A         B         C         D         E         F         G         H
1    186000 speed of light
2     0.333 one third
3       5.3%interest
4   $21,000 salary
5 *********today
```

c. Press **L** and Lotus will present the following set of label-alignment options:

```
B2: 'one third                                                   MENU
Left  Right  Center
Left-align labels in cells
       A         B         C         D         E         F         G         H
1    186000 speed of light
2     0.333 one third
3       5.3%interest
4   $21,000 salary
5 *********today
```

d. Press **C** to indicate centered labels, and Lotus will ask for range to be affected, starting with the current cell:

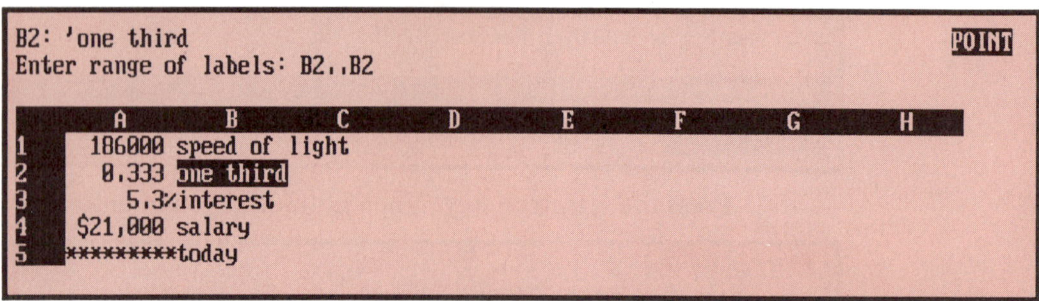

e. Press the <Down> arrow three times, highlighting the range B2..B5:

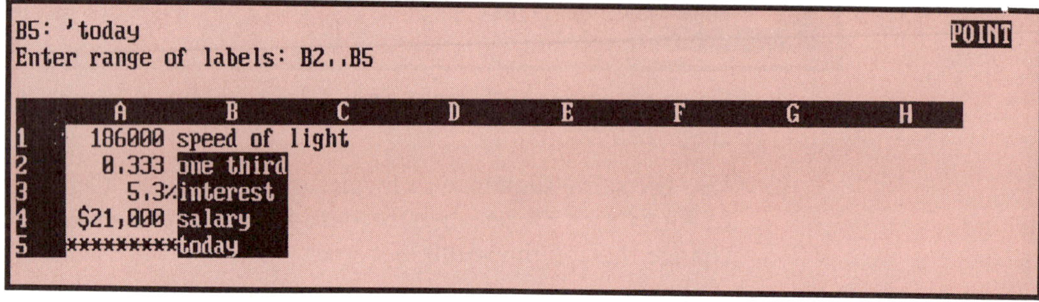

f. Press the <Enter> key to conclude the command.

6. Next, change the width of column A to 12.

   a. Move the cell pointer to column A.

   b. Press **/W** and Lotus will present the following submenu:

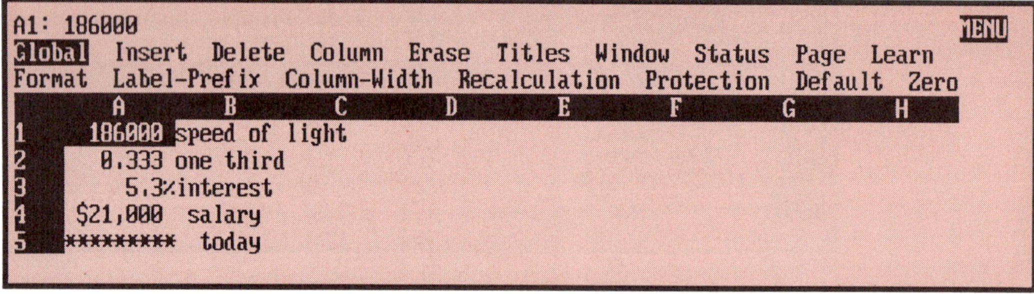

   c. Press **C** to call the Column submenu:

```
A1: 186000                                                    MENU
Set-Width  Reset-Width  Hide  Display  Column-Range
Specify width for current column
        A         B         C         D         E         F         G         H
1     186000 speed of light
2      0.333 one third
3        5.3%interest
4    $21,000  salary
5  *********  today
```

d. Press **S** to indicate that you want to set the width of the current column, and Lotus will ask you to indicate the desired width:

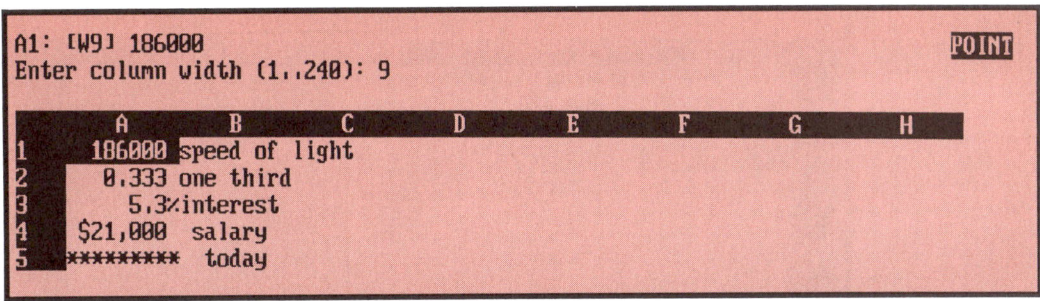

e. Press the <Right> arrow three times; you can see the effect on the worksheet:

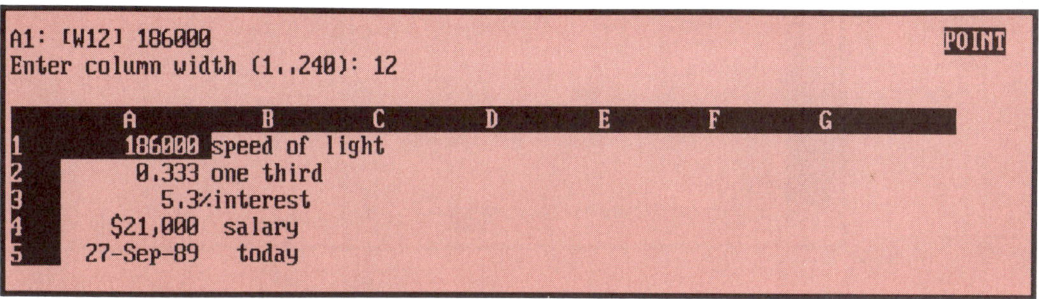

f. Press the <Enter> key to conclude the command.

7. Give the **/W**orksheet **C**olumn **S**et-Width command again to change the width of column B to 15.

8. Your worksheet should now look like Figure 4-3, except that the date in cell A5 is different. Note the entry in the control panel area. The cell pointer is pointing to cell A4. The `(C0)` indicates that the cell is formatted with Currency, 0 decimals format; `[W12]` indicates the column width.

9. Save your work with the file name FORMATS. **/Q**uit to exit to the 1-2-3 Access System. Exit to the operating system. Remember to back up your work.

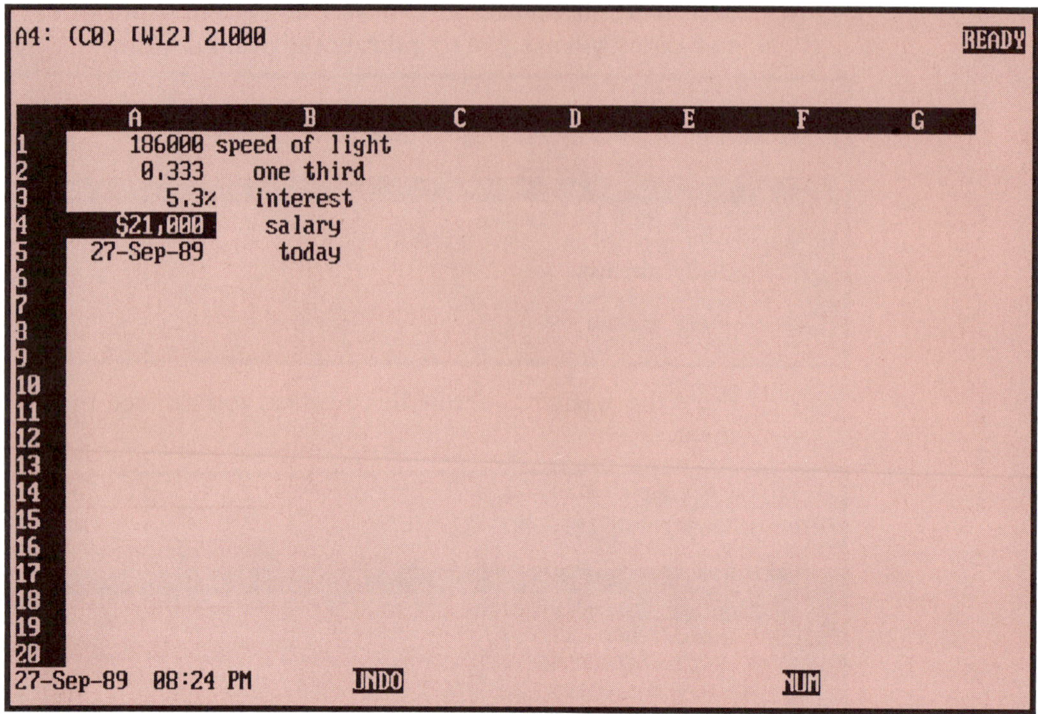

Figure 4-3 The Worksheet after Formatting

EXERCISE: DATE AND CURRENCY FORMATS

1. If you are not continuing from the previous Guided Activity, follow the startup procedure outlined in Unit 1 to load Lotus and enter the 1-2-3 program. If you are continuing from a previous activity or exercise and already have a worksheet on the screen, use the command /**W**orksheet **E**rase **Y**es to clear the screen. (*Remember*: Save it before erasing it.)

2. Use the @NOW function to enter today's date into cell A1. Use the @DATE function to enter your birth date into cell A2. Format both of these to date formats. In A3, enter the difference, which is how many days old you are. Format A3 to Fixed, 0 decimals.

3. Use the /**W**orksheet **I**nsert command to insert a row at row 1, which should cause your work in Step 2 to move down into cells A2, A3, and A4. (You must be in row 1 before using this command.) Insert 2 columns at column A, which moves the previous work into column C. Move the cell pointer to C4, and notice that the formula changed to reflect the new cell positions.

4. Enter the following data in columns E and F of your worksheet, starting in cell E1.

```
Revenue     45000.18
Expenses    38905.33
Income
```

In F3, put the formula that computes income as the difference between revenue and expenses. Format the three values to Currency, 2 decimal places, and change the width of column F to 15. Finally, change the value of revenue to **35000.55** and note what happens to the value and the format of income.

5. /File Save your worksheet with the name MOREFORM.

EXERCISE: THE PERFECT JOB (II)

1. If you are not continuing from the previous Exercise or Guided Activity, follow the startup procedure outlined in Unit 1 to load Lotus and enter the 1-2-3 program.
2. Retrieve the JOBS worksheet created in the Exercise at the end of Unit 2.
3. Format the dollar amounts to Currency, 2 decimal places. These cells will show a series of asterisks because the formatted numbers are too wide for the columns.
4. Change the width of column D to accommodate the formatted numbers. Use the command that changes only one column. Set the width so that there is a space between the $ and the label entries in column C.
5. Save the worksheet.

REVIEW QUESTIONS

1. What are the characteristics of general, fixed, currency, percent, and date formats?
2. What is a range?
3.* What command changes the numeric display format of the entire worksheet?
4. What command changes the numeric display of a specific portion of the worksheet?
5.* What command inserts a row into the worksheet?
6. What command deletes a worksheet column?
7.* What command erases a specific area of the worksheet?
8. What command erases the entire worksheet?
9.* What command reformats values within a specified range?
10. What command realigns labels within a specified range?

DOCUMENTATION RESEARCH

Using the reference manual, find and record the page number of each of the commands discussed in this Unit. I recommend you also write the page number by the discussion of the command, above.

1. /Worksheet Global Format — which cells are not affected by this command?
2. /Worksheet Global Column-Width — which columns are not affected by this command?
3. /Worksheet Insert — how does this command affect functions and formulas?
4. /Worksheet Delete — what happens to formulas that refer to cells in deleted rows or columns?
5. /Worksheet Column — what is the column width after you choose Reset?
6. /Worksheet Erase — what happens once this command is executed?
7. /Worksheet Status — what is the relationship between the amount of main memory a worksheet occupies and the size of the worksheet file created by /File Save?
8. /Range Format — regardless of the format chosen, 1-2-3 remembers the value with full precision. How many decimal places are remembered?
9. /Range Erase — what happens to formulas that refer to cells in the erased range?
10. /Range Label — what is the effect of this command on labels subsequently entered in the range?
11. /Range Name Create — can the same range have more than one name?

UNIT 5

PRINT COMMAND

In this unit we discuss the various options of the **/P**rint command. This command allows you to print all or a part of the worksheet on paper or to a disk file. In Part 3, we discuss the **Allways** Add-In program that provides for more sophisticated output.

LEARNING OBJECTIVES

1. At the completion of this unit, you should know
   a. what a sticky menu is,
   b. what the various **/P**rint submenu items do.
2. At the completion of this unit, you should be able to
   a. print all or a portion of a worksheet,
   b. enter printer control codes directly into a worksheet.

IMPORTANT COMMANDS

/Print
/Worksheet **P**age

/PRINT COMMAND

The **/P**rint command allows you to transfer all or a portion of your worksheet either to paper or to a disk file for later printing. The parameters (discussed below) are stored with the worksheet, so reprinting after revisions is quite easy.

When you issue the **/P** command, you are asked whether you wish to send the output to Printer or File:

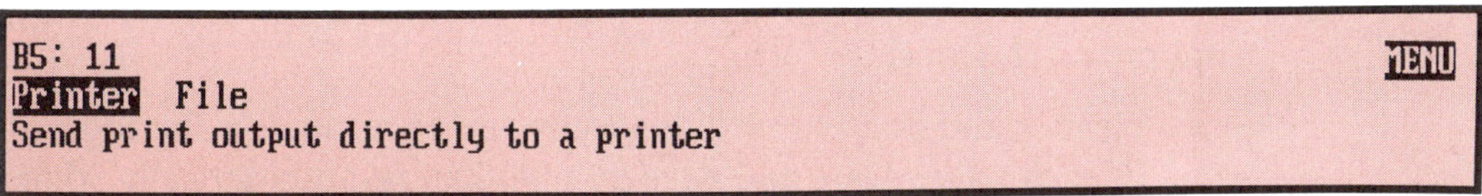

If File is chosen, you are asked to supply the file name:

```
B5: 11                                                            EDIT
Enter name of text file:
```

Files are handy because they can be integrated into other documents, for example as a table in a report. /Print File creates a file with .PRN extension (see Unit 15). /Print Printer is more common: normally you want a paper copy of your output.

Once printer or file is chosen, you are presented with the following submenu:

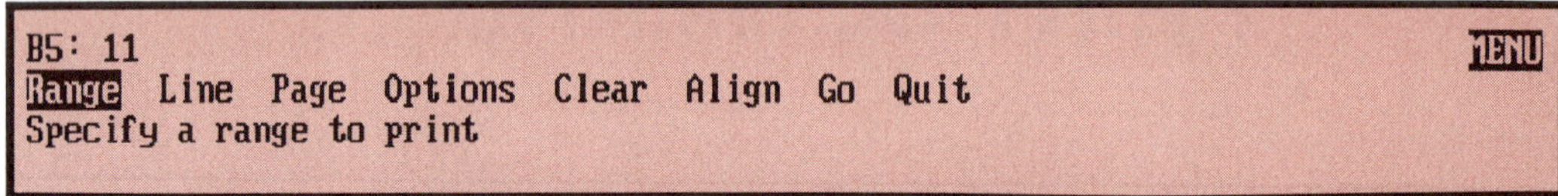

This menu is above a **Print Settings Sheet**. The entire settings sheet is illustrated in Figure 5-1. (The settings sheet in Figure 5-1 shows entries necessary to print the BULL worksheet.) The /Print menu is a **sticky menu**. This is unlike the commands discussed to this point, where you proceed directly through a menu (e.g., /Range Format Fixed 0) and are returned to the READY mode after the last parameter. In sticky menus, you are continually returned to a submenu such as the one above. To exit a sticky menu, choose the Quit option. After each of the following actions, Lotus returns to the submenu above.

Range must be specified the first time you print from a given worksheet. As usual, this is the upper left and lower right corners. You specify the range by pointing or typing. I recommend that you use the cursor to point so you see exactly what is being included in the print range. The specified range is remembered and saved when you do a /File Save operation and you need not specify it again unless you forget to save the file or change your mind about what should be printed.

Line and Page advance the paper in the printer. Note that 1-2-3 assumes that the paper is at the top of the page when you begin a session, and keeps track of page number and position on the page after that. Lotus automatically skips over the perforation. If you move the paper in the printer (by turning the knob or using controls on the printer) Lotus will not know where the paper is in the printer, and will print blank lines in the middle of your output because it thinks it has reached the end of a page.

To reset top-of-page and page number, move the paper and give the Align command. If you move the paper by turning the platen or by the switches on the printer, you must select this command because Lotus does not know that you have moved the paper.

There are a number of Options that can be set and removed (use Clear to undo options). The most useful are

- Header and Footer, used to specify text to appear in the top or bottom ten lines of each page. Date and page number can be automatically added.
- Margins, used to specify top, bottom, left, and right margins; especially the right margin when using wide paper or compressed print.

- **B**orders, used to specify rows and/or columns that are printed at the top and/or left of each page. Allows you to duplicate the effect of titles, very useful when you have long columns that go from page to page.
- **O**ther **A**s-Displayed, the default.
- **O**ther **C**ell-Formulas, which prints the cell contents (formulas, labels, values) instead of the results. These are printed one cell per line, not in the normal matrix. This is useful for **debugging** (i.e., finding errors in formulas) and **documentation** (i.e., providing a record of how the spreadsheet is constructed).
- **O**ther **F**ormatted, the default.
- **O**ther **U**nformatted, which ignores the page length, margins, headers, etc. to give a **continuous** printout. Saves time and paper.
- **S**etup, which allows you to send an initialization string to the printer. This is especially useful when you wish to print wide worksheets (e.g., 132 columns) on 8.5-inch-wide paper. For many printers, use the setup string **`\015`** which causes the printer to print in compressed print (approximately 17 characters per inch).
- **P**g-Length, which allows you to specify non standard page lengths so Lotus knows where the perforation is.

After you have specified the range and any options, choose **G**o to print.

Normally, you use **P**age to eject the page after printing (your instructor might direct otherwise).

When you are finished printing, choose **Q**uit to return to spreadsheet operations.

GUIDED ACTIVITY: USING THE /PRINT COMMAND

This activity provides practice in using the **/P**rint command.

1. Before starting this activity, determine what steps are necessary to use the printer. (Your instructor or lab supervisor will provide the answers.)
   a. How do you turn on the power?
   b. If the printer is shared by more than one computer, how do you get it to select your computer?
   c. Who is responsible for loading paper into the printer? If you are, how is paper loaded?
   d. What do the switches on the printer do?
   e. Is there anything else that you must do before printing?
   f. Is compressed type printing possible? If so, what must you do to print in compressed type?

2. Sign out the Lotus 1-2-3 manual and software. Follow the startup procedure outlined in Unit 1 to load Lotus and enter the 1-2-3 program. Use the data disk that has the BULL.WK1 file from Unit 2.
3. /File **R**etrieve BULL.
4. Prepare the printer for operation.
5. Do the following to print the worksheet. Watch the effect on the screen.
   a. Give the **/P** command; Lotus asks for a destination:

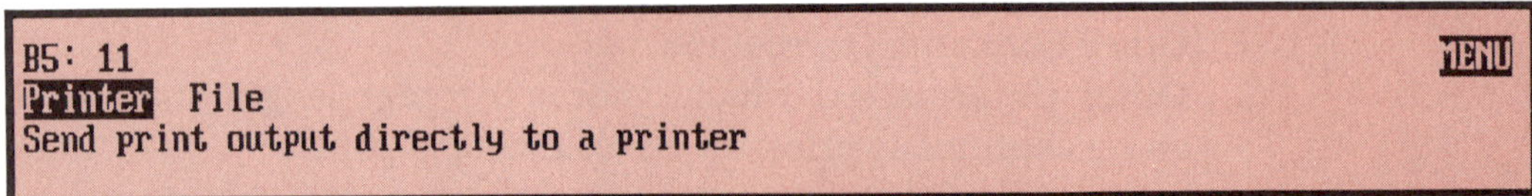

   b. Press **P** (Printer); Lotus presents the **/P**rint menu:

```
B5: 11                                                    MENU
Range  Line  Page  Options  Clear  Align  Go  Quit
Specify a range to print
```

   c. Press **R** (Range); Lotus displays the spreadsheet, with the cell pointer on the cell where it was when you initiated the **/P**rint command:

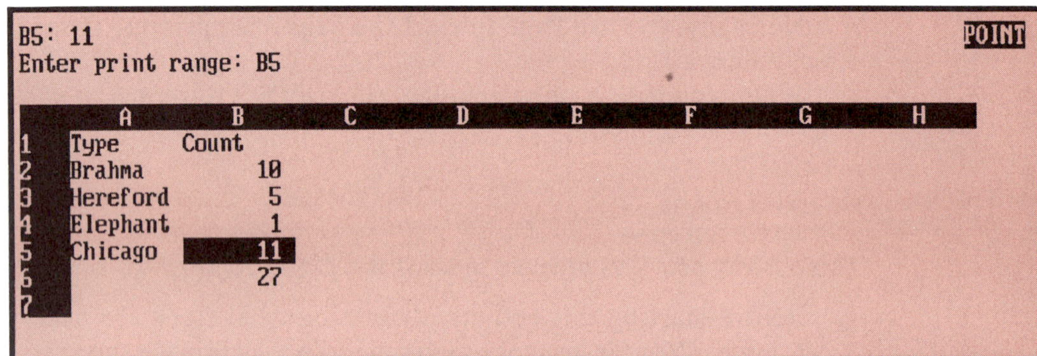

   d. Indicate the range to be printed by moving the cell pointer to cell A1, press a period to anchor the range, move to cell B6:

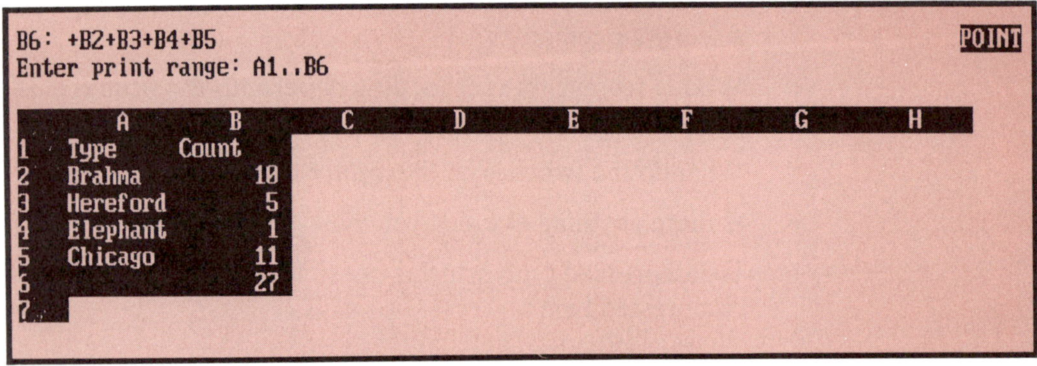

e. Press <Enter>. Lotus now displays the range on the Print Settings sheet (see Figure 5-1).

f. Press **G** (Go) to print.

g. Press **L** (Line) three times to move the paper forward.

h. Press **Q** (Quit) to exit to READY mode.

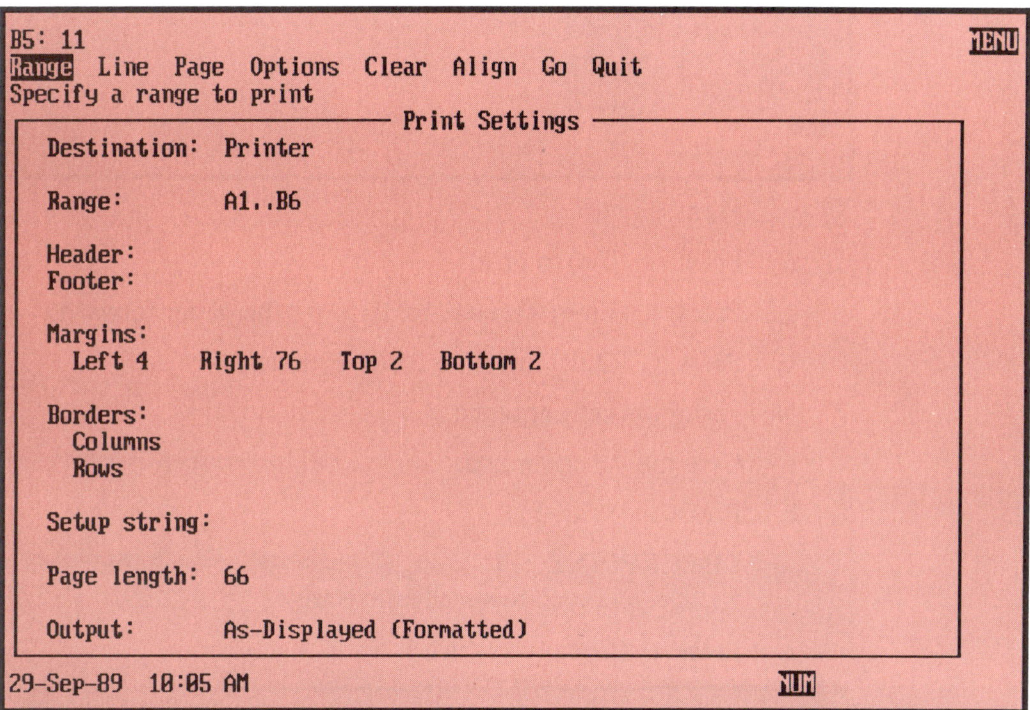

Figure 5-1 The Print Settings Sheet

6. Do the following to print the worksheet again:

a. Give the **/P** command.

b. Press **P** (Printer).

c. Press **R** (Range).

d. Notice that the previous range is highlighted (Lotus has remembered the previous range so you do not need to respecify the range each time you print).

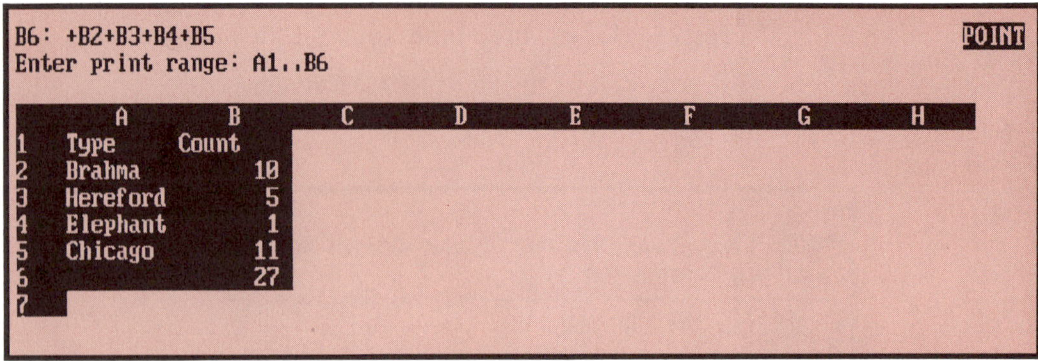

e. Press <Enter>.

f. Press **G** (Go) to print.

g. Press **L** (Line) three times to move the paper forward.

h. Press **Q** (Quit) to exit to READY mode.

7. Now, print the cell contents:

a. Give the **/P** command.

b. Press **P** (Printer).

CHECKPOINT

5a. Do you need to specify the Range?

c. Press **O** (Options), which is a sticky submenu:

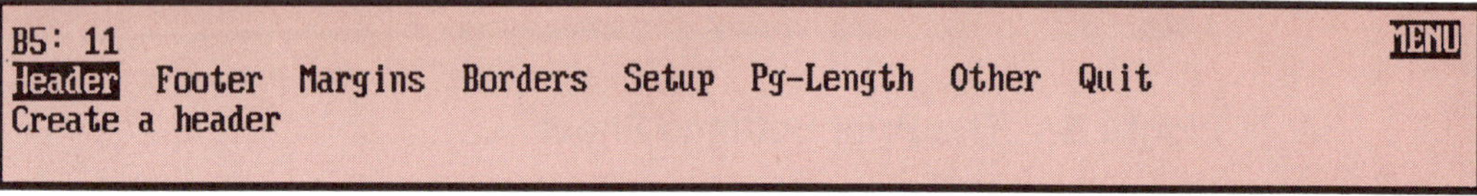

d. Press **O** (Other); Lotus displays yet another menu:

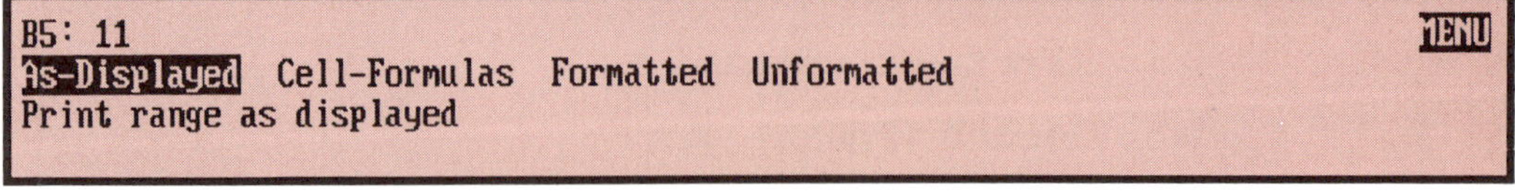

e. Press **C** (Cell-Formulas); Lotus returns to the Options submenu.

f. Press **Q** (Quit) to return to main **/P**rint menu.

g. Press **G** (Go) to print.

h. Press **L** (Line) three times to move the paper forward.

8. You should still be at the main **/P**rint menu. Next change the option back to As-Displayed so that later printouts will print the results, not the formulas.

a. Press **O** (Options), which is a sticky submenu.

b. Press **O** (Other).

c. Press **A** (As-Displayed).

d. Press **Q** (Quit) to return to main /**P**rint menu.

e. Press **Q** (Quit) to exit to READY mode.

9. Finally, print in compressed type style (your instructor will tell you to skip this step if your printers do not support compressed type style):

   a. Give the **/P** command.

   b. Press **P** (Printer).

   c. Press **O** (Options), which is a sticky submenu.

   d. Press **S** (Setup); Lotus prompts for the setup string:

```
B5: 11                                                        EDIT
Enter setup string:
```

   e. Enter the setup string, which you learned in step 1f.

   f. Press the <Enter> key after entering the setup string.

   g. Press **Q** (Quit) to return to main /**P**rint menu.

   h. Press **G** (Go) to print.

   i. Press **P** (Page) to move the paper forward to the top of the page.

   j. Press **Q** (Quit) to exit to READY mode.

10. /**F**ile **S**ave the worksheet with the name BULL. The most recent /**P**rint settings are saved with the file, so next time you /**F**ile **R**etrieve the file you do not need to specify Range and Options.

11. /**Q**uit to exit to the 1-2-3 Access System. Exit to the operating system. Remember to back up your work.

ENTERING PRINTER CONTROL CODES INTO THE BODY OF THE WORKSHEET

You can enter directly into the worksheet certain printer control codes that change the effect of the printer when the document is printed. One of the control codes that is entered is the **page break code**. This code is normally entered using the /**W**orksheet **P**age command. To use this command, move to column A in the row that you want to be the first row on the new page, that is, the row below where you want the page to end. Then give the /**W**orksheet **P**age command. The worksheet below this point moves down (as if you had inserted a row) and the cell in column A of the row displays a double colon and has **|::** in the cell as its entry. (On your computer screen and keyboard the vertical bar may be separated into two pieces, not one solid line as printed here.) Make no other entries in the row with the **::** because Lotus does not print anything that appears in the row.[1]

In addition, **printer setup codes** can be entered into worksheet cells. These codes have the effect of changing printer characteristics (usually font or pitch) in the middle of a printing job. For most dot-matrix printers, entering the label

```
||\015
```

shifts the printer into compressed print. On the screen display, this code is displayed as `|\015`. The first vertical bar is similar to a label alignment character (i.e., **'**, **"**, or **^**). Later (further down) in the worksheet, enter the label

```
||\018
```

to return to normal width print.

EXERCISE: PRINTING A HEADER

This exercise requires you to add a print header to the file HAROLD, then print the worksheet. Not all necessary keystrokes are listed in the following instructions. Practice "Heads-Up" computing as you accomplish this exercise and you will see how to get from one instruction to the next.

1. If you are not continuing from the previous Guided Activity, follow the startup procedure outlined in Unit 1 to load Lotus and enter the 1-2-3 program.
2. Retrieve the file HAROLD. If you have not already done so, change the width of column A so the entire text of the labels is visible.
3. Enter **/Print Printer Options Header**. When Lotus prompts for the header, enter

    `Harold's G.P.A. as of @||Page #`<Enter>

4. Instruct Lotus as to the **R**ange to be printed (the whole worksheet).
5. Print the worksheet. Notice the effect of the special characters entered in the header:

    `@` enters the current date.
    `|` separates header elements into left, center, and right-justified.
    `#` enters the page number.

6. Eject the page.
7. Save the file.
8. Exit Lotus.

---

1. You might put a comment in the row, however, for example: `This page contains the anticipated cash flows under the most optimistic conditions.`

REVIEW QUESTIONS

1.* What is a sticky menu?

2.* What is the **/Print** . . . **Range** submenu item used for?

DOCUMENTATION RESEARCH

Using the reference manual, find and record the page number of each of the commands discussed in this Unit. I recommend you also write the page number by the discussion of the command, above.

1. How would you put the current date in the **/Print** . . . **Footer**?
2. What are the page layout options?
3. How do you remember and clear print specifications?

APPLICATION B

POOR RICHARD'S (II)

In this exercise, you make modifications to the worksheet you created in Application A. Then you are introduced to one of the most useful facets of Lotus 1-2-3: the ability to seek a desired result by changing an input variable.

1. Follow the startup procedure outlined in Unit 1 to load Lotus and enter the 1-2-3 program.
2. Retrieve the AUTO worksheet you created in Application A.
3. Change the Trade in Allowance to **1900**.
4. Your accountant has pointed out two errors in AUTO. Correct your worksheet.
   a. The correct formula for Percent Profit is

   $$\frac{\text{Net Price - Net Cost}}{\text{Net Price}}$$

   b. In cell C18, the function that computes payments based on principal, interest, and term was incorrect because it did not consider sales tax. Change the formula so that the principal amount is *Net Price + (Sales Tax Rate times Net Price)*. (*Note*: You must still use the @PMT function; the arguments for interest and term do not change.)
5. Use the **/R**ange **F**ormat command to format all dollar amounts in currency format with 2 decimal places and all percent figures in percent format with 1 decimal place. You must use the **/W**orksheet **C**olumn **S**et-Width command to change the width of column C to accommodate the reformatted numbers. Your final sheet should look like Figure B-1.
6. Use the **/P**rint command to print a copy of the entire worksheet.

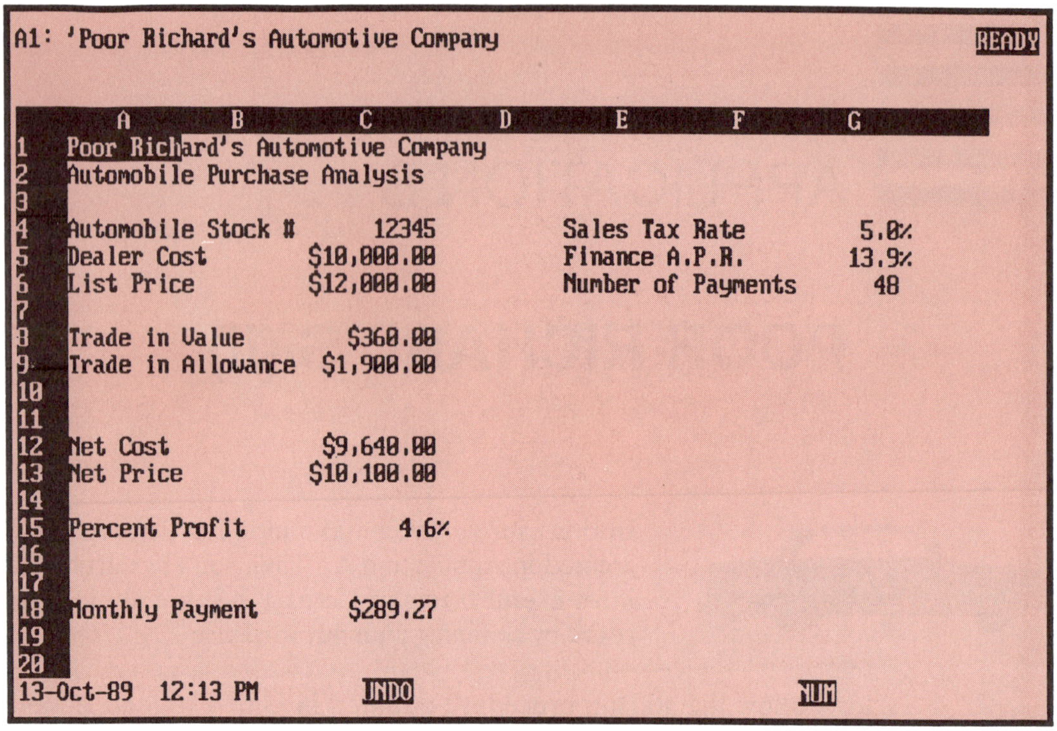

```
A1: 'Poor Richard's Automotive Company                                    READY

     A         B         C         D         E         F         G
1   Poor Richard's Automotive Company
2   Automobile Purchase Analysis
3
4   Automobile Stock #        12345          Sales Tax Rate          5.0%
5   Dealer Cost          $10,000.00          Finance A.P.R.         13.9%
6   List Price           $12,000.00          Number of Payments       48
7
8   Trade in Value          $360.00
9   Trade in Allowance    $1,900.00
10
11
12  Net Cost              $9,640.00
13  Net Price            $10,100.00
14
15  Percent Profit             4.6%
16
17
18  Monthly Payment         $289.27
19
20
13-Oct-89  12:13 PM           UNDO                            NUM
```

Figure B-1 The Worksheet after Formatting

7. One of the selling points of spreadsheet programs is that they facilitate **what-if calculations**. The user is able to see the effect of changing one number on all other results in the spreadsheet. This facility is especially useful when a certain goal (e.g., minimum profit of 10%) is sought. Step 8 asks you to perform a simple what-if procedure.

8. Now enter the number **2500** as the Trade in Allowance. Notice what happens to the Percent Profit. Keep changing the Trade in Allowance number in increments of 100 until you discover the maximum Trade in Allowance that gives Poor Richard a 10.0% or greater profit. Assume that the other three variables contributing to the function are fixed.

9. /Print your worksheet again.

10. When you are finished, save your work one last time.

11. /Quit to exit to the 1-2-3 Access System. Exit to the operating system. Remember to back up your work.

PART II

INTERMEDIATE SPREADSHEET OPERATIONS AND GRAPHICS

In this part, we continue our discussion of spreadsheet operations. Unit 6 is dedicated to two new commands: /Copy and /Move. Two important concepts are presented in Unit 7: Cell Addresses and Recalculation. It is necessary to understand these concepts before you progress from the simple worksheets created in Part 1. The graphics capabilities of Lotus are presented in the two final units of this part.

The application exercises in this part require you to develop a worksheet with sophisticated formulas and require you to develop and print graphs. When you complete this part, you will have been exposed to almost all the Lotus 1-2-3 spreadsheet operations.

UNIT 6

COPY AND MOVE COMMANDS

In this unit, we complete the basic set of spreadsheet commands. These commands enable you to quickly build spreadsheets with multiple similar formulas and to rearrange cell entries.

LEARNING OBJECTIVES

1. At the completion of this unit, you should know
   a. the variations of the /Copy command,
   b. how the /Copy command affects cell addresses,
   c. how the /Move command affects cell addresses,
   d. the difference between /Copy and /Move; when to choose one or the other.
2. At the completion of this unit, you should be able to
   a. copy a portion of the worksheet to another place on the worksheet,
   b. move a portion of the worksheet to another place on the worksheet.

IMPORTANT COMMANDS

/Copy
/Move

/COPY COMMAND

The /Copy command is used to create new cell entries that are copies of existing entries. Be careful using the /Copy command, because whatever existed in the cell prior to copying is erased. The /Copy command automatically adjusts most cell formulas to reflect new positions on the worksheet. See Unit 7 for a discussion of this feature and how to control it.

Prior to issuing the /Copy command, move the cursor to the cell in the upper left corner of the range you are copying. If you are copying one cell, move to that cell. If you are copying a column, move to the top cell in the portion of the column you are copying. If you are copying a row, move to the leftmost cell in the portion of the row you are copying.

If you forget to move to the proper cell, press the <Esc> key once and you can change the cell at the beginning of the range by moving the cell pointer. Or, simply type the range address.

Once you type **/C**, you are asked to specify a **FROM range** and a **TO range**. There are four variations of the /Copy operation:

- From one cell to another cell.
- From one cell to several other cells.
- From one range to one cell.
- From one range to another range.

The manner in which the source (from) and destination (to) ranges are specified determines which variation you are using. Each of these variations is illustrated in the Guided Activities that follow.

GUIDED ACTIVITY: PRELIMINARY ENTRIES IN THE SPREADSHEET

Our discussion of the /Copy command will center around the steps necessary to build a simple income statement. See Figure 6-8 for the end product.

1. Follow the startup procedure outlined in Unit 1 to load Lotus and enter the program.
2. Set the global format to fixed, 0 decimal places.
3. Make the entries displayed in Figure 6-1.
   a. To enter the label in A2, you must precede the entry with a ' (single quotation) mark so Lotus does not attempt to interpret it as a value.
   b. The labels in the following cells are right-justified and must be preceded by " (double quotation) marks: B4, A6..A8, A11..A13, A16..A18.
   c. Numbers are entered in B6, B7, B11, and B12.
   d. Enter the formula that sums Sales and Service in B8.
4. Save the worksheet with the name RB90PROJ.

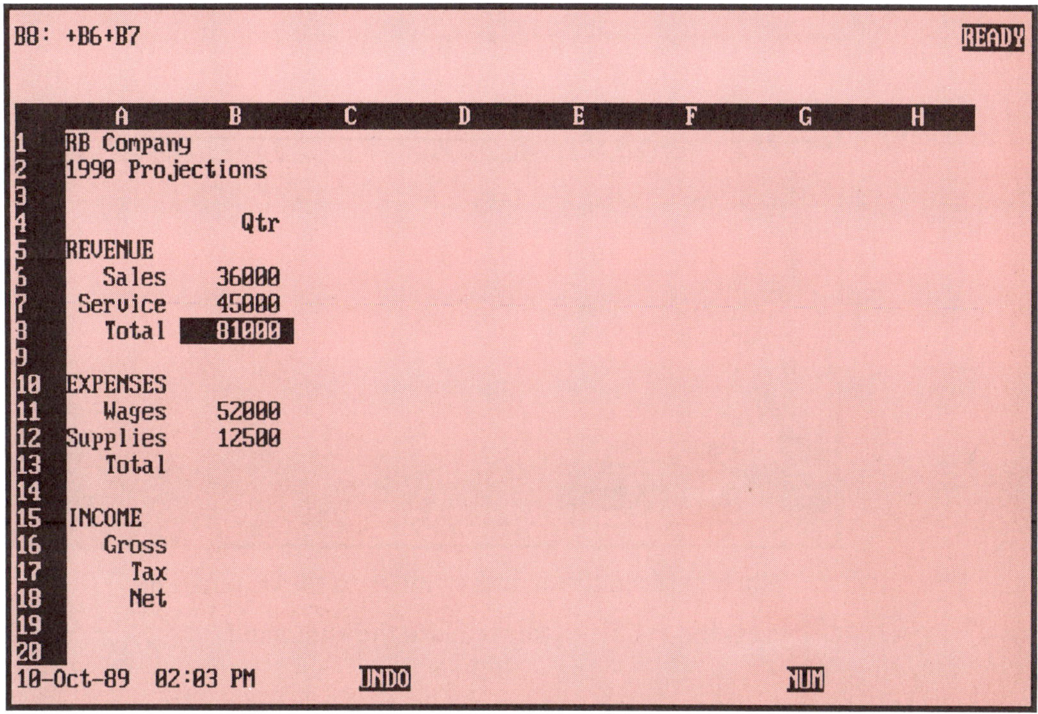

Figure 6-1 Spreadsheet with Preliminary Entries

GUIDED ACTIVITY: COPYING FROM ONE CELL TO ANOTHER CELL

In cell B8, Total Revenue is calculated with the formula **+B6+B7**. Since the same basic formula is used to compute Total Expenses in B13, we can use the /Copy command to copy *from one cell to another cell.*

1. If you are not continuing from the previous Guided Activity, load Lotus and retrieve RB90PROJ.

2. Move the cell pointer to B8.

3. Type **/C**. Lotus responds:

```
B8: +B6+B7                                          POINT
Enter range to copy FROM: B8..B8
```

   Note that Lotus assumes you want to copy from the cell the cursor is in.

4. Press the <Enter> key, which tells Lotus that you are copying a range of one cell. Lotus responds:

```
B8: +B6+B7                                          POINT
Enter range to copy TO: B8
```

5. Press the <Down> arrow key five times, moving the cell pointer to cell B13:

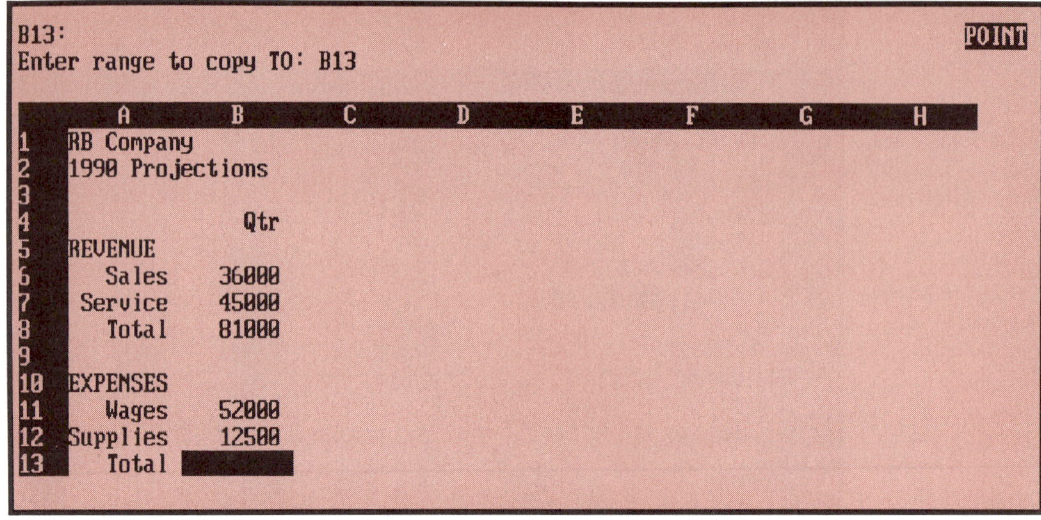

You have used the arrows to move to the destination.

6. Press the <Enter> key to close the command.

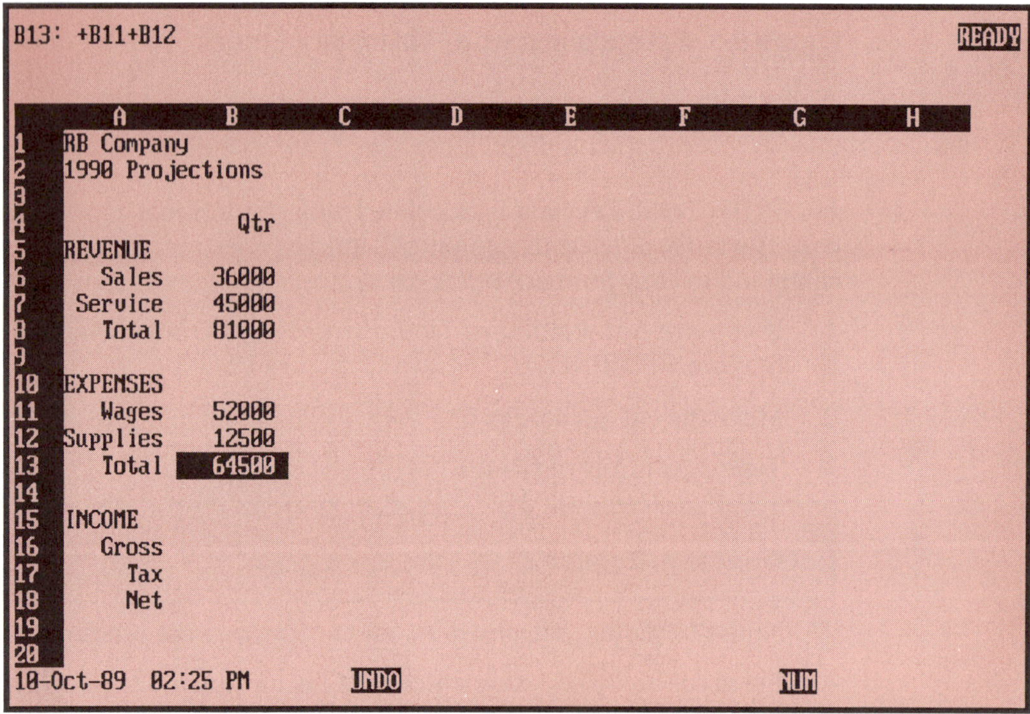

Figure 6-2 After Copying from Cell B8 to Cell B13

7. Use the arrow keys to move to cell B13. The formula in B13 is **+B11+B12**. Note that the cells referenced in the formula have adjusted relative to the formula's new position. The spreadsheet should now look like Figure 6-2.

   ✔CHECKPOINT

   6a. How does the formula in B13 differ from the original formula in B8? In what ways is it similar?

8. Save your work before proceeding.

GUIDED ACTIVITY: COPYING FROM ONE CELL TO SEVERAL OTHER CELLS

Next, we wish to duplicate the **Qtr** heading across columns C through E. Thus, we will make a copy *from one cell to several other cells*.

1. If you are not continuing from the previous Guided Activity, load Lotus and retrieve RB90PROJ.
2. Move the cell pointer to B4.
3. Type **/C**. Lotus responds by indicating the current cell as the cell to copy from.
4. Press the <Enter> key to accept this single-cell range. Lotus next asks for the range to copy to.
5. Press the <Right> arrow once, highlighting cell C4.
6. Press a period to anchor the range.
7. Press the <Right> arrow twice more to highlight the range C4..E4:

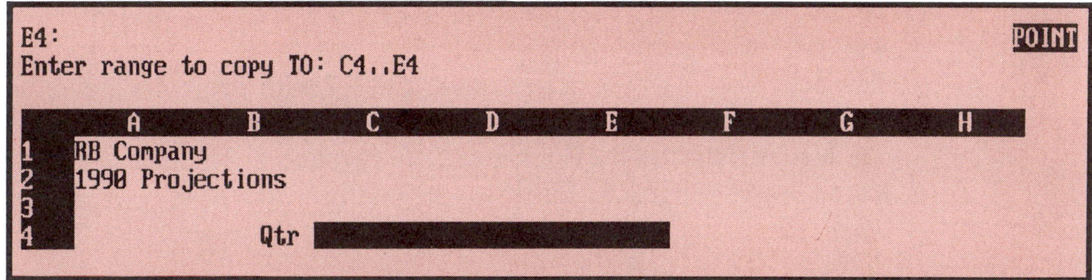

   You have used the arrows to move to the first cell of the destination range, anchored with a period, and arrowed to the last cell of the destination range.

8. Press the <Enter> key to close the command.
9. The spreadsheet should now look like Figure 6-3.
10. Save your work before proceeding.

When copying to or from a range, remember to **anchor** the upper/left cell of the range with a period before you point to the lower/right cell.

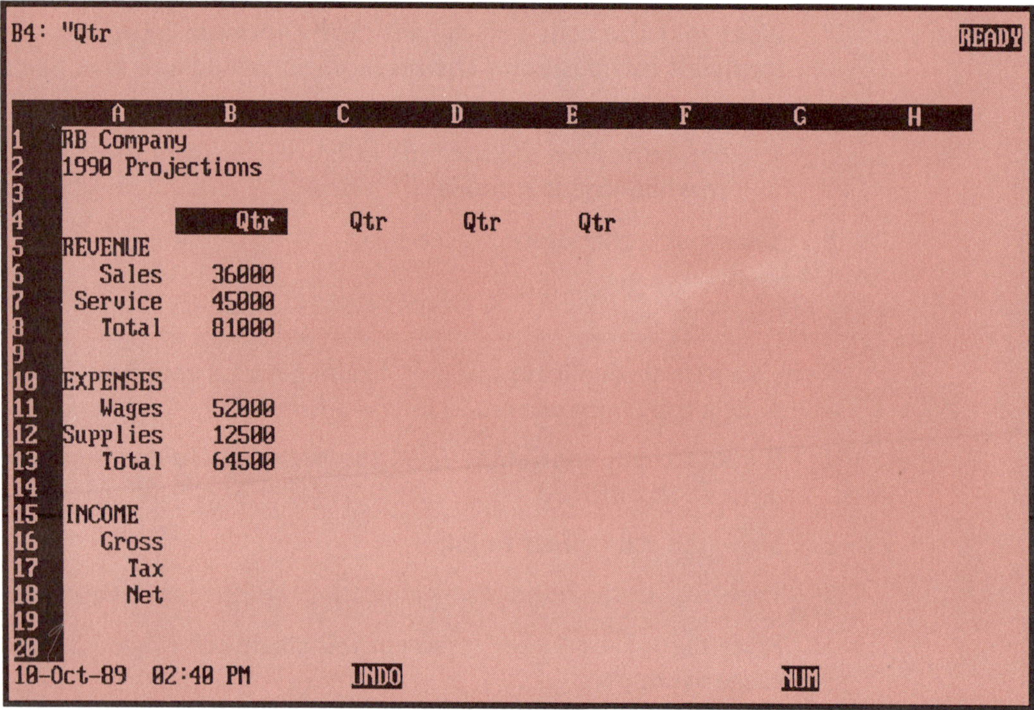

Figure 6-3 After Copying from Cell B4 to Cells C4..E4

GUIDED ACTIVITY: COPYING FROM ONE CELL TO SEVERAL OTHER CELLS

The next step is to fill in the range C6..E7 with projected revenues. The formula **+B6*1.05** is entered in C6. (The company expects each quarter's revenue to be 5% higher than the previous quarter's revenue.) This same formula can be copied to the entire range. Again this is a situation where we copy *from one cell to several other cells*.

1. If you are not continuing from the previous Guided Activity, load Lotus and retrieve RB90PROJ.
2. Move the cell pointer to C6.
3. Enter the formula **+B6*1.05** in cell C6.
4. Type **/C**. Lotus responds by indicating the current cell as the cell to copy from.
5. Press the <Enter> key to accept this single-cell range. Lotus next asks for the range to copy to.

6. Press a **.** (period) to anchor the destination range at the current cell, then highlight the remainder of the destination range (C6..E7):

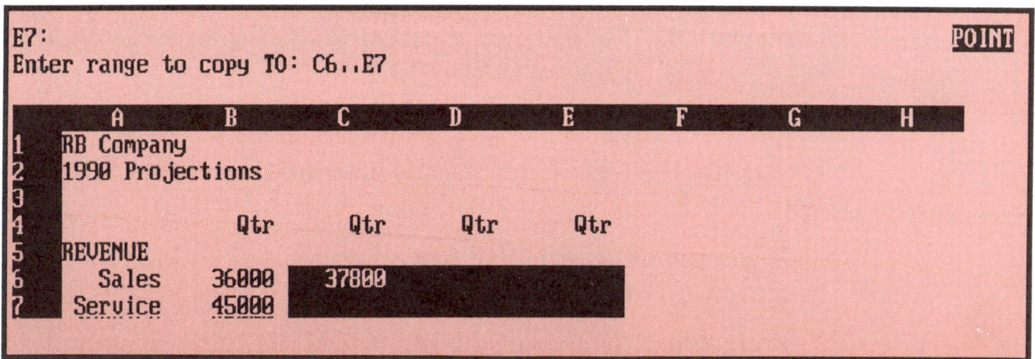

7. Press the <Enter> key to close the command.
8. Use the arrow keys to move around in the range C6..E7.

CHECKPOINT

6b. How are the formulas in C6..E7 different from the original formula in C6? How are they similar?

9. At this point the worksheet should look like Figure 6-4. Save your work before proceeding.

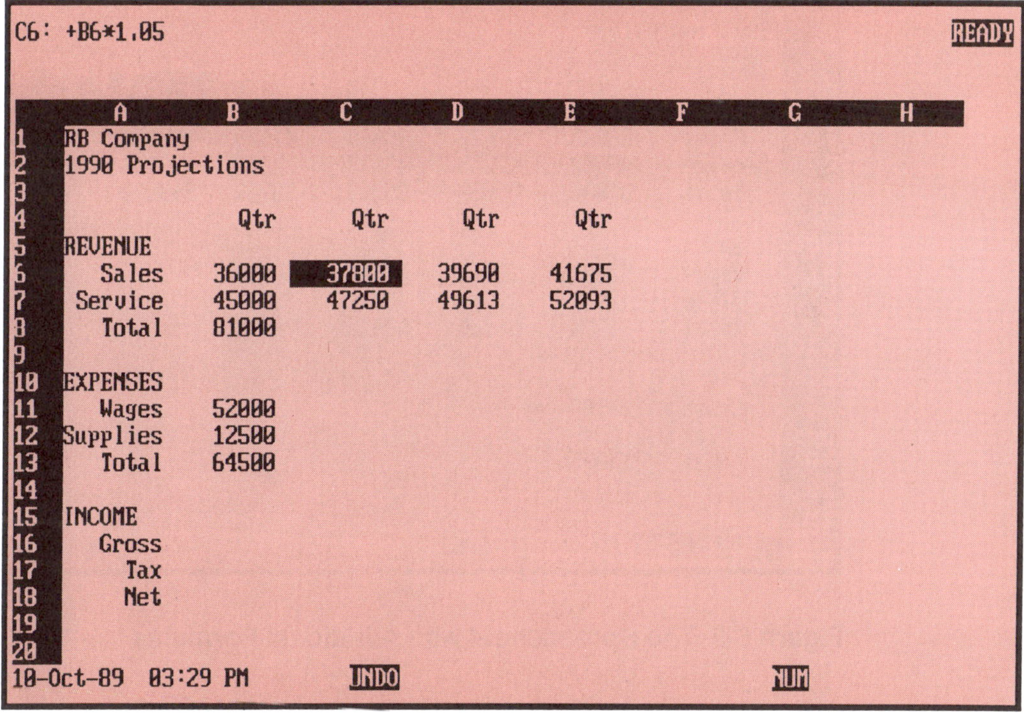

Figure 6-4 After Copying from Cell C6 to Cells C6..E7

In this example we have duplicated a single cell throughout a block. The cell itself is one corner of the block. If you look at any of the entries in the range we have just created, you note that each formula multiplies the cell to the left (i.e., the previous quarter) by 1.05. For instance, the formula in E7 is **+D7*1.05**.

GUIDED ACTIVITY: ADDING ADDITIONAL FORMULAS

Next, we use the techniques already illustrated to add more formulas to the worksheet.

1. If you are not continuing from the previous Guided Activity, load Lotus and retrieve RB90PROJ.
2. Projected Expenses in the range C11..E12 are computed as 1.03 times the previous quarter. Enter the formula **+B11*1.03** in C11. Copy this to C11..E12.
3. Copy the formula in B8 to C8..E8.
4. Copy the formula in B13 to C13..E13.

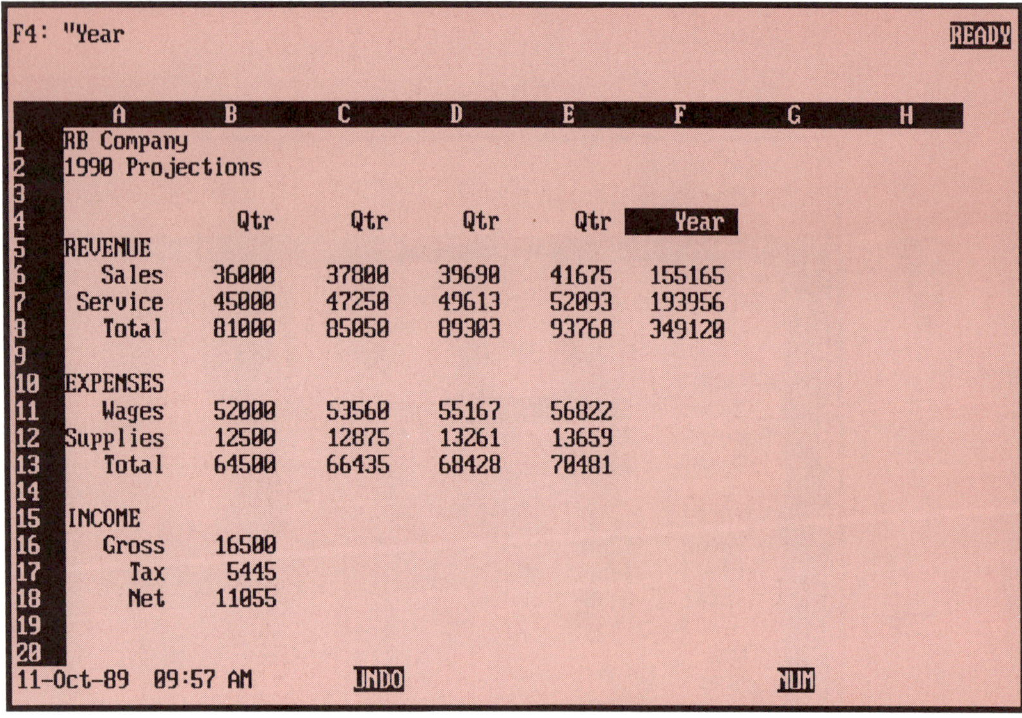

F4: "Year READY

	A	B	C	D	E	F	G	H
1	RB Company							
2	1990 Projections							
3								
4		Qtr	Qtr	Qtr	Qtr	Year		
5	REVENUE							
6	Sales	36000	37800	39690	41675	155165		
7	Service	45000	47250	49613	52093	193956		
8	Total	81000	85050	89303	93768	349120		
9								
10	EXPENSES							
11	Wages	52000	53560	55167	56822			
12	Supplies	12500	12875	13261	13659			
13	Total	64500	66435	68428	70481			
14								
15	INCOME							
16	Gross	16500						
17	Tax	5445						
18	Net	11055						
19								
20								

11-Oct-89 09:57 AM UNDO NUM

Figure 6-5 The Spreadsheet with Additional Formulas

5. Enter these formulas in the INCOME section:

- Gross Income (B16) is Total Revenue less Total Expenses: **+B8-B13**
- Tax (B17) is 33% of Gross Income: **+B16*.33**
- Net Income (B18) is Gross Income less Tax: **+B16-B17**

6. Enter the formula **@SUM(B6..E6)** in F6 and copy it to F7..F8.
7. Enter the label **"Year** in cell F4.
8. The worksheet should now look like Figure 6-5.
9. Save your work before proceeding.

GUIDED ACTIVITY: COPYING FROM A RANGE TO A CELL

The formulas in F6..F8 can be duplicated in the area F11..F13. This requires that we copy *from one range to one cell.*

1. If you are not continuing from the previous Guided Activity, load Lotus and retrieve RB90PROJ.
2. Move the cell pointer to F6.
3. Type **/C**. Lotus responds by indicating the current cell as the cell to copy from.
4. Press the <Down> arrow twice to highlight the range F6..F8:

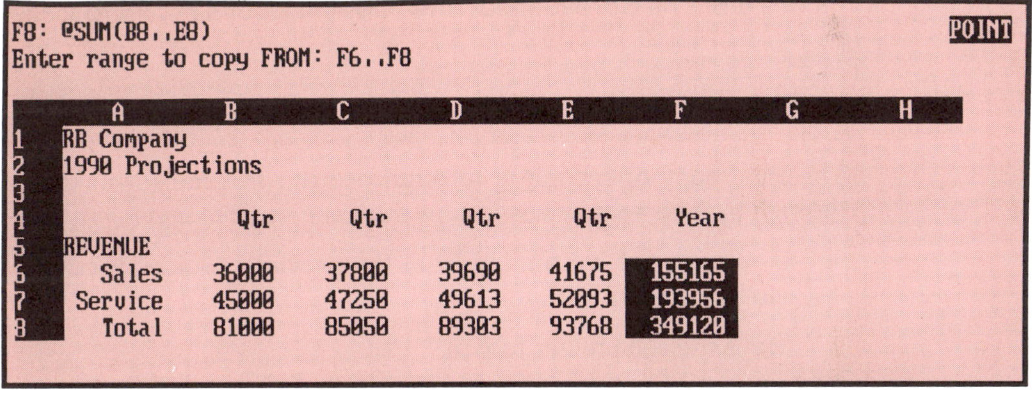

5. Press the <Enter> key to accept the range. This tells Lotus that you are copying a range of three cells. Lotus next asks for the range to copy to.
6. Press the <Down> arrow key to move the cell pointer to F11, then press the <Enter> key. Lotus executes the copy.
7. The spreadsheet should now look like Figure 6-6.

Even though you specified only one cell in the destination range, the entire source range was copied, yielding a three-cell destination range, the same size as the source range.

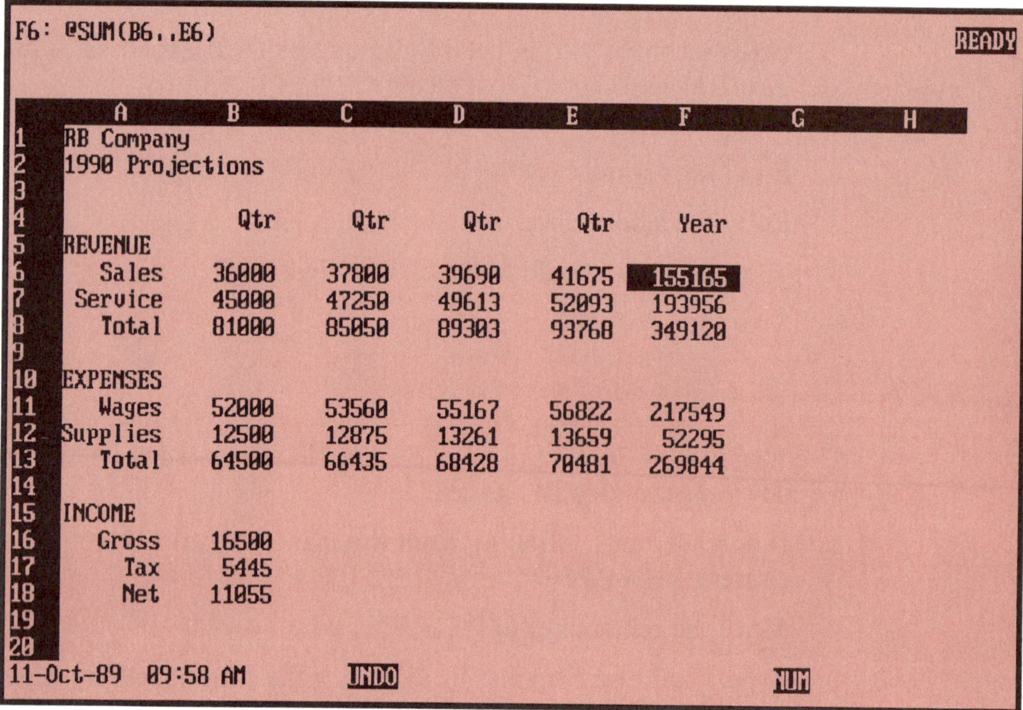
F6: @SUM(B6..E6) READY

	A	B	C	D	E	F	G	H
1	RB Company							
2	1990 Projections							
3								
4		Qtr	Qtr	Qtr	Qtr	Year		
5	REVENUE							
6	Sales	36000	37800	39690	41675	155165		
7	Service	45000	47250	49613	52093	193956		
8	Total	81000	85050	89303	93768	349120		
9								
10	EXPENSES							
11	Wages	52000	53560	55167	56822	217549		
12	Supplies	12500	12875	13261	13659	52295		
13	Total	64500	66435	68428	70481	269844		
14								
15	INCOME							
16	Gross	16500						
17	Tax	5445						
18	Net	11055						
19								
20								

11-Oct-89 09:58 AM UNDO NUM

Figure 6-6 The Spreadsheet after Copying Cells F6..F8 to Cells F11..F13

GUIDED ACTIVITY: COPYING FROM A RANGE TO A RANGE

The final copy operation is to duplicate the Income formulas across columns C through F. This requires us to copy *from one range to another range*.

1. If you are not continuing from the previous Guided Activity, load Lotus and retrieve RB90PROJ.
2. Move the cell pointer to B16.
3. Type **/C**. Lotus responds by indicating the current cell as the cell to copy from.
4. Press the <Down> arrow twice to highlight the range B16..B18, then press the <Enter> key. Lotus next asks for the range to copy to.
5. Press the <Right> arrow key once to move the cell pointer to the upper left cell of the range (C16).
6. Press a **.** (period) to anchor the range.

7. Press the <Right> arrow three times to highlight the range C16..F16:

```
F16:                                                          POINT
Enter range to copy TO: C16..F16

     A          B        C        D        E        F       G      H
1  RB Company
2  1990 Projections
3
4               Qtr      Qtr      Qtr      Qtr      Year
5  REVENUE
6     Sales     36000    37800    39690    41675    155165
7   Service     45000    47250    49613    52093    193956
8     Total     81000    85050    89303    93768    349120
9
10 EXPENSES
11    Wages     52000    53560    55167    56822    217549
12 Supplies     12500    12875    13261    13659     52295
13    Total     64500    66435    68428    70481    269844
14
15 INCOME
16    Gross     16500
```

8. Press the <Enter> key to complete the command.

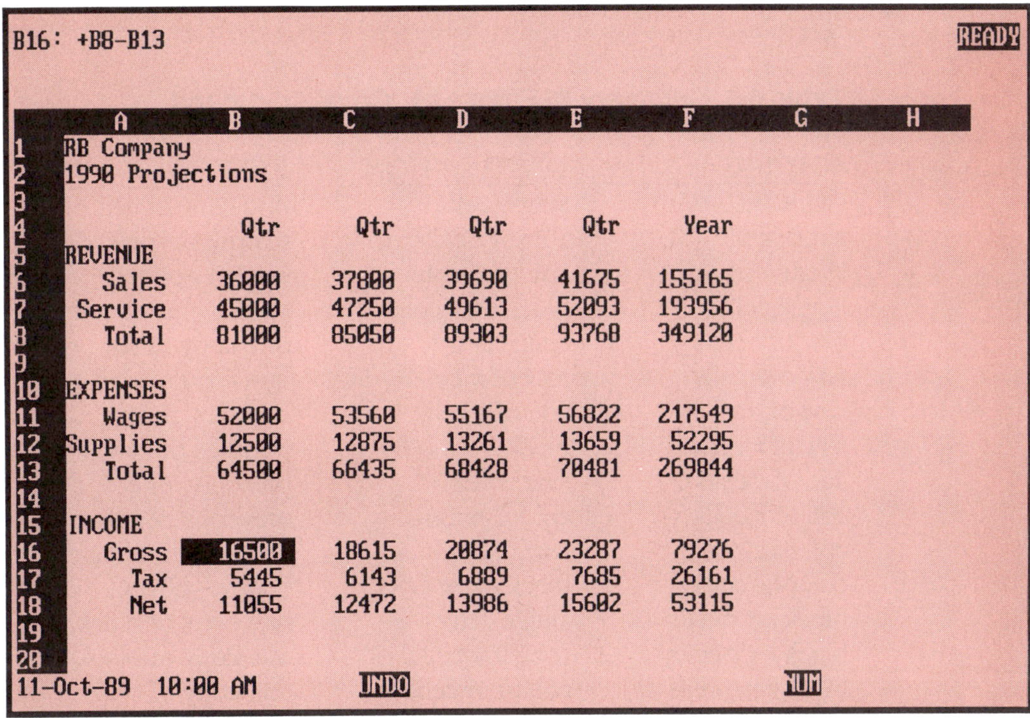

B16: +B8-B13 READY

	A	B	C	D	E	F	G	H
1	RB Company							
2	1990 Projections							
3								
4		Qtr	Qtr	Qtr	Qtr	Year		
5	REVENUE							
6	Sales	36000	37800	39690	41675	155165		
7	Service	45000	47250	49613	52093	193956		
8	Total	81000	85050	89303	93768	349120		
9								
10	EXPENSES							
11	Wages	52000	53560	55167	56822	217549		
12	Supplies	12500	12875	13261	13659	52295		
13	Total	64500	66435	68428	70481	269844		
14								
15	INCOME							
16	Gross	16500	18615	20874	23287	79276		
17	Tax	5445	6143	6889	7685	26161		
18	Net	11055	12472	13986	15602	53115		
19								
20								

11-Oct-89 10:00 AM UNDO NUM

Figure 6-7 The Spreadsheet after Copying Cells B16..B18 to Cells C16..F18

9. The spreadsheet should now look like Figure 6-7. Save your work before proceeding.

In this Guided Activity, a column range has been copied into a row range. Four copies of the column are made — as many copies as there are columns in the destination range.

GENERAL RULES FOR COPYING

Together, these examples illustrate a general rule of copying:

> *Starting at each cell of the 'TO' range, 1-2-3 attempts to place a copy of the entire 'FROM' range.* (quoted from the Lotus manual)

Where there was one source cell and one destination cell, one copy was made because there is only one cell in the destination range. In the next activity, there was one source cell and three destination cells; therefore, three copies of the source range were made. Then, a single-cell source range was copied six times into the destination range. Whenever the source is a single cell, the number of copies is the number of cells in the destination range.

Where the source was a range of cells but the destination was one cell, the source was copied once into the destination range. In the last activity, the source range was copied four times because the destination range was four columns. See Table 6-1 for general rules for copying.

Table 6-1 Summary of Effects of /Copy Command

SOURCE	DESTINATION	EFFECT
single cell	single cell	one copy of cell
single cell	row of *r* cells	*r* copies of cell
single cell	col. of *c* cells	*c* copies of cell
single cell	block *r* x *c* cells	*r* x *c* copies of cell
row of *r* cells	single cell	one copy of row, *r* cells across
row of *r* cells	row of *n* cells	one copy of row, *r* cells across
row of *r* cells	col. of *c* cells	*c* copies of row, *r* cells across
row of *r* cells	block *n* x *c* cells	*c* copies of row, *r* cells across
col. of *c* cells	single cell	one copy of col., *c* cells down
col. of *c* cells	col. of *m* cells	one copy of col., *c* cells down
col. of *c* cells	row of *r* cells	*r* copies of col., *c* cells down
col. of *c* cells	block *r* x *m* cells	*r* copies of col., *c* cells down
block *r* x *c* cells	single cell	one copy of block, *r* by *c*
block *r* x *c* cells	row of *n* cells	one copy of block, *r* by *c*
block *r* x *c* cells	col. of *m* cells	one copy of block, *r* by *c*
block *r* x *c* cells	block *n* x *m* cells	one copy of block, *r* by *c*

c and *m* refer to number of cells down the column.
r and *n* refer to number of cells across the row.

/MOVE COMMAND

The /Move command operates in the same manner as the /Copy command. There are, however, two major differences in effect. First, the source range is erased. Second, some cell references in a /Move operation are treated as if they are absolute: if the formula `+A2+B2` is moved from cell A1 to cell F25, the result in F25 is `+A2+B2`. The cell reference is changed, however, if the referenced cell is part of the block being moved. For instance, if the formula `+A2+B2` is in cell A1, and both A1 and A2 (but not B2) are moved to F25, then the result in F25 is `+F26+B2`.

The effect is that you have the same number of cell entries referencing the same information after the move.

GUIDED ACTIVITY: MOVING A RANGE

Continuing with our income statement spreadsheet, we decide to move A1 and A2 to C1 and C2 so they are centered over the data.

1. If you are not continuing from the previous Guided Activity, load Lotus and retrieve RB90PROJ.

2. Move the cell pointer to A1.

3. Type **/M**. Lotus responds by indicating the current cell as the cell to move from:

4. Press the <Down> arrow key once to highlight the range A1..A2:

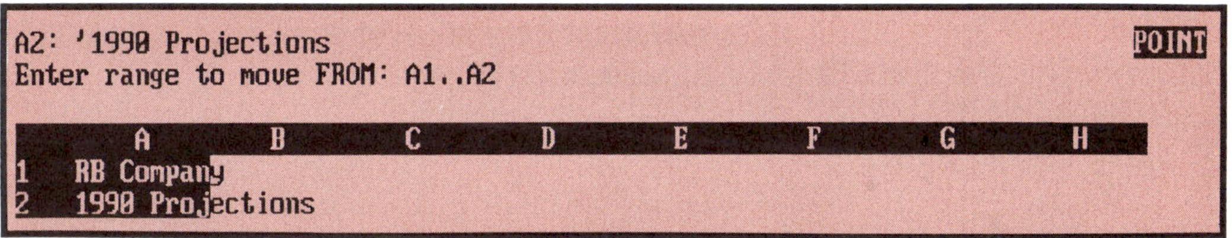

5. Press the <Enter> key to accept the range. This tells Lotus that you are moving a range of two cells. Lotus next asks for the range to move to.

6. Press the <Right> arrow key two times to move the cell pointer to C1:

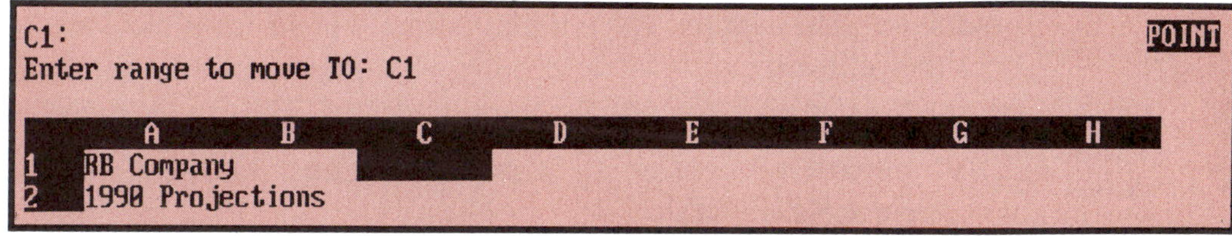

7. Finally, press the <Enter> key. Lotus executes the move.

8. The spreadsheet should now look like Figure 6-8. Notice that A1..A2 are now empty.
9. Save your work.

```
A1:                                                              READY

         A        B        C        D        E        F        G        H
1                          RB Company
2                          1990 Projections
3
4                 Qtr      Qtr      Qtr      Qtr      Year
5    REVENUE
6       Sales     36000    37800    39690    41675    155165
7     Service     45000    47250    49613    52093    193956
8       Total     81000    85050    89303    93768    349120
9
10   EXPENSES
11      Wages     52000    53560    55167    56822    217549
12   Supplies     12500    12875    13261    13659     52295
13      Total     64500    66435    68428    70481    269844
14
15   INCOME
16      Gross     16500    18615    20874    23287     79276
17        Tax      5445     6143     6889     7685     26161
18        Net     11055    12472    13986    15602     53115
19
20
11-Oct-89  10:12 AM          UNDO                           NUM
```

Figure 6-8 The Spreadsheet after Moving Range A1..A2 to C1
This is the Finished Spreadsheet.

GUIDED ACTIVITY: SENSITIVITY ANALYSIS

Finally, we check our income statement spreadsheet to see how sensitive it is to fluctuations in the wage expense. This worksheet shows steadily rising income because initial revenues are higher than initial expenses, and revenues grow at 5% per quarter while expenses grow at only a 3% per quarter rate. In this activity, we determine what happens if the initial estimate of wages is too low. In the first activity in the following unit, we determine what happens if the rates of change are not correct.

1. If you are not continuing from the previous Guided Activity, load Lotus and retrieve RB90PROJ.
2. Move the cell pointer to cell B11.
3. Enter the number **70000** in B11.

4. Notice that the Gross Income for the first quarter changes to `-1500`, Taxes are `-495` (that is, a tax credit), and Net Income is `-1005` (a loss).

5. Notice further that the company still makes a profit: net income for the year (cell F18) is `2661`.

6. Increase the wage expense in B11 in increments of `100` until the Net income for the year changes from positive to negative. This demonstrates the effect of varying wage levels on profitability for the company.

7. Save the worksheet with this latest change. We do further sensitivity analysis in Unit 7.

8. This completes the guided activities for this unit. /**Q**uit to exit to the 1-2-3 Access System. Exit to the operating system. Remember to back up your work.

/COPY VERSUS /MOVE

/**C**opy is normally used to replicate the same formula to several places in the worksheet. /**C**opy is most useful when building a worksheet. /**M**ove is often done purely for visual reasons: cells are moved because they *fit* better in one place than another.

EXERCISE: A SALES WORKSHEET (I)

1. If you are not continuing from the previous Guided Activity, follow the startup procedure outlined in Unit 1 to load Lotus and enter the 1-2-3 program. If you are continuing from a previous activity or exercise and already have a worksheet on the screen, use the command /**W**orksheet **E**rase **Y**es to clear the screen. (*Remember*: Save it before erasing it.)

2. Enter the following information into your worksheet, starting in cell A1. (Enter the column headings in A1..D1 and the items and costs down columns A and B.)

```
Item      Price      Tax      Total
Computer        895
Monitor         278
Printer         449
Desk            199
TOTAL:
```

3. Sales tax is 5% of the price. In C2, enter the formula for sales tax on the computer: **`+B2*.05`**.

4. In D2, place the formula that adds the price and the sales tax.

5. /**C**opy the formulas from C2..D2 to C3..C5. Mentally check the results. For instance, the tax on the desk should be about $10, and the total for the desk should be about $209.

6. In the row labeled `TOTAL:`, enter a function that sums the price column, then /**C**opy that formula to the other two columns. Again, mentally check the results.

7. Format the dollar amounts to Currency, two decimal places. Change column widths as necessary. Use the /**R**ange **L**abel command to right-justify the labels in columns B, C, and D.

8. Next, use the /**M**ove command to reposition the entire table to B11. (B11 is the upper-left corner.) Look at the formulas (which are now in columns D and E): Did they change to reflect the new cell locations? If necessary, change column widths.

9. /**F**ile **S**ave as COMPCOST.

EXERCISE: THE PERFECT JOB (III)

1. If you are not continuing from the previous Exercise or Guided Activity, follow the startup procedure outlined in Unit 1 to load Lotus and enter the 1-2-3 program.

2. Retrieve the JOBS worksheet created in the Exercises at the end of Unit 2 and 4.

3. You would like to adjust the salaries by some factor of the cost of living in the different cities. You decide to use data from the *Places Rated Almanac*.[1] The first step is to add the following to your worksheet:

```
My Job Prospects
=====================================================================================
Company City     Title          Salary Adj. Sal.   Index Housing      Food    Other
-------------------------------------------------------------------------------------
Arthur's Chicago Manager   $25,000.00                        131       100      106
Freddy's Seattle Buyer     $26,300.00                        122       103      112
Mack's   Bangor  Associate $22,135.00                         87        94       97
Mickey's L.A.    Partner   $24,900.00                        166        95      105
Al's     Memphis Executive $21,467.00                         84       103       97
```

4. In the Index column, Chicago row, create a formula that computes the index as

$$\frac{2 \cdot \text{Housing} + 2 \cdot \text{Food} + \text{Other}}{5}$$

You should obtain the answer `113.6`. Copy this formula to the other cities. If you have done this correctly, you should obtain the result `94.2` for Memphis.

5. Next, compute adjusted salaries. The adjusted salary is 100 times salary divided by the index. For Seattle, you should obtain the result `$23,398.57`.

6. Format the Adjusted Salary column to Currency, 2 decimal places and adjust the column width as necessary.

7. Save the worksheet.

---

1. Boyer, Richard and David Savageau, *Places Rated Almanac*, Second Edition. Chicago: Rand McNally, 1985. A newer edition of this book is now available.

REVIEW QUESTIONS

1. What are the four variations of the /Copy command?
2. How does the /Copy command affect cell addresses in formulas in the destination range?
3. How does the /Move command affect cell addresses of cells external to the range being moved?
4. How does the /Move command affect cell addresses of cells internal to the range being moved?
5. What is the difference between /Copy and /Move?

6.* When would you choose the /Copy command?

7.* When would you choose the /Move command?

DOCUMENTATION RESEARCH

Using the reference manual, find and record the page number of each of the commands discussed in this Unit. I recommend you also write the page number by the discussion of the command, above.

1. /Copy — how does this command help you enter a set of *similar* but not identical calculations?
2. /Move — what happens if you move TO a cell that is referred to in a previously existing formula?

UNIT 7

CELL REFERENCE AND CALCULATION

Lotus 1-2-3 is a very well designed spreadsheet. In most of the earlier spreadsheets, the user had to carefully arrange values that would be used in formulas in other cells of the spreadsheet. Lotus 1-2-3 uses a natural order of recalculation, which means that the user need not worry about the relative placement of values that are used in later formulas.

Lotus also provides the ability to replicate formulas and values from one cell to one or more other cells. This allows the user to build the formula once, then copy that formula to many cells, greatly expediting the worksheet development process.

This elegance is not without its cost, however. To effectively use the powers of Lotus, the user must understand the methods of calculation and cell reference used by Lotus.

LEARNING OBJECTIVES

1. At the completion of this unit, you should know
   a. the distinctions among the three types of cell addresses,
   b. when to use mixed or absolute addresses instead of relative addresses,
   c. when to use manual instead of automatic recalculation,
   d. what natural order of recalculation is,
   e. what a circular reference is.
2. At the completion of this unit, you should be able to
   a. enter a formula containing relative, absolute, and mixed addresses using the pointing method,
   b. change the recalculation method from manual to automatic, and vice versa,
   c. change the recalculation method to rowwise or columnwise,
   d. change the recalculation method to a specific number of iterations.

IMPORTANT COMMAND

/**W**orksheet **G**lobal **R**ecalculation

CELL ADDRESSES

A cell address included in a formula can be one of three types:

- **Relative address** (normal).
- **Absolute address.**
- **Mixed address.**

Recall the example from Unit 2: we want to put the sum of cells A2 and B2 into cell A1. Using the pointing method, we enter the formula:

Move to cell A1		
Press	**+**	*Lotus is ready for a formula,*
	<Down>	*move to A2,*
	+	*begin next address; cell pointer returns to A1,*
	<Down> <Right>	*move to B2,*
	<Enter>	*enters formula and calculates result in A1.*

The result in A1 is `+A2+B2`.
Lotus does not remember this as `+A2+B2`, however, but rather as + *down-1 & same column* + *down-1 & right-1*. If we /Copy the formula from cell A1 to another place on the worksheet, say cell F25, then Lotus still remembers the formula as + *down-1 & same column* + *down-1 & right-1*. In F25, the formula reads `+F26+G26`.

RELATIVE CELL ADDRESSES

The example above illustrates how Lotus normally handles cell addresses in formulas: as relative movements from the cell in which the formula resides. **Relative addressing** occurs irrespective of the method used to input the formula. Both pointing and typing methods yield a relative address.

If you do not intend to /Copy the formula, then relative addresses are fine. On many occasions, however, you build a set of formulas that you want to duplicate elsewhere in the spreadsheet. In some cases, relative addresses are acceptable, but in other cases they are not.

ABSOLUTE CELL ADDRESSES

When an **absolute cell address** appears in a formula, that address does not change as the formula is copied to other places in the spreadsheet. For instance, you might put a percentage value in cell A2 that is used in several places in your worksheet. As you /Copy formulas from one place to another, you do not want the reference to cell A2 to change.

To indicate to Lotus that cell A2 is an absolute rather than a relative address, it must be entered into the formula as **$A$2**. The $ sign tells Lotus that this is an absolute address, not to be changed in a /Copy procedure.

Following our earlier example, if cell A1 contains the formula `+$A$2+B2` and we /Copy that formula to cell F25, then the result is `+$A$2+G26`. Notice that the relative component of the address (B2) changes (to G26), but the absolute ($A$2) does not change.

MIXED CELL ADDRESSES

A third possibility is that you wish to hold the row (or column) absolute while allowing the column (or row) to vary relative to the address. This is called a **mixed cell address**, and is obtained by putting the $ prior to the item that does not vary:

$A2 *column A is constant, row varies.*

A$2 *row 2 is constant, column varies.*

Continuing with our example, if cell A1 contains the formula `+$A2+B2` and we /Copy that formula to cell F25, then the result is `+$A26+G26`. Notice that the relative component of the first address (row 2) changes (to row 26), but the absolute (column A) does not change.

What would be the result if cell A1 contains the formula `+A$2+B2` and we /Copy that formula to cell F25?

EXAMPLE

If you put money into a savings account paying compound interest, compounded yearly, then the ending balance (principal + interest) is expressed by the algebraic formula

$$\text{bal} = \text{inv} \cdot (1 + \text{int})^n$$

where *bal* is ending balance, *inv* is initial investment, *int* is periodic interest rate, and *n* is number of periods. Your boss would like you to build a table that shows the effect of leaving various amounts of money, from $10 to $100, in a savings account for one to five years. She tells you to assume a 5.25% interest rate and yearly compounding.

You put the interest rate in cell A1 (see Figure 7-1). Then you put the amounts in column A, from A3 to A12, and the years in row 2, from B2 to F2. The formula for $10 invested for 1 year is to be put into cell B3. If you were to use relative addresses, the formula would be

`+A3*(1+A1)^B2`

That formula could not be copied to the other cells in the table, however, because the addresses of the cells would then point to the wrong cells for investment, interest, and number of periods. Therefore, you decide to try to use mixed and absolute addresses.

First, identify the address(es) in the formula that should remain constant wherever the formula appears. In this case, we want A1 to remain constant because the same interest rate is used for all calculations. Make a note that we want $A$1 in the final formula. Neither A3 nor B2 should be absolute addresses, however, because the investment and the term vary.

Second, look for addresses that must refer to the same row as they are copied down a column. In this case, row 2 contains the number of years, and each of the numbers in row 2 applies to all entries in the column below that number. Therefore, the term (B2) must always refer to row 2 as we /Copy the formula from row 3 to row 12. Thus, the formula must include the term B$2.

Finally, look for addresses that must refer to the same column as they are copied across a row. Here, the investment (A3) must always refer to column A (the amount invested) as we /Copy the formula from column B to column F. Thus the formula must include the term $A3.

The final formula is

+$A3*(1+$A$1)^B$2

You build this worksheet with mixed and absolute addresses in Application C.

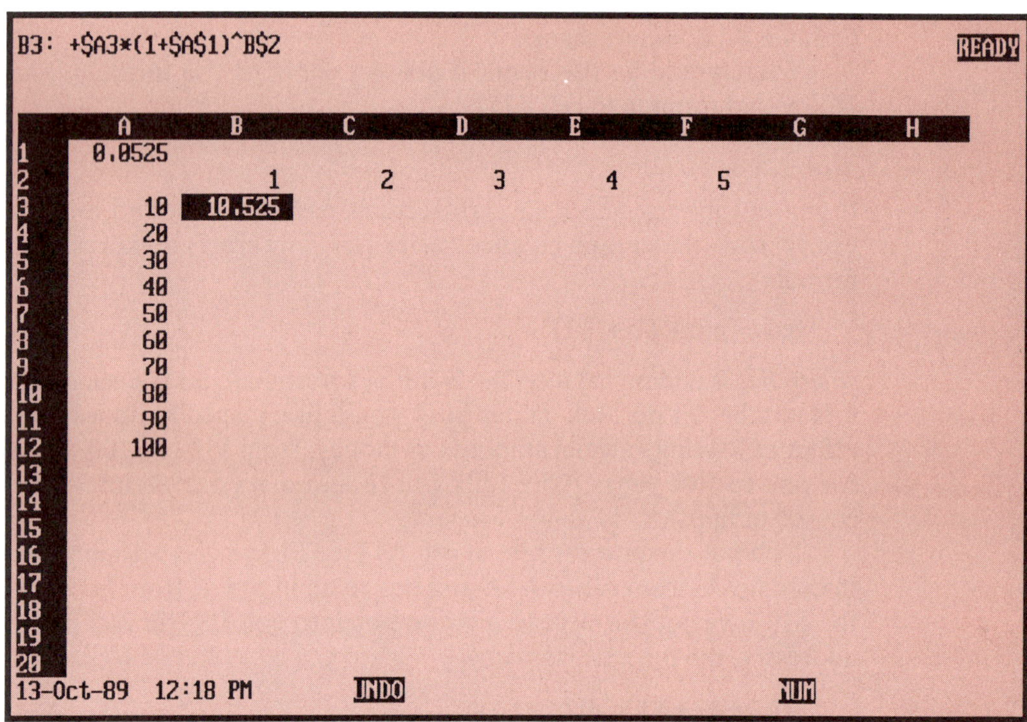

Figure 7-1 A Worksheet with Mixed and Absolute Addresses

ENTERING ADDRESSES INTO FORMULAS

The preferred method for entering addresses, relative, absolute, or mixed, into formulas is the pointing method. The type of address can be changed by pressing the <ABS (F4)> key while pointing at the cell. Assume that we want the formula `+$A3*(1+$A$1)^B$2` in cell B3. The method is as follows:

Move to cell B3

Press	**+**	*Lotus is ready for a formula.*
	<Left>	*Cell pointer moves to A3,*
	<ABS (F4)> key	*changes A3 to $A$3,*
	<ABS (F4)>	*changes $A$3 to A$3,*
	<ABS (F4)>	*changes A$3 to $A3.*
	***(1+**	*Begin next address,*
	<Up><Up><Left>	*moves to A1,*
	<ABS (F4)>	*changes A1 to $A$1.*
	)^	*Begin next address,*
	<Up>	*moves to B2,*
	<ABS (F4)>	*changes B2 to $B$2,*
	<ABS (F4)>	*changes $B$2 to B$2.*
	<Enter>	*Enters formula into B3.*

The result in cell B3 is `+$A3*(1+$A$1)^B$2`.

GUIDED ACTIVITY: CELL ADDRESSES

This activity requires you to employ absolute and mixed cell addresses in a revision of the RB90PROJ spreadsheet developed in Unit 6.

1. Follow the startup procedure outlined in Unit 1 to load Lotus and enter the 1-2-3 program.
2. Retrieve RB90PROJ.
3. Change the value for wages (cell B11) to **`52000`**. Check the net income for the year (cell F18). If the value is not `53115`, check all entries against Figure 6-8 and re-enter the values shown in Figure 6-8.
4. Put the label **`Projected Growth`** in cell G4. Change the width of column G to 17.
5. Enter **`5%`** (or, **`.05`**) in G5, and **`3%`** in G10. These are projected growth Figures for revenues and expenses, respectively. Format these two cells to Percent, one decimal place.
6. Change the formula in C6 to **`+B6*(1+$G$5)`**. The value displayed in the cell should remain `37800`.
7. Copy the formula from C6 to the range C6..E7.

   CHECKPOINT

   7a. What should the formula in E7 be?
8. Change the formulas in C11..E12 so they refer to G10. The spreadsheet should now look like Figure 7-2.
9. Save the spreadsheet. Continue to use the name RB90PROJ.

```
C11: +B11*(1+$G$10)                                                    READY

      A         B        C        D        E        F           G
 1                     RB Company
 2                     1990 Projections
 3
 4                Qtr      Qtr      Qtr      Qtr      Year Projected Growth
 5  REVENUE                                                        5.0%
 6     Sales    36000    37800    39690    41675   155165
 7   Service    45000    47250    49613    52093   193956
 8     Total    81000    85050    89303    93768   349120
 9
10  EXPENSES                                                       3.0%
11     Wages    52000    53560    55167    56822   217549
12  Supplies    12500    12875    13261    13659    52295
13     Total    64500    66435    68428    70481   269844
14
15  INCOME
16     Gross    16500    18615    20874    23287    79276
17       Tax     5445     6143     6889     7685    26161
18       Net    11055    12472    13986    15602    53115
19
20
13-Oct-89  10:50 AM         UNDO                           NUM
```

Figure 7-2 Modified RB Company Projections Worksheet

10. These modifications allow us to change the projected growth value in one cell (either G5 or G10) and see the impact on the "bottom line." For instance, notice what happens if the projected growth rate for expenses is 10% (enter **10%** in cell G10).

11. We can modify the values in six cells and test a wide variety of situations. Under which of the following sets of values will RB Company have a positive net income for the year? After you enter each set of values, print the worksheet.

a.	REVENUE	Sales	36000	Service	45000	Growth	5%
	EXPENSES	Wages	52000	Supplies	12500	Growth	6%
b.	REVENUE	Sales	36000	Service	45000	Growth	5%
	EXPENSES	Wages	52000	Supplies	32500	Growth	6%
c.	REVENUE	Sales	36000	Service	35000	Growth	7%
	EXPENSES	Wages	52000	Supplies	22500	Growth	3%
d.	REVENUE	Sales	36000	Service	45000	Growth	5%
	EXPENSES	Wages	52000	Supplies	12500	Growth	10%

12. Reset the worksheet to the original figures and save it again.

RECALCULATION

There are three aspects of recalculation: method, order, and iterations. Normally the worksheet is recalculated every time an entry is made or edited, using a natural order, with each cell recalculated only once. Each of the three aspects can be changed independently of the others: Method can be manual or automatic; order can be natural, rowwise, or columnwise; and iterations can be from 1 to 50.

MANUAL VERSUS AUTOMATIC RECALCULATION

Each time a cell is input or edited, Lotus recalculates all the entries in the worksheet that are dependent on that cell. This is generally desired, but **automatic recalculation** after every change can become noticeably slow if the worksheet is large or has complicated formulas. When desired, the **/W**orksheet **G**lobal **R**ecalculation command can be used to establish **manual recalculation** (**/WGRM**). A `CALC` indicator appears in the lower right corner of the screen when changes have been made that require recalculation. The worksheet is recalculated only when the <CALC (F9)> key is pressed.

NATURAL ORDER OF RECALCULATION

Unlike earlier spreadsheet programs, Lotus uses a **natural order of recalculation**. What this means is that all cells referred to in a cell formula are recalculated before the cell is recalculated. If the formula `+$A3*(1+$A$1)^B$2` is in cell B3, cells A1, A3, and B2 are recalculated before cell B3 is recalculated. If there were a formula in B2, say `+C2*A9`, then both C2 and A9 would be recalculated before B2. Natural order of recalculation handles almost all spreadsheet situations.

CIRCULAR REFERENCES

Problems arise when a **circular reference** exists. For instance, we might have the following situation:

cell	contents
A1	**+A2**
A2	**+A1**

Here, the value of A1 depends on the value of A2. But the value of A2 depends on the value of A1. Which comes first, the chicken (A1) or the egg (A2)?

The following is a more complex and less obvious situation:

cell	contents
A1	**+A2+B2**
A2	**.0525**
A9	**+A1*2**
B2	**+C2*A9**
C2	**1.29**

When Lotus tries to recalculate this, the following happens. First it goes to cell A1, but finds that it must go to cells A2 and B2 first. A2 is no problem, because it contains a constant value, but Lotus must go to cells C2 and A9 before it can calculate B2. C2 also contains a constant value, but A9 contains a formula that requires

Lotus to evaluate A1 first. Lotus then goes to cell A1, but finds that it must go to cells A2 and B2 first. A2 is no problem, because it contains a constant value, but Lotus must go to cells C2 and A9 before it can calculate B2. C2 also contains a constant value, but A9 contains a formula that requires Lotus to evaluate A1 first. Lotus then goes to cell A1. . . .

Actually, Lotus is too smart to spend its time running around in circles without complaint. Given the situations described, Lotus displays `CIRC` in the lower right corner of the screen; indicating that a **circular reference** occurs in the worksheet. Usually, circular references are unintentional and indicate that there is an error in the worksheet. To locate where the circular reference starts, you can use the /**W**orksheet **S**tatus command (see Unit 12).

Unless you have intentionally constructed a system of simultaneous equations (which *do* require a circular reference), you should search through your spreadsheet for the culprit. Often, the circular reference is created by a /**C**opy command. HINT: Always /**F**ile **S**ave your spreadsheet immediately prior to /**C**opying; then you can /**F**ile **R**etrieve a previous version if you cannot discover the problem.

SIMULTANEOUS EQUATIONS

If the system of simultaneous equations is intentional, then you must use the /**W**orksheet **G**lobal **R**ecalculation command to insure that Lotus does things in the order you wish. Recalculation can be set to Rowwise (**/WGRR**) or Columnwise (**/WGRC**), and the number of Iterations can also be specified (**/WGRI**).

Rowwise vs. Columnwise Recalculation. When rowwise recalculation is specified, the worksheet is recalculated across rows, from top to bottom: cell C1 is recalculated before cell A3 is recalculated. When columnwise recalculation is specified, the worksheet is recalculated down columns, from left to right: cell A3 is recalculated before cell C1 is recalculated.

Note that row- vs. columnwise recalculation is important only when three conditions are all present:

- There is a circular reference.
- The computations are in more than a single row.
- The computations are in more than a single column.

Example. There are occasions when simultaneous equations are necessary. Consider the situation where a company must have a certain amount of money to operate for a period of time, and must borrow to achieve this level of operating capital. Interest must be paid on the borrowed amount, however, and the amount of the interest payment must be added to the amount of operating capital needed. A portion of the worksheet might look like this:

cell	contents	explanation
A1	`1000000`	operating capital needs excl. interest
A2	`50000`	cash on hand
A3	`+A1-A2+A4`	amount to borrow
A4	`0.10*A3`	interest on amount borrowed

For an intellectual exercise, ponder the following: Where is the circular reference? Why does the formula in A3 include a reference to A4? Try working this problem by hand, then put it into a spreadsheet (see the following Guided Activity).

For this problem, does it matter whether or not recalculation is set to rowwise or columnwise?

GUIDED ACTIVITY: RECALCULATION

This activity requires you to use the recalculation command.

1. If you are continuing from the previous Guided Activity, save RB90PROJ, then use the command /**W**orksheet **E**rase **Y**es to obtain a clear worksheet. If you are not continuing from the previous Guided Activity, follow the startup procedure outlined in Unit 1 to load Lotus and enter the 1-2-3 program.
2. Using the /**W**orksheet **G**lobal **F**ormat command, set the default value format to currency, 2 decimal places. Using the /**W**orksheet **G**lobal **C**olumn-Width command, set the column width to 20 characters.
3. Recall the example of a simultaneous equation presented above:

   > Consider the situation where a company must have a certain amount of money to operate for a period of time, and must borrow to achieve this level of operating capital. Interest must be paid on the borrowed amount, however, and the amount of the interest payment must be added to the amount of operating capital needed.

4. Build a worksheet with the following entries:

cell	contents
A1	`1000000.00`
B1	`operating capital needs excl. interest`
A2	`50000.00`
B2	`cash on hand`
A3	`+A1-A2+A4`
B3	`amount to borrow`
A4	`0.10*A3`
B4	`interest on amount borrowed`

5. Note the `CIRC` indicator in the lower right of the screen (Figure 7-3). If you entered the entries in the order A1, B1, A2, . . . A4, B4, the `CIRC` indicator appeared immediately after you made the entry in A4. At that point, the value of A3 is `$950,000.00`, and the value of A4 is `$95,000.00`. After making the entry in B4, the numbers change to what you see in the figure.

CHECKPOINT

7b. Where is the circular reference?

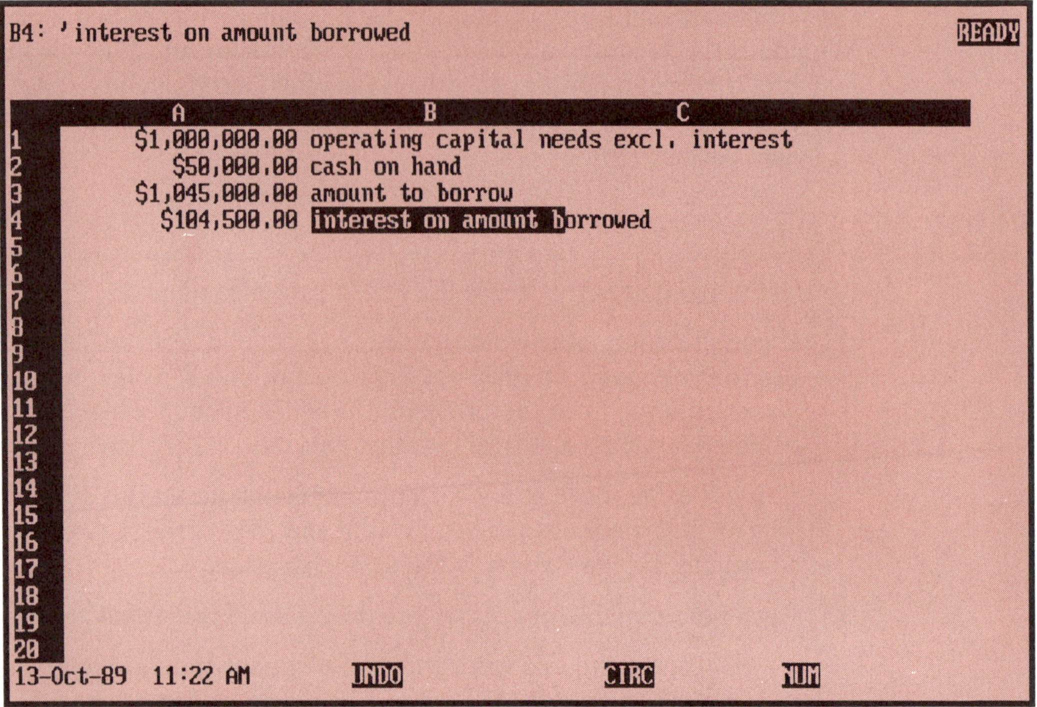

Figure 7-3 A Worksheet with Simultaneous Equations

6. Press the <CALC (F9)> key a few times and watch the numbers in A3 and A4 increase. The increase is less each time, which means that there is some point at which the increase in the amount to borrow is so small as to be meaningless. Continue to press <CALC (F9)> until the amount to borrow remains constant for three consecutive presses. The amount to borrow should be `$1,055,555.56`.

7. Now we want to restart the process and use iterative calculations. First, use /**R**ange **E**rase to erase the formula in cell A4. Notice that the `CIRC` goes away. Next, use the /**W**orksheet **G**lobal **R**ecalculation **I**teration command to set number of iterations to `20`. Finally, reenter the formula **`0.10*A3`** into cell A4. Note that the final answer, `$1,055,555.56`, appears instantly.

8. Save your work with the file name RECALC. Print a copy of the worksheet.

9. Now, change your operating capital needs (cell A1) to `$100,000.00`. The worksheet should quickly calculate a new amount to borrow, `$55,555.56`.

10. Save your work again. Print a copy of the worksheet.

11. /**Q**uit to exit to the 1-2-3 Access System. Exit to the operating system. Remember to back up your work.

EXERCISE: SALES BY STATE

This exercise requires you to develop a worksheet that compares sales by state.

1. If you are not continuing from the previous Guided Activity, follow the startup procedure outlined in Unit 1 to load Lotus and enter the 1-2-3 program. Or, after you have saved RECALC, use the /**W**orksheet **E**rase command to erase the worksheet.
2. Make the following entries in cells A1..B8 (`Sales by ... Region` all goes in A1).

```
Sales by State, Western Region
Alaska          198
California     2593
Hawaii          231
Idaho           165
Oregon          508
Washington      552
TOTAL
```

3. Adjust the width of column A to accommodate the state names.
4. In B8, enter a formula that sums the state figures.
5. In C2, enter a formula that computes the percentage of sales in Alaska. As you enter the formula, think about relative and absolute addressing, and how you can create a formula that can be copied to the rest of the states.
6. Format C2 to percent, 1 decimal place.
7. /**C**opy C2 to C3..C8. Note that the format is copied also. You should have `100.0%` in C8.
8. Save your worksheet with the name WESTREG.

EXERCISE: A SALES WORKSHEET (II)

1. If you are not continuing from the previous Exercise or Guided Activity, follow the startup procedure outlined in Unit 1 to load Lotus and enter the 1-2-3 program.
2. Retrieve the COMPCOST worksheet that you created in Unit 6.
3. Modify COMPCOST so that the sales tax percentage is in a separate cell and all formulas in the "Tax" column refer to that cell.
4. Save the spreadsheet.

REVIEW QUESTIONS

1. What are the three types of cell addresses, and what are the distinctions among the three types of cell addresses?
2.* When do you use mixed or absolute addresses instead of relative addresses?
3.* How does the /Copy command affect relative cell addresses?
4.* How does the /Copy command affect absolute cell addresses?
5.* How does the /Copy command affect mixed cell addresses?
6.* When do you use manual instead of automatic recalculation?
7. What is the natural order of recalculation?
8. What is a circular reference?
9. Assume that cell C8 contains the formula `+C9+B8`.
   a.* Express the formula in terms of relative movements from C8.
   b.* If the formula is copied to cell D8, what is the formula in D8?
10. Assume that cell C8 contains the formula `+C9+$B$8`.
    a. Express the formula in terms of relative movements from C8.
    b. If the formula is copied to cell D8, what is the formula in D8?
11. Assume that cell C8 contains the formula `+C9+$B8`.
    a. Express the formula in terms of relative movements from C8.
    b. If the formula is copied to cell D8, what is the formula in D8?
12.* What command is used to alter the recalculation method?

DOCUMENTATION RESEARCH

Using the reference manual, find the discussion of circular references and the /**W**orksheet **G**lobal **R**ecalculation command.

APPLICATION C

COMPOUND INTEREST (I)

In this exercise you build a new spreadsheet using many of the commands and concepts discussed in this part. You enter a formula containing absolute and mixed addresses, copy that formula, and print the resulting worksheet.

1. Follow the startup procedure outlined in Unit 1 to load Lotus and enter the 1-2-3 program.
2. For this exercise, we complete the example that was discussed in Unit 7. You might wish to review the situation presented in that unit before proceeding.
3. In cell A1, enter the figure **.0525** (5.25%).
4. In cells A3..A12, enter the figures **10, 20, 30, . . . 100.**
5. In cells B2..F2, enter the figures **1, 2, . . . 5.**
6. In cell B3, enter the formula **+$A3*(1+$A$1)^B$2** using the <Arrow> keys to point to the cells and the <ABS (F4)> key to create the absolute and mixed references. Check the formula carefully. Your worksheet should now look like Figure 7-1.
7. Copy from cell B3 to B4..B12.
8. Copy from cells B3..B12 to C3..F3.

9. Look at the formula in F12. It should be

   +$A12*(1+$A$1)^F$2

   If not, repeat steps 6-8.

10. Format cell A1 to percentage with 3 decimal places format. Format range A3..F12 to currency format with 2 decimal places.

11. When your worksheet looks like Figure C-1, save it as COMPOUND and print a copy..

12. /Quit to exit to the 1-2-3 Access System. Exit to the operating system. Remember to back up your work.

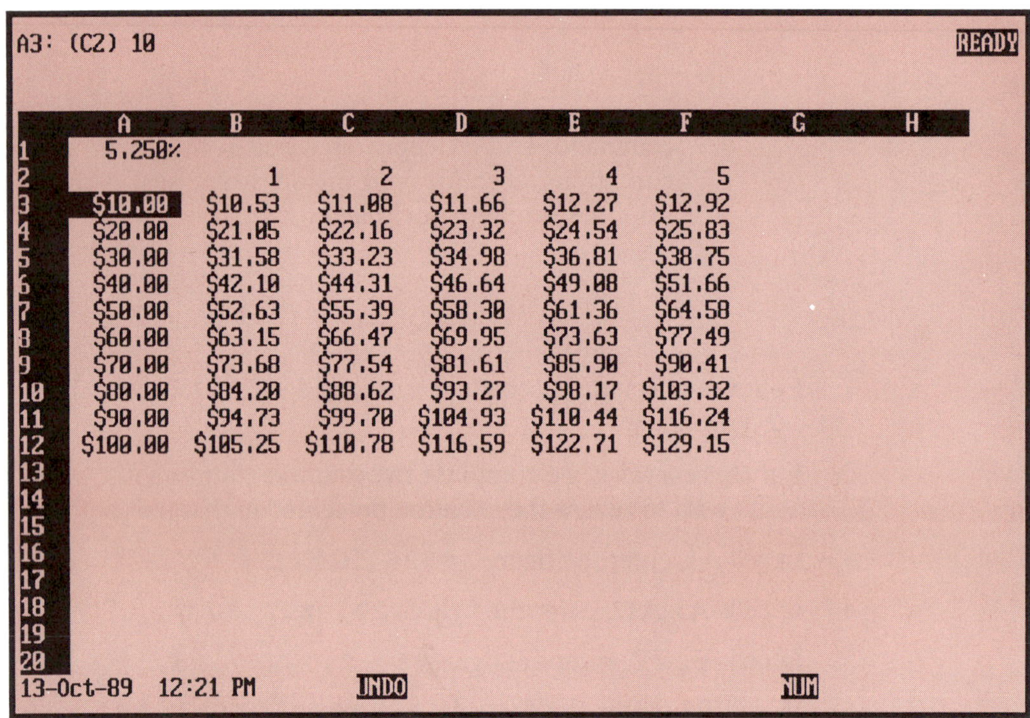

A3: (C2) 10 READY

	A	B	C	D	E	F	G	H
1	5.250%							
2		1	2	3	4	5		
3	$10.00	$10.53	$11.08	$11.66	$12.27	$12.92		
4	$20.00	$21.05	$22.16	$23.32	$24.54	$25.83		
5	$30.00	$31.58	$33.23	$34.98	$36.81	$38.75		
6	$40.00	$42.10	$44.31	$46.64	$49.08	$51.66		
7	$50.00	$52.63	$55.39	$58.30	$61.36	$64.58		
8	$60.00	$63.15	$66.47	$69.95	$73.63	$77.49		
9	$70.00	$73.68	$77.54	$81.61	$85.90	$90.41		
10	$80.00	$84.20	$88.62	$93.27	$98.17	$103.32		
11	$90.00	$94.73	$99.70	$104.93	$110.44	$116.24		
12	$100.00	$105.25	$110.78	$116.59	$122.71	$129.15		
13								
14								
15								
16								
17								
18								
19								
20								

13-Oct-89 12:21 PM UNDO NUM

Figure C-1 The Finished Worksheet

UNIT 8

SCREEN GRAPHICS

Lotus allows us to draw graphs on the computer monitor (screen) if we have the proper hardware in the computer, and on paper if we have the right kind of printer or plotter. In this unit, we discuss the preparation of graphs on the computer screen: an essential first step even if the ultimate objective is a paper copy of the graph.

LEARNING OBJECTIVES

1. At the completion of this unit, you should know the five types of graphs and the appropriate uses of each.
2. At the completion of this unit, you should be able to
   a. define any of the types of graph,
   b. add titles and legends to the graph,
   c. save the graph for later printing,
   d. name the graph for later recall.

IMPORTANT COMMAND

/Graph

STEPS IN CREATING A GRAPH

Before Lotus can draw a graph, the numbers that comprise the graph must be entered in the worksheet. There are four general steps in defining or preparing a graph:

1. Enter the numbers (or formulas) into the worksheet.
2. Tell Lotus the type of graph you wish to draw.
3. Tell Lotus where the data to be graphed exist.

4. (optional) Define parameters such as titles, scaling, color, and legend.

The first three steps can be performed in any order, but each must be performed before you can view the graph. The fourth step can be performed after you have initially viewed the graph. Any of the four can be changed if you wish.

A1: 'MONTH READY

	A	B	C	D	E	F	G
1	MONTH	GENERAL	BUSINESS	CONVENTION			
2	Jan	225	309	88			
3	Feb	747	303	571			
4	Mar	578	521	211			
5	Apr	370	222	287			
6	May	519	546	837			
7	Jun	382	815	354			
8	Jul	604	228	524			
9	Aug	520	537	85			
10	Sep	700	660	921			
11	Oct	431	439	743			
12	Nov	1260	717	414			
13	Dec	673	991	712			
14							
15							
16							
17							
18							
19							
20							

13-Oct-89 02:51 PM UNDO NUM

Figure 8-1 The Worksheet with Hotel Guest Data

WORKSHEET PREPARATIONS

The data to be graphed generally lie in a row, a column, or parallel rows or columns. To illustrate the operation of the /Graph command, we assume that you operate a hotel which has three general classes of guests: general public (who pay full rate), business customers (who pay a lower rate), and convention customers (who pay the lowest rate). You have data that show how many of each group stayed in your hotel last year.

You might build a worksheet such as that illustrated in Figure 8-1. There are several ways of looking at these data. For instance, you might want to compare the three types of customers for each month, or for the year. You might want total registration per month, regardless of type. You might want total registration per year, by type. Note that sometimes we look across a row (e.g., who gave us the most business in January?). Other times, we look down a column (e.g., which month has the highest business registration?). And sometimes we need numbers that are not yet computed (e.g., which month has the highest total registration?).

/GRAPH COMMAND

Once **/G** is typed, you are presented with the following menu:

```
A1: 'MONTH                                                              MENU
Type  X  A  B  C  D  E  F  Reset  View  Save  Options  Name  Group  Quit
View the current graph
```

This is another **sticky menu**. To exit, you must select **Quit**.

GRAPH TYPE

We usually start the graph definition process by specifying **Type**. Each type of graph has its virtues, constraints, and limitations. See Figures 8-2 to 8-6 for illustrations of the various types of graphs.

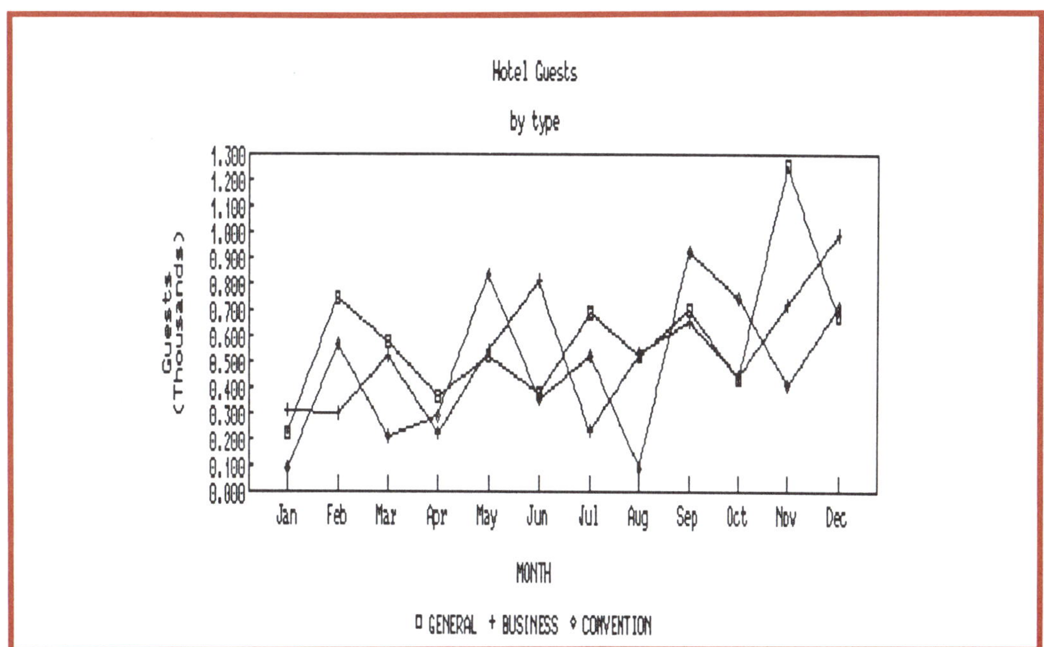

Figure 8-2 Line Graph. Line graphs are good for showing trends, such as the profit line graph shown in many business cartoons. Up to six lines can be drawn, representing six types of data (e.g., type of hotel guest). Line graphs can be drawn with lines, lines and symbols, symbols only, or labels in lieu of lines or symbols.

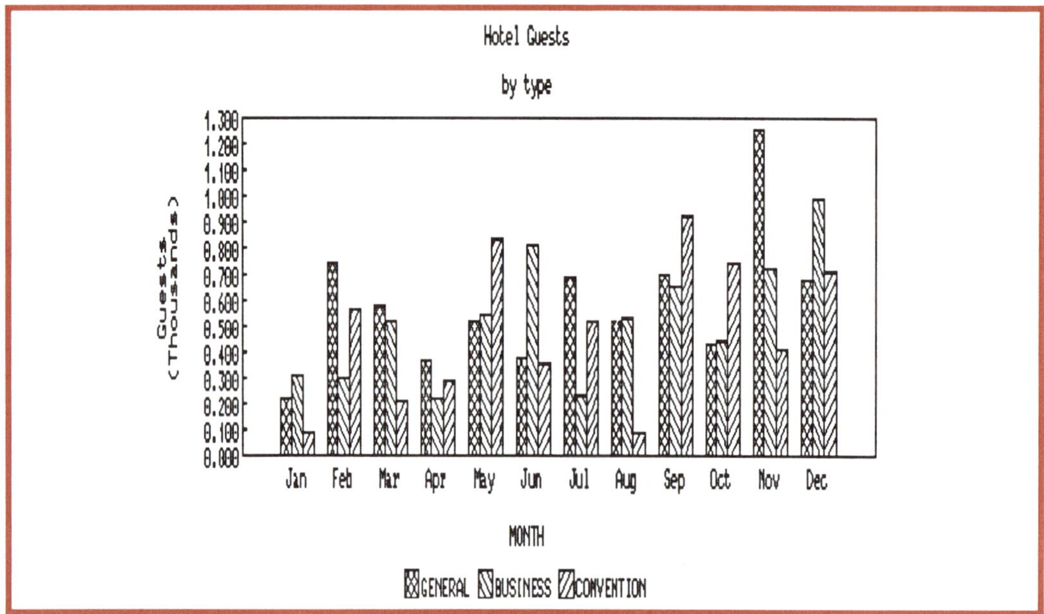

Figure 8-3 Bar Graph. **Bar** graphs use bars of varying heights to indicate amount. Again, six sets of data can be plotted; the bars are of different colors or patterns to indicate the different types of data, and they are side by side across the graph.

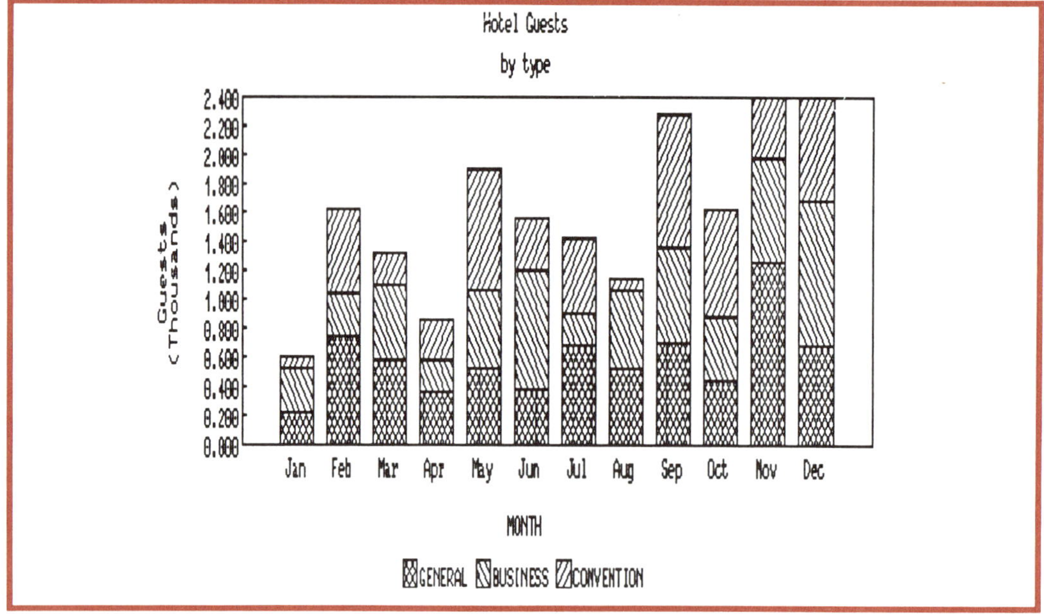

Figure 8-4 Stacked Bar Graph. **Stacked Bar** graphs are similar to bar graphs, except that all data common to a given row or column are in one bar, with colors or pattern varying in the bar according to data set. Stacked bar graphs are good for showing totals with their component parts; for instance, you could stack all three types of guests by month to show total hotel registration for each month.

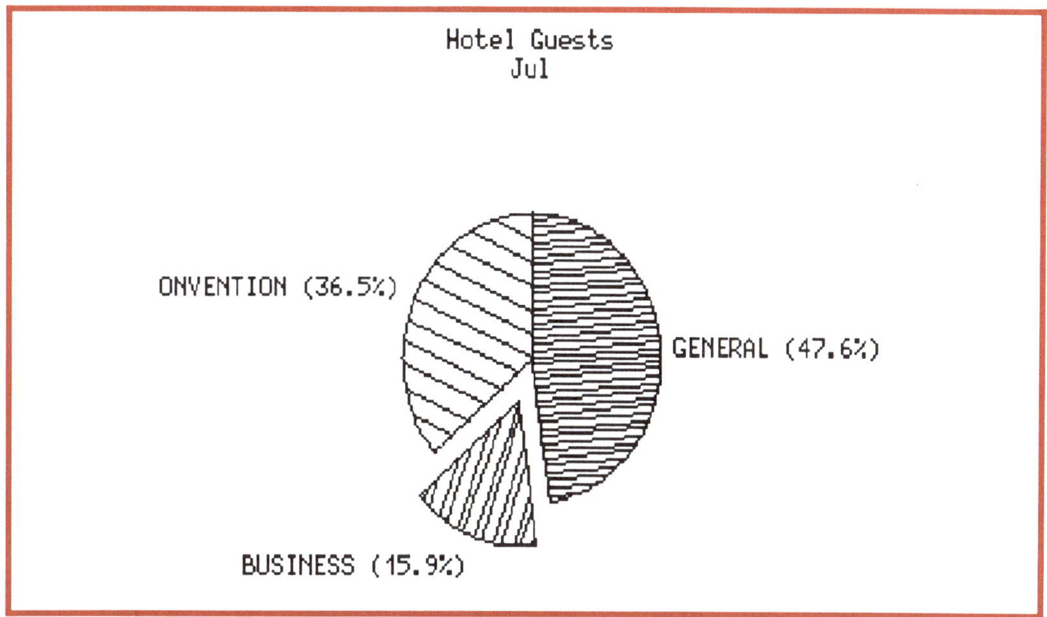

Figure 8-5 Pie Graph. **Pie** graphs are used to show relative proportions of the whole, for one range only. Only the A range data are graphed. For instance, a pie graph could show the relative proportion of guests in each category for the month of July. *Note*: In the graph shown in this figure, the "C" is missing from "Convention." When Lotus tries to fit the graph on the screen, it may not display some characters. These characters are still in the description of the graph, however, and will reappear when we later print the graph (see the next unit).

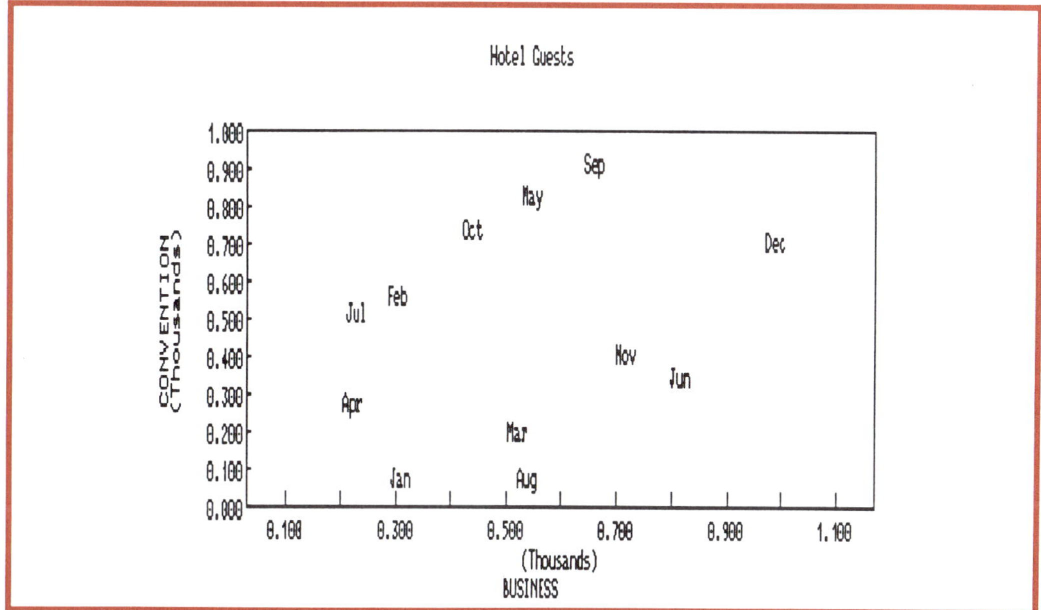

Figure 8-6 XY Graph. **XY** graphs are used to plot numeric functions and other data in which thc horizontal axis (called the X range and discussed below) is numeric rather than label. Each point on the graph (which is usually a symbol or data-

label) represents a pair of numbers, one from the X range (reading across the bottom; business in this example) and the other from one of the six data ranges (reading up the left side; convention in this example). Up to six different lines (data ranges) can be included. XY graphs are sometimes called **scatterplots** and are used to show the relationship between two sets of numbers, for example, the relationship between numbers of business and convention guests. In the graph in Figure 8-6 you interpret the point labeled "Sep" as meaning that there were approximately 700 business and 900 convention guests in September. Notice that the number of convention guests tends to rise as the number of business guests rises.

DATA RANGES

After specifying type, you must specify ranges that contain the data. Each range is specified in the same manner from the main **/G**raph menu:

1. Press the letter of the range.
2. Type or point to the first cell in the range.
3. Anchor with a period.
4. Type or point to the last cell in the range.
5. Finally enter the range by pressing <Enter>.

X range contains the labels or numbers that identify the data in the graph. In our example, the X range would usually be defined as the column containing the month abbreviations (i.e., A2..A13). For XY-type graphs, the X range must be values (not labels). For other types of graphs, the X range can be either values or labels.

A . . . F ranges contain the data to be plotted. In our example, each column of numbers would become a range (i.e., the A range is B2..B13, the B range is C2..C13, etc.).

Use **G**roup to set all data ranges at once:

1. Press **G**.
2. Type or point to the first cell in the range (cell A2 in our example).
3. Anchor with a period.
4. Type or point to the last cell in the range (cell D13).
5. Enter the range by pressing <Enter>.
6. Lotus then asks if the data are arranged in columns or rows. In our example, select **C**olumnwise because each column is a separate data range.

The left column (or the top row) is the X range, and each succeeding column (or row) are the A through F ranges. The **G**roup option is a shortcut when all the data are in adjacent columns or rows. When the data are not adjacent, you must specify each range.

To remove a specific range or to cancel the graph options use **R**eset.

DISPLAYING THE GRAPH

View is used to draw the graph on the screen. If you are using two monitors, the graph appears on the color/graphics monitor. If you are using only one monitor connected to a color/graphics adapter, the worksheet clears from the screen and the graph is drawn. In this latter case, pressing any key returns you to the worksheet. After viewing your graph, you might decide to make some changes and view again. Note: if you do not have a color/graphics adapter in your computer, you cannot view the graph. You can still define the graph type, ranges, and options and save it for later printing.

To view the most recent graph, press the <GRAPH (F10)> key from the READY mode. Press <Space> or any other key to return to READY mode.

SAVING THE GRAPH FOR PRINTING

Save saves the graph as currently defined into a file with a .PIC extension. This **picture file** can be used by PrintGraph to print the graph on a printer. If you later make changes to the graph, you must save it again if you wish to print those changes. Also, unless you have a color printer or plotter, choose B&W from the Options. Otherwise your graph will print in all black bars.

Note that /Graph Save is not a substitute for /File Save. /Graph Save saves a picture file, but does not save the worksheet itself. /File Save saves the worksheet and the /Graph settings in a **worksheet file**. Many a hapless worksheetist, including yours truly, has forgotten to /File Save before /Quitting and lost a substantial amount of work. Both the worksheet and the picture files can have the same file name, because the extensions are different. If I am creating only one picture from a worksheet, I usually save both worksheet and picture with the same name. Of course, where you are creating many pictures from the same worksheet, you must use different names. *Remember*: /Graph Save *is not a substitute for* /File Save.

KEEPING MULTIPLE GRAPHS WITH ONE WORKSHEET

Name suboptions allow the maintenance of several graphs with one worksheet. Named graphs are stored with the worksheet (i.e., with the /File Save command); they are not separate disk files.

- Create attaches a name to the current type, ranges, and options, allowing them to be recalled later with the Use suboption.
- Use retrieves a previously named graph and draws it on the screen.
- Delete erases a named graph.
- Reset erases all named graphs.

/Graph Name differs from /Graph Save: Save creates a picture file for printing; Name attaches an internal label to a set of graph characteristics, which are saved with the worksheet file.

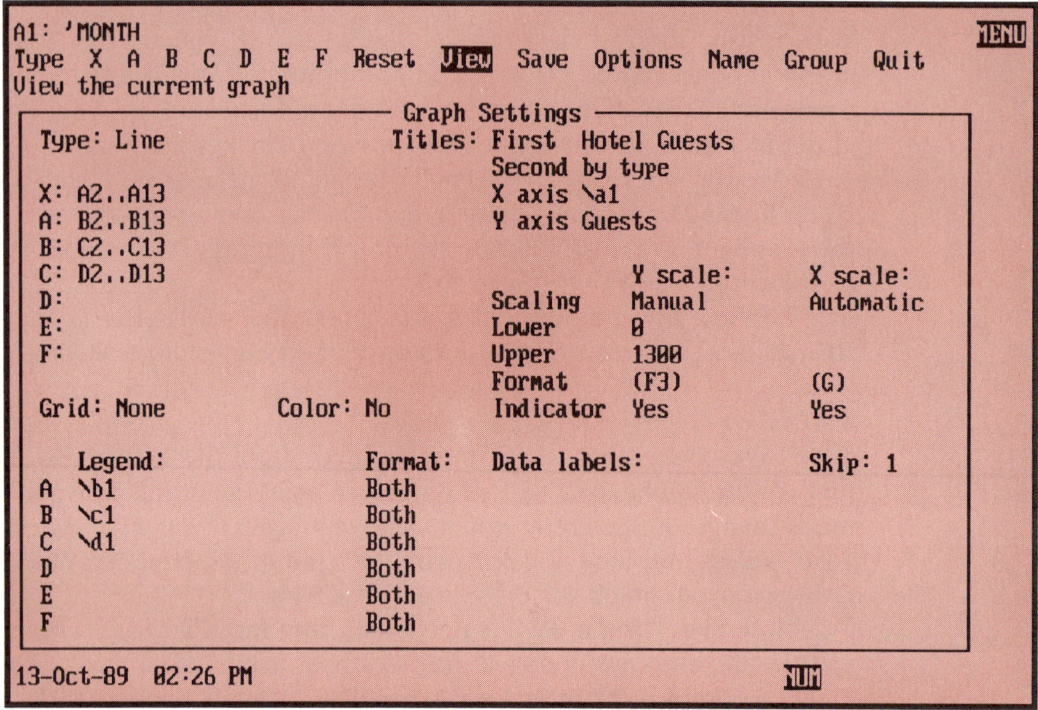
A1: 'MONTH
MENU
Type X A B C D E F Reset View Save Options Name Group Quit
View the current graph
Graph Settings
Type: Line
Titles: First Hotel Guests
Second by type
X axis \a1
Y axis Guests
X: A2..A13
A: B2..B13
B: C2..C13
C: D2..D13
D:
E:
F:
Y scale:
X scale:
Scaling Manual Automatic
Lower 0
Upper 1300
Format (F3) (G)
Indicator Yes Yes
Grid: None
Color: No
Legend:
Format:
Data labels:
Skip: 1
A \b1 Both
B \c1 Both
C \d1 Both
D Both
E Both
F Both
13-Oct-89 02:26 PM
NUM

Figure 8-7 The Graph Settings Screen (for the Graph in Figure 8-2)

OPTIONS TO ENHANCE THE GRAPH

Options allow you to add titles, legends, and data-labels, and to control the presentation of the data. The **Graph Settings** screen (Figure 8-7) displays the current status of all options and data ranges. Among the options are

- Legend, which puts information to identify the various data ranges at the bottom of the graph. This can be color or pattern for bar graphs, or line color or symbol for line and XY graphs. The contents of a cell can be used as a legend. For instance, if the label `'Convention` were in cell D1, **`\D1`** could be specified as the legend for the range containing convention data. If the contents of D1 are subsequently changed, the legend automatically changes also.
- Format, used to specify the presentation of data points in line and XY graphs. Choose lines, symbols, lines and symbols, or neither.
- Data-Labels, used to specify a range of cells whose contents are used to label the data points of a range. Use Data-Labels if you specify Format Neither. Data-Labels and Format Neither are illustrated in Figure 8-6.
- Titles, which allows you to specify two title lines for the graph and titles for both horizontal and vertical axes. As is the case with legends, the contents of a cell can be used for any of these; specify as **`\A1`**.

- Grid, which allows the inclusion or removal of grid lines running horizontally, vertically, or both.
- Scale, which allows some flexibility in specifying upper and lower limits for the X and Y axes (which are automatically scaled otherwise) and for spacing of entries on the X axis (with the Skip suboption). In Figure 8-6, the X scale is manually set to a lower limit of 100 and an upper limit of 1100. (Lotus adds additional space before and after the limits on the X axis.) Format is a suboption to scale that allows specification of one of the Lotus formats for X or Y axis numbers.
- Color and **B&W**, which select display characteristics, relevant for color monitors only. **B&W** uses crosshatching patterns to differentiate among data ranges. Unless a color plotter is available, always select **B&W** before doing a /Graph Save.

LEAVING THE GRAPH MENU

Quit returns you to the worksheet READY mode. Remember that you can re-display the most recent graph by pressing the <GRAPH (F10)> key.

SPECIAL TECHNIQUES

Two techniques deserve additional discussion. The first is the use of **Data-Labels** in line and XY graphs, and the second is the use of a B range to achieve special effects with pie graphs.

USING DATA-LABELS

The Data-Labels option provides a method for identifying each individual point on a graph. Data-Labels are different from legends, which are below the graph and identify the different ranges of data. Data-Labels appear on the graph to identify specific points. For instance, in Figure 8-6 we have used data-labels to identify which point corresponds to which month. The data-labels are contained in a range that is parallel to the data being plotted. To achieve the result in Figure 8-6, the graph type is XY, the X range is the column of business customers, the A range is the column of convention customers, and the data-labels (for the A range) are the column of month names. To suppress lines and symbols, the /Graph Options Format Neither command is also necessary.

EXPLODING PIE GRAPHS

Although a pie graph displays only one range of data (the A range), you can designate a B range that specifies **shading patterns** and **exploded segments**. To do so, designate the X and A ranges as usual, then designate a B range that parallels the A and X ranges and contains shading information. For instance, the following ranges were used to create the graph that is illustrated in Figure 8-5:

X Range	B1..D1
A Range	B8..D8
B Range	B21..D21, containing the following data:
	B21 1
	C21 103
	D21 7

Note that the B Range data were entered in a row below the remainder of the data. Adding a new range for shading and explosion would normally be necessary; the shading patterns would seldom be contained otherwise in your normal data range. Adding 100 to the shading value produces an exploded segment, as illustrated. You should experiment with all the shading patterns (numbered 0 through 7) to determine those most suitable.

GUIDED ACTIVITY: GRAPHING RB COMPANY DATA

This activity requires you to explore the screen graphics commands of Lotus 1-2-3.

1. Follow the startup procedure outlined in Unit 1 to load Lotus and enter the 1-2-3 program.
2. Retrieve the RB90PROJ worksheet used in Units 6 and 7.
3. To draw a line graph of the data . . .
   a. Give the /Graph command.
   b. The menu pointer is pointing at the **Type** option. Press <Enter> to select the type, <Arrow> to highlight **Line** (the menu pointer usually points at Line), then press <Enter>. You return to the main /Graph menu.
   c. Move the menu pointer to **X** and press <Enter>. To indicate that the X range is B4..E4, <Arrow> to cell B4, type a period to anchor the range, <Arrow> to E4, and press <Enter> to close the range. You return to the main /Graph menu; the X range is identified on the Graph Settings screen.
   d. Move the menu pointer to **A** and press <Enter>. Indicate the A range as B8..E8.
   e. Move the menu pointer to **B** and press <Enter>. Indicate the B range as B13..E13.
   f. Indicate the C range as B16..E16.

g. Move the menu pointer to **V**iew and press <Enter>. You see the graph displayed on the screen; it should look like the figure below except that you must still define the legend.

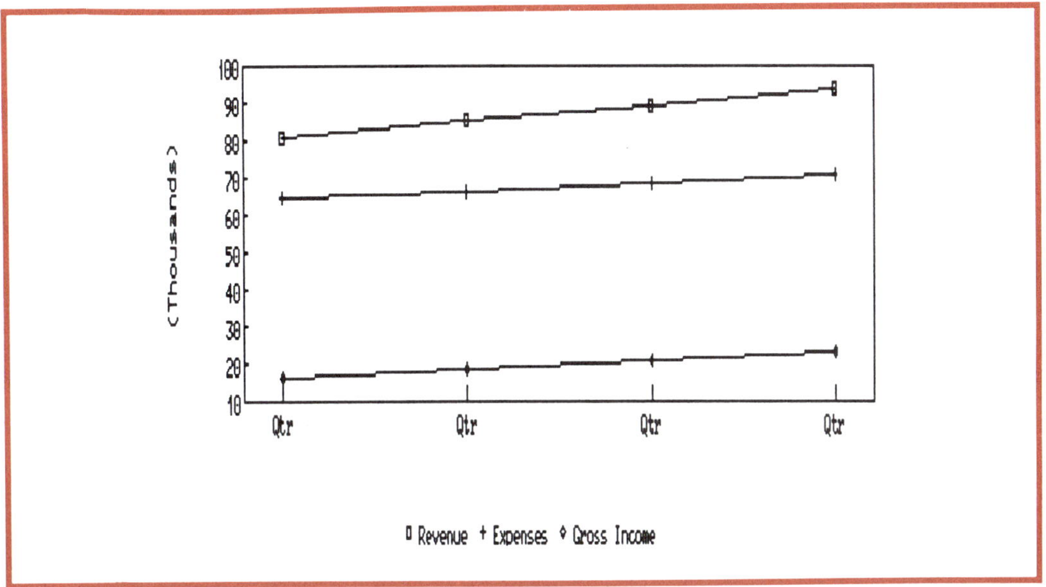

h. Look at your graph. There should be three lines. The line marked with a box is the A-range data, the line marked with a cross is the B-range data, and the line marked with the diamond is the C-range data. Depending on your computer system, the lines may be different colors. The X-range labels are underneath the graph.

i. Unless you have two monitors, you must press the <Space> bar to go back to the Graph Settings screen. Move the menu pointer to **O**ptions and press the <Enter> key. Highlight **L**egend, then press <Enter>. Highlight **A**, then press <Enter>. Enter the legend **Revenue**. You are returned to the options menu. Highlight **L**egend, then press <Enter>. Highlight **B**, then press <Enter>. Enter the legend **Expenses**. Enter **Gross Income** as the legend for the C range.

j. **Q**uit from the options menu, then select **V**iew. The graph should now look like the illustration above.

k. Press the <Space> bar if necessary to return to the Graph Settings sheet, then select the **Q**uit option to return to the READY mode.

4. Save the worksheet (/**F**ile **S**ave command).

5. To draw a bar graph of the data . . .

   a. Give the /**G**raph command.

   b. The menu pointer is pointing at the **T**ype option. Press <Enter> to select the type, highlight **B**ar, then press <Enter>. You return to the main /Graph menu.

c. Move the menu pointer to **View** and press <Enter>. You see the graph displayed on the screen; it should look like the figure below.

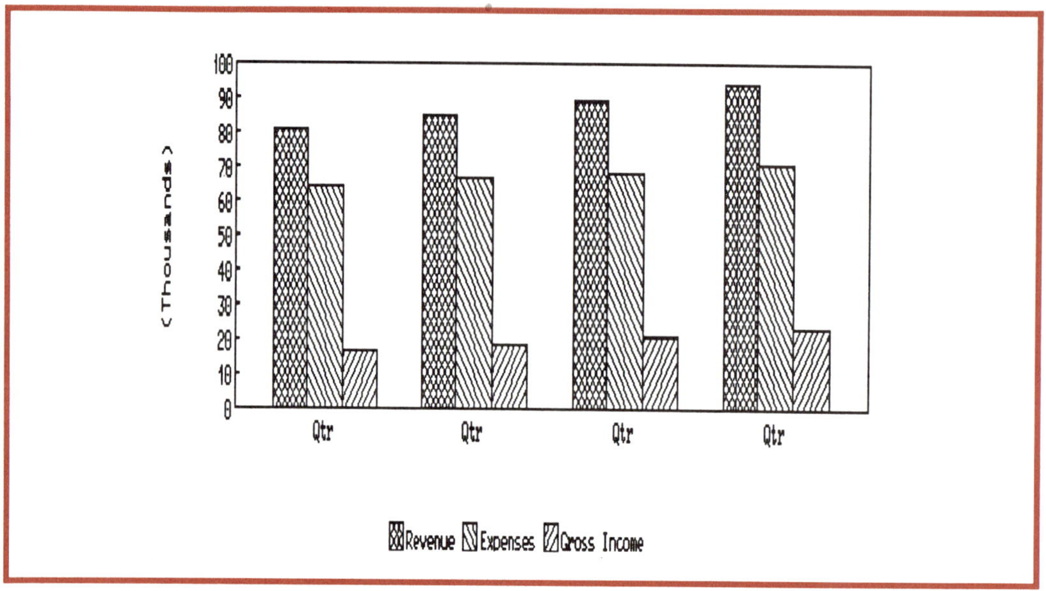

d. Look at the graph. There should be four sets of three bars. In each set, the bar on the left is the A-range data, Revenue, the center bar is the B-range data, Expenses, and the right bar is the C-range data, Gross Income. The legend from the previous graph is still in effect. Again, depending on your system, the bars should be different colors or different patterns.

e. You did not have to respecify the X-, A-, B-, and C-range data because Lotus remembered those ranges.

f. Unless you have two monitors, you must press the <Space> bar to go back to the Graph Settings screen.

g. To facilitate later use of this graph, we assign it a name. Select the **N**ame option, then **C**reate, and then enter the name **BAR** (press the <Enter> key after typing the name).

h. Select the **Q**uit option to return to the READY mode.

6. Save the worksheet.

7. Press the <GRAPH (F10)> key. What happens? Press the <Space> bar to return to READY mode.

8. For a stacked-bar graph, we use the two components of Revenue: Sales and Service. Use **/G**raph **R**eset **G**raph to clear all ranges and options. Change the graph type to **S**tack-Bar. Then define the **X** range as B4..E4, the **A** range as B6..E6, and the **B** range as B7..E7. Establish A- and B-range legends as A6 and A7, respectively (*remember*: use the form **\A6** to use cell contents as a legend). View the graph; it should look like the figure below. The tops of the bars effec-

tively show the total Revenue for each quarter, and the component parts of the bars show the relative contributions of the two sources. Name this graph **SBAR** Quit to return to the READY mode.

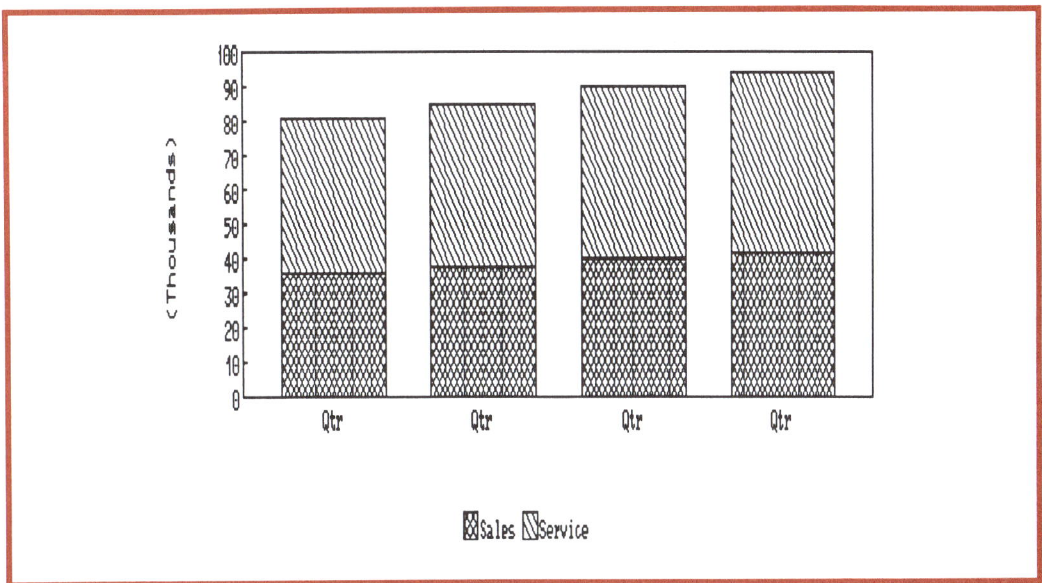

9. Save the worksheet.

10. Our next graph is a pie chart illustrating the relative proportions of Revenue devoted to Wages, Supplies, Tax, and Net Income for the year. We must create a new data range to bring these four values and associated labels together because they are not adjacent in the worksheet. Enter the following formulas in the cells indicated:

Cell	Formula	Cell	Formula
J1	**+A11**	K1	**+F11**
J2	**+A12**	K2	**+F12**
J3	**+A17**	K3	**+F17**
J4	**+A18**	K4	**+F18**

This portion of the worksheet should look like the following:

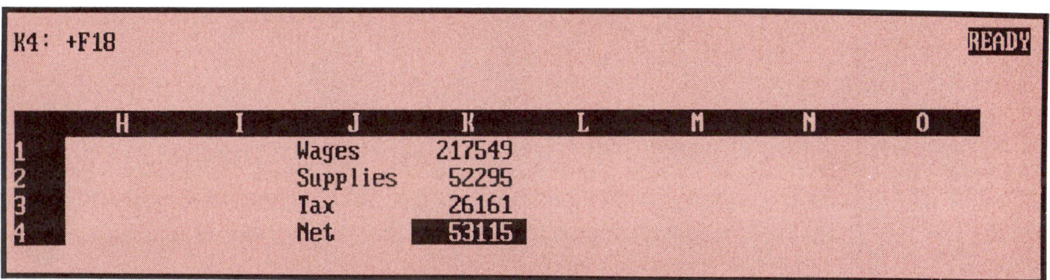

The rest of the task is easy. First, /Graph **R**eset **G**raph. Set the graph type to **P**ie, define the X range as J1..J4 and the A range as K1..K4. View the graph. It should look like the following. This graph illustrates the relative proportions of the four factors. Name this graph **PIE**.

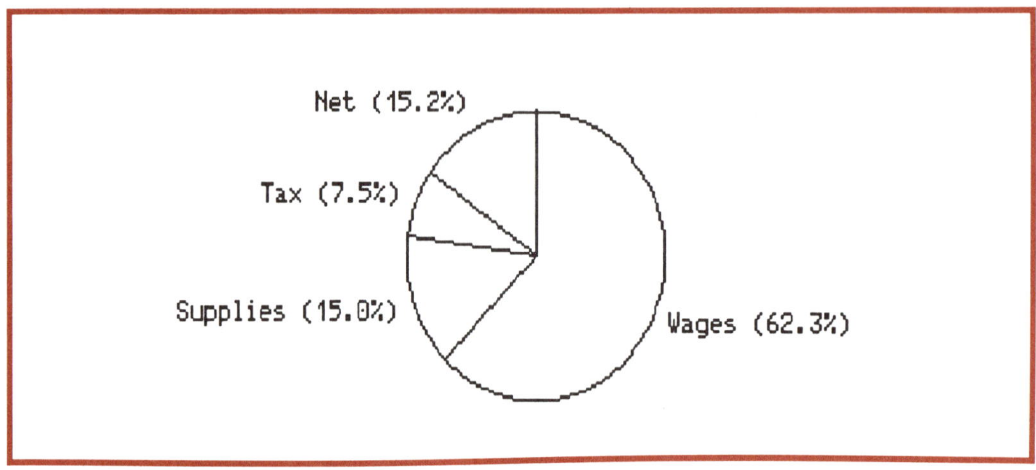

11. Save the worksheet.

12. Next, we create an XY graph showing the relationship between the four uses of Revenue and Total Revenue. Reset the graph. Change the graph type to **XY**. X range is B8..E8; A range is B11..E11; B range is B12..E12; C range is B17..E17; D range is B18..E18. Set the legends to A11, A12, A17, and A18. View; the graph should look like the following. Name the graph **XY**.

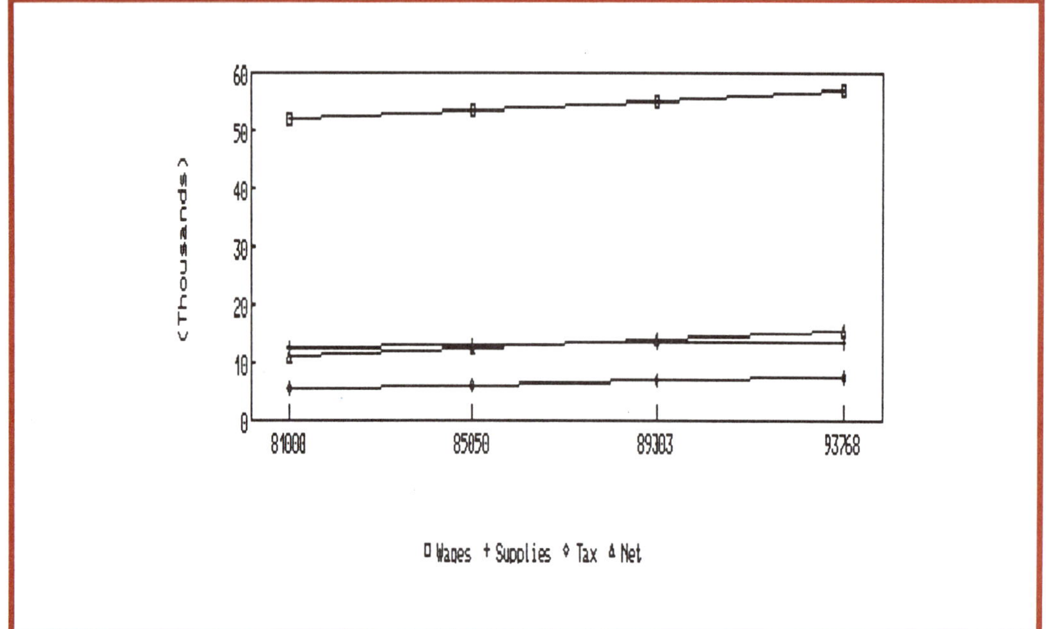

13. Save the worksheet.

GUIDED ACTIVITY: ADDING OPTIONAL FEATURES TO THE GRAPHS

In this activity we add titles and other features to some of the graphs.

1. If you are not continuing from the previous Guided Activity, load Lotus and retrieve RB90PROJ.
2. Enter the command /**G**raph **N**ame **U**se. Highlight the name PIE, then press the <Enter> key. Lotus should display the pie chart you created in the previous Guided Activity.
3. Press the <Space> bar if necessary to return to the Graph Settings screen.
4. You would like each segment of the pie to have a different pattern and you want the Net [Income] segment to be exploded (pulled out from the remainder of the pie). To accomplish this:
   a. **Q**uit from the Graph Settings screen.
   b. Move the cell pointer to cell L1.
   c. Make the following entries:

Cell	Value
L1	**1**
L2	**2**
L3	**3**
L4	**104**

   Note that these patterns parallel the labels and data in columns J and K. Net Income, which we want pulled out, is in K4 so we add 100 to the pattern code in L4.

   d. Enter the command /**G**raph **B** and indicate that the B range is L1..L4.
   e. Select **V**iew; the graph should now contain a different pattern in each segment, and the slice labeled "Net" should be pulled out from the remainder:

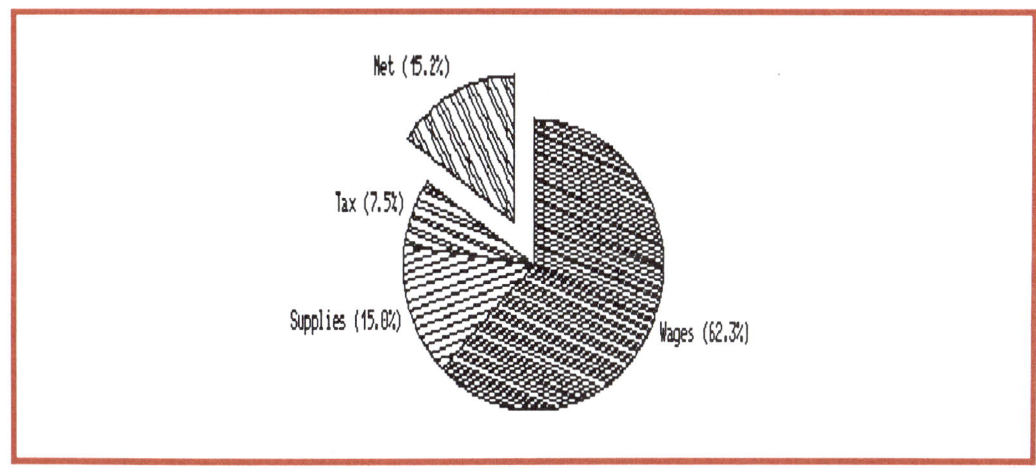

f. (If necessary, press the <Space> bar to return to the Graph Settings sheet.) Select **N**ame then **C**reate, highlight PIE, and press <Enter>. Note that you must re-create the name after changing the graph.

5. Save the worksheet before proceeding.

✔ CHECKPOINT

8a. What steps must you follow to save the worksheet?

6. Next we want to add features to the bar graph. Enter the command /**G**raph **N**ame **U**se. Highlight the name BAR, then press the <Enter> key. Lotus should display the bar graph you created in the previous Guided Activity.
7. Press the <Space> bar if necessary to return to the Graph Settings screen.
8. To add titles to the bar graph:
   a. Highlight **O**ptions and press <Enter>.
   b. Highlight **T**itles and press <Enter>.
   c. Highlight **F**irst and press <Enter>.
   d. Enter **\C1** for the first title.
   e. Highlight **T**itles and press <Enter>.
   f. Highlight **S**econd and press <Enter>.
   g. Enter **\C2** for the second title.
   h. Highlight **Q**uit and press <Enter>.
   i. Highlight **V**iew and press <Enter>. The contents of cell C1 and C2 should appear above the graph.
9. To change the format of the Y scale:
   a. Highlight **O**ptions and press <Enter>.
   b. Highlight **S**cale and press <Enter>.
   c. Highlight **Y**-Scale and press <Enter>.
   d. Highlight **F**ormat and press <Enter>.
   e. Highlight **F**ixed and press <Enter>.
   f. Enter **3** for the number of decimal places.
   g. Highlight **Q**uit and press <Enter>.
   h. Highlight **Q**uit and press <Enter>.

i. Highlight **V**iew and press <Enter>. The graph should look like the one below; notice that the format of the numbers on the vertical axis has changed:

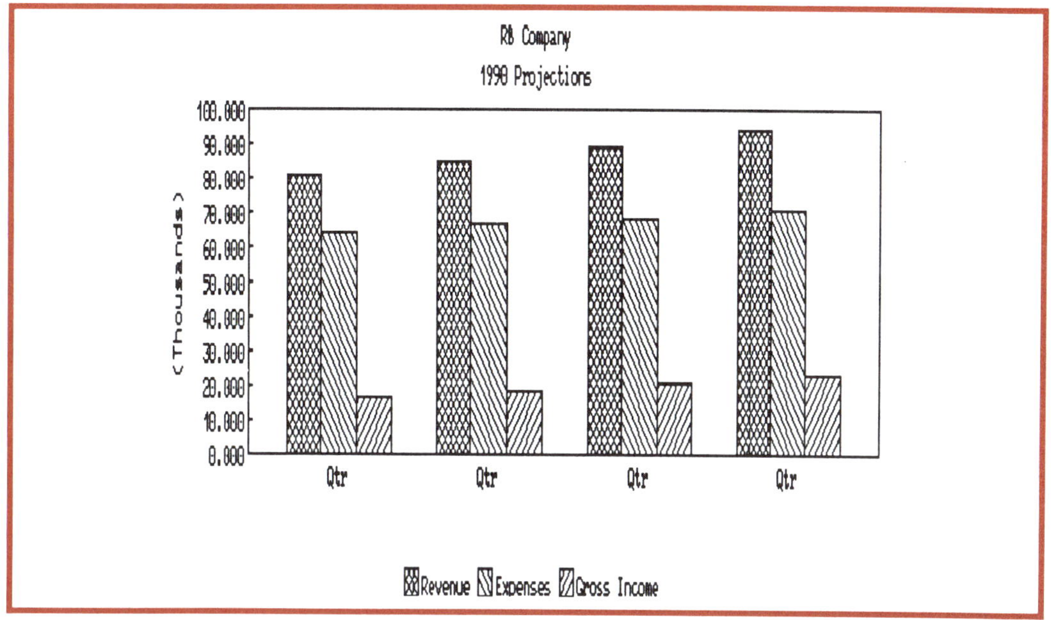

j. (If necessary, press the <Space> bar to return to the Graph Settings sheet.) Select **N**ame, then **C**reate, highlight BAR, and press <Enter>.

10. Save the worksheet before proceeding. *Remember*: You must **/F**ile **S**ave or the graph names you created will be lost.

GUIDED ACTIVITY: SAVING GRAPH PICTURE FILES

In this activity we save the four named files in a form that can be printed.

1. If you are not continuing from the previous Guided Activity, load Lotus and retrieve RB90PROJ.
2. Enter the command **/G**raph **N**ame **U**se. Highlight the name PIE, then press the <Enter> key. Lotus should display the pie chart you created in the previous Guided Activity.
3. Press the <Space> bar if necessary to return to the Graph Settings screen.
4. Choose the **S**ave option, type **RB_PIE**<Enter>.
5. You have created a file named RB_PIE.PIC that contains the information necessary to print the pie chart.
6. In succession, use the other three named graphs (BAR, SBAR, and XY) and save them with the names RB_BAR, RB_SBAR, and RB_XY. We will print these graphs in Unit 9.

7. When you are finished, **Q**uit from the **/G**raph main menu, then save your worksheet one last time.
8. **/Q**uit from spreadsheet mode, then **E**xit to the operating system. When you back up your work, copy both .WK1 and .PIC files.

EXERCISE: GRAPHING STATE SALES DATA

In this exercise you create graphs illustrating the differences among the state-by-state sales data you entered in the worksheet in Unit 7.

1. Retrieve the WESTREG file you created in Unit 7.
2. Create a pie graph that shows the relative proportion of sales for each state. Each state should have a different pattern, and California should be exploded. You need a new column of data (for the B-range patterns). Name this graph PIE and save it as PIE.PIC for later printing.
3. Create a bar graph that compares California to all other states. You must create new ranges of data to accomplish this. Name this graph BAR and save it as BAR.PIC.
4. Remember to save the worksheet file.

EXERCISE: THE PERFECT JOB (IV)

Create a graph that illustrates the levels of salary and adjusted salary for the five jobs in the JOBS worksheet. It is up to you to determine the graph type, data ranges, and what options are needed. Save the graph for later printing.

EXERCISE: A SALES WORKSHEET (III)

Create a graph that shows the relative proportion of the cost (before tax) of each of the components of the computer system in the worksheet COMPCOST. Create a second graph that includes one additional segment: the total amount of sales tax paid on the purchase. Save the graphs for later printing.

REVIEW QUESTIONS

1. What are the five types of graphs?
2. Which type of graph would you use to illustrate each of the following? There are no single correct answers to most of these, although there are arguably preferable answers.
   a.* Relative proportion of tax revenue from individuals, partnerships, corporations, and other sources.
   b.* Growth and decline of college-age population.
   c.* Revenues of three different divisions over a five-year period.
   d.* Total revenue from all divisions over a five-year period.
   e.* Relationship between unemployment level and welfare expenditures.

3.* What is the difference between **/File Save** and **/Graph Save**?

4. What is the difference between **/Graph Save** and **/Graph Name**?

5.* If your worksheet is saved under the name MINE, can you also save a graph under the name MINE? Why or why not?

6. If your worksheet is saved under the name MINE, can you also name a graph with the name MINE? Why or why not?

7. What is the difference between data-labels and legends?

DOCUMENTATION RESEARCH

Using the reference manual, find and record the page number of the command and the types of graph discussed in this unit. I recommend you also write the page number by the discussion of the command and graphs, above.

1. **/Graph** — how can you make 1-2-3 forget the graph settings?
2. Line — what are the four format options?
3. Bar — how many sets of data can be displayed?
4. Stacked bar — how can you change the color or pattern of the bars?
5. Pie — how many sets of data can be displayed?
6. XY — what is the fundamental difference between this type and the other types of graph?

UNIT 9

PAPER GRAPHICS

This unit deals with the creation of paper copies of graphs. We discuss PrintGraph, which is a program separate from the 1-2-3 program, and is called from the 1-2-3 Access System.

LEARNING OBJECTIVE

At the completion of this unit, you should be able to print a copy of a previously saved graph.

IMPORTANT COMMAND

PrintGraph

WORKSHEET PREPARATION

The PrintGraph operation is invoked from the 1-2-3 Access System menu. Before you print a graph, however, you must have used the **/G**raph **S**ave command. While in the worksheet, specify the graph using the normal commands: Type, X and A-F ranges, and Options (Legend, Format, Data-Labels, Titles, Grid, Scale, Color). Then **/G**raph **S**ave the graph into a file, which is given the .PIC extension automatically. You are now ready to exit to the Access System and print your graph.

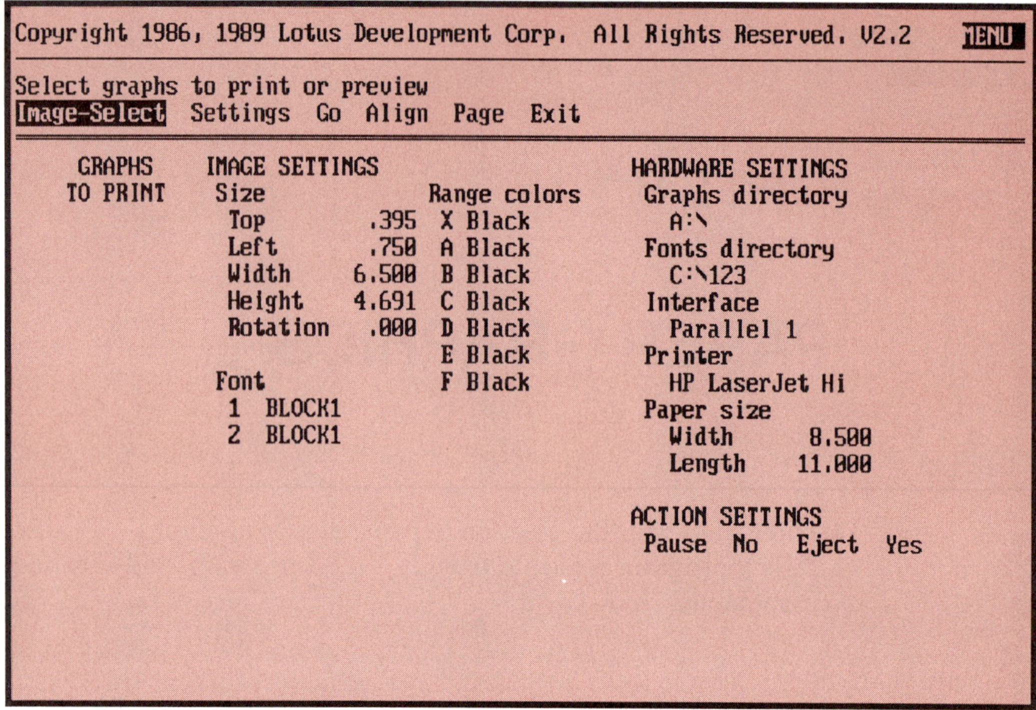

Figure 9-1 The Lotus PrintGraph Menu

PRINTING OPERATIONS

To choose PrintGraph from the Access System menu, use the <Arrow> keys to highlight PrintGraph; then press <Enter> to initiate the PrintGraph program.[1] You see the PrintGraph main menu (Figure 9-1). This menu allows you to do many things, most of which you can ignore for your first graphs.

- Image-Select asks you to select the files to be printed. The process of selecting files is discussed below.
- Settings allows you to change the manner in which the graph is printed, and is discussed in detail below.
- Go prints your selected graph(s).
- Align sets current printer or plotter position as top-of-page.
- Page moves paper to top-of-page.
- Exit returns you to the 1-2-3 Access System menu, from which you can enter 1-2-3 or exit to the operating system.

---

1. If you are working on a floppy disk system, Lotus asks you to insert the PrintGraph Disk; do so, then press <Enter>.

DESIGNATING GRAPHS TO PRINT

Normally, the first action after loading PrintGraph is to select the graphs to be printed. Check to ensure the Graphs Directory entry on the right of the screen indicates the disk that contains your .PIC files (e.g., A:\ in Figure 9-1).[1] If the directory is correct, highlight **Image-Select** and press <Enter>. When you are in the select option, you are presented with a list of all .PIC files on the disk. (See Figure 9-2.) You are instructed how to indicate which to print. If you do not remember which file has the graph you wish to print, highlight one of the candidates and press the <GRAPH (F10)> key. The graph is loaded and drawn (assuming you have a color/graphics monitor).

To select a single graph, highlight the graph file name and press the <Enter> key. To select more than one graph, highlight each in turn and press the <Space> bar to mark. A # (pound sign) is placed next to marked files. Generally, it is best to print only one graph at a time until you are familiar with the program.

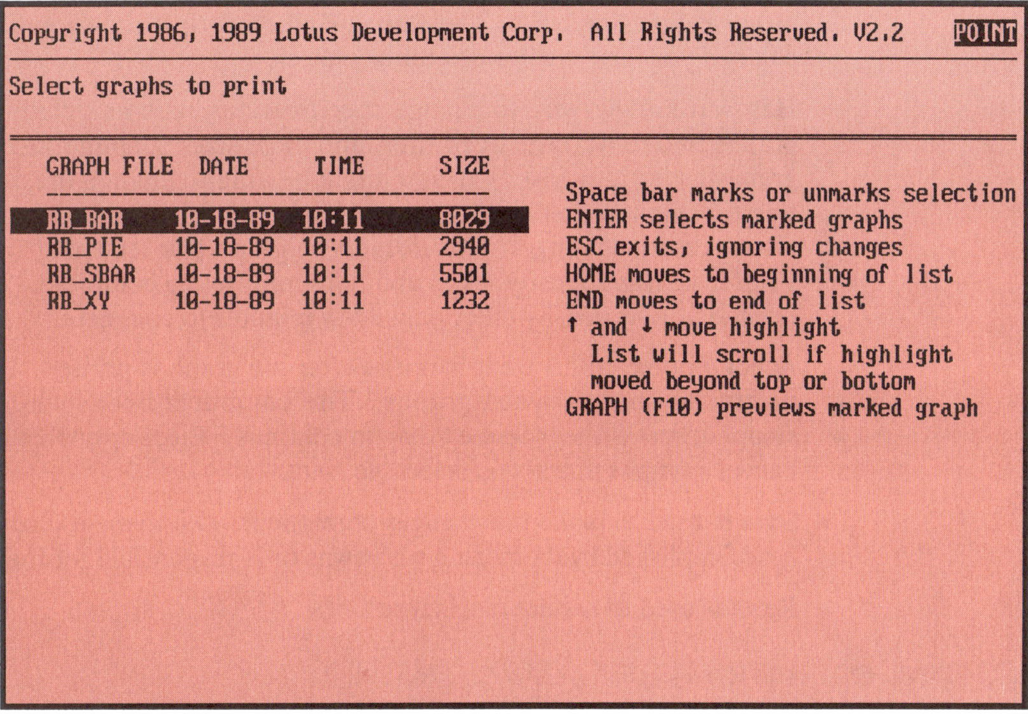

Figure 9-2 Designating Graphs to Print

1. If the drive is incorrect, you or the person responsible for the software must change it. Discuss this with your instructor.

PRINTGRAPH SETTINGS

Most of the flexibility of PrintGraph is contained in the Settings menu choice. When you choose Settings, you are presented with the following submenu:

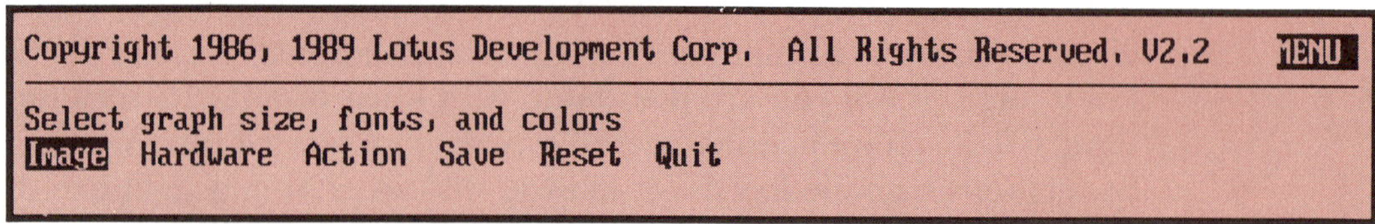

- Image allows you to change the Size of the output, the Font (i.e., type style), and the Range-Colors (if you are using a color printer or plotter). The Size options are Full, Half, Manual. If you choose Manual you are able to select Height, Length, Left margin size, Top margin size, or Rotation. Rotation allows you to turn the printed image (normally 90 degrees is chosen) to achieve a larger size. The Font option lets you select one font (Font 1) for the first line of the title and another (Font 2) for the rest of the graph. The available fonts are Block, Bold, Forum, Lotus, Roman, Italic, and Script. Most of the fonts can be either regular or bold. The Range-Colors option allows you to select graph colors if you have a color printer or plotter.
- Hardware allows you to change specifications such as default directories for graphs and fonts, type of printer, and page size. Depending on how the program was initially installed, you might be able to change the printer specification to yield a higher quality graph. Higher density yields greater quality, but it also takes much longer. For instance, a graph printed using an IBM Graphics Printer at High density takes about 45 minutes to complete. The same graph printed at Low density takes only a few minutes to complete.
- Action options affect what happens after the graph is printed. Pause causes the printer to stop between graphs. The computer beeps while the printer is stopped; press the <Space> bar to continue. Eject option causes a form feed between graphs unless you select No eject.
- Save is used to make the changes permanent. (Permanent changes are normally accomplished by the person who owns or is responsible for the software.)
- Reset is used to restore original settings.

PLOTTING OPERATIONS

You might have access to a **plotter**, a device that uses pens to draw graphs. The PrintGraph program supports plotters as well as printers, and the operation is virtually identical. The Settings Hardware option might have to be used to select the proper device, and you might want to use Settings Image Range-colors to define the colors. For solid bars in color, you must use the /Graph Options Color command while in 1-2-3, prior to the /Graph Save.

QUALITY OF PRINTED GRAPHS

The quality of printed graphs is usually much better than the graphs displayed on the screen. Lotus has more control over the size of lines used to form bars, symbols, and characters. Even graphs that do not fit on the screen will often print OK. For instance, the following is a copy of the pie chart we first saw in Figure 8-5. Note that the missing C has returned and that all the lines and letters look better. Although the quality of the printed graph is dependent on the printer, even inexpensive printers can produce acceptable graphs. Ask your instructor about the equipment available to you.

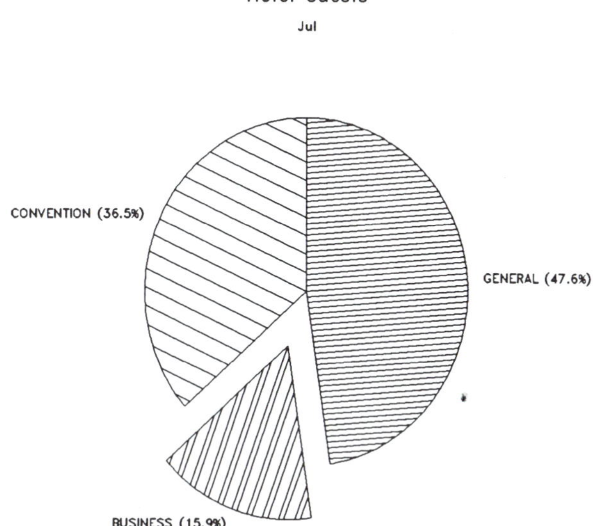

GUIDED ACTIVITY: PRINTING GRAPHS

This activity requires you to print previously saved graphs.

1. Follow the startup procedure outlined in Unit 1 to load Lotus to the 1-2-3 Access System Menu. When you are at that menu, 1-2-3 is highlighted. Use the <Arrow> keys to highlight PrintGraph; then press <Enter> to initiate the PrintGraph program. If Lotus asks you to insert the PrintGraph Disk, do so, then press <Enter>

2. After the program is loaded, you see the PrintGraph menu screen. Put the disk containing the .PIC file from Unit 8 in the drive indicated for the Graphs Directory.

3. Image-Select is highlighted. Press <Enter> and you are presented a list of all .PIC files on your disk. Follow the instructions to select the file to be printed (select RB_BAR) and return to the main menu.

4. Arrow to Go; press <Enter>; and watch your graph be printed. Simple.

CHECKPOINT

9a. If you do not like the graph, how can you change it?

5. When the graph is finished, **Page** ejects the remainder of the page. You might choose **Settings Image Font** and change the fonts. Depending on your printer, the effects might be attractive or unreadable.
6. Select and print each of the other graphs.
7. Once you are finished printing graphs, **Exit** returns you to the 1-2-3 Access Menu, from which you can exit to the operating system or choose 1-2-3 to do further spreadsheet work.

EXERCISES: PRINTING GRAPHS

Print the graphs you saved in the Unit 8 Exercises.

DOCUMENTATION RESEARCH

Using the reference manual, find and record the page number of the program discussed in this unit. I recommend you also write the page number by the discussion of the program, above.

1. What happens to variables such as height, width, and rotation when you select Full or Half size options?
2. When would you set the Pause option to Yes?
3. When would you set the Eject option to Yes?

APPLICATION D

THE HOTEL MANAGER

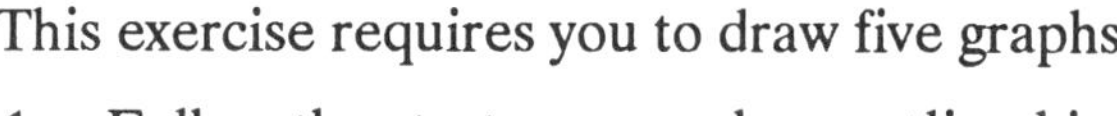

This exercise requires you to draw five graphs.

1. Follow the startup procedure outlined in Unit 1 to load Lotus and enter the 1-2-3 program.
2. Refer to the Hotel Customer Data that was presented in Figure 8-1. Create a worksheet with the file name HOTEL with that data.
3. Create the following graphs. Some of your graphs will look like those in Unit 8, but others will look different. Use the **/G**raph **N**ame command to name each graph so you can maintain all of the graphs with the worksheet. Also, **/G**raph **S**ave each of the five with a unique name (e.g., HOT_BAR, HOT_SBAR, etc.) while you are still in the 1-2-3 spreadsheet mode so they can be printed.
   - A bar graph depicting guests by type by month (HINT: The X range is the column with month names).
   - A stacked bar graph depicting the total patronage for each month.
   - A line graph showing guests by type, as well as total patronage, by month (HINT: You need another column of data).
   - A pie chart showing the relative proportion of each type of guest for the total year (HINT: You need another row of data).
   - An XY graph comparing General and Business registrations for each month of the year.

   For each graph, make liberal use of titles, legends, and any other appropriate options. Use the **/G**raph **O**ptions **S**cale command to set both X and Y axis formats to 3 decimal places.
4. Make printed copies of the graphs.

PART III

ADVANCED SPREADSHEET AND DATABASE OPERATIONS

The **3** in Lotus 1-2-3 stands for database management. Although the database capabilities of Lotus are modest, they are a rather convenient addition to the spreadsheet and graphics components. In this part, we discuss the **/D**ata commands.

This part also deals with advanced techniques that enhance your ability to create sophisticated worksheets. These techniques — Lotus functions, advanced **/W**orksheet, **/R**ange, and **/F**ile commands, and macros — allow you to work faster and achieve more impressive results.

The first exercise in this part provides practice in using the **/D**ata functions: sorting; determining the distribution of responses; filling a range with a sequence of numbers; and computing a table of values. The next exercise is devoted to macro commands. The final two exercises are designed to integrate much of what you have learned in this manual.

Before you start doing the Guided Activities, Exercises, and Applications in this part, you must copy five data files to your data disk. You should have done this in Unit 2, but if not see page 30 and follow the instructions in Step 6 on that page.

UNIT 10

DATA COMPUTATION OPERATIONS

This unit deals with those /**D**ata commands that are more related to computation than to selection. These commands allow you to fill a range with a series of numbers, to compute the values of a formula over a range of variables, to determine the distribution of values among a set of ranges, to manipulate matrices of numbers, and to perform multiple regression. Two related /**R**ange commands are also presented.

LEARNING OBJECTIVES

1. At the completion of this unit, you should know how to write a formula with one or two variables.
2. At the completion of this unit, you should be able to
   a. fill a range with a series of numbers,
   b. compute a one-variable data table,
   c. compute a two-variable data table,
   d. compute a data distribution,
   e. transpose or invert a matrix,
   f. multiply two matrices,
   g. perform a multiple regression,
   h. convert a series of formulas to their values.

IMPORTANT COMMANDS

/**D**ata **F**ill
/**D**ata **T**able **1**
/**D**ata **T**able **2**
/**D**ata **D**istribution
/**D**ata **M**atrix
/**D**ata **R**egression
/**R**ange **T**rans
/**R**ange **V**alue

CREATING A RANGE OF VALUES

/**D**ata **F**ill is used to fill a row or column range with a series of ascending or descending numbers. /**R**ange **V**alue is used to convert a series of formulas to their values.

The /**D**ata **F**ill command is used when the difference between each value in the series is constant. After giving the /**DF** command, you must specify a range, a start value, a step value, and a stop value. The step value can be either positive or negative.

The start and step values must be precise, but either the range or the stop value can be imprecise. Lotus erases the range, then fills the range from the top or left cell with the start value, incrementing by the step value, until the stop value is reached or the end of the range is reached, whichever happens first.

For instance, say you wanted to build a series of numbers from 0 (zero) to 100,000 with an increment of 400, starting at cell B5 and continuing down column B. In this case we know the start, step, and stop values, so we do not need to determine the end of the range. When asked to specify the range, place the cursor in B5, enter a period to anchor, then press <End><Down><Enter> to indicate that the range extends to the bottom of the worksheet. The values fill the range B5..B255. This operation is illustrated in the following Guided Activity.

Alternatively, you might wish to build a series of 11 dates starting with @NOW and having increments of one week (7). The sequence is to start in C2 and continue to M2. In this case, we know the start and step values and the number of values (therefore the range). For the step value, we enter **7**; for the stop value, we enter a large number (say, **1000000**). This operation is also illustrated in the following Guided Activity. Because date values are numbers, you must use the /**R**ange **F**ormat command to reformat the row to a readable form.

When the interval between numbers in the series is not constant, you might be able to build a series of formulas that yields the desired sequence. Then you can use the /**R**ange **V**alue command to copy the values of formulas to a separate place on the worksheet, leaving the formulas intact. Or, you can copy the range over itself, replacing the formulas with their values and eliminating the original formulas.

For instance, you might wish to create a list containing every Monday, Wednesday, and Friday in 1990, starting in cell A1 and proceeding down column A. In A1, put the function for the first relevant date in 1990 (Monday, January 1), **@DATE(90,1,1)**. In A2, put the formula **+A1+2**, which computes the serial number of Wednesday, January 3. The formula **+A2+2** occupies A3. In A4 you can enter a formula that adds seven to the value three cells above, that is, **+A1+7**. This formula can be copied as far as necessary, in this example from A4 to A5..A157. Now, start the /**R**ange **V**alue command. The `range to copy FROM` is A1..A157. The `range to copy TO` is A1. The result is that the formulas are replaced by their values. Although slightly more complex than /**D**ata **F**ill, the result is the same: a series of constant values.

/**D**ata **F**ill and /**R**ange **V**alue commands are especially useful for building a series of numbers for the /**D**ata **T**able and /**D**ata **D**istribution commands discussed below.

GUIDED ACTIVITY: CREATING A RANGE OF VALUES

This activity requires you to use **/Data Fill** and **/Range Value** commands to create several ranges of values.

1. Follow the startup procedure outlined in Unit 1 to load Lotus and enter the 1-2-3 program. If you are continuing from a previous activity or exercise and already have a worksheet on the screen, use the command **/Worksheet Erase Yes** to clear the screen. (*Remember*: Save it before erasing it.)

2. Build a series of numbers from 0 (zero) to 100,000 with an increment of 400, starting at cell B5 and continuing down column B.

   a. Move the cell pointer to cell B5.

   b. Enter **/DF**. Lotus asks for the fill range:

```
B5:                                                              POINT
Enter fill range: B5
```

   c. Press a period to anchor the fill range at B5, then press <End><Down><Enter> to highlight the range B5..B8192. Lotus then asks for a start value:

```
B5:                                                              EDIT
Enter fill range: B5..B8192
Start: 0
```

   d. Press the <Enter> key to accept zero as the start value. Lotus next asks for a step:

```
B5:                                                              EDIT
Enter fill range: B5..B8192
Start: 0                Step: 1
```

   e. Type **400**<Enter>. Lotus next asks for the stop value:

```
B5:                                                              EDIT
Enter fill range: B5..B8192
Start: 0                Step: 400               Stop: 8191
```

   f. Type **100000**<Enter>. Lotus then fills the range from B5 to B255 with values from 0 to 100,000 in increments of 400. (See Figure 10-1.)

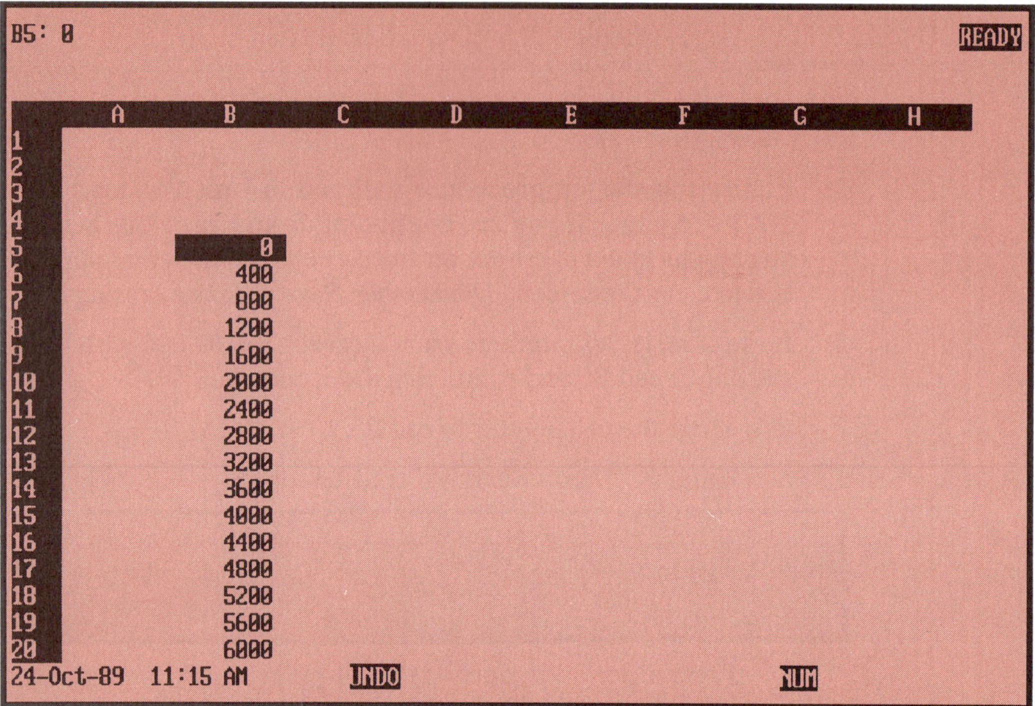

Figure 10-1 Result of the First /DataFill Command

3. Press <End><Down> to move to the bottom of the data column. You should end up in cell B255, which has a value of 100,000. Press the <Up> arrow key several times to move up the column, assuring yourself that each cell contains a constant value that is 400 different from the cells above and below. When you are convinced, press the <Home> key to return to the top of the worksheet.
4. Save your work with the name DATACOMP.
5. Now, build a series of 11 dates, starting with @NOW and having increments of one week. The sequence is to start in C2 and continue to M2.
   a. When you give the **/DF** command, notice that Lotus remembers the previous range:

   b. Press the <Esc> key to cancel (**unanchor**) the previous range, arrow to C2, press a period, arrow to M2, and press the <Enter> key.

c. For the start value, enter **@NOW**; for the step, enter **7**; and for the stop value, enter a very large number, for example **1000000**:

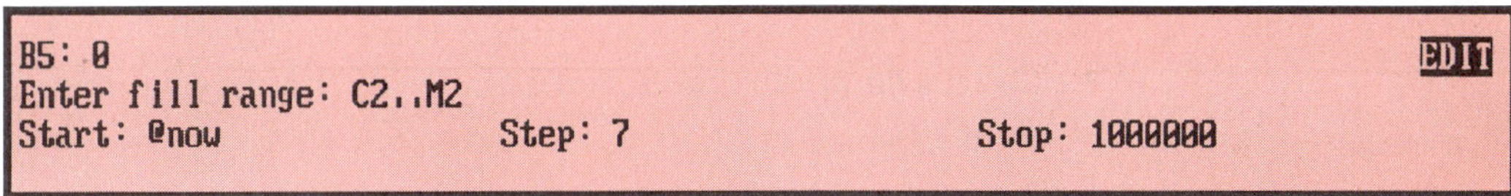

d. Lotus will then compute the results, illustrated in Figure 10-2. The date values will be different from those in the illustration.

CHECKPOINT

10a. Why are the dates different?

10b. How can you format the row of dates to a readable form?

e. Format the dates to **Date2** format (DD-MMM).

f. Note that the dates created by this command are constant values, not formulas. Thus, if you retrieve this spreadsheet tomorrow, the date in C2 will not change to tomorrow's date, it will remain today's date.

6. Save your work before proceeding.

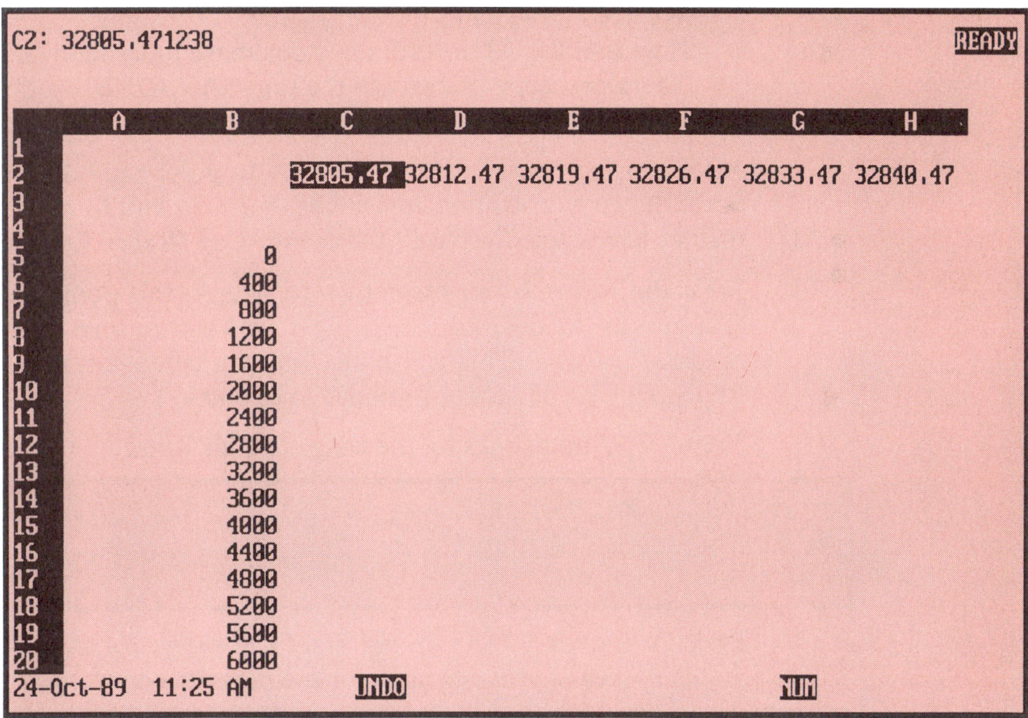

Figure 10-2 The Result of the Second /DataFill Command

7. In column A, starting in cell A1, build a list of dates that includes every Monday, Wednesday, and Friday in 1990. The first date is Monday, January 1.

   a. Move the cell pointer to A1. Enter the function **@DATE(90,1,1)** in that cell. This computes the serial number of the date January 1, 1990 (which is a Monday).

   b. Move to A2. Enter **+A1+2** in that cell. This calculates the serial number of the day two days later than the date in cell A1.

   c. Use the /Copy command to copy the formula from A2 to A3.

   d. Move to A4. Enter **+A1+7** in that cell. This calculates the serial number of the day one week later than the date in cell A1.

   e. Use the /Range Format command to format the range A1..A4 to Date1 (DD-MMM-YY). Use the /Worksheet Column Set-Width command to change the width of Column A to 10.

   f. The next step is to copy the formula in A4 to a range that will include all dates in 1990. Unless you are very smart, you probably do not know how many cells it will take. Here's how I figured out how far to copy the formula:

      - There are 52 weeks, plus a few extra days, in a year.
      - We need three dates for every week.
      - If we multiply 53 times 3, we should have more than enough rows.
      - Therefore, copy from A4 to the range A5..A159.
      - If we have copied too far, use /Range Erase to erase the excess.

   g. After copying, press <End><Down> to go to the bottom of the column. Since the copy operation copies both formula and format, it is easy to see that we have copied two cells too many. Use /Range Erase to erase them.

   h. Press the <Home> key to return to A1. At this point, we have *formulas* that give us the desired dates. Next, we want to turn those formulas into *constant values*. (This will make the worksheet recalculate faster since Lotus will have 157 fewer formulas to calculate.)

   i. Enter **/RV**. Lotus asks for the range to copy from:

```
A1: (D1) [W10] @DATE(90,1,1)                                    POINT
Enter range to copy FROM: A1..A1
```

   j. Press <End><Down> to highlight the range A1..A157, then press the <Enter> key. Lotus next asks for the range to copy to:

```
A1: (D1) [W10] @DATE(90,1,1)                                    POINT
Enter range to copy TO: A1
```

k. Press the <Enter> key to accept A1 as the range to copy to. Just as with the /Copy command, if the source range is more than a single cell, only the upper/left cell of the destination range need be indicated. Thus, Lotus will convert each formula in the original range to its current value, then place that value in the corresponding cell in the destination range. Since the source and destination ranges are the same, the formulas are replaced by their values (and the formulas no longer exist).

l. The worksheet should now look like Figure 10-3. Use the arrow keys to move down the range, convincing yourself that the formulas have been replaced by values. Press the <Home> key to return to A1.

8. Save your work again.

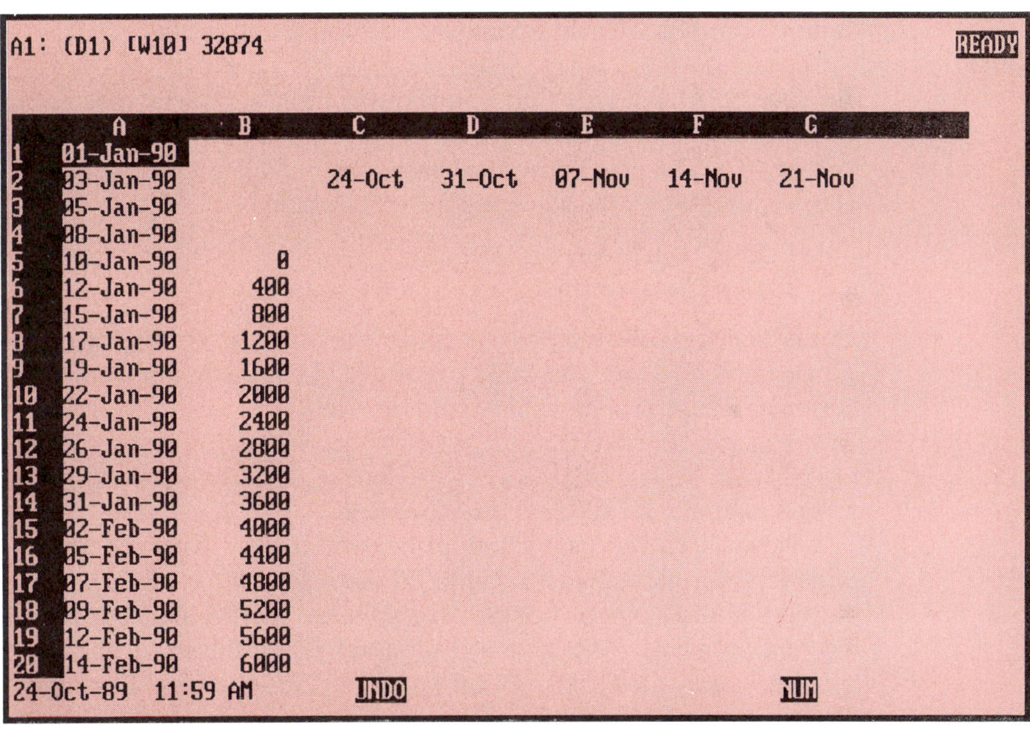

Figure 10-3 Result of the /RangeValue Command

ONE-VARIABLE TABLE

Data tables are a powerful tool for performing **what-if** analyses. You can see how results change as the value of one (or two) variables change.

/Data Table **1** is used to evaluate the impact of one or more values of one variable in one or more formulas. In the language of mathematics, these are equations with one unknown. When complete, the table is structured as follows:

blank	formula_a	formula_b	*etc.*
value_1	result_{a1}	result_{b1}	
value_2	result_{a2}	result_{b2}	
value_3	result_{a3}	result_{b3}	
etc.			

The top row of the table contains formulas. We want to determine the results of these formulas as one of the variables in the formulas changes. For instance, we might want to see how cost and revenue change as the level of sales changes (see the example that follows). The left column of the table contains a set of values for the variable. The results area will contain the result of the formulas when the variable has the various values. Thus result_{a1} is the value of formula_a when the variable has value_1.

When you construct a data table, you need enter only the formulas and the values. The **/D**ata **T**able **1** command computes the results.

An Example. Assume that you want to build a table whose columns contain the cost and revenue of differing levels of sales, from 0 (zero) to 100,000 units, at intervals of 400. The cost to produce each item is $125 and the selling price is $200. If *x* is the amount sold, the algebraic formulas would be

$125x$ for total cost.
$200x$ for total revenue.

Lotus does not allow us to use *x* as a part of a formula, however. Instead, a cell name must be used. Assuming that cell X1 is vacant, we can use that cell in the formula. The Lotus formulas would then be

```
125*X1        200*X1
```

In this example, X1 is called the **input cell.**

Now, choose an empty area of the worksheet. The area must be three columns wide (two formulas plus one) and 252 rows deep (251 values plus one). This area is called the **table range**. For our example, we use B4..D255 as the table range. Cell B4 remains blank. We have already used **/D**ata **F**ill to fill the range B5..B255 with numbers **`0, 400, ... 100000.`** Place the formulas into cells C4 and D4. Return the cursor to cell B4.

Now (finally!) you can issue the **/DT1** command. When asked for the table range, type or point to B4..D255. When asked for the input cell, type or point to X1. Lotus calculates the results and place them in cells C5..D255. This operation is illustrated in the following Guided Activity.

Lotus remembers the most recent **/D**ata **T**able **1** or **/D**ata **T**able **2** operation. To repeat the most recent operation (for instance, after changing the formulas or the values in the first column), press the <TABLE (F8)> key. Note that Lotus does not recalculate the table when you change the value of any cell that would affect the table's results. The table is not recalculated until you press <TABLE (F8)>.

GUIDED ACTIVITY: A ONE-VARIABLE TABLE

In this activity we create a one-variable data table.

1. If you are not continuing from the previous Guided Activity, load Lotus and retrieve DATACOMP.

2. Build a table whose columns contain the total cost and revenue of differing levels of sales, from 0 (zero) to 100000 units, at intervals of 400. Use B4..D255 as the table range. The cost to produce each item is $125 and the selling price is $200. If x is the amount sold, the formulas would be

   $125x \quad 200x$

   CHECKPOINT

   10c. What are the Lotus formulas?

3. We will use the previously entered range of values as one part of the table. Recall that the range B5..B255 contains a series of numbers ranging from 0 (zero) to 100,000 in increments of 400.

4. The next step is to enter the Lotus formulas one row above and one column right of the lowest value. Therefore, enter **125*X1** in cell C4, and **200*X1** in cell D4.

5. Move the cell pointer to B4.

6. To compute the table:

   a. Enter the sequence **/DT1**. Lotus asks for a table range:

   b. Highlight the table range. Rather than trying to remember the exact range, use the cursor movement keys to help:

      i. While still in B4, press a period to anchor the range.

      ii. Press <Down><End><Down> to highlight the entire column of values.

      iii. Press the <Right> arrow key twice (because there are two formulas). The control panel should now show the range B4..D255.

      iv. Press the <Enter> key to enter the range.

   c. Lotus next asks for the input cell:

   d. Type **X1**<Enter> or point to cell X1. (This is one time when typing is preferred because the cell is far from the table area.)

e. Lotus completes the table, with the result illustrated in Figure 10-4. Arrow around in the results area. Notice that the results area contains constant values, not formulas. If you were to change one of the formulas in row 4, you would have to recompute the table.

B4: READY

	A	B	C	D	E	F	G
1	01-Jan-90						
2	03-Jan-90		24-Oct	31-Oct	07-Nov	14-Nov	21-Nov
3	05-Jan-90						
4	08-Jan-90		0	0			
5	10-Jan-90	0	0	0			
6	12-Jan-90	400	50000	80000			
7	15-Jan-90	800	100000	160000			
8	17-Jan-90	1200	150000	240000			
9	19-Jan-90	1600	200000	320000			
10	22-Jan-90	2000	250000	400000			
11	24-Jan-90	2400	300000	480000			
12	26-Jan-90	2800	350000	560000			
13	29-Jan-90	3200	400000	640000			
14	31-Jan-90	3600	450000	720000			
15	02-Feb-90	4000	500000	800000			
16	05-Feb-90	4400	550000	880000			
17	07-Feb-90	4800	600000	960000			
18	09-Feb-90	5200	650000	1040000			
19	12-Feb-90	5600	700000	1120000			
20	14-Feb-90	6000	750000	1200000			

24-Oct-89 02:51 PM UNDO NUM

Figure 10-4 The Result of the /DataTable1 Command

7. Save your work before proceeding.
8. You decide to raise the price to $210. Change the formula in D4 to **210*X1**. Notice that the results in the column below D4 do not change. Press the <TABLE (F8)> key. This causes Lotus to recalculate the table results using the new price.
9. Save the worksheet.

TWO-VARIABLE TABLE

/Data Table **2** is used to evaluate the impact of one or more values of two variables in one formula. This is called an equation with two unknowns. When complete, the table is structured as follows:

formula	value_{b1}	value_{b2}	*etc.*
value_{a1}	$\text{result}_{a1,b1}$	$\text{result}_{a1,b2}$	
value_{a2}	$\text{result}_{a2,b1}$	$\text{result}_{a2,b2}$	
value_{a3}	$\text{result}_{a3,b1}$	$\text{result}_{a3,b2}$	
etc.			

The top-left cell contains a single formula. We want to determine the results of this formula as two of the variables in the formula change. For instance, we might want to see how monthly payment changes as a result of different principal amounts and interest rates (see the example that follows). The left column of the table contains a set of values for one of the variables. The top row contains a set of values for the other variable. The results area will contain the result of the formula when the variables have the various values. Thus $\text{result}_{a1,b1}$ is the value of the formula when one variable has value_{a1} and the other variable has value_{b1}.

When you construct a two-variable data table, you need enter only the formula and the values. The **/D**ata **T**able **2** command computes the results.

An Example. Assume that you want to build a table whose columns contain the monthly payments on various principal amounts at various interest rates for 60 months. The principal amounts are $5000 to $25,000 in increments of $2000 and the interest rates are 7.5% to 17.5% in increments of 1.0%. Recall that the Lotus function is

```
@PMT(prn,int,term)
```

Again, Lotus requires cell names in the formula. Assuming that cells X1 and Y1 are vacant, we can use them as the arguments to the function. The Lotus formula would then be

```
@PMT(X1,Y1/12,60)
```

In this example, X1 is called **input cell 1** and Y1 is **input cell 2**.

Now, choose an empty area of the worksheet. The area must be twelve columns wide (eleven values of *int* plus one) and twelve rows deep (eleven values of *prn* plus one). This area is the **table range**. For our example, we use H21..S32 as the table range. Cell H21 contains the @PMT formula. Use **/D**ata **F**ill to fill the range H22..H32 with numbers **5000, 7000, ..., 25000.** Use **/D**ata **F**ill to fill the range I21..S21 with numbers **.075, .085, ..., .175.** Return the cursor to cell H21.

Now you can issue the **/DT2** command. When asked for the table range, type or point to H21..S32. When asked for the input cell 1, type or point to X1. When asked for the input cell 2, type or point to Y1. Lotus calculates the results and places them in cells H22..S32. This operation is illustrated in the following Guided Activity.

Lotus remembers the most recent **/D**ata **T**able **1** or **/D**ata **T**able **2** operation. To repeat that most recent operation (for instance, after changing the formula or the values in the first row or column), press the <TABLE (F8)> key. Lotus does not recalculatc the table when you change the value of any cell that would affect the table's results. The table is not recalculated until you press <TABLE (F8)>.

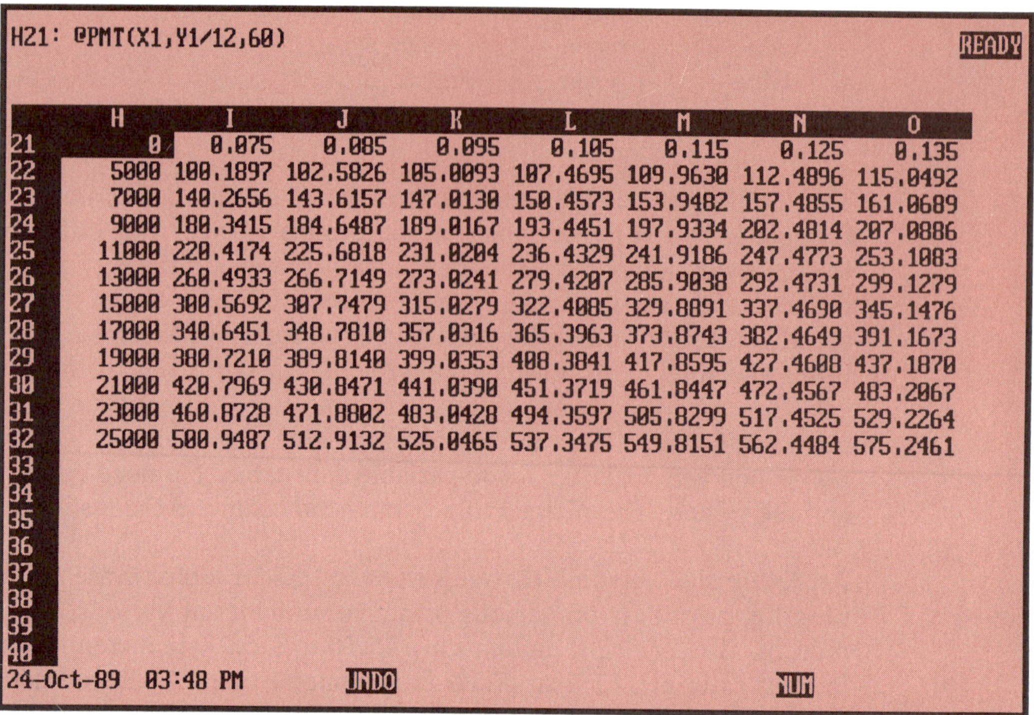

H21: @PMT(X1,Y1/12,60) READY

	H	I	J	K	L	M	N	O
21	0	0.075	0.085	0.095	0.105	0.115	0.125	0.135
22	5000	100.1897	102.5826	105.0093	107.4695	109.9630	112.4896	115.0492
23	7000	140.2656	143.6157	147.0130	150.4573	153.9482	157.4855	161.0689
24	9000	180.3415	184.6487	189.0167	193.4451	197.9334	202.4814	207.0886
25	11000	220.4174	225.6818	231.0204	236.4329	241.9186	247.4773	253.1083
26	13000	260.4933	266.7149	273.0241	279.4207	285.9038	292.4731	299.1279
27	15000	300.5692	307.7479	315.0279	322.4085	329.8891	337.4690	345.1476
28	17000	340.6451	348.7810	357.0316	365.3963	373.8743	382.4649	391.1673
29	19000	380.7210	389.8140	399.0353	408.3841	417.8595	427.4608	437.1870
30	21000	420.7969	430.8471	441.0390	451.3719	461.8447	472.4567	483.2067
31	23000	460.8728	471.0802	483.0428	494.3597	505.8299	517.4525	529.2264
32	25000	500.9487	512.9132	525.0465	537.3475	549.8151	562.4484	575.2461
33								
34								
35								
36								
37								
38								
39								
40								

24-Oct-89 03:48 PM UNDO NUM

Figure 10-5 The Result of the /DataTable2 Command

GUIDED ACTIVITY: A TWO-VARIABLE TABLE

In this activity we create a two-variable data table.

1. If you are not continuing from the previous Guided Activity, load Lotus and retrieve DATACOMP.

2. Follow the example discussed above for the **/D**ata **T**able **2** command to build a table whose columns contain the monthly payments on various principal amounts at various interest rates for 60 months. The principal amounts are $5000 to $25,000 in increments of $2000 and the interest rates are 7.5% to 17.5% in increments of 1.0%. Use H21..S32 as the table range.

3. You should be able to complete this activity without detailed instructions. The result should look like Figure 10-5.

4. Save your work. This completes our work with DATACOMP.

DISTRIBUTION OF DATA

When we ask questions such as "How many people have salaries in the ranges $10,000 to $20,000 and $20,000 to $30,000?" we are asking for a **distribution** of the raw data. The **/Data Distribution** command is used to compute the distribution of values of a range of numbers.[1] When complete, the distribution table is structured as follows:

$cutpoint_1$	$count_1$
$cutpoint_2$	$count_2$
$cutpoint_3$	$count_3$
blank	$count_4$

The left column contains a series of **cutpoints**. The right column contains the count of the number of values that are greater than the cutpoint in the row above and less than or equal to the cutpoint in the same row: thus $count_1$ is the number of values less than or equal to $cutpoint_1$; $count_2$ is the number of values greater than $cutpoint_1$ and less than or equal to $cutpoint_2$; and so on. Notice that there is one more count than cutpoint. This last count ($count_4$ in this example) contains the number of values greater than the last cutpoint ($cutpoint_3$ in this example).

When you construct a data distribution table, you need enter only the cutpoints (and, of course, the raw data). The **/Data Distribution** command computes the counts.

An Example. Assume that you have a list of employees and one of the columns is *salary*. You want to know how many persons are earning salaries in the ranges 0.00 to 9,999.99, 10,000.00 to 19,999.99, 20,000.00 to 29,999.99, . . . 90,000.00 to 99,999.99, and greater than 100,000.00.

The salary data are contained in the column range D2..D39. This is the **values range**.

Find an empty area of the worksheet, say J1..K11, which is two columns wide and as long as the number of intervals (including the last *greater than* interval). In the left column of this area, place the cutpoints of all but the last intervals. In this example, we could use **/Data Fill** to fill range J1..J10 with start value of **9999.99**, step of **10000**, and end value of **99999.99**. This column (J1..J10) is the **bin range**. Note that the bin range does not include the second column nor the last row of the *empty area*.

Now give the **/DD** command. When asked for the values range, type or point to D2..D39. When asked for the bin range, type or point to J1..J10. Lotus counts the number of values in the values range that are less than or equal to the first value in the bin range, and puts the result in K1. Lotus then proceeds down the bin range column, counting the number of values range values that fall into the relevant ranges range values that fall into the relevant ranges and placing the results in the K column. On reaching the end of the bin range, Lotus counts all values that are

1. The numbers that are counted for the distribution are in a separate range of the spreadsheet.

greater than the last cutpoint (99,999.99) and places that count in the cell (K11) one row down from and one column to the right of the last entry in the bin range. This operation is illustrated in the Guided Activity that follows.

Lotus remembers the bin and values ranges, but does not recalculate the distribution table when changes are made to the values range. To recalculate the distribution table, give the command **/DD**<Enter> <Enter>.

GUIDED ACTIVITY: COMPUTING A DATA DISTRIBUTION TABLE

In this activity we compute a data distribution table.

1. If you are not continuing from the previous Guided Activity, load Lotus.
2. Retrieve the file NAMELIST (this is one of the files you should have copied to your data disk in the Guided Activity called "File Retrieval and Backup" on pages 29-31).
3. Note that this file has four columns of data. Arrow to the "Salary" column (D). Press <End> <Down> to see how far down the data go. (You should go to cell D39.) Press the <Home> key to return to cell A1.
4. Before computing the data distribution table, we must build the bin range.
   a. Move the cell pointer to cell J1.
   b. Use the **/Data Fill** command to fill the range J1..J10 with the cutpoints. Use a start value of **9999.99**, a step of **10000**, and an end value of **99999.99**:

```
J1:                                                                  EDIT
Enter fill range: J1..J10
Start: 9999.99            Step: 10000               Stop: 99999.99
```

5. Next, compute the table.
   a. Give the **/DD** command. Lotus asks for the values range:

```
J1: 9999.99                                                          POINT
Enter values range: J1
```

   b. Type or point to D2..D39, then press <Enter>. Next, Lotus asks for the bin range. Type or point to J1..J10:

```
J10: 99999.99                                                        POINT
Enter values range: D2..D39          Enter bin range: J1..J10
```

   c. After you press <Enter> the distribution table is computed. The result appears in Figure 10-6.
6. Save the worksheet.

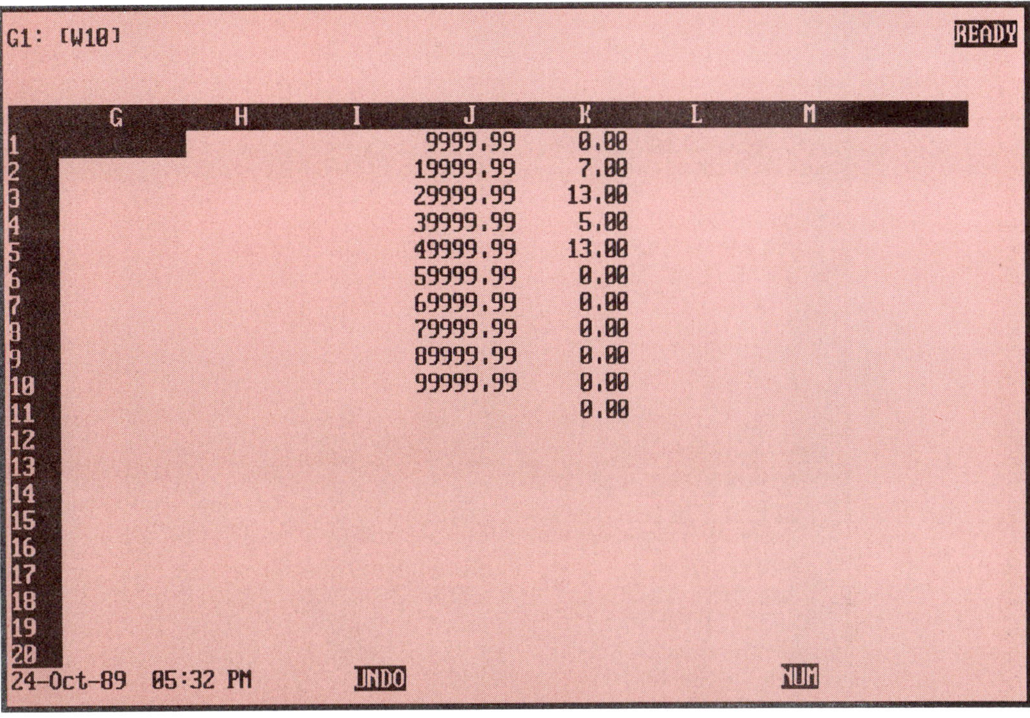

Figure 10-6 The Result of the /DataDistribution Command

MATRIX OPERATIONS

Lotus 1-2-3 provides two commands that deal with matrices of data. These commands are used for specialized applications, such as statistics and graphics. If you do not *know* you need to use these commands, then you probably do not need to use them. On the other hand, these commands provide a substantial bonus to those who do need to use matrix operations in their work.

The /**R**ange **T**rans command is used to **transpose** a matrix of data, that is, to copy a block of data to another location, exchanging rows for columns and vice versa. *Formulas in cells that are transposed are converted to their values in the destination range.*

The /**D**ata **M**atrix command is provided to allow the multiplication and inversion of matrices. The largest matrix that can be used in this command is 90 by 90. Only square matrices can be inverted. When multiplying matrices, the number of columns in the first matrix must equal the number of rows in the second matrix. Both operations are initiated by the /**D**ata **M**atrix command. To invert a matrix, you are asked to specify the range to invert and the upper left corner of the area to hold the result. To multiply two matrices, you are asked to indicate both matrices, then the upper left cell of the range to hold the answer.

A1: [W20] 'Name READY

	A	B	C	D	E	F
1	Name	1989	1990			
2	AMER. HOME PRODUCTS	109.6	107.3			
3	AMERICAN EXPRESS	-154.7	-139.1			
4	AMERICAN TELEPHONE	61.9	65.4			
5	ATLANTIC RICHFIELD	-457.1	-567.8			
6	BRISTOL-MYERS	265.8	314.9			
7	BRITISH PETROLEUM	-242.3	-267.4			
8	COCA-COLA	-288.0	-349.7			
9	DOW CHEMICAL	-122.6	-126.2			
10	DU PONT	-398.9	-493.8			
11	EASTMAN KODAK	271.1	303.2			
12	EXXON CORP.	-72.1	-78.9			
13	FORD MOTOR	-409.0	-332.0			
14	GENERAL ELECTRIC	412.3	438.6			
15	GENERAL MOTORS	60.1	69.9			
16	GENERAL TELEPHONE	419.4	407.5			
17	GETTY OIL	487.6	593.0			
18	GULF OIL	335.6	273.5			
19	HEWLETT-PACKARD CO.	-226.4	-247.3			
20	INT'L BUSINESS MACH.	-491.0	-502.5			

25-Oct-89 08:54 AM UNDO NUM

Figure 10-7 The PORTFOLI Worksheet

MULTIPLE REGRESSION

The /Data Regression command is used to compute simple or multiple regression statistics. (If you have not had a class in statistics, the concept of regression might be new to you.) This discussion uses the PORTFOLI worksheet, a portion of which is illustrated in Figure 10-7. In this case, we wish to compute the relationship between 1989 ratings in column B and predicted 1990 ratings in column C. For /Data Regression to function, we must have at least two columns of data, one of which is the **dependent variable** (in this case, the predicted 1990 ratings) and the other(s) the **independent variable(s)**.

When the **/Data Regression** command is given, the menu and **Regression Settings** screen illustrated below appears.

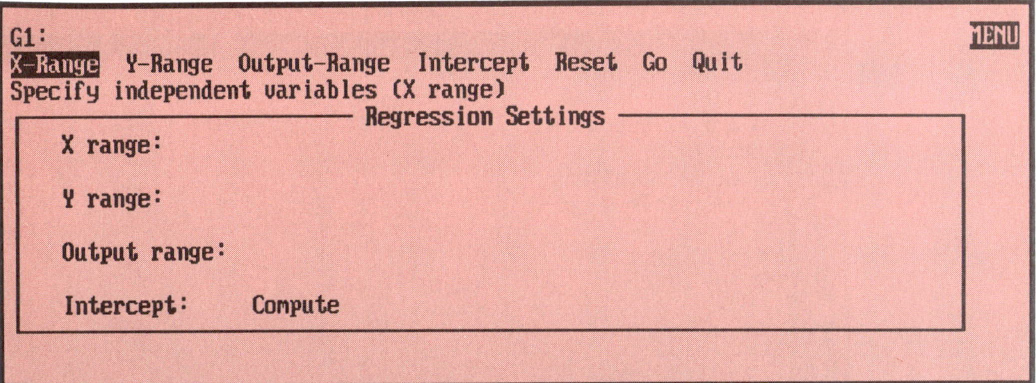

The **X**-Range is defined as the column or columns (maximum 16) containing the independent variable data. In this case, the range was specified as B2..B38. The **Y**-Range is the column containing the dependent variable data (C2..C38). The **O**utput-Range is the area of the worksheet where the regression results are written. Only the top-left cell need be specified. The output will be nine rows by a minimum of four columns. Each independent variable after the second adds a column to the width (i.e., four independent variables occupy six columns in the output range). Make sure that the output range is empty (or contains nothing you want to keep) because it is erased when the regression results are computed. The **I**ntercept option is usually ignored except when the intercept must be set to some number such as zero. For this problem, the Regression Settings screen looks like the following when complete:

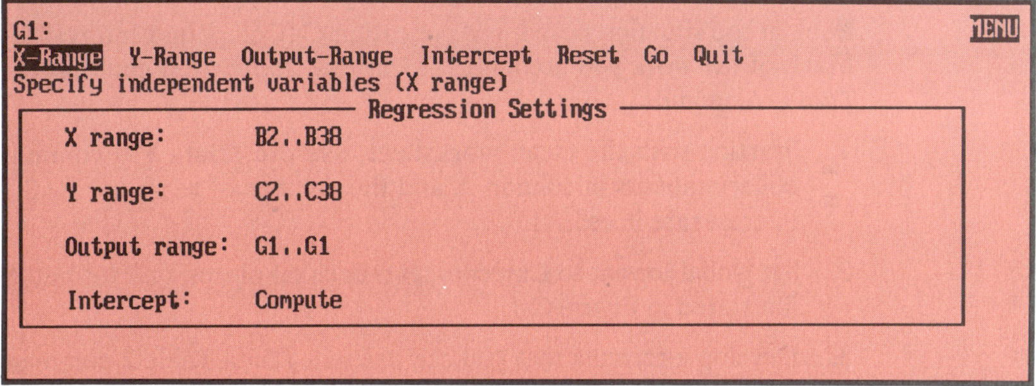

As usual, the **G**o choice causes the regression to be computed. Since many regression statistics are in the range 0 (zero) to 1 (one), it is a good idea to format the output range to Fixed, 3 decimal places. The (formatted) output from the regression is illustrated in Figure 10-8. **R**eset clears all settings. **Q**uit returns to the READY mode without computing the regression.

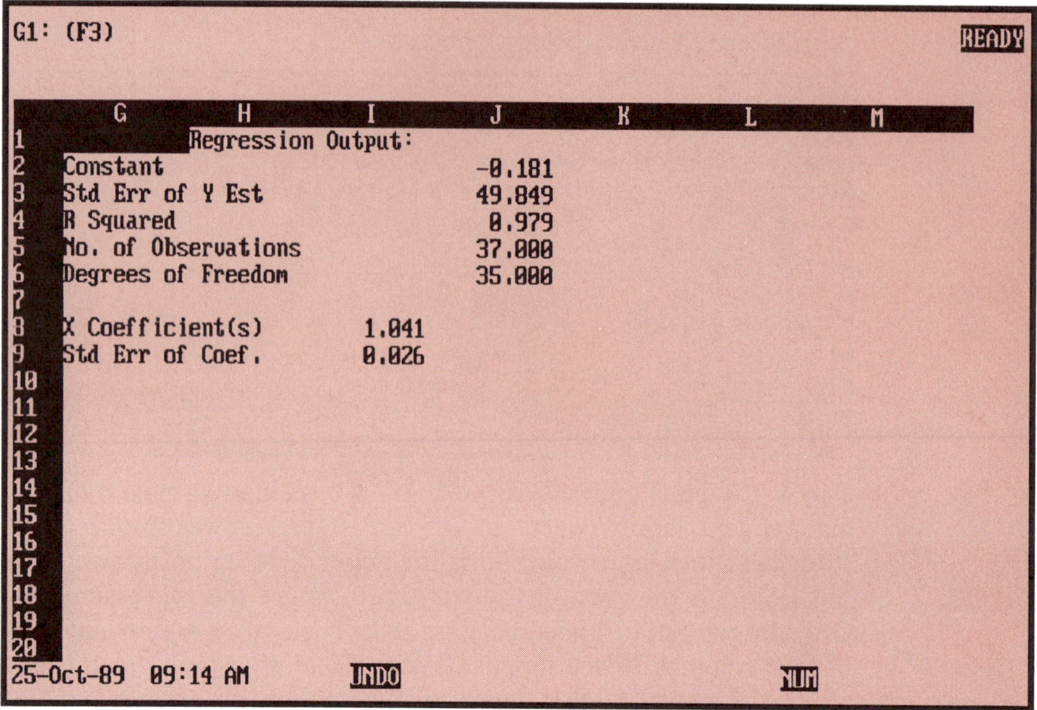

Figure 10-8 Output of the /DataRegression Command

EXERCISE: COMPOUND INTEREST REVISITED

Look at the situation posed in Application C [Compound Interest (I), pages 113-14]. Much of the work you accomplished in that application could have been done with /Data commands.

1. Starting with the clean worksheet, use the /**D**ata **F**ill command to enter the dollar amounts in column A and the number of years in row 2. Also, enter the interest rate in cell A1.
2. Set global format to Currency, two decimal places, and format A1 and B2..F2 as illustrated in Figure C-1.
3. Develop a formula that you can use in a /**D**ata **T**able **2** command and place the formula in A2.
4. Use the /**D**ata **T**able **2** command to calculate the table. Your result should look like Figure C-1, except that the formula in A2 displays some value [probably 0 (zero)].
5. Save your work with the file name COMPOX.

EXERCISE: A SALES WORKSHEET (IV)

Look at the COMPCOST worksheet used in several previous Exercises. Any time you have the same basic formula copied down a column you should consider changing the worksheet to use the /**D**ata **T**able **1** command. In this case, we can enter the formula for Tax in D12[1] and the formula for Total in E12 and compute the values for rows 13-15 using the /**D**ata **T**able **1** command.[2] After entering **/DT1**, indicate that the table range is C12..E15 and the input variable is C12.

REVIEW QUESTIONS

1. Write formulas for the following functions, which can be used in /**D**ata **T**able **1** or /**D**ata **T**able **2** commands. Use X1 as input cell 1 and, where necessary, Y1 as input cell 2.
   a.* The total cost of producing *x* units, where the total cost is the sum of a constant (fixed) cost of $40,000 and a cost per unit of $69.95.
   b.* The amount of a monthly payment on principal of *x* at *y* percent per annum interest for 3 years.
2. You wish to /**D**ata **F**ill a series of cells, beginning with A1, with the series 0.0, 0.1, . . . 1.0. What do you specify as the
   a.* start value?
   b.* step value?
   c.* stop value?
   d.* range?
3. You wish to compute a data distribution of ages: 14 and below, 15-24, 25-34, . . . 65-74, 75 and over. Assume that ages are expressed in integers.
   a.* If the bin range starts in cell K1, where does it stop?
   b.* What value appears in each cell from K1 to K10?

DOCUMENTATION RESEARCH

Using the reference manual, find and record the page number of each of the commands discussed in this unit. I recommend you also write the page number by the discussion of the command, above.

1. /**D**ata **F**ill — are the resulting numbers constants or formulas?
2. /**R**ange **V**alue — is the numeric format of the original formulas copied?
3. /**D**ata **T**able **1** — if the input cell contains a value, what happens to that value during the execution of this command?

---

1. These cell addresses assume that you moved the table as instructed in Step 8 of the Exercise on pages 97-98.

2. This is a small worksheet and you don't gain much using a data table, but consider how useful this would be if you had 100 items on the worksheet.

4. /Data **T**able **2** — must the upper left cell of the table range contain the formula to be evaluated?
5. /Data **D**istribution — what is the value of blank and label cells in the values range?
6. /**R**ange **T**rans — what command should you use if the original range contains formulas?
7. /Data **M**atrix — what is the relationship between the number of columns in the first-specified matrix and columns in the second-specified matrix?
8. /Data **R**egression — what is the minimum size of the output range?

UNIT 11

DATA SELECTION OPERATIONS

This unit deals with those /Data commands and functions that are designed to allow rudimentary database management capabilities. These commands allow you to sort information, select certain items from a list based on criteria you specify, and compute statistics for a portion of the list.

LEARNING OBJECTIVES

1. At the completion of this unit, you should know
   a. definitions of various database terms,
   b. how to specify criteria using label-match, number-match, and formula-comparison methods.
2. At the completion of this unit, you should be able to
   a. sort a data range using one or two keys,
   b. establish and specify input, output, and criterion ranges,
   c. find records that match specific criteria,
   d. extract records that match specific criteria,
   e. compute statistics on records that match specific criteria.

IMPORTANT COMMANDS

/Data Sort
/Data Query

TERMINOLOGY

Before discussing the commands, we should define a few terms. These definitions are specific to Lotus 1-2-3; other database management systems use some of these terms somewhat differently. A sample database is illustrated in Figures 11-1a and 11-1b.

1-2-3 Database: a cell range of one or more columns and two or more rows. The top row of a 1-2-3 database contains field names, all other rows contain data. In the example, the database is the range A1..D39. Field names are Name, Dept, Phone, and Salary.

Record: each row of data below the first row; a set of information to be processed as a unit. For instance, row 2 contains all information pertaining to Daniel Smith: his name, department, phone, and salary.

Field: each column of the database. The field name is the first row of the column, subsequent rows contain fields within records. The field name must be a label; all other entries can be labels, formulas, or numbers but should be consistent within a field (down a column). In this example, the fields are Name, Dept, Phone, and Salary.

Input Range: a named or specified range, usually the same range as the database, that contains the field names row and the records to be processed.

Criterion Range: a named or specified range that contains field names in the first row and criteria in subsequent rows. Field names must match exactly the field names in the input range. Criteria can be label-match, number-match, or formula-comparison. See the section entitled *Specification of Criteria*, below.

Output Range: some /Data commands require an output range because they copy records to this area for further processing. The first row of the output range contains the field names of the fields to be copied. You do not need to put all field names in this area, and those fields (columns) whose names do not appear are not copied. The field names that are specified must match the field names in the input range exactly, including capitalization.

SORTING

The /Data Sort command is used to sort the records (rows) according to one or two keys (columns). A **Data-Range** and **Primary-Key** must be specified the first time this command is used. Subsequent sort operations use the same range and key unless you specify new ones or give the reset subcommand. Once the /DS command is given, a **Sort Settings** screen appears. The /Data Sort menu is a **sticky menu**, illustrated in Figure 11-2.

Data-Range is the named or specified range that holds the data to be sorted, usually all columns of all rows in the database, except *field names should not be included in the Data-Range*. To sort the example database, we would specify A2..D39 as the Data-Range.

Primary-Key is the field (column) by which the records are sorted. Place the cell pointer anywhere in the column containing the Primary-Key and press <Enter>; then indicate your choice of ascending or descending sort order by pressing **A** or **D**, followed by <Enter> again. To sort our example database by Name, we would place the cell pointer in column A, press <Enter>, press **A** for ascending (A . . . Z) order, and press <Enter> again.

A1: [W24] 'Name READY

	A	B	C	D	E	F
1	Name	Dept	Phone	Salary		
2	Smith, Daniel	Executive	3283	48,597		
3	Brosmer, Emily	Executive	3169	40,741		
4	Stone, Jessica	Executive	3959	36,471		
5	Obudzinski, Tom	Executive	3342	32,239		
6	Braun, Kathleen	Executive	3541	17,386		
7	Ross, Kelly	Finance	3196	44,661		
8	Gregory, Lisa	Finance	3328	32,318		
9	Schon, Jeffrey	Finance	3885	27,923		
10	Salisbury, Patricia	Finance	3995	24,430		
11	Kolb, Lodewyk	Marketing	3996	41,907		
12	Broekhuizen, Matthew	Marketing	3383	36,805		
13	Parent, Sarah	Marketing	3160	29,103		
14	Parker, Timothy	Marketing	3830	23,919		
15	Knowles, Steven	Marketing	3330	15,425		
16	Hibscher, Jessica	Personnel	3966	43,647		
17	Handel, Adam	Personnel	3814	28,076		
18	Arnett, Tobie	Personnel	3197	18,011		
19	Ross, Shannon	Production	3883	48,229		
20	Black, Melissa	Production	3392	47,877		

25-Oct-89 09:38 AM UNDO NUM

Figure 11-1a A Lotus 1-2-3 Database

A21: [W24] 'Poll, Seanna READY

	A	B	C	D	E	F
21	Poll, Seanna	Production	3081	46,794		
22	Treffinger, Alexis	Production	3370	44,838		
23	Blair, Patrick	Production	3792	44,711		
24	Perlewitz, Tyler	Production	3422	43,700		
25	Ernster, Ray	Production	3165	42,541		
26	Skyles, Giuseppe	Production	3686	41,421		
27	Cammizzo, Adrienne	Production	3139	32,231		
28	Lacy, Andrea	Production	3017	28,411		
29	Jenks, Michael	Production	3732	27,577		
30	Gosman, Matteah	Production	3100	24,255		
31	Baim, Daniel	Production	3335	24,045		
32	Yap, John	Production	3400	23,671		
33	Pinto, Stephen	Production	3647	22,654		
34	Crome, Katherine	Production	3788	21,307		
35	Hart, Joseph	Production	3648	20,455		
36	McNamara, Ian	Production	3645	13,464		
37	Squires, Katharine	Production	3527	13,318		
38	Melnikov, Amy	Production	3315	11,845		
39	Behrens, Meredith	Production	3171	11,416		
40						

25-Oct-89 09:38 AM UNDO NUM

Figure 11-1b A Lotus 1-2-3 Database (continued)

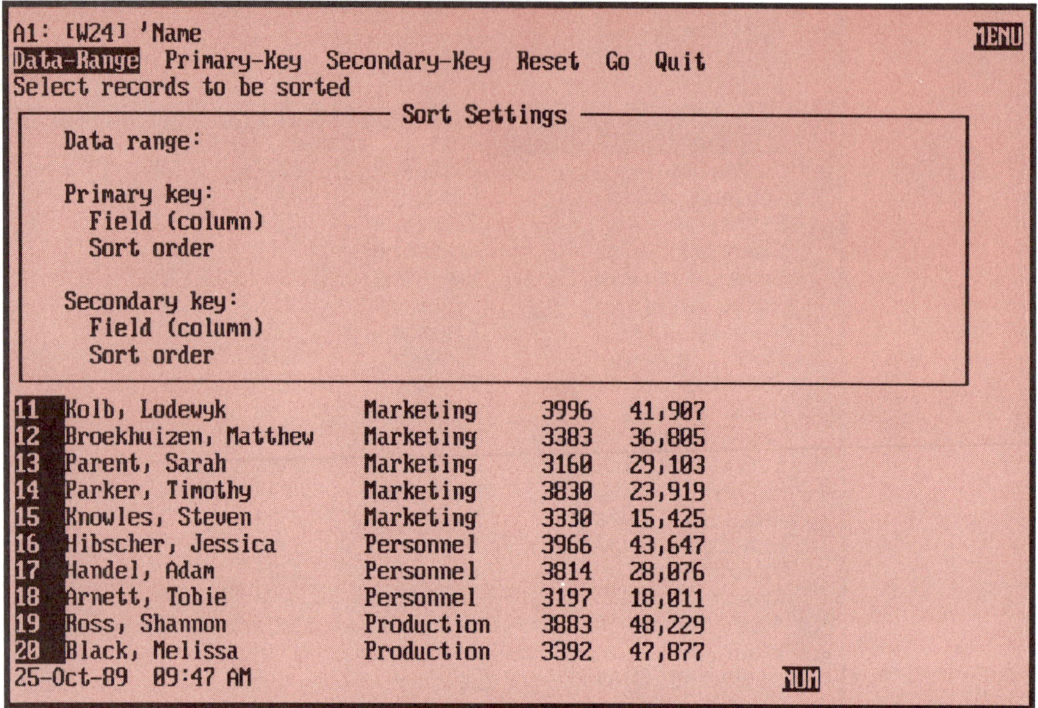

Figure 11-2 The /DataSort Menu and Settings Screen

Secondary-Key is used to break ties in the Primary-Key. This is optional, and is specified in the same manner as the Primary-Key. Be advised that the Secondary-Key breaks exact ties only. Numbers that have been rounded for display format might appear to be equal, but might not be equal and would frustrate your attempts to break ties.

Reset is used to cancel (forget) Data-Range and keys.

Go initiates the sort operation.

Quit returns to ready mode.

GUIDED ACTIVITY: SORTING

This activity requires you to sort the data in a worksheet.

1. Follow the startup procedure outlined in Unit 1 to load Lotus and enter the 1-2-3 program.
2. Retrieve NAMELIST.
3. Notice that this is the same database discussed in this unit. Verify that the database occupies the range A1..D39 by arrowing around.
4. Using /Data Sort, sort the data by salary from highest to lowest. Remember that the Data-Range does not include row 1.

11a. What is the Data-Range?

a. Give the **/DS** command.

b. **D**ata-Range is highlighted; press **D** and Lotus displays the worksheet for you to highlight or type the data-range.

c. Move the cell pointer to A2, press a period to anchor, then press the following sequence of keys (watch the screen as you do so):

<End> <Down> <End> <Right> <Enter>

Notice that pressing the <End> key and then an arrow key moves the cell pointer to the end of a set of occupied cells in the direction of the arrow. The range A2..D39 should have been highlighted and should now appear in the Sort Settings screen as the data-range.

d. Press **P** (for **P**rimary-Key). Move the cell pointer to any cell in column D (Salary) and press <Enter>. Lotus next asks for sort order:

```
A1: [W24] 'Name                                                  EDIT
Primary sort key: D1                    Sort order (A or D): A
```

Press **D**<Enter> for descending (highest to lowest).

e. Press **G** (for **G**o). Lotus sorts the data and returns you to the READY mode. The spreadsheet should look like Figure 11-3.

5. Save the file.

```
A1: [W24] 'Name                                                  READY

            A                 B          C       D       E       F
1   Name                    Dept       Phone   Salary
2   Smith, Daniel           Executive   3283   48,597
3   Ross, Shannon           Production  3883   48,229
4   Black, Melissa          Production  3392   47,877
5   Poll, Seanna            Production  3081   46,794
6   Treffinger, Alexis      Production  3370   44,838
7   Blair, Patrick          Production  3792   44,711
8   Ross, Kelly             Finance     3196   44,661
9   Perlewitz, Tyler        Production  3422   43,708
10  Hibscher, Jessica       Personnel   3966   43,647
11  Ernster, Ray            Production  3165   42,541
12  Kolb, Lodewyk           Marketing   3996   41,907
13  Skyles, Giuseppe        Production  3686   41,421
14  Brosmer, Emily          Executive   3169   40,741
15  Broekhuizen, Matthew    Marketing   3383   36,805
16  Stone, Jessica          Executive   3959   36,471
17  Gregory, Lisa           Finance     3328   32,318
18  Obudzinski, Tom         Executive   3342   32,239
19  Cammizzo, Adrienne      Production  3139   32,231
20  Parent, Sarah           Marketing   3160   29,103
25-Oct-89  10:25 AM        UNDO                          NUM
```

Figure 11-3 After the /DataSort Operation

SPECIFICATION OF CRITERIA

The /Data Query command and the database statistical functions depend on criteria for selection of records. Criteria are specified in a **criterion range**, which is an area of the worksheet with one or more field names and one or more criteria. There are three types of criteria: label-match, number-match, and formula-comparison.

LABEL-MATCH CRITERIA

Label-match criteria are used to select records according to the value of a label field. For instance, to select all persons in the Production Department, we put the field name in one cell, say F1, and the label to be matched in the cell below, which would be F2.

For selection to occur, the label in the input range must match the label in the criterion range exactly, including any trailing spaces. The only exceptions are when one of the three following special characters is used in label-match criteria:

- ? matches any single character, so that **`Sm?th`** matches `Smith` and `Smyth`, but not `Smythe`.
- * matches all characters to end of label, so that **`P*`** matches `Personnel` and `Production`, but not `planning` (because of the case of the letters).
- ~ accepts all labels except those that match the following characters, so that **`~P*`** accepts all that do not begin with a capital P.

The following is an example of a label-match criterion:

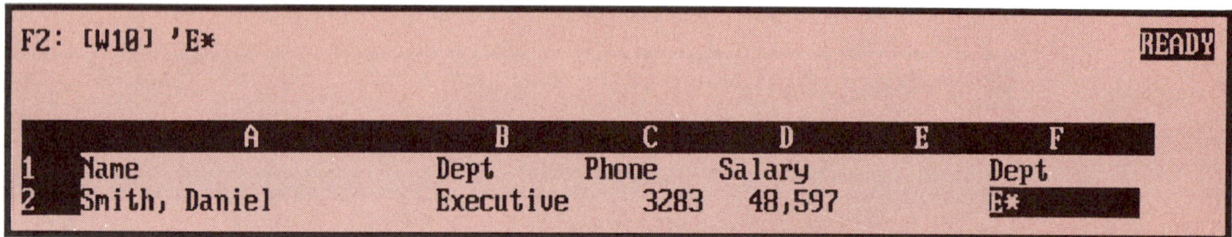
F2: [W10] 'E* READY

	A	B	C	D	E	F
1	Name	Dept	Phone	Salary		Dept
2	Smith, Daniel	Executive	3283	48,597		E*

Note that the effect of cells F1..F2 is to match all departments with a capital `E` as the first letter.

NUMBER-MATCH CRITERIA

Number-match criteria are used to select records according to the value of a numeric field (either constant value or formula). For instance, to select all persons whose phone number is 3383, we would put **Phone** in the top row of the criterion range and **3383** in the row below:

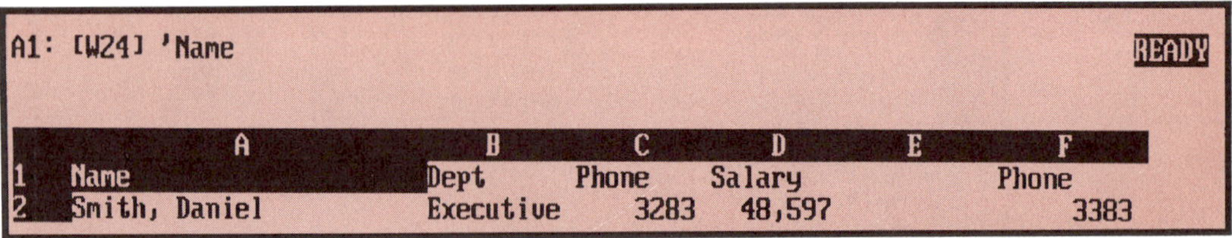
A1: [W24] 'Name READY

	A	B	C	D	E	F
1	Name	Dept	Phone	Salary		Phone
2	Smith, Daniel	Executive	3283	48,597		3383

FORMULA-COMPARISON CRITERIA

Formula-comparison criteria are used to select records according to the value of a numeric field (either constant value or formula). Instead of a simple match, however, records are selected if the result of the formula is true (or any number other than zero).

When specifying formula-comparison criteria, the formula should test the first record (second row) of the database. In other words, to test salary, we use the cell D2 in the formula. For instance, to select all persons whose salary is greater than $35,000.00, we would use the formula **+D2>35000**. This particular criterion is illustrated in Figure 11-4 (cells F41..F42).

It is possible to make across-field comparisons using formula-comparison criteria. If a database had fields for salary and bonus, it would be possible to select those persons whose bonus exceeded their salary. For instance, if our database had bonus in column E, then the criterion would be **+E2>D2**. Although the field name in the first row of the criterion range is ignored for formula-comparison criteria, I recommend that you use something meaningful.

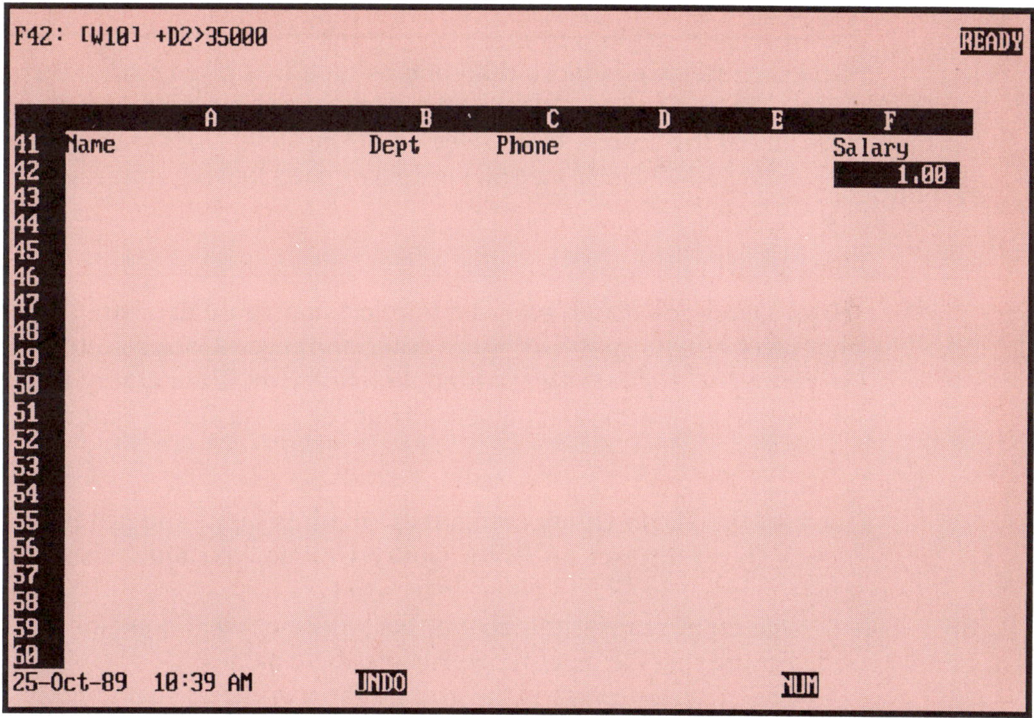

Figure 11-4 /DataQuery Criterion and Output Ranges
The Criterion Range is F41..F42
The Output Range is A41..C41

MULTIPLE CRITERIA

The examples above all use a single criterion. It is possible to establish multiple criteria, such as `Production` Dept *and* `Salary>35000`, by using multiple fields (columns) in the criterion range (E41..F42):

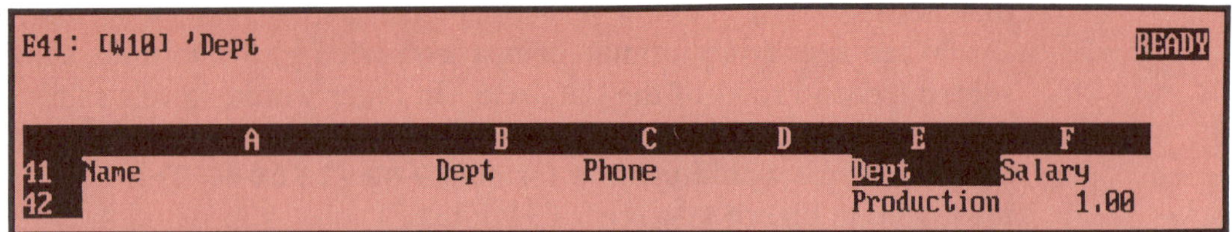

It is also possible to establish alternate criteria, such as `Production` Dept *or* `Salary>35000`, by using multiple rows in the criterion range (E41..F43):

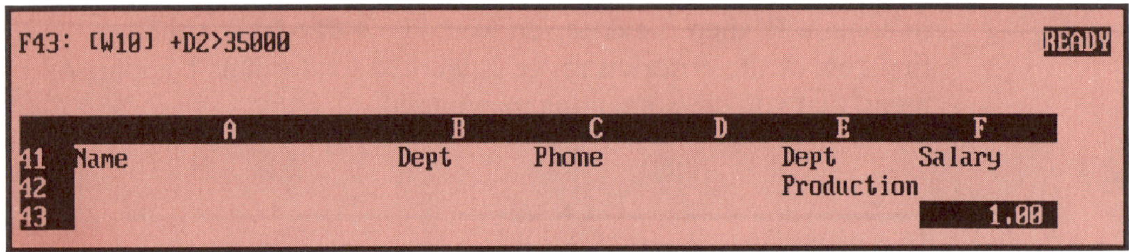

When criteria are in more than one column in a given row, a record must pass all criteria to be selected. When the criteria are in more than one row, a record must pass any of the criteria to be selected. Consider: Does your ideal mate need to be rich *and* good-looking (one row) or rich *or* good looking (two rows)?

QUERIES

/**D**ata **Q**uery commands are used to select only those database (input range) records that meet criteria specified in the criterion range. Once selected, those records can be viewed with /**D**ata **Q**uery **F**ind, deleted with /**D**ata **Q**uery **D**elete, or written to an output range with /**D**ata **Q**uery **E**xtract or /**D**ata **Q**uery **U**nique.

PREPARATION

Each of the /**D**ata **Q**uery commands requires input and criterion ranges. To use /**D**ata **Q**uery **E**xtract or /**D**ata **Q**uery **U**nique, you must also prepare an output range.

The **input range** is the area of the worksheet that contains the data to be queried. Ensure that the input range includes field names.

The **criterion range** is the area of the worksheet that contains the criteria for selection. See *Specification of Criteria*, above, for details on how to prepare the criterion range.

The **output range** is an empty area of the worksheet that holds the records selected by /**D**ata **Q**uery **E**xtract or /**D**ata **Q**uery **U**nique procedures. The output range contains a row of field names, and is usually otherwise empty. If it is not empty, Lotus erases it when the extract or unique procedure starts.

Generally, the output range is specified as the row of field names only, which means that Lotus uses all rows below the field name row to hold output. Field names in the output range must match exactly the field names in the input range, although all fields need not appear. Only those that are named are output.

See Figure 11-4 for an example of output and criterion ranges. Note that these are below the database (A1..D39), that the output range (A41..C41) contains only three of the field names, and that the criterion range (F41..F42) is based on a formula comparison of the salary field (**+D2>35000**). Because the comparison is True for D2, the value `1.00` shows on the worksheet.

RANGE SPECIFICATION

Once the ranges are established on the worksheet, you can give the **/**Data **Q**uery command. You are presented with the following sticky menu and the **Query Settings** screen:

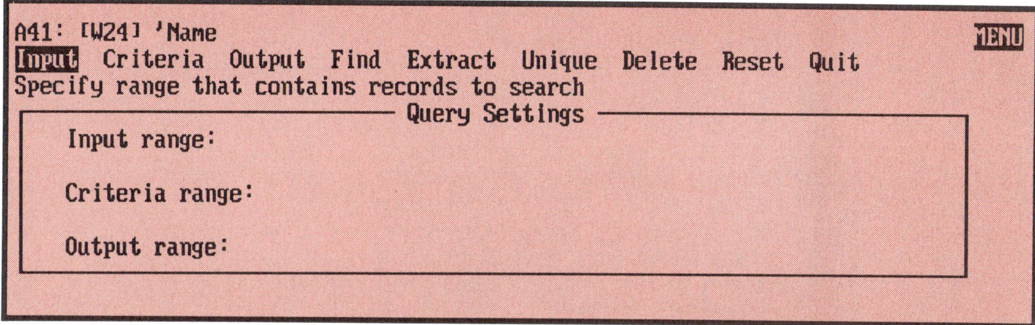

The first time you use **/**Data **Q**uery, you must specify input, criterion, and (usually) output ranges. Choose each option in turn and type or point to the relevant range. These ranges do not need to be specified again unless you wish to change them.

OPERATIONS

Once the ranges are specified, choose **F**ind, **E**xtract, **U**nique, **D**elete, **R**eset, or **Q**uit.

Find moves you to the uppermost record in the database (input range) that meets the criteria. Use the <Up> and <Down> arrow keys to move to other records. With this option you can also edit fields (cells) of found records. To do so, move to the record to be edited, highlight the particular cell you wish to edit by pressing <Left> and <Right>, then press the <EDIT (F2)> key and edit as usual. Press <Enter> to continue with the find process. Press <Enter> (again) to return to the **/**Data **Q**uery menu.

Extract copies all records that match the criteria into the output range. The result of **/**Data **Q**uery **E**xtract is illustrated in Figure 11-5.[1] Once the records are in the output range, you can edit the records or do whatever you wish with them after you **Q**uit from the **/**Data **Q**uery menu).

Unique yields the same result as Extract, except that duplicate records are not copied.

Delete deletes records in the input range that match the criteria: be careful with this one! (Generally, do a **/**File **S**ave before a **/**Data **Q**uery **D**elete.)

Reset is used to cancel the range settings.

1. To remove the setting screen, press the <WINDOW (F6)> key. To recall the settings screen press <WINDOW (F6)> again.

Quit returns you to the READY mode.

Lotus remembers the most recent **/D**ata **Q**uery operation. To repeat that most recent operation (for instance, after changing the criterion), press the <QUERY (F7)> key.

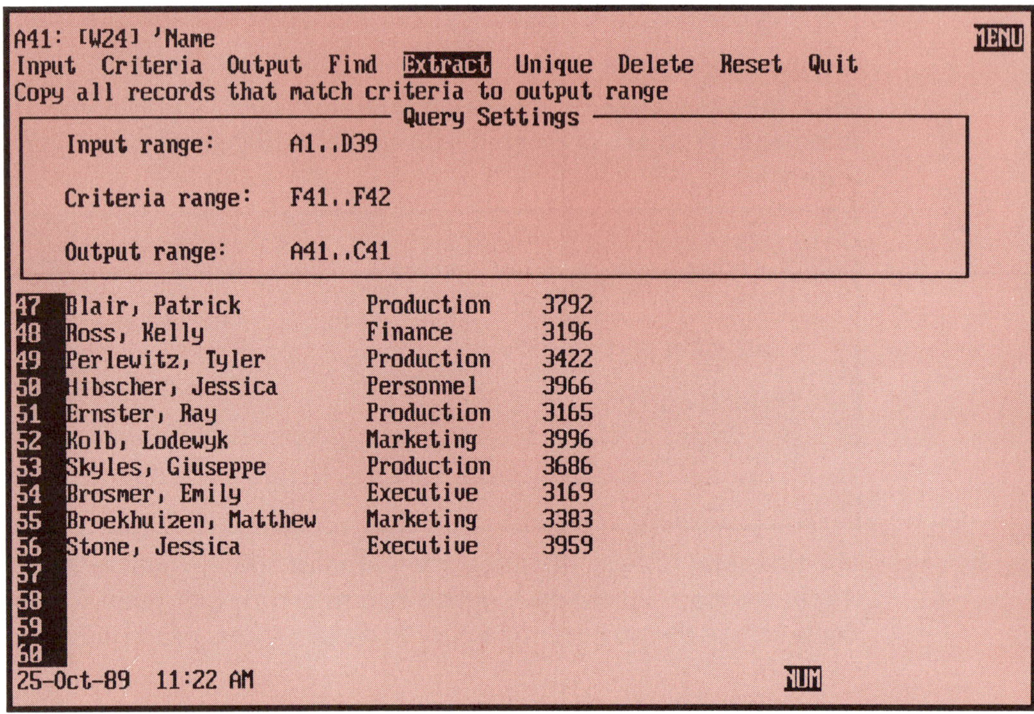

Figure 11-5 Result of the /DataQueryExtract Operation

GUIDED ACTIVITY: QUERY OPERATIONS

This activity requires you to use several of the database selection commands.

1. If you are not continuing from the previous Guided Activity, load Lotus and retrieve NAMELIST.

2. Using **/D**ata **Q**uery **F**ind, find all persons who earn more than 35,000.

   a. Before entering the command, you must prepare a criterion range. In cell F41, enter the field name `Salary`. In cell F42, enter the appropriate formula.

   CHECKPOINT
   11b. What formula do you put in the criterion range?

   b. Give the `/DQ` command.

   c. On the menu that appears, select **I**nput and indicate that the input range is A1..D39. (Remember, the input range includes the row with field names.)

d. Next, select **C**riteria and indicate that the criterion range is F41..F42.

e. Now, select **F**ind. Lotus will display the database and highlight the first record that meets the criterion:

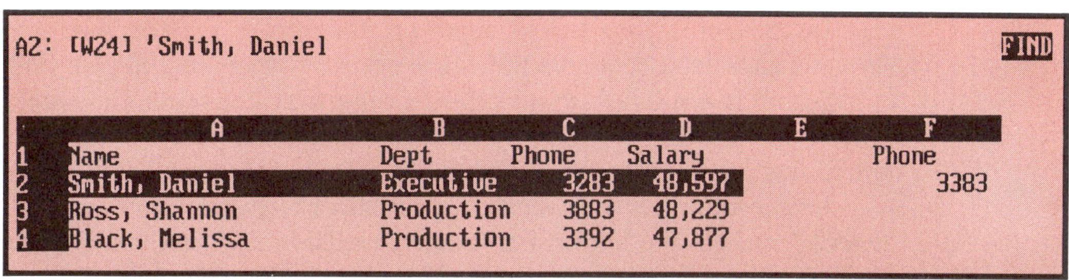

f. Press the <Up> and <Down> arrows to see which records Lotus allows you to highlight. Since the database was sorted by salary in the last Guided Activity, all the salaries that meet the criterion are at the top. You should not be able to move the highlight above row 2 nor below row 16. (If you can move below row 16, your criterion is incorrect.)

g. Press the <Enter> key to return to the menu and settings screen.

3. Using **/D**ata **Q**uery **E**xtract, extract the Name, Dept, and Phone of all persons who earn more than 35,000.

   a. Before we extract, we must create an output range. Select **Q**uit if you are still at the **/D**ata **Q**uery menu.

   b. Using the **/C**opy command, copy the first three field names (Name, Dept, and Phone) from the range A1..C1 to the range A41..C41. Using the **/C**opy command ensures that you duplicate the original field names *exactly* in the output range. The lower part of your spreadsheet should now look like Figure 11-4.

   c. Now, give the **/DQ** command.

   d. On the menu that appears, select **O**utput and indicate that the output range is A41..C41.

   e. Select **E**xtract. The result is illustrated in Figure 11-5.

   f. Press the <WINDOW (F6)> key. The Query Settings screen will be removed and you can see the worksheet. Press the <WINDOW (F6)> key again to redisplay the Query Settings screen.

   g. Select **Q**uit.

4. Change the criterion in F42 to **+D2>45000**.

5. Press the <QUERY (F7)> key. Only four records should be extracted.

6. Change the criterion in F42 so that all who make *less than* $20,000 are selected and extract again.

7. Print a copy of the output range, then save the worksheet.

DATABASE STATISTICAL FUNCTIONS

Note: The database statistical functions are more complex than the statistical functions discussed earlier in this book. If possible, use the statistical functions (@AVG, @COUNT, etc.) rather than the functions discussed below.

In the definitions below, *input,offset,criterion* are the means by which Lotus knows which fields (columns) of which records (rows) to average, sum, etc.

Input is a named or specified range that contains all rows of interest and columns containing criterion fields and the field to be averaged, summed, etc. See the discussion of input range in the **/D**ata **Q**uery command section, above.

Offset identifies the specific field relative to the leftmost column. An offset of 0 (zero) indicates the leftmost column; an offset of 5 indicates the fifth column from the left, the sixth column overall. The offset column is the column that is summed, averaged, etc.

Criterion is a named or specified range that contains selection criteria. See section entitled *Specification of Criteria* above.

@DAVG(input,offset,criterion) *the average value* of the items in *offset* column of *input* range that meet the *criterion*. For example, **@DAVG(A1..D39,3,F1..F2)** averages the values of those cells in the range D2..D39 (column D is the third column from the left) that meet the criterion established in F1..F2 (this example is discussed in more detail below).

@DCOUNT(input,offset,criterion) *the number of items* in the *offset* column of *input* range that meet the *criterion*. For example, **@DCOUNT(A1..D39,2,F1..F2)** counts the number of cells in the range C2..C39 that contain data (i.e., are not empty) and meet the criterion established in F1..F2.

@DMIN(input,offset,criterion) *the minimum value* in the *offset* column of *input* range that meets the *criterion*. For example, **@DMIN(A1..D39,2,F1..F2)** displays the minimum value of those cells in the range C2..C39 that meet the criterion established in F1..F2.

@DMAX(input,offset,criterion) *the maximum value* in the *offset* column of *input* range that meets the *criterion*. For example, **@DMAX(A1..D39,2,F1..F2)** displays the maximum value of those cells in the range C2..C39 that meet the criterion established in F1..F2.

@DSTD(input,offset,criterion) *the standard deviation* of the items in the *offset* column of *input* range that meet the *criterion* (N weighted). For example, **@DSTD(A1..D39,3,F1..F2)** displays the standard deviation statistic for those cells in the range D2..D39 that meet the criterion established in F1..F2.

@DSUM(input,offset,criterion) *the sum* of the items in the *offset* column of *input* range that meet the *criterion*. For example, **@DSUM(A1..D39,3,F1..F2)** displays the sum of those cells in the range D2..D39 that meet the criterion established in F1..F2.

@DVAR(input,offset,criterion) *the variance* of the items in the *offset* column of *input* range that meet the *criterion* (N weighted). For example, **@DVAR(A1..D39,3,F1..F2)** displays the variance of those cells in the range D2..D39 that meet the criterion established in F1..F2.

Example. Assume that you have been asked to compute the average salary of all persons in the Executive Dept. This example is illustrated in Figure 11-6. You use F1..F2 as the criterion range. In F1, you put the field name, **Dept**, and in F2 you put the label-match criterion, **E***. (This criterion would not suffice if the organization had an Ecology Dept.) You put the formula in cell F7 and labels in F5 and F6 to identify the value. The appropriate formula is

@DAVG(A1..D39,3,F1..F2)

which translates to *Average all numbers in the third column from the left in range A1..D39 that meet the criteria specified in range F1..F2 and put the result in this cell.* The result appears instantly. To compute the average salary of all persons in the Finance Dept., all you have to do is change the label in cell F2 to **F*** or **Finance**.

```
F7: [W10] @DAVG(A1..D39,3,F1..F2)                                   READY

             A                     B          C        D       E       F
1   Name                  Dept        Phone   Salary          Dept
2   Smith, Daniel         Executive    3283   48,597          E*
3   Ross, Shannon         Production   3883   48,229
4   Black, Melissa        Production   3392   47,877
5   Poll, Seanna          Production   3081   46,794          Dept Avg
6   Treffinger, Alexis    Production   3370   44,838          Salary
7   Blair, Patrick        Production   3792   44,711          35086.00
8   Ross, Kelly           Finance      3196   44,661
9   Perlewitz, Tyler      Production   3422   43,700
10  Hibscher, Jessica     Personnel    3966   43,647
11  Ernster, Ray          Production   3165   42,541
12  Kolb, Lodewyk         Marketing    3996   41,907
13  Skyles, Giuseppe      Production   3686   41,421
14  Brosmer, Emily        Executive    3169   40,741
15  Broekhuizen, Matthew  Marketing    3383   36,805
16  Stone, Jessica        Executive    3959   36,471
17  Gregory, Lisa         Finance      3328   32,318
18  Obudzinski, Tom       Executive    3342   32,239
19  Cammizzo, Adrienne    Production   3139   32,231
20  Parent, Sarah         Marketing    3160   29,103
26-Oct-89  12:00 PM       UNDO                            NUM
```

Figure 11-6 The @DAVG Function

GUIDED ACTIVITY: DATABASE STATISTICAL FUNCTIONS

This activity requires you to use database statistical functions in a worksheet.

1. If you are not continuing from the previous Guided Activity, load Lotus and retrieve NAMELIST.
2. Using @DAVG(input, offset, criterion), compute the average salary of all persons in the Executive Dept. as illustrated in Figure 11-6.
3. Now change the criterion so that the average is of all persons in the Marketing Dept.
4. Save the file. This completes the Guided Activities in this unit.

EXERCISE: MORE DATABASE EXERCISES

In this exercise, we continue to use the NAMELIST file.

1. If you are not continuing from the previous Guided Activity, load Lotus and retrieve NAMELIST.
2. Sort the database by department in descending order of salary (i.e., highest salary at top). *Hint*: You need two keys, with the Dept column being the primary key.
3. Determine the maximum, mean (average), and minimum of the salaries in each department. This requires five criterion ranges and fifteen functions. Put your criteria in rows 1 and 2, starting with cell H1. Put your functions in rows 3, 4, and 5, starting with H3. Put the labels **`Maximum`** in G3, **`Mean`** in G4, and **`Minimum`** in G5.
4. Save your work.

EXERCISE: THE PERFECT JOB (V)

Do the following to further analyze your job prospects:

- Sort the data in descending order of Salary. Make sure you include all necessary columns in the Data-Range.
- Extract a list of jobs (Company, City, Title, Salary, and Adj. Sal.) for which the adjusted salary is greater than or equal to $23,000. This action is complicated by the line of `------` in row 4. The Input range is A3..E9 and the criterion should refer to row 4; even though that row does not contain data the extract operation will still function correctly.

Save the file when you are finished.

REVIEW QUESTIONS

1. Define the following database terms:
   a. 1-2-3 Database
   b. Field Name

  c. Record
  d. Field
  e. Input Range
  f. Criterion Range
  g. Output Range

2. For this question, assume that your criterion range is K1..K2 and that you are using the database discussed in this unit. To establish each of the criteria listed below, what would you put in K1 and what would you put in K2?
   a.* Select everyone whose last name is `Ross`.
   b.* Select everyone whose last name is not `Ross`.
   c.* Select everyone whose telephone number is `3883`.
   d.* Select everyone in the `Personnel` Dept.
   e.* Select those whose salary is less than $20,000.

3. To sort by salary, from highest to lowest, what would you specify as
   a.* the Data-Range,
   b.* the Primary-Key,
   c.* the sort order?

4. To determine the lowest phone number in the Production Dept.,
   a.* what function would you use,
   b.* how would you specify the criterion range?

DOCUMENTATION RESEARCH

Using the reference manual, find and record the page number of each of the commands discussed in this unit. I recommend you also write the page number by the discussion of the command, above.

1. /**D**ata **S**ort — if your primary key column contains blank cells, labels, and values and is sorted in ascending order, which is first (top) and which is last in the resulting range?

2. /**D**ata **Q**uery
   a. Is capitalization important in the specification of field names?
   b. When specifying formula criteria, how must you refer to cells within the database, and how must you refer to cells outside of the database?
   c. What happens to data in the output range when you select **E**xtract or **U**nique?
   d. If you want the output range to extend to the bottom of the worksheet, how many rows do you specify?
   e. Which is the only option that affects (changes) the input range?

3. How can you combine database statistical functions with data table commands?

APPLICATION E

PREDICTING THE FUTURE

In this exercise, you perform sorting and distribution operations on an existing database.

1. Start Lotus and retrieve PORTFOLI.

2. Note that this worksheet is a database with three fields: Name, 1989, 1990. Even though the last two field names appear to be numbers, they are really labels. Verify this by looking at cell C1. The entries are stock name, 1989 rating, and 1990 (predicted) rating, respectively. The first 20 rows of the worksheet are illustrated in Figure E-1.

3. Use the /**D**ata **D**istribution command to compute the number of stocks whose 1990 ratings are in each of the following intervals: less than or equal to -250, greater than -250 and less than or equal to 0, greater than 0 and less than or equal to 250, and greater than 250. Start the bin range in cell E1.

4. Use /**D**ata **S**ort to sort the database in descending order of 1989 ratings. Ensure that the Data-Range includes all three columns (but not the distribution table) and all 37 rows (but not the field names).

5. /**P**rint the entire sorted worksheet, including the distribution table. Circle the name of the stock with the tenth highest rating in 1989.

6. Use the /**D**ata **R**egression command to compute the association between the 1989 ratings (independent) and the 1990 ratings (dependent). Start the **O**utput-range in cell E11, and format the output to *fixed, 3 decimal places*. /**P**rint the results.

7. Save your work.

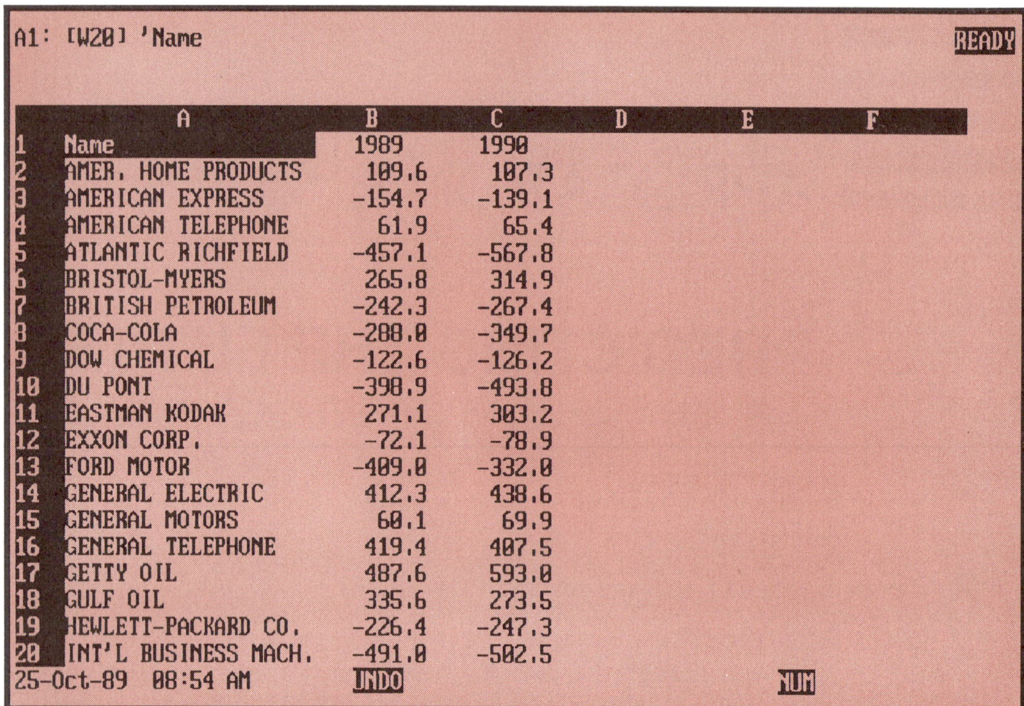

Figure E-1 The PORTFOLI Worksheet

UNIT 12

ADVANCED WORKSHEET OPERATIONS

In this unit, you learn about advanced operations available through the /Worksheet command. These options affect what you see on the screen through global formats, titles that do not scroll off the screen, and split windows on the worksheet.

LEARNING OBJECTIVES

At the completion of this unit, you should be able to

a. set the global worksheet format to any of the available choices,
b. change the global column width,
c. hide columns,
d. suppress the display of zero values,
e. change the default label prefix,
f. use titles to freeze column or row labels,
g. split the screen into two windows.

IMPORTANT COMMANDS

/**W**orksheet **C**olumn
/**W**orksheet **G**lobal
/**W**orksheet **S**tatus
/**W**orksheet **T**itles
/**W**orksheet **W**indow
/**P**rint . . . **O**ptions **B**orders

WORKSHEET GLOBAL SETTINGS

The default settings for many worksheet characteristics can be changed using the **G**lobal option of the /**W**orksheet command. After you enter the **/WG** command, a menu and the **Global Settings** screen appears (Figure 12-1).

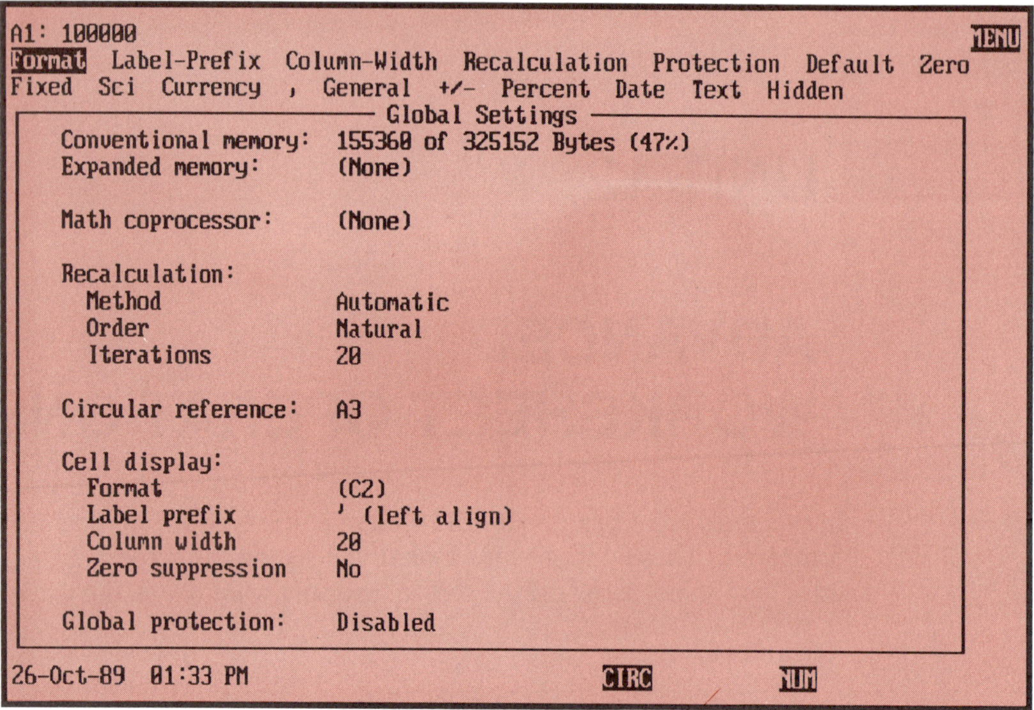

Figure 12-1 The /WorksheetGlobal Menu and the Global Settings Screen
This is the Global Settings Screen for the RECALC Worksheet.

/Worksheet Global Format allows you to specify the format for all numbers not specifically formatted by a /Range Format operation. We discussed the most common formats in Unit 4. The complete set of formats available are

- *Fixed format* displays numbers with a fixed number of decimal places. Set to 0 (zero) decimal places for integers.
- *Sci (Scientific) notation format* is for the engineers.
- *Currency format* puts dollar signs in front, negative values in parentheses, and as many decimal places as you specify.
- , *Comma format* is the same as currency without the dollar sign.
- *General format* displays as many decimal places as fit or as are needed (the default).
- *+/- format* yields a horizontal bar graph if the column is wide enough.
- *Percent format* converts real numbers to percentages and puts a percent sign after the right digit. Again, you specify the number of decimal places.

- *Date formats* convert the result of the @NOW and @DATE(. . .) functions (which is an integer in the range 1 to 73049) to a readable format, such as `01-Jan-87`, `01-Jan`, or `Jan-87`. There are also *DateTime formats* that allow the display of time in several formats. Time is generated with the @TIME(. . .) and @NOW functions.
- *Text format* displays formulas instead of the numeric results of the formulas.
- *Hidden format* removes from view the contents of all cells not otherwise formatted (with the /**R**ange **F**ormat command). The cell contents are still *there*, however, and the cell can be referenced by other cells (as in formulas).

/**W**orksheet **G**lobal **L**abel-Prefix allows you to change the default **label alignment** from left-aligned to centered or right-aligned. This affects only those labels that are entered subsequent to the command. If you have already entered labels, use /**R**ange **L**abel to realign a range of labels.

/**W**orksheet **G**lobal **C**olumn-Width is used to change the width of all columns not specifically set by the /**W**orksheet **C**olumn **S**et-Width command. **Column width** can vary from 1 to 240 characters.

/**W**orksheet **G**lobal **R**ecalculation was discussed in Part 2. Remember that setting **recalculation** to **M**anual speeds development of a large worksheet.

/**W**orksheet **G**lobal **Z**ero **Y**es displays nothing (i.e., a blank space) in cells that have the value 0 (zero). Or, enter /**W**orksheet **G**lobal **Z**ero **L**abel to specify a label to be displayed in cells that have a zero value (e.g., you could have Lotus display `-0-` instead of `0`). Redisplay zero values with /**W**orksheet **G**lobal **Z**ero **N**o (which means, "do not suppress zeros").

A related command is /**W**orksheet **C**olumn **H**ide, which hides (i.e., does not display or print) entire columns. Hidden columns are made temporarily visible during commands such as /**C**opy which require a view of the entire worksheet. Permanent visibility is restored with the /**W**orksheet **C**olumn **D**isplay command. Hidden format, Column Hide, and Zero are useful for removing clutter from the worksheet.

WORKSHEET STATUS

The /**W**orksheet **S**tatus command also displays the Global Settings screen, but does not allow you to change any settings. This is a shortcut if you want to see current conditions without changing anything. It also helps you in eliminating a **circular reference** condition by indicating one of the cells in the loop and gives you a place to start checking the formulas to determine which is incorrect (assuming that the circular logic is unintended). The /**W**orksheet **S**tatus command for the RECALC worksheet is shown in Figure 12-2. (See Unit 7 for a discussion of this worksheet.) Note that the screen indicates a circular reference in cell A3, which is one of the cells in the (intentional) circular reference in that worksheet.

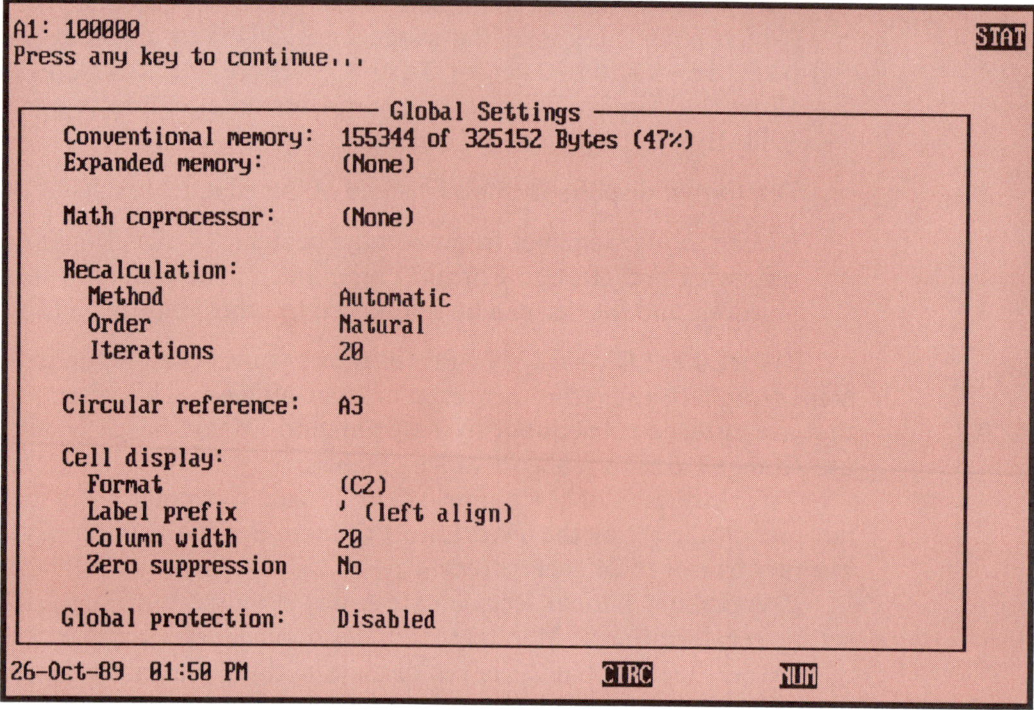
A1: 100000
STAT
Press any key to continue...
Global Settings
Conventional memory: 155344 of 325152 Bytes (47%)
Expanded memory: (None)
Math coprocessor: (None)
Recalculation:
Method Automatic
Order Natural
Iterations 20
Circular reference: A3
Cell display:
Format (C2)
Label prefix ' (left align)
Column width 20
Zero suppression No
Global protection: Disabled
26-Oct-89 01:50 PM
CIRC
NUM

Figure 12-2 The /WorksheetStatus Global Settings Screen
This is the Global Settings Screen for the RECALC Worksheet.

WORKSHEET TITLES AND PRINT BORDERS

The two operations discussed here make it easier to understand the information contained in a large worksheet. **Titles** are placed on the screen and **Borders** are printed to provide a frame of reference for worksheet information.

WORKSHEET TITLES

When your worksheet is longer than 20 rows, it might be difficult to remember which column is which as you move down the column and the information in the top rows scrolls off the screen. The same problem occurs when the worksheet is wider than the number of columns that fit on the screen. The /Worksheet Titles command allows you to specify rows and/or columns that remain on the screen. As you move the cell pointer to a cell that is not on the screen, the title area appears to be fixed and the nontitle area seems to slide under the title area.

For example, remember the PORTFOLI worksheet used in Application E. The column headings are in row 1, and there are over 20 rows in the worksheet. As we move to the bottom of the list, the column headings scroll off the screen. To freeze the column headings, do the following:

1. Move to A2, the first row that we do not want to freeze.

2. Give the command **/WTH**, which establishes a horizontal title above where the cell pointer is.

The PORTFOLI worksheet with horizontal titles appears in Figure 12-3. It is also possible to establish vertical titles (**/WTV**) and both horizontal and vertical titles (**/WTB**). **/WTC** clears previously established titles.

Once titles have been established, it is not possible to move into the title area using the keypad arrows. The <Home> key takes you to the upper left cell of the nontitle area. Commands that ask you to specify a range (such as /**C**opy, /**M**ove, and /**R**ange) allow you to <Arrow> into the title area.

If you must make a change to a cell in the title area, use the <GOTO (F5)> key to move to that cell. You see the title area twice until you move far enough away to scroll the screen.

When you save the file, the titles are saved with it. When you retrieve the file, the titles are still in effect.

PRINT BORDERS

When your worksheet is too big to print on one page, you might wish to specify borders as a /**P**rint . . . **O**ption. Do not include the border rows or columns in your print range, or you will print them twice.

A38: [W20] 'WAL-MART STORES READY

	A	B	C	D	E	F
1	Name	1989	1990			
20	INT'L BUSINESS MACH.	-491.0	-502.5			
21	INT'L TELEPHONE	-458.4	-380.7			
22	JOHNSON&JOHNSON	-484.0	-517.3			
23	MERCK & CO	199.7	245.0			
24	MINNESOTA MINING&MFG	-139.6	-141.9			
25	MOBIL CORP.	-381.6	-383.7			
26	MOTOROLA,INC.	443.6	346.0			
27	PFIZER, INC.	-328.3	-322.6			
28	PHILIP MORRIS	-58.0	-56.9			
29	PROCTER&GAMBLE	-462.1	-465.2			
30	REYNOLDS INDUSTRIES	-215.1	-200.4			
31	SCHLUMBERGER, LTD.	-144.7	-179.8			
32	SEARS, ROEBUCK	432.8	439.3			
33	STANDARD OIL (CALIF)	-3.5	-3.3			
34	STANDARD OIL (IND.)	287.1	346.3			
35	STANDARD OIL (OHIO)	-190.6	-162.8			
36	TEXACO, INC.	-479.1	-580.1			
37	UNION PACIFIC CORP.	-386.8	-450.3			
38	WAL-MART STORES	-415.3	-360.9			

26-Oct-89 02:00 PM UNDO NUM

Figure 12-3 A Worksheet with a Horizontal Title
Note that rows 2-19 are not displayed.

WORKSHEET WINDOWS

Windows allow you to see two parts of the worksheet at once. For instance, you might have a *bottom line result*, such as profit, that you are trying to maximize by changing numbers in various parts of the worksheet. With the /**W**orksheet **W**indow command, you can split the screen into two panels, freeze one (the *bottom line*), and move about in the other. As you make changes in one window, you see the result in the other.

/**W**orksheet **W**indow **H**orizontal creates a horizontal break at the cell pointer location, pushing succeeding rows down and putting a new set of column heading letters where the succeeding row had been. The cell pointer remains in the upper window. /**W**orksheet **W**indow **V**ertical has a similar effect.

Once windows are established, you might decide that you want movements in one window to cause parallel movements in the other window. Or, you might decide that you want movements in the windows to be independent. If you want the display in the second window to remain fixed and not scroll parallel to movements in the first window, use the /**W**orksheet **W**indow **U**nsync command. To direct parallel movements, use the /**W**orksheet **W**indow **S**ync command.

```
C26: +B26+C25                                                              READY

             A          B        C        D        E        F        G
1   My Budget
2                      Jan      Feb      Mar      Apr      May      Jun
3   ------------------------------------------------------------------------
12  Expenses
13  -------------
14  Books           400.00
15  Dates            25.00    25.00    25.00    25.00    25.00    25.00
16  Groceries       200.00   200.00   200.00   200.00   200.00   200.00
17  Movies           20.00    20.00    20.00    20.00    20.00    20.00
18  Room            275.00   275.00   275.00   275.00   275.00   275.00
19  Sports           30.00    30.00    30.00    30.00    30.00    30.00
20  Travel          300.00                     600.00            300.00
21  Tuition        2500.00
22                ----------------------------------------------------------
23     TOTAL EXP.  3750.00   550.00   550.00  1150.00   550.00   850.00
24
25           NET:   250.00   -50.00   -50.00   -50.00   -50.00   -50.00
             A          B        C        D        E        F        G
25           NET:   250.00   -50.00   -50.00   -50.00   -50.00   -50.00
26       BALANCE:   250.00   200.00   150.00   100.00    50.00     0.00
26-Oct-89  02:04 PM        UNDO                           NUM
```

Figure 12-4 A Worksheet with Titles and a Window
Note that rows 4-11 are not displayed and that row 25 is in both windows.

If you are working in one window and wish to work in the other, press the <WINDOW (F6)> key once. Press it again when you are ready to return to the first window.

The windows can have different column-widths, title rows/columns, and global display formats. To alter the **/W**orksheet settings for a window, move the cell pointer into that window (via <WINDOW (F6)>) and issue the appropriate **/W** command.

See Figure 12-4 for an example of a worksheet with a horizontal window.

When you save the file, the windows are saved with it. When you retrieve the file, the windows are still in effect.

GUIDED ACTIVITY: ADVANCED WORKSHEET COMMANDS

This activity requires you to use several of the **/W**orksheet commands in a worksheet.

1. Follow the startup procedure outlined in Unit 1 to load Lotus and enter the 1-2-3 program.
2. Retrieve PORTFOLI.
3. Follow the instructions above to set a horizontal title below row 1. Once the title is set, move the cell pointer down to cell A38. The screen should look like Figure 12-3.
4. Use the **/W**orksheet **G**lobal **C**olumn-Width command to change the default column width to 15. Note that column A does not change width because the width was set individually, using the **/W**orksheet **C**olumn **S**et-Width command.
5. Split the screen vertically:
   a. Move the cell pointer into column B.
   b. Give the **/W**orksheet **W**indow **V**ertical command.
   c. Observe the effect, illustrated in Figure 12-5.
   d. Use the <WINDOW (F6)> key to move the cell pointer into the right window.
   e. Press the <Left> arrow key; you should now see column A in both windows.
   f. Move the cell pointer <Up> beyond the currently displayed row; notice a corresponding movement in the other window.
   g. Experiment with more cell pointer movements; notice the effect on the display in the two windows.
6. Save the file with the name WINDOWS.
7. **/Q**uit and Exit. Remember to back up your work.

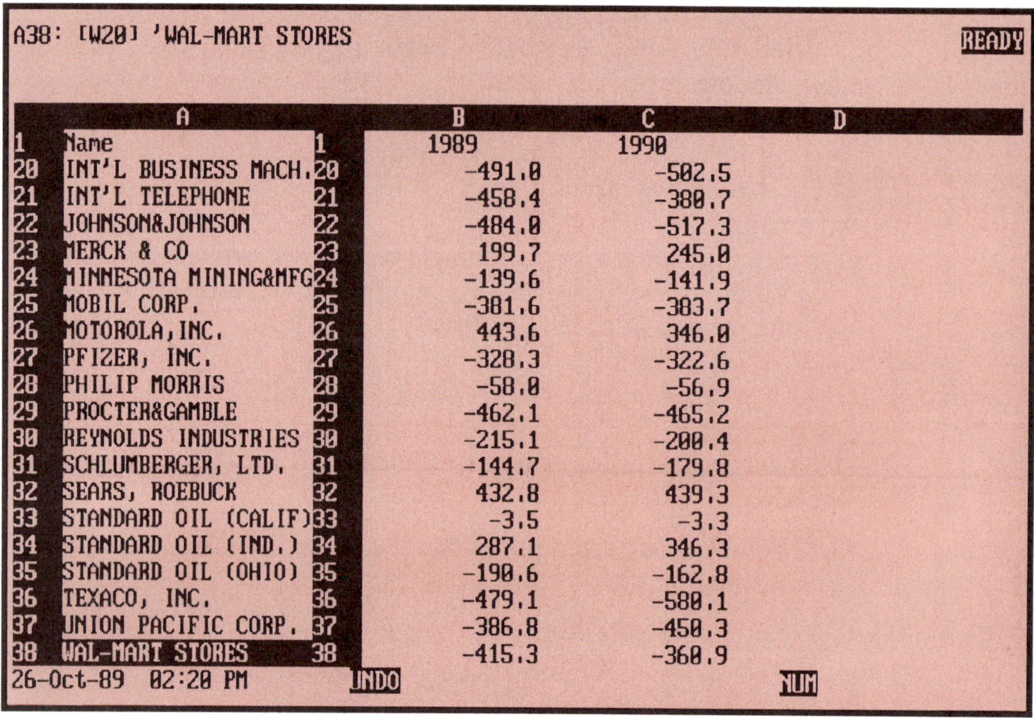
A38: [W20] 'WAL-MART STORES READY

	A		B	C	D
1	Name	1	1989	1990	
20	INT'L BUSINESS MACH.	20	-491.0	-502.5	
21	INT'L TELEPHONE	21	-458.4	-380.7	
22	JOHNSON&JOHNSON	22	-484.0	-517.3	
23	MERCK & CO	23	199.7	245.0	
24	MINNESOTA MINING&MFG	24	-139.6	-141.9	
25	MOBIL CORP.	25	-381.6	-383.7	
26	MOTOROLA, INC.	26	443.6	346.0	
27	PFIZER, INC.	27	-328.3	-322.6	
28	PHILIP MORRIS	28	-58.0	-56.9	
29	PROCTER&GAMBLE	29	-462.1	-465.2	
30	REYNOLDS INDUSTRIES	30	-215.1	-200.4	
31	SCHLUMBERGER, LTD.	31	-144.7	-179.8	
32	SEARS, ROEBUCK	32	432.8	439.3	
33	STANDARD OIL (CALIF)	33	-3.5	-3.3	
34	STANDARD OIL (IND.)	34	287.1	346.3	
35	STANDARD OIL (OHIO)	35	-190.6	-162.8	
36	TEXACO, INC.	36	-479.1	-580.1	
37	UNION PACIFIC CORP.	37	-386.8	-450.3	
38	WAL-MART STORES	38	-415.3	-360.9	

26-Oct-89 02:20 PM UNDO NUM

Figure 12-5 The Worksheet with a Vertical Window

REVIEW QUESTIONS

1.* What is the difference between comma and currency formats?

2.* Which columns do not have their widths changed by the /Worksheet Global Column-Width command?

3.* If the cell pointer is in cell C5 and you use the /Worksheet Titles Horizontal command, which rows are frozen?

DOCUMENTATION RESEARCH

Using the reference manual, find and record the page number of each of the commands discussed in this unit. I recommend you also write the page number by the discussion of the command, above.

1. Worksheet Titles — can you move into the title area when using the pointing method to indicate a cell or range?
2. /Worksheet Window — when you Clear windows, which set of settings remains?
3. /Worksheet Global Zero — how can you prevent inadvertent writing-over of hidden zeros?
4. /Worksheet Column Hide — is it possible to hide more than one column at once?

UNIT 13

ADVANCED RANGE OPERATIONS

In this unit, you learn about advanced operations available through the /**R**ange command. These options facilitate your ability to deal with a complex worksheet of many parts, and also affect the manner in which data can be entered or changed in the worksheet.

LEARNING OBJECTIVES

At the completion of this unit, you should be able to

a. name worksheet ranges,
b. use named ranges in formulas,
c. use named ranges as destinations,
d. use named ranges in commands,
e. establish protected cells,
f. toggle worksheet protection on and off,
g. establish a form-oriented data entry system,
h. search and replace cell contents.

IMPORTANT COMMANDS

/**R**ange **N**ame
/**R**ange **P**rot
/**R**ange **U**nprot
/**W**orksheet **G**lobal **P**rotection
/**R**ange **I**nput
/**R**ange **S**earch

RANGE NAMES

We hinted at the virtues of named ranges in Part 1. As your worksheet grows, it becomes more and more useful to have a quick method of referring to specific portions of the worksheet.

For instance, you might have built a worksheet to calculate federal income taxes, and have separate areas on your worksheet for Form 1040, Schedule A, Schedule D, Form 2441, and so on. As you work on your taxes, you would like some easy way to jump from Form 1040 to Schedule D, and back again. Or, you might have built a worksheet containing a pet store inventory, grouped into classes such as rodent, bird, fish, etc. As you manage your inventory, you would like to be able to write formulas quickly to sum the cost of all the rodents you have in stock.

Your life will be easier if you take the time to create range names. It is easier to name ranges as you build the worksheet, but ranges can be named any time.

NAMING RANGES

To name a range, move the cell pointer to the upper left corner of the range to be named, give the /**R**ange **N**ame **C**reate command, and indicate the lower right corner of the range. You can remove the name from a specific range using /**R**ange **N**ame **D**elete and from all ranges with /**R**ange **N**ame **R**eset. /**R**ange **N**ame **L**abels can be used to assign names from adjacent cells. /**R**ange **N**ame **T**able creates a table in the worksheet with the names and addresses of currently active ranges. If you later add or delete a range, you must use the command again. This is useful for debugging large worksheets.

USING NAMED RANGES IN FORMULAS

Many Lotus functions allow the use of range names as arguments. To use a range name as an argument, simply type the range name where you would normally type addresses. In the following examples, assume that you have named the range Q5..Q20 as WEST.

UNNAMED RANGE	NAMED RANGE
@IRR(0.10,Q5..Q20)	@IRR(0.10,WEST)
@SUM(Q5..Q20)	@SUM(WEST)
@DAVG(Q5..Q20,1,A1..B2)	@DAVG(WEST,1,A1..B2)

USING NAMED RANGES AS A DESTINATION

Recall the tax form example. If you name the ranges with names such as FORM1040, SCHEDA, etc., then it is very easy to jump about. Press the <GOTO (F5)> key, then the <NAME (F3)> key and you are presented with a list of named ranges. Arrow to the desired one and press <Enter>. The cell pointer jumps to the upper left corner of the chosen range.

USING NAMED RANGES IN COMMANDS

Almost all Lotus commands make use of ranges:

/**R**ange	all subcommands
/**C**opy	FROM and TO ranges
/**M**ove	FROM and TO ranges
/**F**ile	Combine and eXtract operations
/**P**rint	Range
/**G**raph	X and A . . . F ranges
/**D**ata	all subcommands

In most cases, when asked for a range, you can use the <NAME (F3)> key to display a list of range names and select the appropriate one.

CELL PROTECTION

Cell protection is used to prevent you or others from making inadvertent changes to protected cells. There are two aspects to cell protection:

- A given cell is either unprotected or protected.
- The entire worksheet is either in the protection-on or the protection-off state.

The normal mode is that all cells are protected, but the worksheet is in protection-off state. A given cell's protected state is irrelevant if the entire worksheet is in the protection-off state.

ESTABLISHING PROTECTED CELLS

The normal sequence of events for using cell protection:

1. As you build the worksheet, make note of those cells that the user will need to change. Recall the Poor Richard's example in Applications A and B. The items to be changed are in cells C4..C9 and G6 (see Figure B-1 on page 80).
2. Either concurrently with step 1 or later, use the /**R**ange **U**nprot command to make these cells unprotected. If you unprotect the wrong cells, use the /**R**ange **P**rot command to reprotect them. The contents of unprotected cells are displayed in a different intensity or color. A U is displayed in the control panel area to indicate the cell is unprotected.
3. Change the worksheet to the protection-on state using the /**W**orksheet **G**lobal **P**rotection **E**nable command. To make changes later, use the /**W**orksheet **G**lobal **P**rotection **D**isable command to change the worksheet to protection-off state.

When this worksheet is /**F**ile **S**aved, the unprotected status of the cells and the protection-on/off status of the worksheet is also saved. When the worksheet is later /**F**ile **R**etrieved, these statuses are still in effect.

DATA ENTRY

It is possible to create a worksheet that provides a form-oriented data entry situation. In such a situation, the user can only enter values or labels in unprotected cells in a specified range.

Once the worksheet has been set up with protected and unprotected cells, as in the discussion above, the /**R**ange **I**nput command is issued. The input range is either named, typed, or pointed to. Cell pointer movement is then restricted to unprotected cells in the input range. Range input is terminated by pressing either <Esc> or <Enter> without first typing or editing an entry.

SEARCH AND REPLACE

Lotus provides the **/Range Search** command to assist you in making changes to a worksheet. This feature is similar to the find and replace feature of most word processors. You can search for and replace a series of characters in label entries or formulas. You cannot search for or replace constant value entries (but you can search and replace a number that is part of a formula).

For instance, you might decide to change the name of the `Production` department (in the NAMELIST file) to `Operations`. To do so:

1. Move the cell pointer to cell B2, the top cell in the range to be replaced. (This step is not required, but makes the rest of the process easier.)
2. Issue the command **/RS**. Lotus asks for the range to be searched:

3. Highlight the range B2..B39. The quick way to do this is to press a period, then <End> <Down> <Enter>.
4. Lotus next asks for the string to search for. Enter **production**:

```
B2: [W10] 'Executive                                    EDIT
Enter string to search for: production
```

5. Press the <Enter> key. You do not need to match the capitalization. Next Lotus asks what kinds of entries should be searched:

```
B2: [W10] 'Executive                                    MENU
Formulas  Labels  Both
Search for string in formulas only
```

6. In this case, only labels need be searched, so press **L**. The next question is whether to **F**ind (only) or find and **R**eplace:

```
B2: [W10] 'Executive                                    MENU
Find  Replace
Highlight search string in the search range
```

7. Press **R**. Lotus prompts for the replacement string; enter **Operations**:

```
B2: [W10] 'Executive                                    EDIT
Enter replacement string: Operations
```

8. Press <Enter>. In the replacement string, you must enter the desired capitalization. Lotus highlights the first match in the search range and gives you several choices:

```
B3: [W10] 'Production                                              MENU
Replace  All  Next  Quit
Replace string and proceed to next matching string in range
             A             B          C        D        E         F
1  Name                 Dept       Phone    Salary            Dept
2  Smith, Daniel        Executive   3283    48,597            E*
3  Ross, Shannon        Production  3883    48,229
4  Black, Melissa       Production  3392    47,877
```

Replace changes the highlighted string and finds the next occurrence. All replaces all matching strings. Next moves to the next match without changing the highlighted string. Quit returns you to READY mode. The safest method is to select Replace and view each entry before changing.

9. If you move through the range with Replace and Next, Lotus will inform you with the message `No more matching strings` when the end of the range is reached. Press the <Enter> key and Lotus will replace the last entry (if you so directed) and then return to READY mode.

There are many uses for the search and replace feature. Not only can you replace the contents of a range of labels, you can also correct a reference to the wrong cell in a range of formulas. You can change a function (e.g., from @PV to @FV). Or, you can use the search feature to search a large worksheet for every place the @PMT function is used.

EXAMPLE USING ADVANCED /WORKSHEET AND /RANGE COMMANDS

The advanced commands discussed in this and the previous unit can be combined to create a useful worksheet. For instance, the timekeeper of an organization might wish to build a worksheet to record the time worked by each individual in a given week. The final worksheet looks like Figure 13-1.

The only things that are input on a weekly basis are the entries in the four columns under `---Hours---` and the date in row 16. The remainder of the worksheet consists of labels (such as the names) and formulas (such as the `---Pay---` columns).

The timekeeper decides to fix rows 1 through 5 and columns A and B as titles. The cell pointer is moved to cell C6 and the /Worksheet Titles Both command is issued. The effect of this command is that all rows above the cell pointer are fixed and all columns to the left of the cell pointer are fixed. The cell pointer cannot be moved into the fixed rows or columns using the <Arrow> keys, but can be moved into those areas using the <GOTO (F5)> key.

The next step is to create two named ranges. The first is named HOURS, and consists of the range C6..F12, the area in which the hours are input. The timekeeper issues the command /Range Name Create, enters the name **`hours`**, and points to the range (as illustrated in Figure 13-2).

The second named range is called DATE and consists of cell C16, which contains the current week's date.

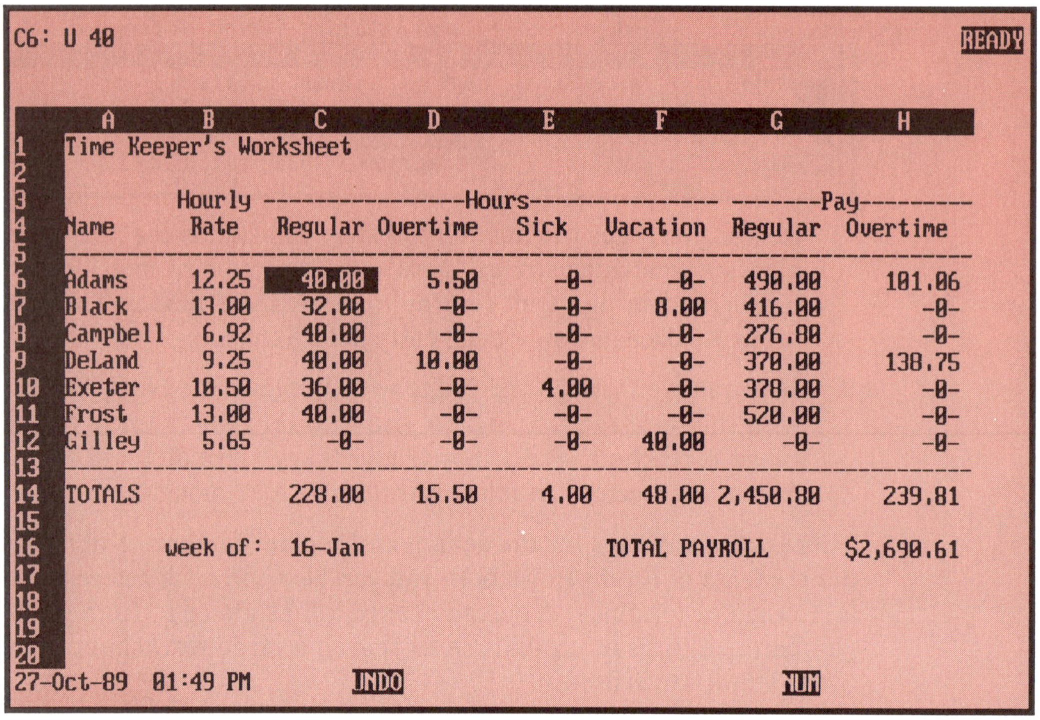

```
C6: U 40                                                                   READY

     A         B        C         D        E        F         G        H
1   Time Keeper's Worksheet
2
3              Hourly ---------------Hours--------------- -------Pay---------
4   Name        Rate  Regular Overtime   Sick   Vacation  Regular  Overtime
5   --------------------------------------------------------------------------
6   Adams      12.25    40.00     5.50     -0-       -0-   490.00    101.06
7   Black      13.00    32.00      -0-     -0-      8.00   416.00       -0-
8   Campbell    6.92    40.00      -0-     -0-       -0-   276.80       -0-
9   DeLand      9.25    40.00    10.00     -0-       -0-   370.00    138.75
10  Exeter     10.50    36.00      -0-    4.00       -0-   378.00       -0-
11  Frost      13.00    40.00      -0-     -0-       -0-   520.00       -0-
12  Gilley      5.65      -0-      -0-     -0-     40.00      -0-       -0-
13  --------------------------------------------------------------------------
14  TOTALS             228.00    15.50    4.00     48.00 2,450.80    239.81
15
16           week of:  16-Jan                  TOTAL PAYROLL       $2,690.61
17
18
19
20
27-Oct-89  01:49 PM          UNDO                           NUM
```

Figure 13-1 The Finished Timekeeper's Worksheet
(After the changes discussed in this unit have been made.)

After the two ranges are named, the timekeeper uses the /**R**ange **U**nprot command to unprotect the cells in the two ranges. For instance, to unprotect the HOURS range:

1. Issue the command **/RU**.
2. Press the <NAME (F3)> key for a list of range names. At this point the worksheet looks like Figure 13-3.
3. Arrow <Right> to the desired range; press <Enter>.

When both ranges have been unprotected, the timekeeper sets the worksheet in the protection-on state with the /**W**orksheet **G**lobal **P**rotection **E**nable command.

The timekeeper makes one additional enhancement before entering data. The /**W**orksheet **G**lobal **Z**ero command is used to change the display of zero values from `0.00` to the Label `"-0-`.

Now the worksheet is ready for the use of the /**R**ange **I**nput command. To input the DATE range, changing from 09-Jan to 16-Jan, do this:

1. Issue the command /**R**ange **I**nput.

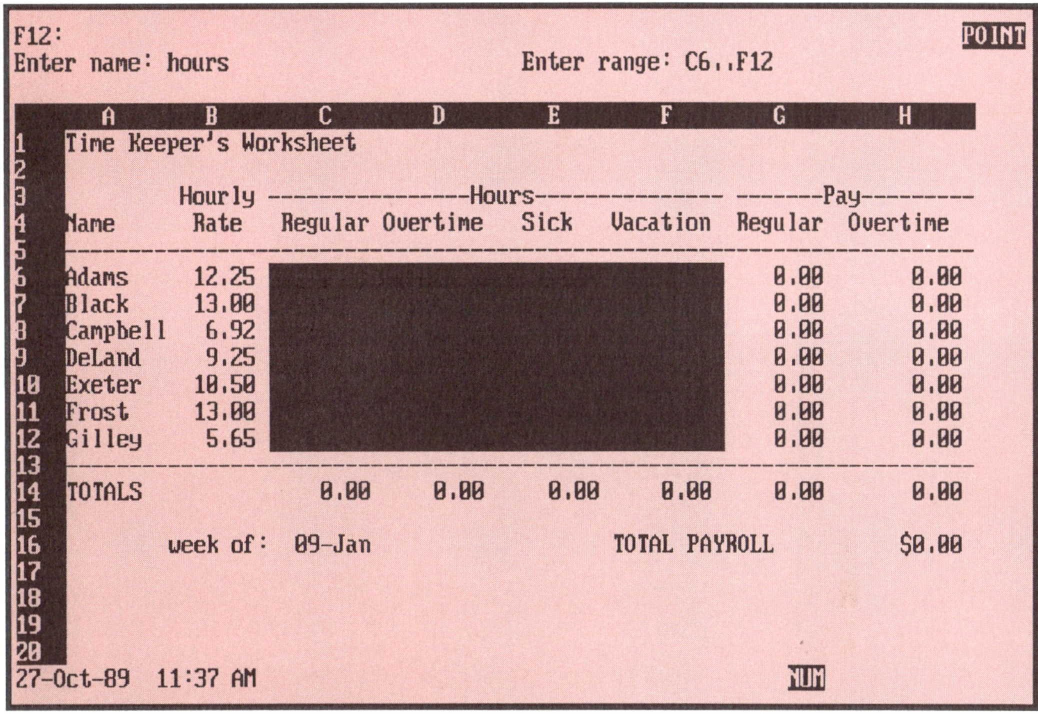

Figure 13-2 Naming a Range

```
C6:                                                              NAMES
Enter range to unprotect:
DATE        HOURS
      A          B        C       D        E        F        G        H
1   Time Keeper's Worksheet
2
3              Hourly ---------------Hours--------------- -------Pay---------
4   Name        Rate  Regular Overtime  Sick   Vacation Regular  Overtime
5   ----------------------------------------------------------------------
6   Adams      12.25                                        0.00      0.00
7   Black      13.00                                        0.00      0.00
8   Campbell    6.92                                        0.00      0.00
9   DeLand      9.25                                        0.00      0.00
10  Exeter     10.50                                        0.00      0.00
11  Frost      13.00                                        0.00      0.00
12  Gilley      5.65                                        0.00      0.00
13  ----------------------------------------------------------------------
14  TOTALS              0.00     0.00     0.00     0.00     0.00      0.00
15
16        week of:  09-Jan              TOTAL PAYROLL              $0.00
17
18
19
20
27-Oct-89   11:39 AM                                    NUM
```

Figure 13-3 The /RangeUnprot Operation

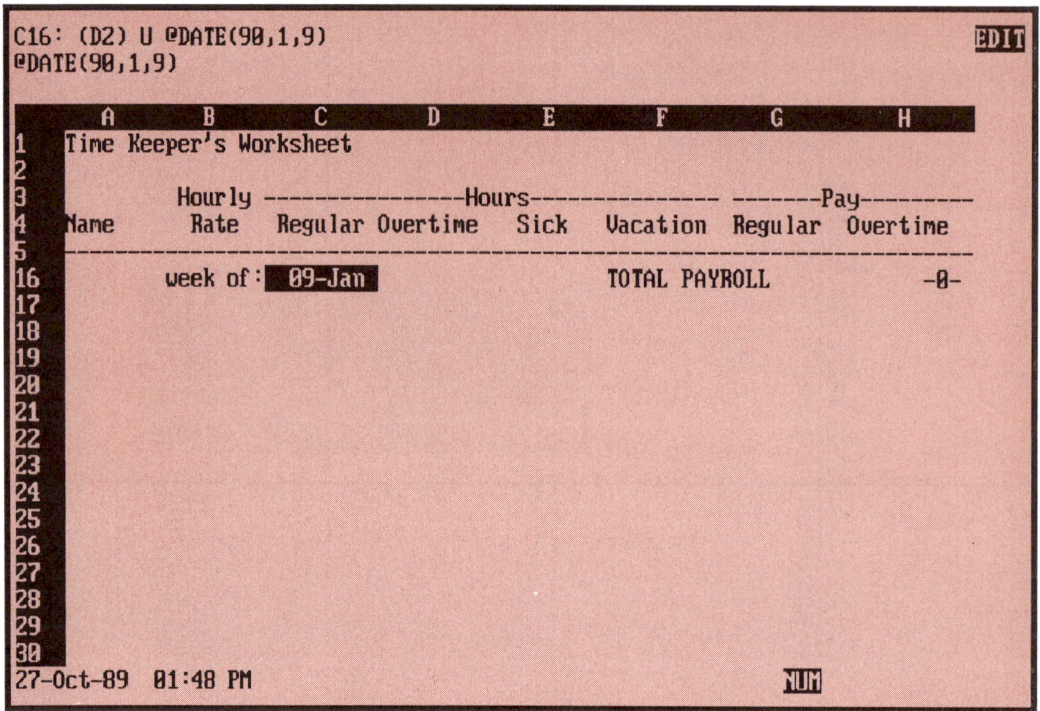

Figure 13-4 During the /RangeInput Operation

2. Press the <NAME (F3)> key for a list of range names.
3. Highlight the desired range; press <Enter>.

After the range name is selected, the input range is moved to the upper left corner of the nontitle part of the worksheet. The easiest way to change the date entry is to press the <EDIT (F2)> key. See Figure 13-4 for an illustration of the process at this point. Notice that the DATE range, which is cell C16, is moved to the upper right portion of the nontitle area (i.e., below row 5 and right of column B). Once the <EDIT (F2)> key is pressed, the mode indicator changes to `EDIT` and the prior entry is put into the second line of the control panel area. At this point, we can change the 9 to 16, then press <Enter>. To terminate the **/R**ange **I**nput operation, press the <Esc> key or press <Enter> again.

Range input to the HOURS range is similar. While in the range input mode, you can arrow around within the designated range, but not outside of the range. The best way to exit range input mode is to press the <Esc> key.

GUIDED ACTIVITY: ADVANCED /WORKSHEET AND /RANGE OPERATIONS

This activity requires you to use several of the advanced range commands to complete the example discussed above.

1. Follow the startup procedure outlined in Unit 1 to load Lotus and enter the 1-2-3 program.

2. Retrieve TIMEKPR. Arrow around, looking at the formulas.
3. Arrow to cell C6.
4. Use the /**W**orksheet **T**itles **B**oth command to fix rows 1 to 5 and columns A and B, as discussed above.
5. Now press the <Up> arrow key. Lotus beeps at you because you are trying to move into the title area.

   CHECKPOINT

   13a. Which of the following are you able to do from cell C6: <Left>, <Right>, <Up>, <Down>?

   Try each of the arrow keys to see what works.
6. Press the <Home> key. Where does the cell pointer move?

   CHECKPOINT

   13b. Why does the cell pointer move to C6?
7. Now you want to name the range C6..F12 as HOME, and cell C16 as DATE. Follow the example discussed above.
8. The next step is to unprotect the cells in the ranges HOME and DATE. Again, follow the example above.
9. Set the worksheet to the protection-on state.

   CHECKPOINT

   13c. What command establishes the protection-on state?

   13d. If you wish to make a change to a protected cell, what must you do first?
10. Use the /**W**orksheet **G**lobal **Z**ero command to display the label `-0-` wherever there is a zero value.
11. Using the /**R**ange **I**nput command, change the DATE range to `16-Jan` and enter the hours so your worksheet looks like Figure 13-1. Where the illustration shows `-0-`, enter the value **0** (zero) — do not enter **-0-**.
12. Save the result under the name TIMEKPR2.

EXERCISE: USING RANGE NAMES IN FORMULAS

This exercise provides a simple illustration of how ranges can be named from adjacent labels and how range names can be used in formulas.

1. Follow the startup procedure outlined in Unit 1 to load Lotus and enter the 1-2-3 program. If you are continuing from a previous activity or exercise and already have a worksheet on the screen, use the command /**W**orksheet **E**rase **Y**es to clear the screen. (*Remember*: Save it before erasing it.)

2. Enter the labels **Revenue, Expenses, Gross, Taxes, Net** down column A, from A2..A6. Use the /**R**ange **N**ame **L**abel **R**ight command to name the adjacent cells in column B (the `label range` is A2..A6). In C5, put the number **42%** and name that cell TAXRATE (one word).
3. In B4, put the formula **+revenue-expenses**. There are four ways to enter this formula:
   - Type the range names and operators, **+revenue-expenses**
   - Type **+**, press <NAME (F3)>, highlight REVENUE, press <Enter>, press **-**, press <NAME (F3)>, highlight EXPENSES, press <Enter>, press <Enter> again
   - Type the cell addresses, **+B2-B3**
   - Point to the cells (as usual)

   In any case, the formula is entered as the range names, making it easy for you to figure out what you intended when you look at this worksheet in six months. In B5, put the formula **+gross*taxrate** In B6, put the formula **+gross-taxes**.
4. /**R**ange **U**nprot the ranges REVENUE, EXPENSES, and TAXRATE (requires three commands). The easiest way to do this is to use the <NAME (F3)> key. After pressing **/RU**, press <NAME (F3)>; highlight the name of the range to unprotect; then press <Enter>. Next, set global protection on. Set global format to comma, 0 decimal places. Format TAXRATE to percent, one decimal place (you can use <NAME (F3)> in this command also). Take a moment to ponder what you have just created: a simple accounting worksheet with all formulas protected.
5. Test your worksheet by entering various combinations of revenue, expenses and tax rates. If tax rate is constant at 42%, which is better: revenue of 10,000 and expenses of 9,000, or revenue of 11,000 and expenses of 9,900?
6. Try to make entries in any protected cell of the worksheet. When finished, save your work with the file name TAXPLAN.

REVIEW QUESTIONS

1.* When can you make changes to a protected cell?

2.* What is the normal (default) state of all worksheet cells?

3. What is the normal (default) protection state?

4.* What key do you press for a list of range names?

5. When would you use the /**R**ange **I**nput capability?

DOCUMENTATION RESEARCH

Using the reference manual, find and record the page number of each of the commands discussed in this unit. I recommend you also write the page number by the discussion of the command, above.

1. /**R**ange **N**ame — how do you remove a name from a named range?
2. /**R**ange **U**nprot — how does the display of unprotected cells differ from the display of protected cells?
3. /**W**orksheet **G**lobal **P**rotection — can you delete columns or rows when protection is enabled?
4. /**R**ange **I**nput — must protection be enabled before this command is used?
5. Find the sections of the reference manual that discuss cell protection. What analogy does Lotus use to describe the protection-on and protection-off states?

APPLICATION F

SPRING BREAK: FLORIDA OR BUST

There are no complex commands or formulas in this exercise, nor are there step-by-step instructions. Your task is to build a worksheet that contains a cash flow projection and to determine how much money is needed to achieve a desired ending balance.

Your parents, being frugal sorts, have come up with a budget for spring semester that provides for all necessities and a modest amount of fun. What they failed to plan for was your trip to Florida for spring break. Staying on campus in March is no fun, especially when everyone else is in Fort Lauderdale.

Here are your sources of income:

Scholarship	$1000	paid in January
Parents	3000	paid in January
	500	paid February through June
	600	additional paid in April
	300	additional paid in June
		the additional amounts are for travel to and from home

Your budget allows for the following expenses:

Tuition	$2500	paid in January
Books	400	paid in January
Room	275	per month (January through June)
Groceries	200	per month
Dates	25	per month
Movies	20	per month
Sports	30	per month

continued on following page

Travel

to school	300 in January
Easter	600 in April
home	300 in June

This budget is displayed in Figure F-1. You notice that every penny of income is used by the end of June. You need $400 in March for your Florida excursion, and therefore must get a job. The problem is to figure out how much per month you must earn to keep the balance above zero. Because too much work affects your social and academic life, you must minimize the amount of work in each month. When you save your worksheet, name it BUDGET.

My Budget	Jan	Feb	Mar	Apr	May	Jun
Income						
Job						
Parents	3000	500	500	1100	500	800
Scholarship	1000					
TOTAL INC.	4000	500	500	1100	500	800
Expenses						
Books	400					
Dates	25	25	25	25	25	25
Groceries	200	200	200	200	200	200
Movies	20	20	20	20	20	20
Room	275	275	275	275	275	275
Sports	30	30	30	30	30	30
Travel	300			600		300
Tuition	2500					
TOTAL EXP.	3750	550	550	1150	550	850
NET:	250	-50	-50	-50	-50	-50
BALANCE:	250	200	150	100	50	0

Figure F-1 The Student Cash Flow Problem

UNIT 14

ADVANCED FILE OPERATIONS

Disk files allow us to save our work from one session to be retrieved in another; to move a portion of one worksheet into another worksheet; to save a copy of a graph for printing; and to share information with programs other than Lotus 1-2-3. In this unit, we discuss the various types of files and the **/F**ile commands.

LEARNING OBJECTIVES

1. At the completion of this unit, you should know
   a. how to identify the purpose a file serves by the file extension,
   b. the differences among **/F**ile **S**ave, **/F**ile **X**tract, and **/P**rint **F**ile, and when each is most appropriate,
   c. the differences among **/F**ile **R**etrieve, **/F**ile **C**ombine, and **/F**ile **I**mport, and when each is most appropriate.
2. At the completion of this unit, you should be able to
   a. list all worksheet files on a disk,
   b. create a table containing information about the files on the disk,
   c. extract a portion of a file and save it on a disk,
   d. combine two files,
   e. print to a disk file,
   f. import a disk file,
   g. use values from other worksheets in the current worksheet.

IMPORTANT COMMANDS

/File **S**ave
/File **X**tract
/Print **F**ile
/File **R**etrieve
/File **I**mport
/File **C**ombine

IMPORTANT COMMANDS

/File List
/File Erase
/File Directory
/File Admin

FILE NAMES AND EXTENSIONS

Most PC-DOS application programs, including Lotus 1-2-3, use the file extension to designate the purpose the file serves, that is, the file type. If you are not familiar with the general rules for file names and extensions, refer to Appendix A in this manual.

DATA DISK FILE TYPES

Three types of files are used by Lotus 1-2-3 to store data on disks. .WK1 files contain the worksheet itself, including global, range, print, data, and graph settings. Files with a .PRN extension contain the output of a print-to-file operation and are also used to import non-Lotus data into Lotus 1-2-3. .PIC files contain data for printing graphs.

/FILE COMMANDS

You are already familiar with /File Save and /File Retrieve commands, which move worksheet files to and from disk storage. Both commands assume a .WK1 extension. You can also use DOS path names in all /File commands that ask for a file name. (Path names are normally used only on hard disk systems, e.g., \BUDGETS\SALES refers to the file SALES.WK1 in the subdirectory BUDGET.)

MOVING DATA FROM MEMORY TO DISK

Three commands take data from the current worksheet and save it in some form on your data diskette.

/File Save saves the entire file to disk. All formulas, formats, /Worksheet, /Print, /Range, /Data, and /Graph settings are saved with the file. Use /File Save when you want to save the entire file (the normal case). Do not use /File Save when you want to save a portion of a file, nor when you want to save the results of formulas rather than the formulas themselves.

/File Xtract is used to save only a portion of the worksheet. With this command, you can save the formulas (**/FXF**) or just the current values of the computations (**/FXV**). In either case, the resulting file is a worksheet file with a .WK1 extension. Formulas, formats, /Worksheet, /Print, /Range, /Data, and /Graph settings are saved with the file. Use /File Xtract when you want to save only a portion of the worksheet, or when you want to save the current values of formulas, not the formulas themselves.

/Print File is used to save the file as a text (**print**) file. The normal /Print output is sent to a disk file with a .PRN extension. The /Print command is discussed in Unit 5. Use /Print File when you want to save a copy of how the worksheet appears, for instance, when you wish to incorporate a worksheet table into a letter you are writing with a word processor.

MOVING DATA FROM DISK TO MEMORY

Three commands take data from the diskette and load it into the computer's memory. The first erases any current worksheet, while the other two add the data to the current worksheet.

/File **R**etrieve moves the file from disk to active memory. Before the file is retrieved, any current worksheet is erased. All formulas, formats, **/W**orksheet, **/P**rint, **/R**ange, **/D**ata, and **/G**raph settings are retrieved with the file. Use **/F**ile **R**etrieve when you are starting a session or when you are through with the current worksheet and want to work on a previously saved worksheet.

The process of combining data from multiple worksheets is called **consolidation**. It is quite important in accounting applications. **/F**ile **I**mport allows you to consolidate data from sources other than Lotus worksheets, while **/F**ile **C**ombine is used to incorporate data from other Lotus worksheets into the current worksheet.

/File **I**mport is used to bring a nonworksheet file into a worksheet (which might be empty, or might already contain data). Files to be imported can be created by a program written in BASIC, by a word processor, or by a database manager; they can also be received from other computers. The file to be imported must have a .PRN extension. (If a file is in the proper format but does not have a .PRN extension, you can use the DOS RENAME command to change the extension.) Files to be imported can be either text (**/FIT**) or numbers (**/FIN**):

- A **Text** file is imported as a column of labels: each line in the input file becomes a row one cell wide in the worksheet file.
- A **Number** file must be specially formatted before it is imported. Label (text) entries must be enclosed in quotes (" . . . "), numeric entries must be separated by either a comma or one or more spaces. Each distinct entry in an imported line becomes a cell in a row; each line in the imported file becomes a row in the worksheet.

The **/F**ile **I**mport commands are used when the data to be brought into the worksheet are not in Lotus .WK1 format. Importation of data into Lotus 1-2-3 is discussed in more detail in the following unit.

/File **C**ombine commands are used to integrate all or a portion of one worksheet file into another. These commands are often used to consolidate the results from different worksheets, such as when preparing a master budget from the budgets of several divisions.

To use the **/F**ile **C**ombine command, first **/F**ile **R**etrieve one worksheet. Then move the cell cursor to the cell where you want the upper left corner of the incoming data to be placed. You have three combination methods; each of the three allows you to bring in an entire file, a named range, or a range specified by cell addresses. The file being combined must be a worksheet.

/File **C**ombine **C**opy: each entry in the incoming file or range replaces the corresponding entry on the present worksheet. Blank cells in the incoming file do not erase occupied cells in the present worksheet. You can combine an entire file (**/FCCE**) or a range (**/FCCN**).

/File Combine Add: the value of each numeric entry (formula or constant) in the incoming file or range is added to a corresponding number or blank entry on the present worksheet. If the present worksheet cell contains a label or formula, the incoming value is discarded. You can add an entire file (**/FCAE**) or a range (**/FCAN**).

/File Combine Subtract: the value of each numeric entry (formula or constant) in the incoming file or range is subtracted from a corresponding number or blank entry on the present worksheet. If the present worksheet cell contains a label or formula, the incoming value is discarded. You can subtract an entire file (**/FCSE**) or a range (**/FCSN**).

Use /File Combine when you want to bring one worksheet into the current worksheet. Note that /Worksheet, /Print, /Range, /Data, and /Graph settings are not combined with the file.

DISK OPERATIONS

The remaining /File commands deal with files stored on the data disk.

/File List lists files of a specified type (Worksheet, Print, Graph, or Other). Use this command to check whether or not a certain file is on the disk.

/File Erase erases a specified file. It is better to do this at the PC-DOS level, but sometimes you need the room and must do it from within Lotus. I use /File Erase only when I am trying to save a worksheet file and Lotus tells me that the disk is full. To avoid losing of my work, I must erase a file on the disk to make room for the worksheet I am currently using. If you must erase a file, erase the least important one, because that file is lost forever from the current diskette. Hopefully, you are able to erase a file that is backed up on another disk.

/File Directory is used to change the directory that Lotus searches for files. This command is normally used only by those with a hard disk system.

/File Admin Table creates a table listing specified types of files and places that table in the worksheet at a location you designate.

LINKING FILES

Lotus permits you to refer to values in another worksheet when building formulas in the current worksheet. This feature is called **linking**. For example, you have a spreadsheet (named INVSTMTS) in which you keep track of your investments (name, quantity, current market value). One of the cells in that spreadsheet contains the current dollar value of the investments (the sum of quantity times value for all items). This cell is named CUR_VAL.

You maintain another spreadsheet (named NETWORTH) that contains your total net worth, that is, how much your home is worth and the amount of mortgage, your savings and retirement account data, and so on. One of the entries on this second spreadsheet is "Current Value of Investments." To ensure that this figure is up to date whenever you work with NETWORTH, you enter a formula that refers to the CUR_VAL range in INVSTMTS:

+<<INVSTMTS>>CUR_VAL

in the cell in NETWORTH that is supposed to contain the current value of investments. Notice that the formula begins with a plus sign, that the file name is enclosed in a pair of less-than and greater-than signs, and that there are no spaces or other punctuation between the file name and the range (cell) name. If INVSTMTS were on a different disk or directory, that information should be included inside the << >> signs.

Although you can use a cell address (e.g., `J35`) in the formula, range names are much better. If you alter the structure of the INVSTMTS file, the cell address might change. But the range name would usually continue to be valid, even if it refers to a different cell.

Whenever you retrieve NETWORTH, it will obtain the current value of the CUR_VAL range in INVSTMTS and place that value in the proper place in NETWORTH. If you are operating in a network or multitasking system where it is possible that the values in INVSTMTS could change while you are working in NETWORTH, use the **/F**ile **A**dmin **L**ink-Refresh command to retrieve the most recently saved value of CUR_VAL.

Linked files have a major advantage over data files that are combined using one of the **/F**ile **C**ombine commands. When you combine files, the data in the combined file reflects the situation at the time the files were combined. If you subsequently change one of the source files, the data in the combined file is no longer accurate. Linked files, however, always use the most recent data and reflect all changes in the source files. **/F**ile **C**ombine is somewhat easier to use, however, because large ranges of data can be addressed at once.[1]

GUIDED ACTIVITY: FILE MANIPULATIONS

This activity requires you to use several of the **/F**ile commands.

1. Sign out the Lotus 1-2-3 manual and software. Follow the startup procedure outlined in Unit 1 to load Lotus and enter the 1-2-3 program. The data disk should have the worksheet files that you created in Unit 7 (RECALC.WK1) and Application C (COMPOUND.WK1).

2. Use the **/F**ile **L**ist **W**orksheet command to list all Worksheet files on the disk. Your display should look similar to the following. (But you will have different files on your disk.) Use the arrow keys to move the cursor around. As you highlight a file, more detailed information about that file appears near the top of the screen.

1. Note: You *cannot* refer to more than one cell in a linking formula, thus a formula such as +<<western>>sales+<<eastern>>sales *does not* work.)

```
A1:                                                                    FILES
Enter extension of files to list: C:\LO22_INS\*.wk?
           COMPOUND.WK1    10/13/89        12:22          3702
AUTO1.WK1       AUTO2.WK1       BULL.WK1        BULL2.WK1       CLASSEX.WK1
COMPCOST.WK1    COMPOUND.WK1    DATACOMP.WK1    DEMOGRAF.WK1    FIG4-1.WK1
FIG7-1.WK1      FORMATS-.WK1    FORMATS.WK1     FUNCTION.WK1    HAROLD.WK1
HOTEL.WK1       JUNK.WK1        NAMELIST.WK1    OPERATOR.WK1    PORTFOLI.WK1
PORTREGR.WK1    RB90PROJ.WK1    RBCOMPAN.WK1    RECALC.WK1      TAXPLAN.WK1
TIMEKPR.WK1     TIMEKPR2.WK1    UNIT3EX.WK1     WINDOWS.WK1
```

Press the <Enter> key to return to the **READY** mode.

3. /**F**ile **R**etrieve RECALC.
4. Use the arrow keys or the <GOTO (F5)> key to move the cursor to cell A7.
5. Use the /**F**ile **C**ombine **C**opy command to copy the **E**ntire-File COMPOUND into the worksheet. The result should look like Figure 14-1.

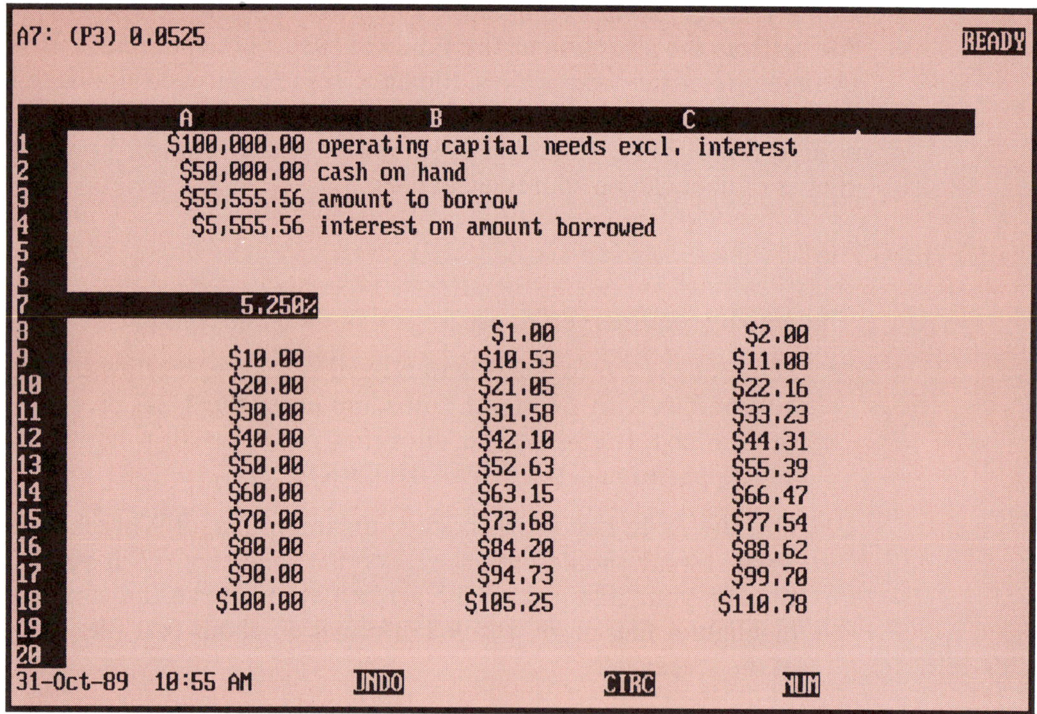

Figure 14-1 The Combined Worksheets

6. Look at the result of this operation. Use the <Arrow> keys to move around in the area occupied by COMPOUND.

CHECKPOINT

14a. Did the formulas in COMPOUND adjust to reflect their new location, or did the absolute and mixed addresses prevail?

14b. Was there any effect on the logic of RECALC?

14c. Why are the columns so wide?

7. Press the <Home> key.
8. Use the **/F**ile **X**tract command to extract the **V**alues of the range A1..F20 into a file called EXTRACT.
9. Save your work with the file name COMBINE.
10. Use the **/F**ile **L**ist command to list all worksheet files on the disk. Are both EXTRACT and COMBINE listed?
11. Use the **/P**rint **F**ile command to print the range A1..F20 to a file called COMBINE. (You can use the same file name, because the worksheet file is called COMBINE.WK1 while the print file is called COMBINE.PRN.)
12. Save the file again.
13. **/F**ile **R**etrieve EXTRACT. Go to some of the cells that used to have formulas. Are there any formulas left? Why not?
14. **/Q**uit to exit to the 1-2-3 Access System. Exit to the operating system.
15. Give the command

    ```
    type b:combine.prn
    ```

    to see the result of the **/P**rint **F**ile command.

EXERCISE: CONSOLIDATING DATA FROM TWO SPREADSHEETS

In this exercise we create two simple worksheets with sales and expenses data, then combine them into a national summary sheet. In practice, the regional worksheets would be much more complex, but this exercise is intended to illustrate the procedure for consolidating data from different worksheets.

1. Starting in cell A1 of a blank worksheet, make the following entries:

    ```
    Western Region
    Sales          15000
    Expenses       10000
    ```

2. Name the range B2..B3 as SUMMARY. Also, use **/R**ange **N**ame **L**abels **R**ight to name cells B2..B3 after the labels in A2..A3. Save the file as WESTERN.
3. Change the entries to read:

    ```
    Eastern Region
    Sales          17000
    Expenses       13000
    ```

4. Save the file with the name EASTERN. (You do not have to rename the ranges before saving the worksheet.)
5. Change the worksheet to read:

```
National Summary
Sales
Expenses
NET
```

   Now, cells B2 and B3 are blank. Put the formula **+sales-expenses** in cell B4.
6. Put the cell pointer in B2. Use the **/F**ile **C**ombine **A**dd **N**amed/Specified-Range command to consolidate the data from the range SUMMARY in each of the regional worksheets (one at a time). The two sales and the two expenses figures should be added and the NET figure should reflect the difference of the sums.
7. Save your work with the name NATIONAL. The next exercise links the NATIONAL worksheet to the two regional worksheets.

EXERCISE: LINKING SPREADSHEETS

In this exercise, we link the data from the two regional worksheets into the NATIONAL worksheet. You must complete the previous exercise before attempting this exercise.

1. If you are not continuing from the previous Exercise, load Lotus and retrieve NATIONAL.
2. Enter the following labels in the cells indicated. Use the " (double quote) mark to right justify the labels:

Cell	Label
D1	West
E1	East
F1	Total

3. Enter the following formula in D2: **+<<western>>sales**
4. Enter similar formulas in D3, E2, and E3. (Note: You *cannot* refer to more than one cell in a linking formula, thus the formula **+<<western>>sales+<<eastern>>sales** *does not* work.)
5. In F2 and F3, sum the two sales and expenses figures. In F4, subtract expenses from sales (you must use the cell addresses, not the range names, in this formula). The values of B4 and F4 should agree.
6. Save the spreadsheet with the name NATIONAL.
7. To this point, you can see that **/F**ile **C**ombine is easier to set up than linking files. The purpose of the next several steps is to show what happens when the regional data change after the files are combined.
8. Retrieve WESTERN and change the sales figure to **18000**.

9. Save WESTERN.

10. Retrieve NATIONAL. Note that the value in D2 changes to 18000, reflecting the change in WESTERN, and the new NET in F4 is 12000. But, the NET in B4 has not changed to reflect the change in WESTERN. (We would have to erase the range B2..B3 and then do the two /File Combine commands again to achieve the proper result in B4.)

11. Save the file again.

REVIEW QUESTIONS

1. What are the differences among /File Save, /File Xtract, and /Print File, and when is each most appropriate?

2. What are the differences among /File Retrieve, /File Combine, and /File Import, and when is each most appropriate?

3. What kind of data is contained in files with the following extensions:
   a. .WK1
   b. .PRN
   c. .PIC

4. What command lists all worksheet files on a disk?

DOCUMENTATION RESEARCH

Using the reference manual, find and record the page number of each of the commands discussed in this unit. I recommend you also write the page number by the discussion of the command, above.

1. **/File Save** — how can you save the file to a disk other than the current default disk (usually the disk in Drive B)?

2. **/File Xtract** — does this command save cell and range names?

3. **/Print File** — what happens if you specify several print ranges, following each with **Go**, before you select **Quit**?

4. **/File Retrieve** — what happens to the current worksheet when you retrieve a new worksheet?

5. **/File Import** — what happens to current worksheet data in the range to which you import data?

6. **/File Combine** — which of the options combines values of formulas and which replaces current cell contents with imported cell contents?

7. **/File List** — what happens if there are no files of the indicated type on the disk?

8. **/File Erase** — what is the purpose of the characters ? and * with this command?

9. **/File Directory** — how do you determine the current directory?

UNIT 15

INTERCHANGING DATA WITH OTHER PROGRAMS

By now, you have seen many ways in which 1-2-3 can assist you in manipulating numbers, with its date arithmetic, financial functions, data tables, graphics, and so on. However, there are many other personal computer software programs that you might have to operate, and there is a good chance that someday you will want to take data generated elsewhere and insert that data into 1-2-3, or to take data from 1-2-3 and send it to another application.

In this unit, we first discuss methods for bringing data from other sources into Lotus 1-2-3; then we discuss a method for exporting 1-2-3 data so that other programs can use it.

LEARNING OBJECTIVES

At the completion of this unit, you should be able to

a. use the Translate program to prepare data for importation into Lotus 1-2-3,
b. use the Translate program to prepare data for exportation from Lotus 1-2-3,
c. import ASCII data from a .PRN file,
d. export ASCII data to a .PRN file.

IMPORTANT COMMANDS

Translate
/**F**ile **I**mport
/**P**rint **F**ile
/**D**ata **P**arse

IMPORTING DATA INTO 1-2-3

The data you wish to manipulate can come from a number of sources:

- VisiCalc or some other spreadsheet, for applications created back in the dark ages before 1-2-3.
- dBASE data files, such as a master accounts or a transaction file.
- BASIC programs that write sequential files.
- WordStar or WordPerfect files; these **word processors** are also good for entering text and data into sequential files.
- The moon, or, at least, a mainframe computer, via a communications package.

The above sources fall into two general categories: program-specific format and ASCII-generic format. The format determines how you incorporate the file into 1-2-3.

PROGRAM-SPECIFIC FORMATS

Most of the database managers and spreadsheets use a specialized format for storing data in disk files, with distinctive file extensions (the characters after the period) used to denote the special format. For instance, dBASE IV uses the extension .DBF, while VisiCalc uses .VC. A number of programs have the ability to store data in the so-called data interchange format, or .DIF, which was developed by the makers of VisiCalc for transfer of numeric data among programs.

Lotus includes a utility program to transfer data between program-specific formats and Lotus 1-2-3 and Symphony worksheet formats.[1] The various formats that Lotus can translate are listed in Figure 15-1.

The transfer is initiated from the 1-2-3 Access System, the menu you see first after typing **LOTUS** at the PC-DOS A>_ prompt. Instead of choosing 1-2-3 (the default), use the <Arrow> keys to move over to Translate and then press <Enter>. Depending on your specific computer system, you might have to switch disks. If this is necessary, 1-2-3 prompts you.

The screen in Figure 15-1 is the first stage of the translate process. The instructions at the bottom of the various translate screens are quite clear and guide you through the various steps. The program also lets you change your mind in several places.

Once you indicate the type of file you wish to translate from, the program displays the possible formats that you can translate to (Figure 15-2). In this unit, we translate from a dBASE III[2] .DBF file to a Lotus 1-2-3 Release 2.2 .WK1 file.

In some cases, Translate will display an informational screen about the translation. After reading the screen, press the <Esc> key to continue.

---

1. If you wish to use a Release 2.2 .WK1 file with Release 1A, you must first use the *Release 2.2* Translate program to convert it. Conversely, a Release 1A .WKS file may be /File Retrieved or /File Combined directly into a Release 2.2 worksheet.

2. dBASE III Plus and dBASE IV use virtually the same file format as dBASE III, so this choice will also translate those dBASE files.

Lotus 1-2-3 Release 2.2 Translate Utility
Copr. 1985, 1989 Lotus Development Corporation All Rights Reserved

What do you want to translate FROM?

1-2-3 1A
1-2-3 2, 2.01 or 2.2
dBase II
dBase III
DIF
Multiplan (SYLK)
Symphony 1.0
Symphony 1.1, 1.2 or 2.0
VisiCalc

Highlight your selection and press ENTER
Press ESC to end the Translate utility
Press HELP (F1) for more information

Figure 15-1 Specifying the Source File Type

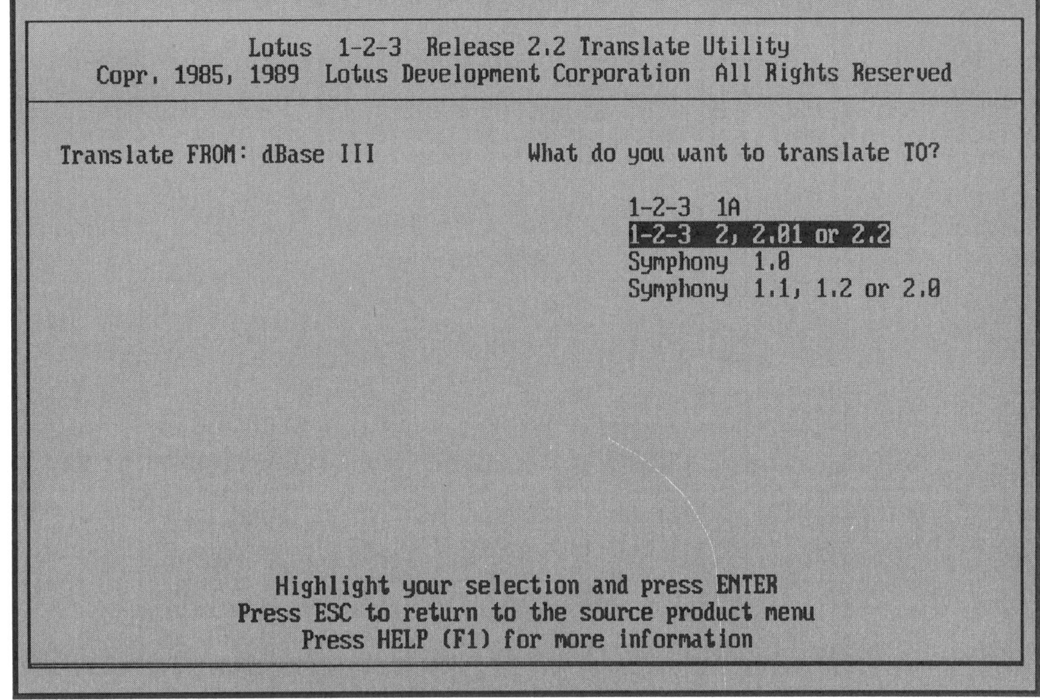

Figure 15-2 Specifying the Target File Type

```
            Lotus  1-2-3  Release 2.2 Translate Utility
   Copr. 1985, 1989  Lotus Development Corporation  All Rights Reserved

Translate FROM: dBase III              Translate TO: 1-2-3 2.2

Source file: A:\*.dbf

 MIL_BANK DBF   4/17/89   8:28a      5465

        ACCOUNTS DBF
        FIN_GOOD DBF
        HUSBANDS DBF
        MIL_BANK DBF
        MIX      DBF
        NAMELIST DBF
        ORDERS   DBF
        —More—

         Highlight the file you want to translate and press ENTER
             Press ESC to edit the source file specification
                   Press HELP (F1) for more information
```

Figure 15-3 Selecting the Source File

```
            Lotus  1-2-3  Release 2.2 Translate Utility
   Copr. 1985, 1989  Lotus Development Corporation  All Rights Reserved

Translate FROM: dBase III              Translate TO: 1-2-3 2.2

Source file: A:\MIL_BANK.DBF

Target file: A:\MIL_BANK.WK1

     Edit the target file specification if necessary and press ENTER
               Press ESC to select a different source file
                   Press HELP (F1) for more information
```

Figure 15-4 Specifying the Target File

Next, Translate displays a list of files of the appropriate source-type on the default disk drive. If there are no files of the appropriate type on the default drive/directory, the following error message is displayed:

```
Translate FROM: dBase III                    Translate TO: 1-2-3 2.2

Source file: C:\L022_INS\*.DBF

        No files were found that match the source file specification
                 If appropriate, insert a new disk and
                 press ENTER to search again, or press
                 ESC to edit source file specification.
```

Since the files to be translated are on the disk in drive A, I pressed the <Esc> key, then edited the drive/directory (to **A:*.DBF**). Then Translate lists all .DBF files (Figure 15-3). Use the arrow keys to move the menu pointer to select the source file. Translate suggests a target file name, which you can change or accept (Figure 15-4). Note that Translate will copy the file to the same disk that it is currently on unless you change the target file name. Press the <Enter> key to accept the suggested name, or use the usual keys to edit the name first.

Translate then asks you if you wish to proceed. As the file is translated, the program keeps your attention by displaying a bar graph showing progress:

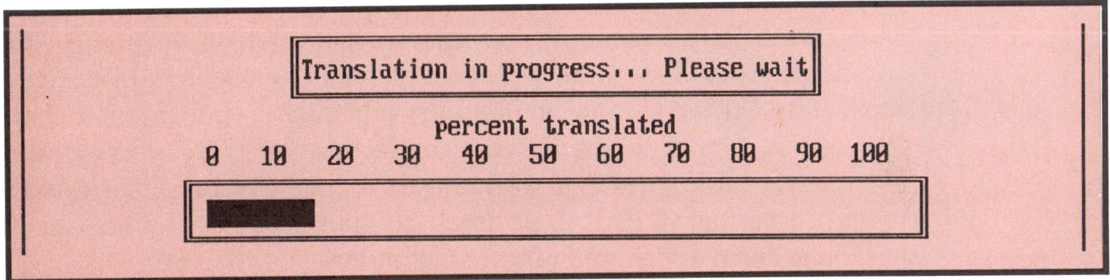

Upon completion, you can perform another translation of the same type, specify a different type of translation (e.g., from Lotus .WK1 to dBASE .DBF), or exit to the 1-2-3 Access System.

You now have a .WK1 (or .DBF or whatever) file that is essentially the same as the source .DBF (or .WK1 or whatever) file. Some VisiCalc functions and formulas do not transfer, nor do deleted dBASE records. As you use the program, it informs you via messages on the screen of other conditions that affect the final result.

To use your .WK1 file, simply return to the 1-2-3 Access System menu, select 1-2-3, and then /File **R**etrieve or /File **C**ombine. You probably need to do a bit of cleaning up of formats, etc., but this is far better than reentering all the data.

ASCII-GENERIC FORMATS

ASCII is the acronym for American Standard Code for Information Interchange. ASCII-generic formatted files are files in which the data is not in a special machine code, but rather in rows and/or columns of plain text. ASCII-generic files are created by BASIC programs as sequential files (but BASIC random access files are not ASCII-generic). WordStar (in the nondocument mode) and WordPerfect (using the

Text In/Out command) create ASCII-generic files. dBASE IV and other database managers can write an ASCII-generic file with commands such as **COPY TO . . . SDF** and **COPY TO . . . DELIMITED**. Also, anything you receive *over the wire* that is in text and numbers can probably be converted to an ASCII-generic format.

Lotus 1-2-3 generates ASCII-generic files when you use the /**P**rint **F**ile command.

If your file contains both text and numbers that you wish to include in your worksheet, you must edit the ASCII-generic file before loading it into 1-2-3, or use the /**D**ata **P**arse command discussed below. Text should be enclosed in double quotes (" . . . "), and text and numbers should be separated by spaces or commas. The file should have a .PRN extension; if it does not, rename it.

Once the file is edited, you are ready to import it into a 1-2-3 worksheet. First, you must be in the 1-2-3 worksheet mode. Move the pointer to the upper left corner of the region you wish the imported file to occupy. Enter the /**F**ile **I**mport command. The first question asks if you are importing text (only) or numbers (and text-labels). Then you type or point to the file name.

The results depend on whether you specified **T**ext or **N**umbers. For text, 1-2-3 creates a left-aligned label for each line in the print file. For numbers, 1-2-3 creates a number entry for each number and a left-aligned label for each " . . . " string. Each line in the print (imported) file generates a row on the worksheet. Anything else is ignored. You might need to experiment a bit to get the results you want.

/DATAPARSE AND ASCII FILE IMPORTATION

The /**D**ata **P**arse command works in conjunction with the /**F**ile **I**mport **T**ext command to make the importation of ASCII-generic data easier. This command separates (**parses**) imported data into value, date, time, and label entries based on a **format line**, and even helps create the format line. This command is useful to those who create tables and lists of numbers using other applications software (such as word processing, statistical, or database management systems), or who capture data in tabular format from mainframe computers.

For example, say you have a file of inventory data on a disk, with each line of the file beginning with a label followed by three numbers:

```
Generic Pet Type          Cost       Qty      Price
Parakeet                  0.99        10       4.99
Hamster                   1.25        15       6.95
Guppy                     0.03       200       0.98
```

You wish to bring these data into Lotus so you can calculate how much you have paid for your inventory and how much money you would make if you sell it all. Before entering Lotus, you renamed this file so it has a .PRN extension.

First, use the /**W**orksheet **E**rase command to give you a clean worksheet (remember to /**F**ile **S**ave before erasing). For this example, I moved the cell pointer to cell A6. Then I used /**F**ile **I**mport **T**ext to bring the file in as a series of labels. You create a column of label entries starting with the cell where the cell pointer was when the command was initiated. Cell A6 now contains the label

```
'Generic Pet Type          Cost       Qty      Price
```

and A7 contains the label

```
'Parakeet                          0.99         10          4.99
```

Keeping the cell pointer in the top cell of the column of imported data (that is, A6), give the **/Data Parse** command. You are presented with this submenu and **Parse Settings** screen:

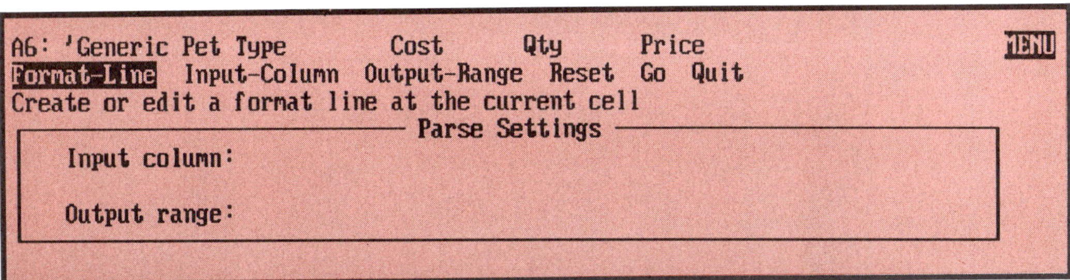

The first step in parsing is to create a format line. The format line is used in subsequent steps to tell Lotus how to divide the text data into label and value **blocks**, with each block occupying a different column in the worksheet after parsing. Lotus creates a "best guess" format line if you select the **F**ormat-Line option. This option yields two further options, **C**reate or **E**dit; choose **C**reate. Lotus inspects the label text in the current cell, creates a format line based on the data in that cell, displaces the text entries one row down, and places the proposed format line in the current cell. You can see the result in Figure 15-5. The data imported into cells A6..A9 have been pushed down one cell, and A6 now contains a format line. Format line symbols have the following meanings:

- L *first character of a label block.*
- V *first character of a value block.*
- D *first character of a date block.*
- T *first character of a time block.*
- S *skip the character below when parsing.*
- > *continuation of a block.*
- * *blank space, currently undefined, that can become part of the block to either side in cells below.*

As it creates the format line, Lotus analyzes each character in the input line. Lotus assumes that blanks separate blocks and replaces them in the format line by the * character. When a number is encountered after a blank, a value, date or time block is started with symbols V, D, or T. When a nonnumeric character is encountered, a label block is started with the L symbol. The block, of whatever type, is continued with > characters until another blank space is encountered.

Format line creation works reasonably well except when there are labels with embedded spaces in the line being analyzed. Note that Lotus separated `Generic Pet Type` into three separate blocks in the initial format line (illustrated in Figure 15-5). It was necessary to edit, using the **F**ormat-line **E**dit subcommand, to achieve the proper format line, which is illustrated in Figure 15-6. When editing format lines, the default is **overstrike** mode and an `OVR` indicator appears in the bottom right of the screen. To edit this particular format line, I moved the cursor to the first `*`, then pressed > (greater-than) signs until I reached the next asterisk. Once the line is edited, terminate editing by pressing <Enter>.

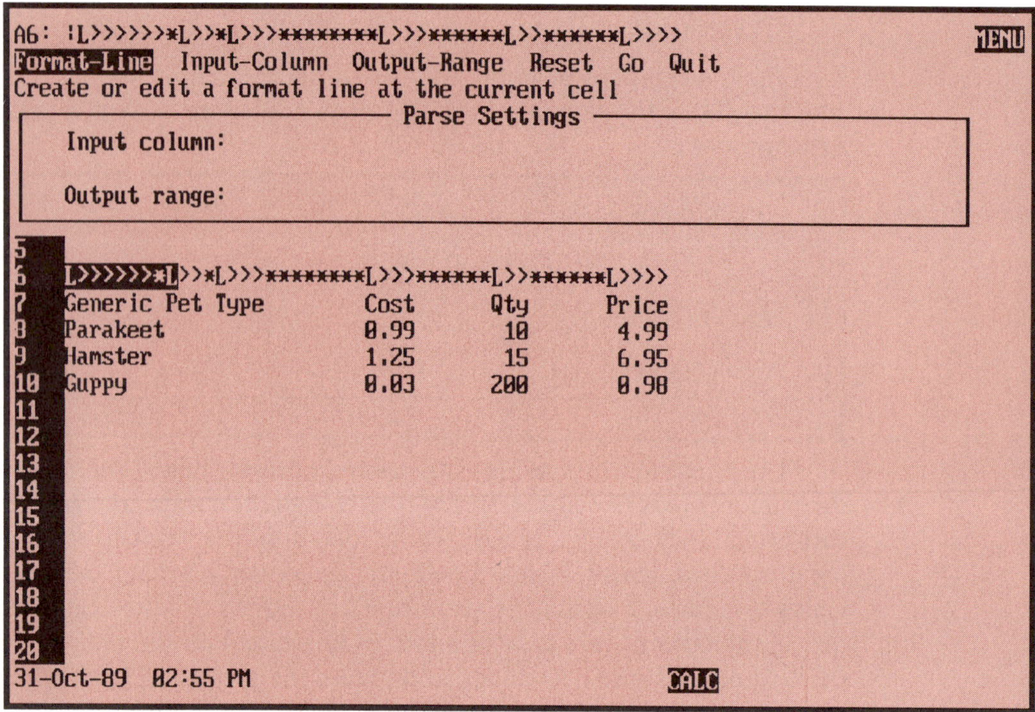

Figure 15-5 /DataParse Settings Screen and Initial Format Line

When you have label column headings over numeric data columns, as in this example, it is necessary to create a second format line, as shown in Figure 15-6. To do so, Quit from the /Data Parse menu, move the cell pointer to the top cell of the next type of column (thus, I moved the cell pointer to A8, the first row that contains numeric data), and give the /Data Parse Format-Line Create command again. This second format line did not require editing.

Once format lines are created and edited, the Input-Column should be specified. The input column is the range containing the format line(s) and all rows of text to be parsed. In this situation, the range was specified as A6..A11. The Output-Range is identified by the upper left cell in the output range (in this case, A15). Finally, the Go option parses the data according to the format line(s) and fills the output range with the data. I had to adjust the width of Column A (using the /Worksheet Column Set-Width command) because the labels in that column were wider than the default width. Note, in Figure 15-6, that the column width of 17 is displayed as `[W17]` in the control panel area when the cell pointer points at a cell in that column. In addition, I used the /Range Label Right command on cells B15..D15 to right-justify the headings over those columns.

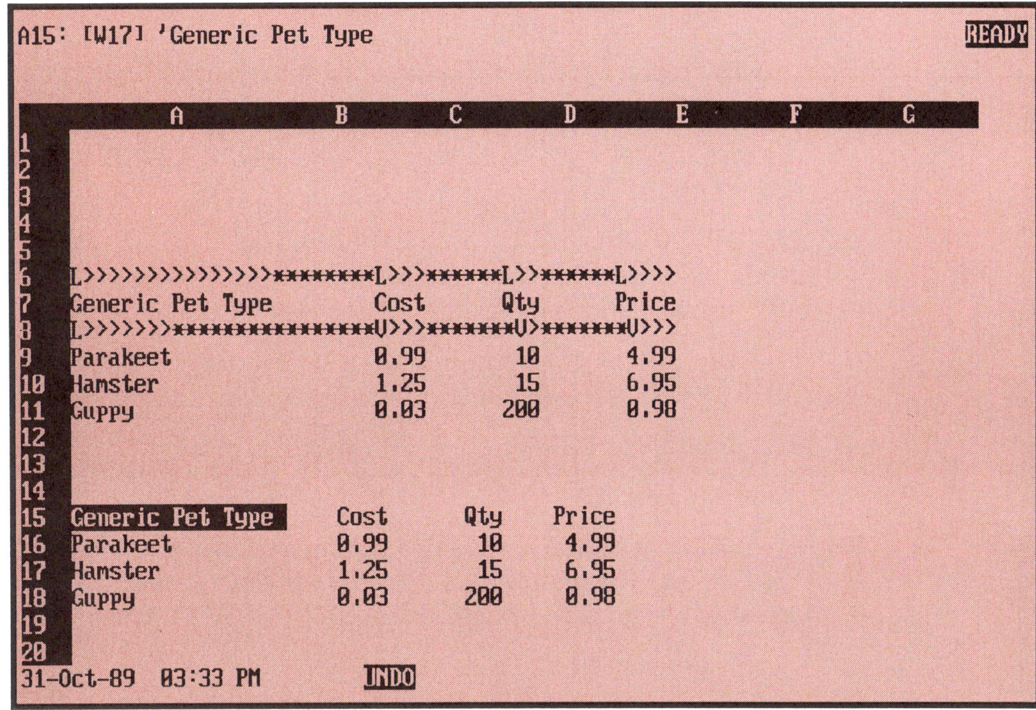

Figure 15-6 Result of /DataParse Command and Additional Editing

Although the /**D**ata **P**arse command might seem difficult, it is by far the easiest way to import tabular ASCII data. On the other hand, when the source of the data can create output in a delimited form (quotes ["] around labels, and commas [,] between data items), /**D**ata **P**arse is not necessary: the data can be directly imported using the /**F**ile **I**mport **N**umbers command. Both dBASE and BASIC can write disk files in this format.

EXPORTING DATA FROM 1-2-3

There are two ways to export data from Lotus 1-2-3 worksheets. The first uses Translate, discussed above. The second uses /**P**rint **F**ile to create an ASCII-generic file that can be directly imported into word processors such as WordStar. These files can also be imported into dBASE III and other database managers if both worksheet and database are structured alike.

/**P**rint **F**ile works just like the more common /**P**rint **P**rinter command. It is generally best, however, to set /**P**rint . . . **O**ptions **O**ther **U**nformatted before printing to eliminate margins and page breaks in the output. These usually cause problems when the file is read later by the other program.

GUIDED ACTIVITY: FILE IMPORT AND EXPORT

This activity requires you to use several file importing and exporting commands.

1. Check your data disk to ensure that it contains the file PETS.PRN (which should have been copied to the disk when you started Part 3). Load Lotus and enter the 1-2-3 program.
2. PETS.PRN is an ASCII file in tabular form. Use the /**F**ile **I**mport **T**ext and /**D**ata **P**arse commands to import the file into your worksheet, starting at location A6, and convert the data to cell entries starting in A15, as discussed above.
3. Use the /**P**rint **F**ile command to print the worksheet to a file named PETS2.PRN (as usual, Lotus automatically supplies the file extension).
4. Save your file as PETS.
5. /**Q**uit and Exit.
6. If you have access to a word processing package, use that package to read the file PETS2.PRN and edit as directed by your instructor. If you do not have access to a word processing package, give the DOS command

   type b:pets2.prn

   to see the result of the /**P**rint **F**ile operation. You will see that Lotus does not print the format lines. That is because any line with a | as the first character is not printed.

REVIEW QUESTIONS

1.* What is the difference between program-specific and ASCII-generic file formats, and how does that difference affect the interchange of data between Lotus and other programs?

2. What other applications software programs are available to you? How can you transfer data between them and Lotus 1-2-3?

DOCUMENTATION RESEARCH

Using the reference manual, find and record the page number of each of the commands discussed in this unit. I recommend you also write the page number by the discussion of the command, above.

1. /**D**ata **P**arse — what is the effect of the **S** character in a format line?
2. /**F**ile **I**mport — what is the effect of a blank line in the file being imported?
3. /**P**rint **F**ile — what effect do current margins have on the resulting file?

UNIT 16

ADVANCED FUNCTIONS

We introduced arithmetic operators and several of the Lotus functions in Unit 3. In this unit, we complete the presentation of operators and functions by discussing lookup tables, string expressions, logical expressions, and advanced mathematical functions.

LEARNING OBJECTIVES

At the completion of this unit, you should be able to

a. design a lookup table,
b. use the lookup functions to extract data from the table,
c. write formulas using logical functions and expressions,
d. write formulas using string functions and expressions,
e. write formulas using advanced mathematical functions.

LOOKUP TABLES

A **lookup table** is a table from which we draw information based on an index number. Most of us are familiar with the concept of such a table, perhaps with a different name. Consider the following examples:

(grades)
0 to 69 = F
70 to 76 = D
77 to 84 = C
85 to 92 = B
93 to 100 = A

(taxes)

if taxable income is over:	but not over:	tax is	of the amount over
0	3,400	0	
3,400	5,500	11%	3,400
5,500	7,600	231 + 12%	5,500
7,600	11,900	483 + 14%	7,600
etc.			

(sales)

Stock no.	Description	Cost	Price
10985	84 Pontiac SW	10000	13950
12000	85 GMC PU	9000	11350
13488	85 Cadillac Cp	14000	19450
etc.			

Each of these examples has a few characteristics in common:

1. An **index** (minimum score, minimum income, stock no.) in the left-hand column that allows us to find data relevant to that index (grade, tax rate, cost, price).
2. The index is a value (not a label).
3. There are no duplicate index values.
4. The table is sorted in ascending index value order.

We can use the @VLOOKUP(x,range,offset) function to extract data from the tables above. In this function, *x* is the index, and can be a constant, a cell reference, or another function. For instance, we might have taxable income in cell B1, which has the range name of INCOME. *Range* is a named or specified (by cell addresses) range. Assume that we have put a tax table in range A8..C11 named TABLEY. *Offset* is the number of columns to the right of the index column (offset for the index column is 0 [zero]).

A worksheet with this example appears in Figure 16-1. Part of the formula in B3 is not visible in that figure; the complete formula is

```
@VLOOKUP(INCOME,TABLEY,1)+@VLOOKUP(INCOME,TABLEY,2)*(INCOME-@VLOOKUP(INCOME,TABLEY,0))
```

For intellectual exercise, you are encouraged to determine how and why this formula works.

Where the *x* (index) argument is not matched exactly, the row chosen by @VLOOKUP is the last row in which the index (left) column value is less than the index argument value. This is generally the desired effect, as in the tax example.

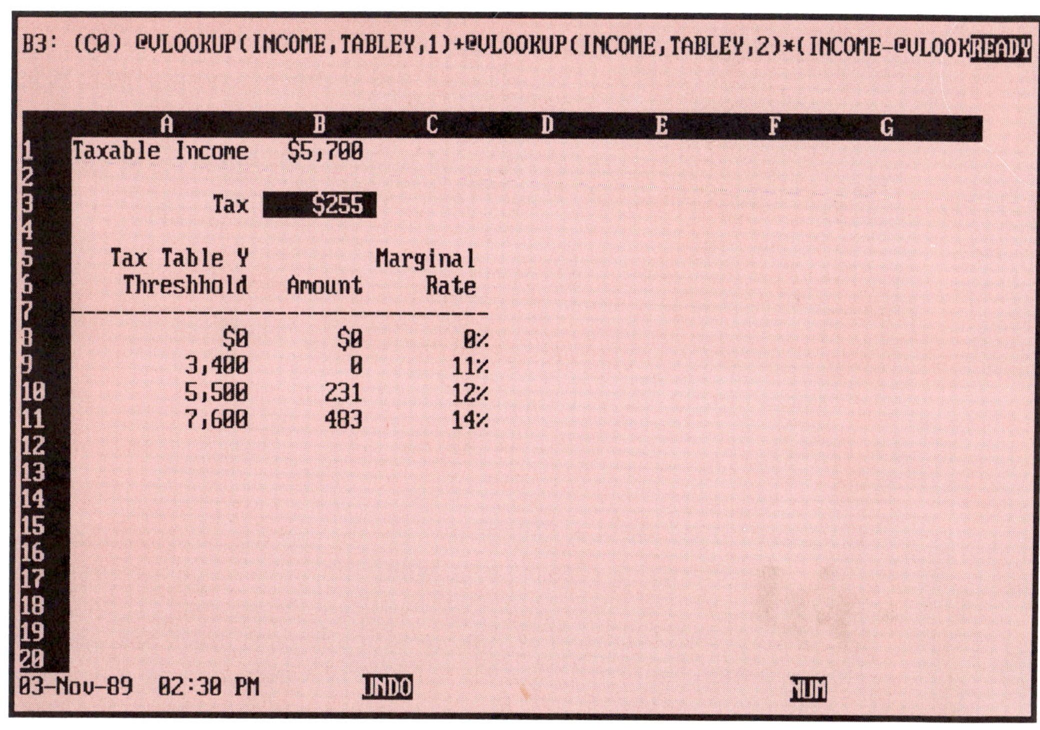

Figure 16-1 Worksheet with a Lookup Table

@VLOOKUP is one of four **choice functions**. The complete set is as follows:

@CHOOSE(x,v0,v1, . . . vn) *select value*: if *x* = 0, then the cell containing this function displays value *v0*; if *x* = 1, then the cell displays value *v1*; and so forth. *x* and *v0 . . . vn* can be constants, other cell addresses, or functions.

@HLOOKUP(x,range,offset) *table lookup with index row*: this function is used to select a value from a table based on the value of *x*.

@VLOOKUP(x,range,offset) *table lookup with index column*.

@INDEX(range,col,row) *value of cell at intersection*: this yields the value of the cell in *range*, *row* rows from the top and *col* columns from the left. For instance, @INDEX(A1..C9,0,0) returns the value of A1, while the result of @INDEX(A1..C9,K3,J9) depends on the values of K3 and J9 as well as the values in the range A1..C9.

GUIDED ACTIVITY: A LOOKUP TABLE

This activity requires you to build a lookup table.

1. Follow the startup procedure outlined in Unit 1 to load Lotus and enter the 1-2-3 program.

2. Build the tax example lookup table discussed above. The worksheet should look like Figure 16-1. In addition to entering the labels, values, and @VLOOKUP formula, you must also adjust the width of column A and name two ranges (INCOME and TABLEY).
3. Once the worksheet is complete, test the function by entering the following numbers in cell B1. Check the function by computing the tax by hand.
   a. **5700**
   b. **3400**
   c. **9000**
4. Save your work with the file name INC_TAX.

LOGICAL EXPRESSIONS

Logical expressions are cell entries combining logical functions and logical operators. Logical expressions are used when the value to be assigned to a cell is dependent on the value of one or more other cells.

There are several situations in which logical functions are necessary. For instance, a merchant might keep a list of credit accounts on a worksheet. One of the columns is the balance due on the account and another is the minimum payment. The minimum payment is one of the following:

- The balance due, if the balance due is less than $20.
- $20, if the balance due is between $20 and $200.
- 10% of the balance due if the balance due is over $200.

As another example, consider the payroll of a small manufacturer. Most employees are paid overtime at the rate of 1.5 times their hourly wage if they work more than 40 hours per week. A few employees, in *Exempt* status, are not eligible for overtime regardless of how many hours they work.

We use these two examples to illustrate the use of logical operators and functions, but first, lists of the operators and functions must be presented.

LOGICAL OPERATORS

The logical operators are as follows. There are three levels of precedence, with the top group (=, <, etc.) having the highest precedence.

Highest Precedence	
=	*Equal to.*
<	*Less than.*
<=	*Less than or equal to.*
>	*Greater than.*
>=	*Greater than or equal to.*
<>	*Not equal to.*

Middle Precedence	
#NOT#	*Logical not* (inverse).

Lowest Precedence

#AND# *Logical and* (both of).

#OR# *Logical or* (either of).

SPECIAL FUNCTIONS

Lotus provides two special functions:

@NA *not available*; sets the value of the cell to NA.

@ERR *error*; sets the value of the cell to ERR. Any cell that depends on this cell via a formula also has the value ERR.

LOGICAL FUNCTIONS

The following logical functions deal with results that can be categorized as true or false.

@FALSE *false*, 0 (zero).

@TRUE *true*, 1 (one).

@IF(cond,x,y) *if the condition is true or not equal to zero, then x; if the condition is false or equal to zero, then y.*

@ISNUMBER(x) *1 (TRUE) if content of x is a value.* Values are generated by numeric entries, formulas, most functions (including @NA and @ERR), and blank cells, which are considered a numeric 0 (zero).

@ISSTRING(x) *1 (TRUE) if content of x is a string (label).* Strings are generated by label entries and the string functions discussed below.

@ISNA(x) *1 (TRUE) if content of x is NA.*

@ISERR(x) *1 (TRUE) if content of x is ERR.*

1-2-3 considers any value that is not equal to zero to be TRUE. The value zero and any formula that yields the result zero is FALSE.

An @IF statement might look like **@IF(a1,b1,c1)**, which means that the cell containing the @IF statement has the value of cell B1 if cell A1 < > 0, and the value of cell C1 if cell A1 = 0.

Another possible @IF statement would be **@IF(a1>a2,b1,c1)**, which takes the value of B1 if A1>A2; otherwise, it takes the value of C1.

Examples of cell entries using logical operators and special and logical functions:

@IF(A1>0,A5,@ERR) yields the value of A5 if A1 is greater than 0; otherwise is ERR.

@IF(@ISERR(C9),A5,0) yields the value of A5 if C9 is ERR; otherwise is 0 (zero).

@IF(A2=A8#AND#A3=A9,@TRUE,@ERR)

yields the value TRUE (1) if both A2=A8 and A3=A9; otherwise is ERR. Because of the order of precedence, the equivalences are evaluated first, then the logical #AND# is evaluated.

When writing complex expressions such as these, it is a good idea to test them with dummy data before entrusting the fortunes of the company to your ability to think logically.

EXAMPLES

The two situations outlined earlier, overtime and minimum payment, are evaluated here.

Overtime. Consider the payroll of a small manufacturer. Most employees are paid overtime at the rate of 1.5 times their hourly wage if they work more than 40 hours per week. A few employees, in *Exempt* status, are not eligible for overtime regardless of how many hours they work.

In this worksheet (illustrated in Figure 16-2), each employee is listed on a separate row. Name and ID number are in columns A and B, the hourly rate is in column C, the exempt status is in column D, and the total hours worked in column E (NOTE: This is *not* the same as the timekeeper's worksheet discussed in Unit 13). Columns A and B are labels, columns C and E are numbers, column D is a series of @TRUE (for exempt) and @FALSE (for nonexempt) entries.

The number of regular hours is computed in column F and the pay for those hours in column G. The number of overtime hours, if any, is computed in column H and the overtime pay, for those who are not exempt, is computed in column I. The following entries would be made in row 2, the first row of data:

- In cell F2: **@IF(D2,E2,@MIN(40,E2))** This translates as follows: If the employee is an exempt employee (i.e., D2 is @TRUE), then all hours (in E2) are regular hours. If the employee is nonexempt, then the number of regular hours is 40 hours or the number of hours worked, whichever is less.
- In cell G2: **+C2*F2** This is the hourly rate times the number of regular hours worked.
- In cell H2: **+E2-F2** This is the difference between total hours (in E2) and those hours that are regular hours. For exempt employees and those nonexempt employees who work 40 hours or less, this is 0 (zero).
- In cell I2: **1.5*C2*H2** This is one and one-half times the hourly rate times the number of overtime hours.

Corresponding entries would be made in the remaining rows of the worksheet. The key to this application is column F. Study the formula carefully. This example is incorporated in the Guided Activity that follows this section.

F2: (F0) [W10] @IF(D2,E2,@MIN(40,E2)) READY

	A	B	C	D	E	F	G	H	I
1	Name	ID No.	Rate	Exempt	Hours	Reg. Hrs.	Reg. Pay	OT Hrs.	OT Pay
2	Walker	13-100	10.00	0	32	32	320.00	0	0.00
3	Xavier	13-108	12.90	0	48	40	516.00	8	154.80
4	Young	01-004	35.00	1	60	60	2100.00	0	0.00
5	Zedeck	02-025	15.00	1	32	32	480.00	0	0.00
6									
7									
8									
9									
10									
11									
12									
13									
14									
15									
16									
17									
18									
19									
20									

03-Nov-89 02:48 PM UNDO NUM

Figure 16-2 The Overtime Worksheet

Minimum Payment. Recall the merchant who keeps a list of credit accounts on a worksheet. In column B is the balance due on the account and in column C is the minimum payment. The minimum payment is one of

- The balance due, if the balance due is less than $20.
- $20, if the balance due is between $20 and $200.
- 10% of the balance due if the balance due is over $200.

Assume that the first row of data is row 2. When there are three choices, as above, we usually need nested @IF statements, that is, one @IF statement contained as an argument to another @IF statement. The trick to building this logic is to momentarily ignore one of the options.

First we write the statement that accomplishes the first condition and part of the second condition:

```
@IF(B2<20,B2,20)
```

Then we include that expression as the false condition argument in an @IF statement dealing with the second and third conditions:

```
@IF(B2>200,.10*B2,@IF(B2<20,B2,20))
```

This can be read as *If the value of B2 (the balance due) is greater than 200, then display 10% of B2; otherwise, if the value of B2 is less than 20, display B2; otherwise display 20.*

GUIDED ACTIVITY: LOGICAL FUNCTIONS

This activity requires you to use logical functions.

1. If you are not continuing from the previous Guided Activity, load Lotus. If you are continuing from the previous Guided Activity, save INC_TAX one last time, then use the /Worksheet Erase command to clear the screen.
2. Build a spreadsheet like that illustrated in Figure 16-2:
   a. All entries in row 1 are labels: A1 and B1 are left-justified; C1..I1 are right-justified.
   b. Adjust the columns widths so columns A through I are visible and all labels in row 1 are readable (you must widen column F and you can make several columns narrower).
   c. The entries in columns A and B are labels, those in columns C and E (below row 1) are values, and those in column D are either @TRUE or @FALSE.
   d. Enter the formulas, discussed in the preceding section, in F2..I2. If you do not obtain the results illustrated in Figure 16-2, carefully check your work.
   e. The formulas can be copied to the range F3..I5.
   f. Format numeric entries to match the illustration.
3. The completed spreadsheet should look like Figure 16-2.
4. Save this worksheet with the name OVERTIME.

STRING REFERENCE, MANIPULATION, AND FUNCTIONS

The ability to refer to and manipulate labels (**strings**) in functions allows you to develop more sophisticated worksheets. A logical formula can return a string. The label contents of a cell can be referred to by another cell. Labels can be entered as usual in cells, but labels used in formulas must be enclosed in double quotation marks (" . . . "). Two labels are combined (**concatenated**) with the & operator. For instance, if cell A1 contains the label `'United Consolidated Industries` and cell F9 contains the label `' Overdrawn`, then

The cell entry **`+A1`**	displays the contents of cell A1 — `United Consolidated Industries` — in the current cell.
The cell entry **`+A1&F9`**	yields `United Consolidated Industries Overdrawn`
The cell entry **`+A1&" Ltd."`**	yields `United Consolidated Industries Ltd.`

The entry **@IF(J1>K1,J1-K1,F9)**
yields the difference if J1 is greater than K1; otherwise, yields `Overdrawn.`

This feature permits you to use the same worksheet to analyze a different company by simply changing the contents of A1, which changes the result displayed by all cells that reference A1. Several functions are provided to further enhance use of string data.

@CHAR(x) *character whose ASCII value is x.* This is often used to create characters that are not directly accessible on the keyboard. For instance, **@CHAR(189)** displays ½ on the screen.[1]

@CODE(string) *ASCII value of first character in string.*

@EXACT(string1,string2) *exact equivalence of two strings*, where exact equivalence includes capitalization. Use of the = operator also checks for equivalence, but ignores capitalization. For instance, if C35 contains `'Polish` and J35 contains `'polish,` then **@IF(C35=J35,@TRUE,@FALSE)** is TRUE; while **@EXACT(C35,J35)** is FALSE.

@FIND(search string,string,start number) *location of search string in another string.* This is used to determine position of the *search string* in the *string*, starting with character at *start number*.

@LEFT(string,n) *first n characters of string.*

@LENGTH(string) *number of characters in string.*

@LOWER(string) *lowercase conversion.* This converts all characters in *string* to lowercase and displays the result. It could be used before an @EXACT comparison. Following above example, **@EXACT(@LOWER(C35),J35)** is TRUE.

@MID(string,start number,length) *middle characters from string*, starting at *start number*, proceeding for *length* characters.

@N(range) *label to value conversion.* This converts label in upper left corner of range to numeric type, with value of 0 (zero), allowing numeric formulas to reference cells that might or might not contain labels.[2] This is often a problem in accounting worksheets, where a balance is computed by adding the previous balance to the current net. In the first period, the cell that would normally contain the previous balance contains a label. (Figure F-1 [page 204] contains an example of this situation.) If the balances are in row 26 and the net amounts are in row 25, the following formula would compute the proper balance for column B and could be copied across the

---

1. Lotus selects characters from the **Lotus International Character Set** (LICS) which is discussed in Appendix 2 of the Lotus *Reference Manual*. These characters differ from the extended character set built into the IBM PC and compatibles.

2. Because Lotus Releases after 2.0 consider any cell with a label to have the numeric value 0 (zero), this function need not be used if you are using Release 2.2.

worksheet: **@N(A26..A26)+B25**. This function converts only one cell, the upper left cell in the range, regardless of the size of the range specified. See also @VALUE.

@PROPER(string) *proper capitalization*. This capitalizes the first letter of each word in *string*. See example in next function.

@REPEAT(string,n) *repeat string*. This repeats the *string n* times. The following example is inspired by the Reference Manual:

@PROPER("SHE LOVES YOU, "&@REPEAT("YEAH ",3))

yields `She Loves You, Yeah Yeah Yeah`

@REPLACE(original string,start number,n,new string) *replace text in string with new string*. This replaces *text* in original string, beginning at character *start number*, for *n* characters, with *new string*.

@RIGHT(string,n) *last n characters in string*.

@S(range) *value to label conversion*. This turns values into empty labels so they can be used in string functions. The only use of this function appears to be prevention of an error caused by referencing a value cell with a string function or operator. As with @CELL, single cell ranges require special notation. This function converts only one cell, the upper left cell in the range, regardless of the size of the range specified. See @STRING for conversion of value to string data.

@STRING(value,n) *value to label conversion*. This creates a string out of a number, allowing specification of *n* decimal places. For instance, if cell X13 contains the current year as a value (e.g., 1990), you could concatenate that to a label entry: **+"Results for "&@STRING(X13,0)**

@TRIM(string) *remove excess spaces*. This removes leading and trailing space characters and converts multiple embedded spaces to single spaces.

@UPPER(string) *uppercase conversion*. This converts all characters in string to uppercase and displays the result.

@VALUE(string) *label to value conversion*. This converts any of the following to values that can be used in numeric computations: **@VALUE("13 3/5")** yields `13.6`; **@VALUE(K9)** yields `10` if cell K9 contains **'10**; **@VALUE("TV")** yields ERR (error).

CELL AND RANGE REFERENCE FUNCTIONS

The functions in this group are used to determine information about the cells and ranges of a worksheet. In general, their use is beyond the scope of this manual.

@@(cell address) *value of cell referenced by cell at cell address*. This allows one cell to reference another cell that contains a value. For instance, if F9 contains the label entry **'K9** and cell K9 contains the value **100**, then a cell containing the function **@@(F9)** would also display the value `100`.

@CELL(attribute,range) *attribute of range*, where range attributes include type of data, contents of cell, numeric format, protection status, and several others. Consult the reference manual for more information and a list of all the attributes. If you want information about a single cell, the *range* must be specified as either **A1..A1** or **!A1**, e.g., **@CELL("FORMAT",!A1)**.

@CELLPOINTER(attribute) *attribute of current cell*, i.e., the attribute (such as address) of the cell where the cell pointer was at the time of the last recalculation.

@COLS(range) *number of columns in a range*: most useful when used with named ranges.

@ROWS(range) *number of rows in a range*: again, most useful when analyzing named ranges.

ADVANCED MATHEMATICAL FUNCTIONS

Lotus provides a number of functions oriented to engineering and other non-business mathematical applications. They are listed here should you have need of them in your academic or professional life.

The terms in parentheses that follow a function are called **arguments** of the function. In the examples below, *x* can be a cell, a constant value, a formula, or another function. For instance, @ABS(x) could be either **@ABS(a10)**, **@ABS(5029)**, **@ABS(a10-b12)**, or **@ABS(@TAN(g9))**.

@ABS(x) *absolute value of x*.

@ACOS(x) *arc cosine of x*, the angle in radians whose cosine is *x*. If *x* is not between -1 and +1, the value is ERR. To convert radians to degrees, multiply [radians]*180/π: for example, if cell H8 contains a cosine, then the angle in degrees is determined by the function **@ACOS(H8)*180/@PI**.

@ASIN(x) *arc sine of x*, the angle in radians whose sine is *x*. If *x* is not between -1 and +1, the value is ERR. To convert radians to degrees, multiply [radians]*180/π: see @ACOS(x) above for an example.

@ATAN(x) *arc tangent of x*, the angle in radians whose tangent is *x*. To convert radians to degrees, multiply [radians]*180/π: see @ACOS(x) above for an example.

@ATAN2(x,y) *arc tangent of y/x*, the angle in radians whose tangent is *y/x*. See the manual for the distinction between this and @ATAN(x). To convert radians to degrees, multiply [radians]*180/π: see @ACOS(x) above for an example.

@COS(x) *cosine of x in radians*. To convert degrees to radians, multiply [degrees]*π/180: for example, if cell G12 has a number in degrees, then the function is **@COS(G12*@PI/180)**.

@EXP(x) *exponential*: e^x.

@INT(x) *integer part of x.* The cell entry **@INT(2.95)** yields the value 2. The cell entry **@INT(-2.95)** yields the value -2.

@LN(x) *log_e of x.*

@LOG(x) *log_{10} of x.*

@MOD(x,y) *x mod y: modular part* (remainder) of *x/y.* The cell entry **@MOD(6,4)** yields the value 2.

@PI π is 3.141592653589794

@RAND *random number* between 0 and 1.

@ROUND(x,n) *round number x to n decimal places.*

@SIN(x) *sine of x in radians.* To convert degrees to radians, multiply [degrees]*π/180: see @COS(x) above for an example.

@SQRT(x) *square root of x.*

@TAN(x) *tangent of x in radians.* To convert degrees to radians, multiply [degrees]*π/180: see @COS(x) above for an example.

EXERCISE: LOOKING UP A STRING VALUE

In this exercise you construct a simple worksheet that looks up a string value.

1. Start with a clear worksheet.
2. Build a worksheet with a lookup table for the assignment of grades, using the cutoff values in the example on page 225. Put the table in cells J1..K5. Assign the name CUTOFF to the table range.
3. Enter the following data in A1..B5:

```
Name      Score
John         92
Paul         73
George       88
Ringo        77
```

4. In C1, enter the label **Grade**. In C2, enter a lookup function that computes John's grade based on his score. For the *range* in the function, use **$CUTOFF**. The $ instructs Lotus to treat the range as an absolute set of references whenever you /Copy the formula. Once the function is working properly (you might test it by changing John's grade to a different number, but remember to change it back to the original 92), /Copy the formula to the other students. You should have their grades instantly.
5. Save your work with the file name GRADES.

EXERCISE: ANOTHER LOGICAL EXERCISE

In this exercise you construct a simple worksheet that uses a logical formula to compute a minimum payment due.

1. Start with a clear worksheet.
2. Make the following entries in A1..C4:

```
Name          Bal Due  Min Pay
Jones             255
Smith              15
Kaczmierk         145
```

3. Following the discussion of "Minimum Payment" on page 231, create a logical function that computes the minimum payment for each of these. (Develop the function in C2, **/**Copy it to C3..C4.)
4. Save this worksheet with the name MINPAY.

REVIEW QUESTIONS

1.* Cells H19 and J19 contain two numbers. Write a logical formula that yields -1 if H19 is not greater than J19, +1 otherwise.

2.* Cell K9 contains a number. Write a logical formula that yields 100 if K9 is greater than zero, NA if K9 equals zero, and ERR if K9 is less than zero. (HINT: The formula has one @IF contained within another @IF.)

DOCUMENTATION RESEARCH

Using the reference manual, find and record the page number of each of the functions discussed in this unit. Write the page number by the discussion of the function, above.

1. What is the maximum value of @ACOS(x)?
2. What are the possible arguments to the function @TRUE?
3. What is the result of a @VLOOKUP function if the index argument is less than the first value in the range?

UNIT 17

MACRO COMMANDS

Macro commands are used for four main purposes: for a repeated entry (i.e., a label that appears in several places on the worksheet); for a repeated command (i.e., a command such as a format command that is used in several places on the worksheet); for a repeated procedure (i.e., a series of commands, such as setting width or setting numeric format and label alignment in a column); and for programming commands (i.e., commands to build a specialized menu and to execute different commands based on menu choice).

LEARNING OBJECTIVES

1. At the completion of this unit, you should know the uses of macro commands.
2. At the completion of this unit, you should be able to
   a. write a macro command for repeated data entry,
   b. write a macro command for repeated command execution,
   c. write a macro command program,
   d. use the learn and step features in macro development.

IMPORTANT COMMANDS

/**R**ange **N**ame **C**reate
/**W**orksheet **L**earn

MACRO COMMANDS

CREATING MACRO COMMANDS

Before they can be used, macros must be created. Macro creation is a two-step process: Enter the macro as a label into one or more spreadsheet cells, then name the range containing the macro. If the macro is lengthy, it can be put into several contiguous cells in the same column; Lotus executes macro instructions from the point of entry until it reaches a blank cell in the column below the point of entry. I usually place macro commands to the right (<Tab> over one or more screens) or below (<PgDn> one or more screens) the main worksheet area. *Make sure that the first cell in the column below the macro is blank.*

You can also "teach" Lotus a macro command by having it record each key pressed as you "demonstrate" the command. This feature is discussed in the section entitled "The Learn Feature" later in this unit.

NAMING MACRO COMMANDS

Once the macro is entered, the top cell of the macro must be named using the /**R**ange **N**ame **C**reate command. Most of the time, you wish to execute the macro from the keyboard. To do so, give the macro a name starting with the \ (**backslash**) character (*not* the / [**frontslash** or **slash**] character!) and one additional character, which is one of the letters of the alphabet. Examples: \A \G \F \c \k, etc. The letters can be entered as upper- or lowercase. Lotus converts them to uppercase. The only nonletter character permissible as a macro name is 0 (zero). A macro named \0 is executed automatically whenever you /**F**ile **R**etrieve the worksheet. If you want to check your macro later, you can locate it quickly by pressing <GOTO (F5)> followed by <NAME (F3)>. The macro ranges appear at the end of the list of range names.

A macro can be assigned any legitimate range name (i.e., multiple characters such as `DATAINP`), not just backslash-single character combinations. The next section tells you how to execute macros with either type of name.

INVOKING MACRO COMMANDS

Once the macro is created and named, it can be invoked by pressing the <Alt> key and the letter. (Hold down the <Alt> key while pressing the letter key.) For instance, to invoke the macro named \Z, you press <Alt-Z>. Whatever you have entered into the cell (range) named \Z is executed.

To invoke a macro with a multiple-character name from the keyboard, you must use the <RUN (Alt-F3)> function key. After pressing <RUN (Alt-F3)>, a list of all named ranges is presented:

Highlight the name of the macro to run and press <Enter>. The macro will be executed.

EXAMPLES OF MACRO COMMANDS

REPEATED LABEL

Suppose that you are making a worksheet and that you must enter the label `'General Fiduciary` in several places on that worksheet. You decide to use a macro to save some typing.

1. Move to an empty area of the worksheet, say cell X1.

2. Type the following in X1: **'General Fiduciary~** <Enter>.
   Note: <Enter> is the keyboard key.
3. Name the range \M using these keystrokes: **/RNC\m**<Enter> <Enter>.
4. Go to wherever you want General Fiduciary to appear.
5. Invoke the macro by pressing <Alt-M>.

You can now move to other places and put General Fiduciary in those places by typing <Alt-M>. This macro stays with the worksheet when you /File Save and returns with the worksheet when you /File Retrieve.

The ~ (**tilde**) character in the macro above indicates where the <Enter> key is pressed during macro execution. As usual, you press <Enter> after typing the text of the macro to enter what you have typed in the status line into the cell. (You can also terminate the entry by pressing one of the arrow keys, as usual.) Almost all keyboard macros need a ~ character to terminate them; the major exceptions are those that end with a cursor movement instruction, such as in the following example.

REPEATED COMMAND

Suppose that you wanted to set the width of several columns to 12 characters. You could give the /Worksheet Column Set-Width command several times, or you could build a macro. Before you build a command macro, you should execute the command once, taking careful notes of every key you press. Then you can create the macro.

1. Move to an empty area of the worksheet, say, cell Z1.
2. Type the following in Z1: **'/wcs12~{right}**<Enter>.
   Note, <Enter> is the keyboard key, **{right}** *is typed by you.*
3. Name the range \C using these keystrokes: **/RNC\c**<Enter><Enter>.
4. Move to wherever you want to set the column width to 12.
5. Invoke the macro by pressing <Alt-C>.

To enter a command into a cell, we must enter it as a label. That means that a label-alignment character (one of ' " or ^) must be typed, as above. If the label-alignment character is not typed, Lotus thinks you are executing a command.

This macro sets the width of the column the cursor is in to 12, then moves the cursor one column to the right. If you have ten columns together that you want to set to 12 columns wide, you simply press <Alt-C> ten times.

The preceding two examples used special key indicators (~ and {right}). These are the method of indicating to Lotus that you want the effect of pressing a special keyboard key in the macro command. A complete list of these indicators appears in Table 17-1. To achieve multiple "presses" of the key, include a number inside the braces: **{right 4}**

Table 17-1 Special Key Indicators for Macro Commands

Macro Entry	Keyboard Equivalent	Macro Entry	Keyboard Equivalent
~	<Enter> key	{up}	<Up> arrow
{down}	<Down> arrow	{left}	<Left> arrow
{right}	<Right> arrow	{home}	<Home> key
{end}	<End> key	{pgup}	<PgUp> key
{pgdn}	<PgDn> key	{esc}	<Esc> key
{del}	<Del> key	{bs}	<Backspace> key
{help}	<HELP (F1)> (function key 1)	{edit}	<EDIT (F2)>
{name}	<NAME (F3)>	{abs}	<ABS (F4)>
{goto}	<GOTO (F5)>	{window}	<WINDOW (F6)>
{query}	<QUERY (F7)>	{table}	<TABLE (F8)>
{calc}	<CALC (F9)>	{graph}	<GRAPH (F10)>
{~}	~ (not interpreted as <Enter>)	{{}	{
{}}	}	{bigright}	<Tab> key
{bigleft}	<Shift-Tab>		

REPEATED COMMAND

As a final example, assume that you want to print a specific range on your worksheet. You must use /**R**ange **N**ame **C**reate to name the range (e.g., OREGON) and then enter and name the following macro: **'/pproregon~gq**. Take a moment to decipher this macro. What does /ppr accomplish? Why is there a ~ (i.e., an <Enter>) after the range name? What does gq accomplish?

THE LEARN FEATURE

With the **learn** feature, Lotus provides the mechanism for developing a macro through demonstration. In short, you instruct Lotus to capture a series of keystrokes in a range of the worksheet as you execute a command. The next time you need to execute the command, simply tell Lotus to repeat the captured data.

There are a few steps necessary to use the learn feature:

1. Enter the command /**W**orksheet **L**earn **R**ange; then designate a blank area on the worksheet to hold the record of commands. The learn range should be *one* column wide and *several* rows long (I recommend a minimum of twenty rows, more for a complicated procedure).

2. Move the cell pointer to wherever in the worksheet you want to "demonstrate" the macro.

3. Press <LEARN (Alt-F5)>. Every subsequent keystroke will be recorded in the learn range until you press <LEARN (Alt-F5)> a second time.

4. After the entire macro has been demonstrated, press <LEARN (Alt-F5)>.

5. Move the cell pointer to the learn range. You can see how the macro was recorded. You can add or delete steps by editing the cells in the learn range. (Make sure you understand how the macro works before changing it.) If you

decide to demonstrate the whole macro again, use /**W**orksheet **L**earn **E**rase to clear the learn range.

6. Use /**R**ange **N**ame **C**reate to assign a name to the macro.
7. Use /**W**orksheet **L**earn **C**ancel to cancel the learn range designation. (This prevents you from accidentally writing over the macro.)
8. Use the macro as necessary.

GUIDED ACTIVITY: MACRO COMMANDS

This activity requires you to use several of the macro capabilities.

1. Follow the startup procedure outlined in Unit 1 to load Lotus and enter the 1-2-3 program.
2. Create a macro to enter the text **`General Fiduciary`**, following the example above. Test your macro by entering General Fiduciary in cells A1, B5, and C8.
3. Create a macro to set column width to 12, following the example above. Test your macro by setting the width of columns C and D to 12.
4. Enter the function **`@NOW`** in cell D3. Enter the function **`@DATE(95,5,14)`** in cell D5. Enter the function **`@DATEVALUE("22-Oct-97")`** in D7.
5. Using /**W**orksheet **L**earn **R**ange, set the learn range to X5..X25.
6. Move the cell pointer to D3.
7. Press <LEARN (Alt-F5)> The indicator **LEARN** should appear at the bottom of the screen.
8. Give the sequence of commands to format the current cell (only) for **D**ate **1** (DD-MMM-YY) format.
9. Press the <Down> arrow once.
10. Press <LEARN (Alt-F5)>. The **LEARN** indicator should disappear from the bottom of the screen.
11. Move the cell pointer to X5. You should see something like `/rfd1~` in X5 and `{D}` in X6. When learning macro commands, Lotus abbreviates (for instance, `{DOWN}` is shortened to `{D}`). If you used the arrow keys or other methods when entering the format command, your macro might not be exactly the same as mine.)
12. Name the range (cell X5) with the name DATEFORM.
13. Move the cell pointer to cell D5.
14. Press <RUN (Alt-F3)>. Highlight **DATEFORM**, then press <Enter> Cell D5 should be formatted and the cell pointer should move to D6.
15. Use the macro to format D7.

16. Give the range A1..D10 the name OREGON. Create a macro in cell D1, naming the macro \P, which prints the range Oregon, following the example above. Test the macro by printing the range twice.
17. Save your worksheet with the name MACRO.

PROGRAMMING WITH MACROS

Much more sophistication is possible with macros. A series of macro programming commands is available. With these, it is possible to write your own menus and to use conditional logic to determine worksheet operations. The Lotus 1-2-3 Release 2.2 manual contains a very extensive discussion of programming with macro commands. The discussion that follows provides only an overview of what the new commands accomplish. If you wish to take full advantage of Lotus macros, consult the reference manual. Examples of programming with macro commands are presented later in this unit and in Application G, which follows.

SCREEN CONTROL COMMANDS

{beep} This command sounds the computer's "bell."

{bordersoff} / {borderson} The first command suppresses display of the worksheet column letters and row numbers. The second command reinstates the display. This provides a more "custom-screen" look to a macro program.

{frameoff} / {frameon} These provide the same function as {bordersoff} and {borderson}.

{graphon} / {graphoff} The first command displays a graph while a macro executes. The second removes the displayed graph.

{indicate *string*} This command changes the indicator in the upper right hand corner of the screen to the *string* of your choice.

{paneloff} / {panelon} The first command suppresses display in the control panel area during macro execution, which speeds up macro execution. Panel display remains suppressed until the second command is encountered or the macro terminates.

{windowsoff} / {windowson} The first command suppresses display in the window area of the screen; which greatly speeds up macro execution because the screen is not redrawn after each step.

KEYBOARD INTERACTION COMMANDS

These commands are designed to accommodate those situations when user input of data or menu choice is necessary.

{?} Causes the computer to pause until <Enter> is struck, accepts input at current cell location.

{break} Produces the effect of pressing <Ctrl-Break>, returning 1-2-3 to the READY mode.

{breakon} / {breakoff} These commands disable or enable the ability to stop macro execution by pressing the <Ctrl-Scroll Lock> (<Break>) key combination. Use {breakoff} in a macro that others will use when you do not want them to be able to stop the macro.

{get *location*} This command causes Lotus to pause for a single keystroke, which is stored in *location*.

{getlabel *prompt-string,location*} This displays *prompt-string*, stores input label at *location*. Same as the **/XL** command.

{getnumber *prompt-string,location*} This displays *prompt-string*, stores input number at *location*. Same as **/XN** command.

{look *location*} This checks to see if a character key has been pressed since the macro began execution; if so, stores the character in *location*.

{menubranch *location*} This passes control to menu at *location*. When menu activity is finished, control reverts to READY mode unless a {branch} sends it elsewhere. Same as **/XM** command.

{menucall *location*} This passes control to menu at *location*. When menu is finished, control returns to statement following (below) the {menucall} command.

{wait *time serial number*} This command causes the macro to suspend operation until the specified time is reached. To wait one minute, use the cell entry **{WAIT @NOW+@TIME(0,1,0)}**.

COMMANDS THAT CONTROL PROGRAM FLOW

These commands direct the sequence of command execution.

{*routine*} Macro execution is sent to the named routine (a named range). Control passes to the statement following this when the routine terminates. Same as **/XC** command.

{branch *location*} Macro execution is sent to *location* for further instructions. This is the equivalent of the **/XG** command and the infamous BASIC language GOTO statement.

{define *location:type* . . . } This is used to receive arguments in routines, the discussion of which is too complex for this text.

{dispatch *location*} This transfers control to cell that is named in *location* cell.

{for *counter-location,start-number,stop-number,step-number,starting-location*} This command repeatedly executes instructions at *starting-location*, counting the iterations in *counter-location*, according to the sequence in *start-number,stop-number,step-number*. The loop is restarted when a blank cell or a {return} is encountered below *starting-location*.

{forbreak} This cancels a {for} loop and transfers control to the statement following the {for}.

{if *condition*} When the *condition* is true, macro execution continues on the same line (i.e., in the same cell) as the {if} statement. If the *condition* is not true, macro execution proceeds to the cell below. The *condition* can be another cell or can be contained in the {if} statement. Read the Lotus manual carefully before trying to get too fancy with these. Same as the **/XI** command.

{onerror *branch-location,message-location*} This allows you to write your macro so it recovers from errors. Again, see the Lotus manual for examples.

{quit} This stops execution of all macros, including sub- and calling routines. Same as the **/XQ** command.

{restart} This is used to cause Lotus to avoid returning to a calling routine from a called subroutine (the name of this command is not particularly descriptive). After this command, the subroutine continues execution to its own end; then the macro ceases, as if a {quit} had been encountered.

{return} This returns to the statement following the {*routine*} or {menucall} statement. This statement is not required if there is a blank cell below the subroutine or menu. Same as the **/XR** command.

{system} This temporarily suspends macro execution and causes a DOS command or program to be executed. When the DOS program ends, control is returned to the macro.

COMMANDS FOR DATA MANIPULATION

These commands move data in the worksheet.

{blank *location*} This does the equivalent of a **/R**ange **E**rase of *location*.

{contents *destination-location,source-location*} This copies contents of *source-location* cell to *destination-location*, converting value data to label data. Format of the data can be specified: see the Lotus manual.

{let *location,number*} This command stores a *number* entry at *location*.

{let *location,string*} This stores a *string* entry at *location*.

{put *location,col-number,row-number,number*} This stores the *number* in the range *location*, offset from the upper left by *col-number* and *row-number*.

{put *location,col-number,row-number,string*} This stores the *string* in the range *location*, offset from the upper left by *col-number* and *row-number*.

{recalc *location*} This recalculates a specified *location* of the worksheet, proceeding row by row.

{recalccol *location*} This recalculates a specified *location* of the worksheet, proceeding column by column.

COMMANDS DEALING WITH FILES

The commands in this section are used to access ASCII files used with other programs. You might use these commands to create a file of data for use with a mail-merge application.

{close} This terminates all further interaction with the currently open file.

{filesize *location*} This stores the size of the currently open file, in bytes, in *location*. Used to ensure that you do not try to read beyond the end of the file.

{getpos *location*} This determines the current position of the file pointer in the open file and stores it in *location*. Used to keep track of where you are in the file.

{open *file-name,access-mode*} This opens a file for reading (only); writing as well as reading; or modification. Access mode codes are R, W, and M respectively. Files opened for writing lose any previous contents; files opened for modification retain their previous contents.

{read *bytecount,location*} This reads the specified number of bytes from the open file and stores the result in *location*.

{readln *location*} This reads a full line (up to an <Enter> character) and stores the result in *location*.

{setpos *file-position*} This moves the file pointer to *file-position* bytes from the beginning of the file.

{write *string*} This writes the *string* to the currently open file, at the file pointer position.

{writeln *string*} This writes the *string* to the currently open file, at the file pointer position. The string is terminated by the carriage return-line feed sequence.

EXAMPLE OF MACRO COMMAND PROGRAMMING: MACRO-DRIVEN INPUT

In this section, we develop the first of two simple examples of macro programming. The first example prompts the user for input of a series of numbers needed to complete a financial statement. The second example illustrates the menu capability of macro programming.

In many situations, persons who are not very familiar with Lotus 1-2-3 are asked to enter data into the program. This process is much easier, and less error-prone, if macro commands are used to manage the interaction between the user and the program. In this example, we develop a series of macro commands that prompt the user for specific values and then store the results in a worksheet. This macro executes automatically when the worksheet is retrieved.

As with any programming assignment, it is useful to begin by laying out the steps to be accomplished. With Lotus, this can often be done by an experienced user (you!) going through the process on a worksheet, carefully recording the steps taken. Where the experienced person "knows" to move the cell pointer and enter a particular number, you wish to develop a program instruction to aid the inexperienced user. Let us begin with a simple spreadsheet (see Figure 17-1).

Once the spreadsheet is constructed, we determine what essential acts are to be performed by the user. In this case, I decided that the cell pointer should move to each of the input cells, which are A1, B5..B6, B10..B14, and C18. (These cells are unprotected. All other cells contain formulas or constant text information and are protected.) As the cell pointer moves, the user should be prompted for the appropriate information and that information should be stored in the proper cell.

The macro commands necessary to make this work are fairly simple. A label is placed in A22 to help us remember what is below. The macro commands themselves are placed in the rows below the worksheet, starting in cell A23 (see Figure 17-2). Cell A23 is assigned the name **\0** (backslash-zero) which means that the macro commands execute automatically when the worksheet is retrieved. In the macros, I capitalized all commands and cell references to differentiate them from the text of the prompts. Capitalization is not necessary, but in this case it is helpful. The commands in A23 accomplish the following:

`{BREAKON}`	Allows user to interrupt macro execution by pressing <Break>.
`{HOME}`	Moves cell pointer to cell A1.
`/WGPE`	Establishes protection-on state.
`{INDICATE "INPUT"}`	Changes mode indicator to `INPUT`.

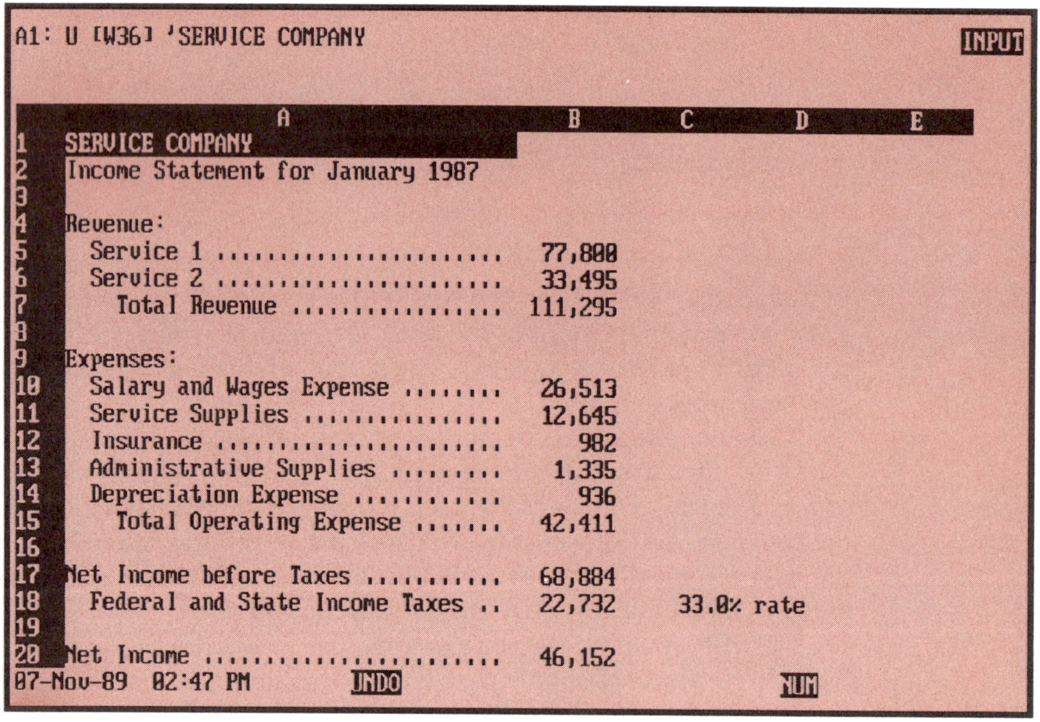

Figure 17-1 Worksheet for Macro Commands

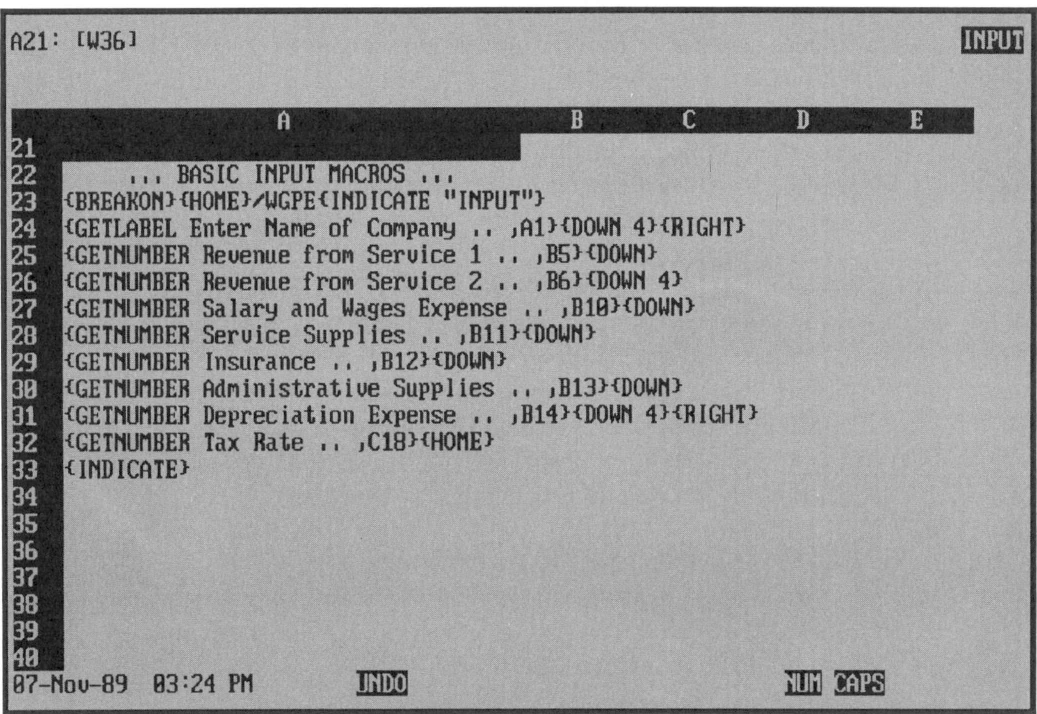

Figure 17-2 Input Macro Section

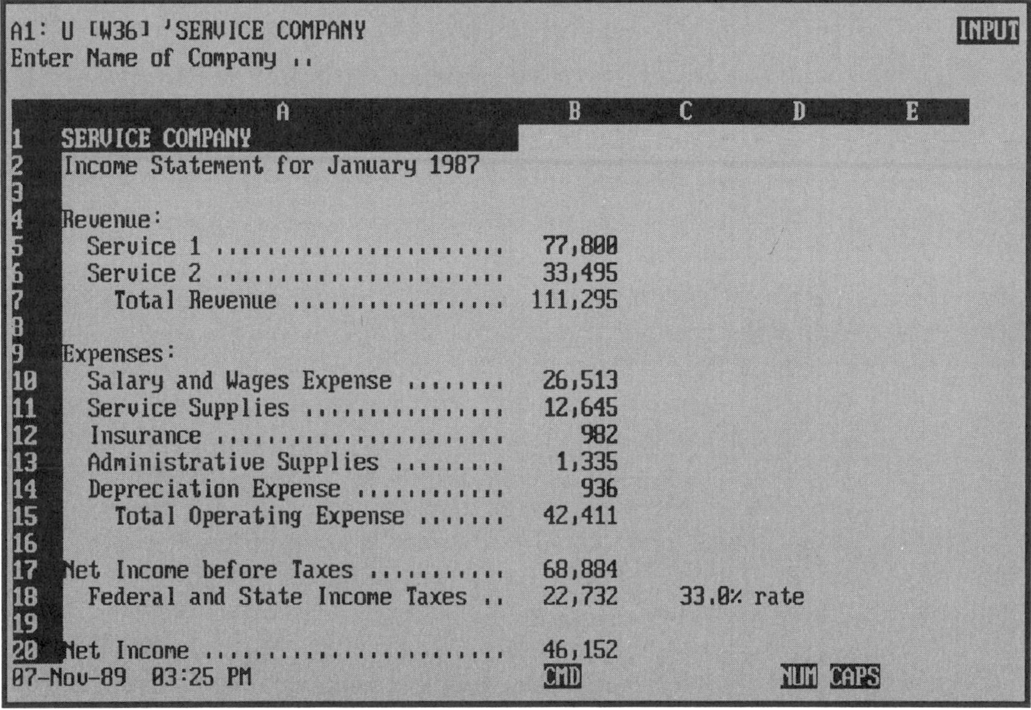

Figure 17-3 The Input Macro in Use

Note that there are no spaces in this entry (except between *indicate* and *input*). Spaces confuse Lotus and usually cause macros to fail.

The rest of the commands should be fairly obvious. Pay special attention to the punctuation in the GET commands. There are spaces before and after the two periods, but not after the comma. The spaces within the prompt are acceptable and make the prompt easier to understand. The space before the comma provides a space between the end of the prompt and where the user enters the information. (You can see this effect in the control panel area in Figure 17-3.) A space after the comma would cause the macro to fail. The final {INDICATE} is used to restore the normal mode indicator (READY).

Once the macro commands are entered and the range named, the worksheet is saved. Next, the worksheet is retrieved and the macro (if named **\0**) executes automatically (see Figure 17-3). You might want to assign an additional name (such as **\I**) to the macro range (cell A23) so that you can execute the macro without continually saving and retrieving.

GUIDED ACTIVITY: MACRO PROGRAMMING

This activity requires you to develop a spreadsheet that uses macro programming commands to control input.

1. Create the worksheet in Figure 17-1 and add the macro program for input (Figure 17-2).

   a. You should be able to determine what formulas are in the worksheet by looking at Figure 17-1 (a real-life situation; often you will be given a finished product and asked to duplicate it with Lotus).

   b. Enter the macro commands illustrated in Figure 17-2. Name your macro (cell A23) as **\I** and test it by reentering the data illustrated in Figure 17-1.

2. When everything works, save the file as MACRO2.

EXAMPLE OF MACRO COMMAND PROGRAMMING: MACRO MENUS

We can extend the above example by providing our user with a menu that offers a number of common choices. For instance, we might want to give the user the ability to **I**nput, **P**rint, **S**ave, **E**xit (to worksheet mode), or **Q**uit (to the 1-2-3 Access System). A macro menu is constructed by putting the one-word choices across one row and extended definitions below. As with Lotus-provided menus, when a choice is highlighted the extended definition appears in the third row of the control panel area. In the column below an extended definition are the commands to be executed if that choice is chosen. The commands are executed down the column until a blank cell or {return} is encountered. The following illustrates the general construction of a macro menu:

CHOICE1	CHOICE2	CHOICE3	CHOICE4	*blank*
DEF'N1	DEF'N2	DEF'N3	DEF'N4	
COMMAND1-1	COMMAND2-1	COMMAND3-1	COMMAND4-1	
COMMAND1-2	COMMAND2-2	*blank*	COMMAND4-2	
COMMAND1-3	*blank*		COMMAND4-3	
blank			*blank*	

The cell containing CHOICE1 determines the address of the menu. This is used in the {menubranch} and /XM commands. When the menu is called, the choices (CHOICE1 . . . CHOICE4; Lotus knows to stop displaying choices when it sees the blank cell to the right of CHOICE4) are displayed on the second line in the control panel area. When CHOICE1 is highlighted by the menu pointer, DEF'N1 (definition 1) appears in the third line. Choosing CHOICE1 causes Lotus to execute the commands starting with COMMAND1-1 and stopping with the blank cell after COMMAND1-3. Control then returns to the cell below the {menubranch} or /XM command.

Several changes are made to the previous worksheet to incorporate a menu. First, I **/M**oved the input procedure to start in cell A27, with the identifying label in A26. A few minor changes were made in the first and last lines of the macro, and the name INPUT was assigned to cell A27.

```
A26:    ^... BASIC INPUT MACRO ...
A27:    '{INDICATE "INPUT"}
A28:    '{GETLABEL Enter Name of Company .. ,A1}{DOWN 4}{RIGHT}
A29:    '{GETNUMBER Revenue from Service 1 .. ,B5}{DOWN}
A30:    '{GETNUMBER Revenue from Service 2 .. ,B6}{DOWN 4}
A31:    '{GETNUMBER Salary and Wages Expense .. ,B10}{DOWN}
A32:    '{GETNUMBER Service Supplies .. ,B11}{DOWN}
A33:    '{GETNUMBER Insurance .. ,B12}{DOWN}
A34:    '{GETNUMBER Administrative Supplies .. ,B13}{DOWN}
A35:    '{GETNUMBER Depreciation Expense .. ,B14}{DOWN 4}{RIGHT}
A36:    '{GETNUMBER Tax Rate .. ,C18}{HOME}
A37:    '{INDICATE}{RETURN}
```

A new startup macro was established at A22..A24, with the name \0 assigned to A23.

```
A22:    ^... STARTUP MACRO ...
A23:    '{BREAKON}{HOME}/WGPE{MENUCALL F27}
A24:    '{BRANCH A23}
```

This has the effect of a continuous loop, always setting break on, homing the cell pointer, enabling worksheet protection, and calling the menu at F27. Once the menu is exited, the entry in A24 sends control back to A23, starting the process again.

The menu itself starts in F27. The left column of the menu deals with Input. (See Figure 17-4 for an illustration of the menu in use.) The entry in F26 is for information only. The entry in F27 is the choice and an extended definition appears in F28 (both of which can be seen in Figure 17-4). The entry in F29, which is executed only when Input is selected, sends control to the named range INPUT (called a **routine**), which, you recall, is our old input macro. When the end of

INPUT is reached (in cell A37), control returns to F30 which is also a {return} command. This command terminates the menu and sends control back to A24.

```
F26:    ^... MENU MACRO ...
F27:    'Input
F28:    'Enter Data Into Income Statement
F29:    '{INPUT}
F30:    '{RETURN}
```

The **P**rint choice is in column G. You should be able to decipher the commands:

```
G27:    'Print
G28:    'Print the Results
G29:    '/PPRA1..D20~GPQ
G30:    '{RETURN}
```

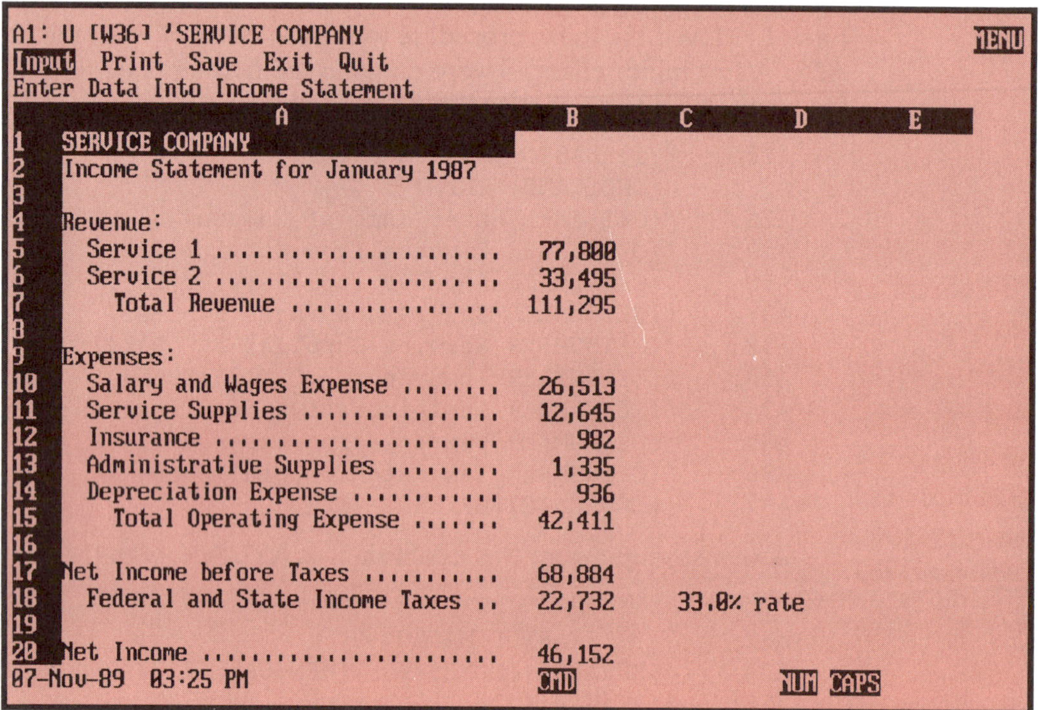

Figure 17-4 The Macro Menu in Use

The **S**ave command is written so that the file is always saved with the name SERVICE. After naming the file, the macro issues the **R**eplace command automatically. In most cases, this is necessary because the file already exists. In some situations, however, the R is unnecessary. The {ESC} after the R has one of two effects: if the R is necessary, then the {ESC} is ignored; if the R is not necessary, then the {ESC} prevents it from being carried into the next command (which might result in its being entered into a cell).

```
H27:    'Save
H28:    'Save the Results
H29:    '/FSSERVICE~R{ESC}
H30:    '{RETURN}
```

The Exit command returns the indicator to normal and quits the whole macro.

```
I27:    'Exit
I28:    'Exit this Menu to READY Mode
I29:    '{INDICATE}~
I30:    '{QUIT}
```

Quit exits 1-2-3. Be careful with a macro like this because your novice user might quit without saving. You might include an automatic save with this macro (using the logic in cell H29).

```
J27:    'Quit
J28:    'Quit 1-2-3
J29:    '/QY
```

The use of macro menus greatly extends the capabilities of Lotus 1-2-3. In this short example we have attempted a modest illustration of how macro commands and macro menus can automate and facilitate worksheet operations.

/X COMMANDS

Lotus 1-2-3 Release 1A provides a series of **/X** commands which allow macro programming. (See Table 17-2.) These commands still function in Release 2.2, although there are alternative commands that have been discussed above.

Table 17-2 /X Commands

Programming Commands	
/XI*condition*~*then*	If . . . then
/XG*location*~	Go to cell or range *location*
/XC*location*~	Call subroutine at cell or range *location*
/XR	Return from subroutine
/XQ	Quit macro
Pause for Input Commands	
{?}	Pause for input and store in current cell
/XM*location*~	Process user-defined menu at cell or range *location*
/XL*message*~*location*~	Accept label entry and store in cell or range *location*
/XN*message*~*location*~	Accept number entry and store in *location*

DEBUGGING MACROS

Like any other computer programming endeavor, creating spreadsheets with macros requires careful thought and extreme precision. All of the macro programming exercises in this book give you *complete* and *exact* texts for the macros, and you might think that accomplishing those exercises would be a simple typing exercise. Even the best typists make mistakes, however, and those mistakes yield macros that do not operate properly.

Determining where errors lie in programs and removing those errors is called **debugging** (i.e., removing the bugs). The first step in debugging is to check all entries for typographical errors and to go through the instructions to ensure that you did not skip a step. If you cannot find the problem this way, then perhaps you can discover the problem by watching the program execute. One of the best aids for debugging is the ability to have the program execute instructions one step at a time. If your program does not work and you cannot find any typographical errors, follow the following steps to isolate the problem:

1. Press <STEP (Alt-F2)>. The indicator `STEP` should appear at the bottom of the screen.
2. Execute the macro. [If the macro is a \0 — autoexecute macro — you can execute it by pressing <RUN (Alt-F3)>.]
3. To cycle the macro through the instructions, press any key. The macro will execute one character or key at a time. You will see the address of the macro instruction and the position in the instruction at the bottom of the screen and the (normal) display of the worksheet at the top.
4. Watch the effect of each command. You will probably see where your macro goes astray and, hopefully, will recognize what character or instruction is causing the problem.
5. When you have seen enough of the macro, press <Ctrl-Break> to stop it. (You might also have to press the <Esc> key.)
6. Press <STEP (Alt-F2)>.
7. Correct the problem and test the macro again.

EXERCISE: MACRO MENU

You must have completed the Guided Activity titled "Macro Programming" before commencing this exercise.

1. Change the MACRO2 worksheet to include the macro menu discussed above.
2. When the menu works, save the spreadsheet as MACRO3.

REVIEW QUESTIONS

1. What are the uses of macro commands?

2.* Write a macro that saves a file with the name MACRO. Assume that the file already exists and that you want to replace the previous version.

DOCUMENTATION RESEARCH

Using the reference manual, find and record the page number of each of the commands discussed in this Unit. I recommend you also write the page number by the discussion of the command, above.

1. /**R**ange **N**ame **C**reate — what would happen if you gave a range the name K9?

2. /**X** and other macro commands — for each of the macro and /**X** commands, determine the equivalent command in another programming language (e.g., BASIC, FORTRAN, COBOL).

APPLICATION G

POOR RICHARD'S (III)

In this exercise, you make modifications to the worksheet you created in Applications A and B. This requires you to use many of the commands and concepts discussed in Part 3. You enter a formula containing a lookup table reference, name several ranges, establish worksheet titles, use query commands, and write several macro commands.

1. Load Lotus and enter the 1-2-3 program. Retrieve the AUTO worksheet you edited in Application B.

2. For most people, creation of a complex, sophisticated worksheet such as this one is an iterative, trial-and-error process. This is what Sherlock Holmes would call *A Two-Pipe Problem* (literally!). The discussion that follows leads you through the steps followed as this worksheet was developed.

   My desire was to build a worksheet that would be fairly foolproof. When the worksheet is retrieved, it should present the user (a car salesperson, not a computer operator) with a short menu with three choices: **S**elect a car, **A**nalyze the purchase, or **E**xit.

   To simplify the process further, the worksheet should contain a list of the inventory and automatically fill in the Dealer Cost and List Price cells, as well as display a description of the car.

3. The first step is to build a table with the inventory list. Follow the example provided as Figure G-1.

   a. **Column H**: Set the width to five characters. The word "Stock" is entered in H2, the remainder of the column is empty.

   b. **Column I**: Set the width to seven characters. Enter the label "No." in I2. The entries in I3..I10 are numbers (not labels).

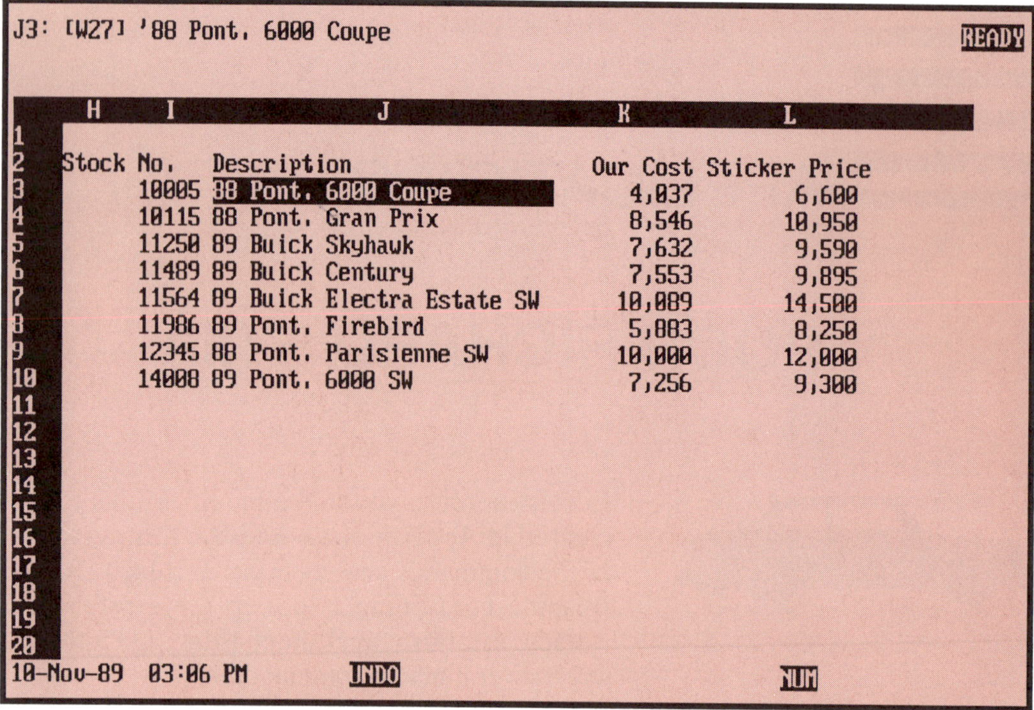

Figure G-1 The Inventory Section
Note: Costs and prices are wild guesses.

c. **Column J**: Set the width to 27 characters. Each entry that starts with a numeral (e.g., "88 Pont. 6000 Coupe") must be preceded by a ' (single quotation) mark.

d. **Column K**: Set the width to 12 characters. Right justify the label entry in K2. The remainder of the data in the column are values set to *comma,0* format.

e. **Column L**: Set the width to 13 characters. Enter label and values as in column K.

4. When the Inventory table is complete, use the /**R**ange **N**ame **C**reate command to name the range I3..L10 as INVENTORY. Do not include row 2 or column H in the named range. Save your work (continue to use AUTO as the file name).

5. Name the cell C4 with the name CASE.

6. At this point, move the cell pointer to A3 and give the /**W**orksheet **T**itles **H**orizontal command.

7. Move the cells containing Sales Tax Rate, Finance A.P.R., and Number of Payments to E16..G18. (You can see where these end up in Figure G-2.)

8. Now we use a lookup function. Note that the Dealer Cost figure is in the second column to the right of the stock number. Go to cell C5. Enter the following function:

   @VLOOKUP($CASE,$INVENTORY,2)

   Convince yourself that this works by changing the stock number (cell C4) a few times and watch the Dealer Cost change. Convince yourself that it does not work perfectly by entering a bogus stock number, such as **11000**. We fix that later. When you have had enough fun, put stock number **12345** in cell C4.

9. Enter a similar function in cell C6 to read the List Price from the INVENTORY range. (You can copy the function from C5, then change the offset.)

10. Enter a similar function in E4 to read the Description.

11. Set the width of column C to 12 characters and column D to 14 characters. The analysis portion of the spreadsheet should now look like Figure G-2.

12. /**R**ange **U**nprot cells C8, C9, and G18. Save your work.

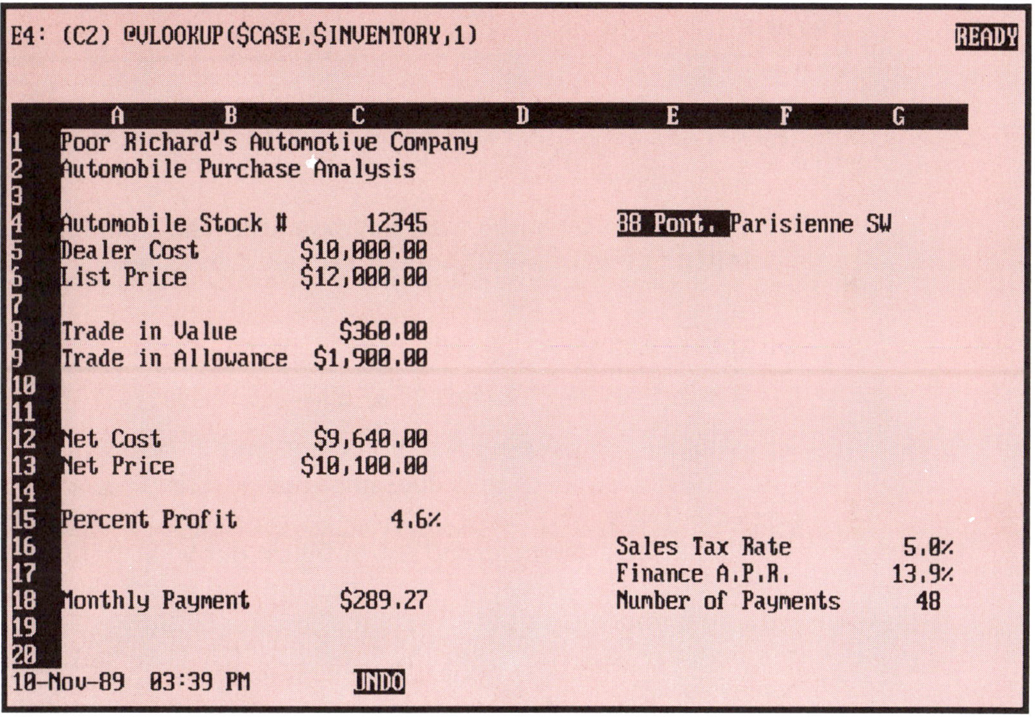

Figure G-2 The Analysis Section

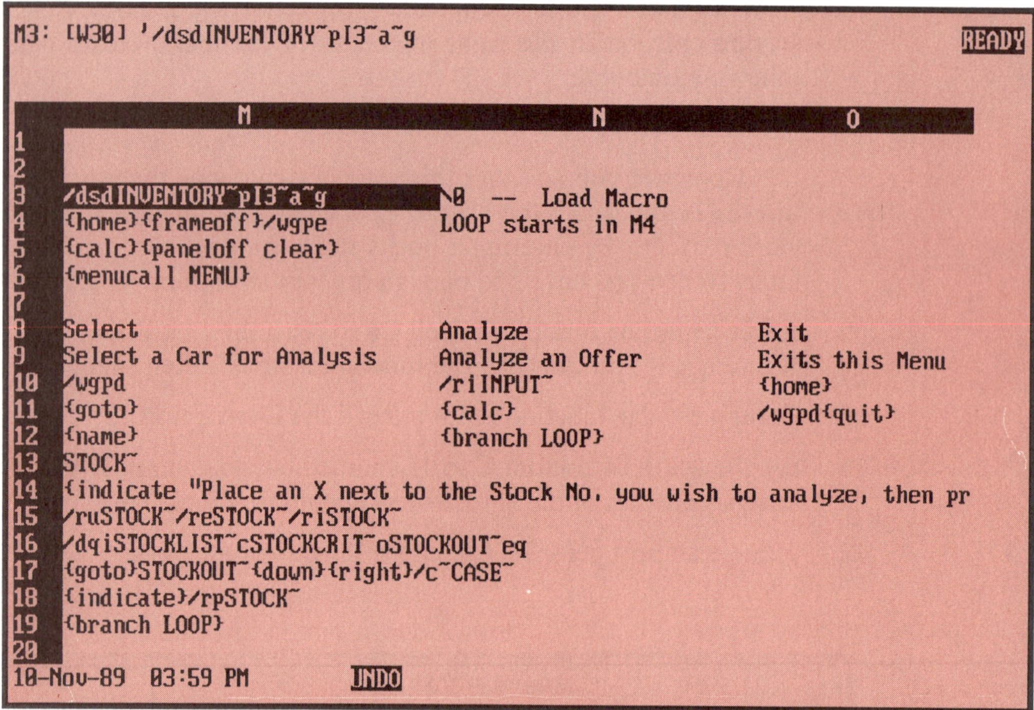

Figure G-3 The Macro Section

13. Now we start to build the macro commands. The completed macro section is illustrated in Figure G-3. Set the following column widths: M - 30, N - 25, O - 17.

14. Go to M3. Enter

    '/dsdINVENTORY~pI3~a~g

    into that cell. Remember that you must type ' (a single quotation mark) to start the entry so that Lotus does not attempt to execute a command when you press the / key.

    Pause for a moment and try to figure out what this macro does. If you cannot break the code, type the command and watch what happens. (As you type, remember that the ~ means press <Enter>.) The reason for this command is to ensure that the inventory list is sorted in ascending stock number order.

    Name this cell \0 (zero). Also name it \M. The first name means that this macro executes whenever the worksheet is retrieved. The second gives us a method for restarting the system without having to retrieve the worksheet again.

15. Make the entries indicated in cells M4..M6. Give cell M4 the name LOOP. After each pass through the menu the macro jumps to M4, where the cell pointer is sent to home (which, because of the titles, is cell A3), the frame (border) is

turned off, and /Worksheet Global Protection is Enabled. In M5, worksheet is recalculated and the control panel cleared. In M6, the menu at location MENU is called.

The entry in cell N3 is a label indicating that M3 contains the \0 macro (when you make this entry, start with a single quotation mark — otherwise you will get a repeating label). The entry in N4 reminds us where the LOOP starts.

16. The menu itself starts in cell M8. The menu has three choices: Select, Analyze, and Exit, entered in cells M8..O8. Extended definitions are entered in cells M9..O9. As with Lotus-provided menus, the extended definition appears in the control panel when the associated choice is highlighted. (See Figure G-5 for an illustration.)

    Name the range M8..O20 as MENU. Make the entries shown in Figure G-3. Be very careful to duplicate exactly what is in the figure (plus the leading ' [single quotation mark], which you cannot see). The entire entry in M14 is not visible; the complete entry is

```
{indicate "Place an X next to the Stock No. you wish to analyze, then press <Enter> twice. "}
```

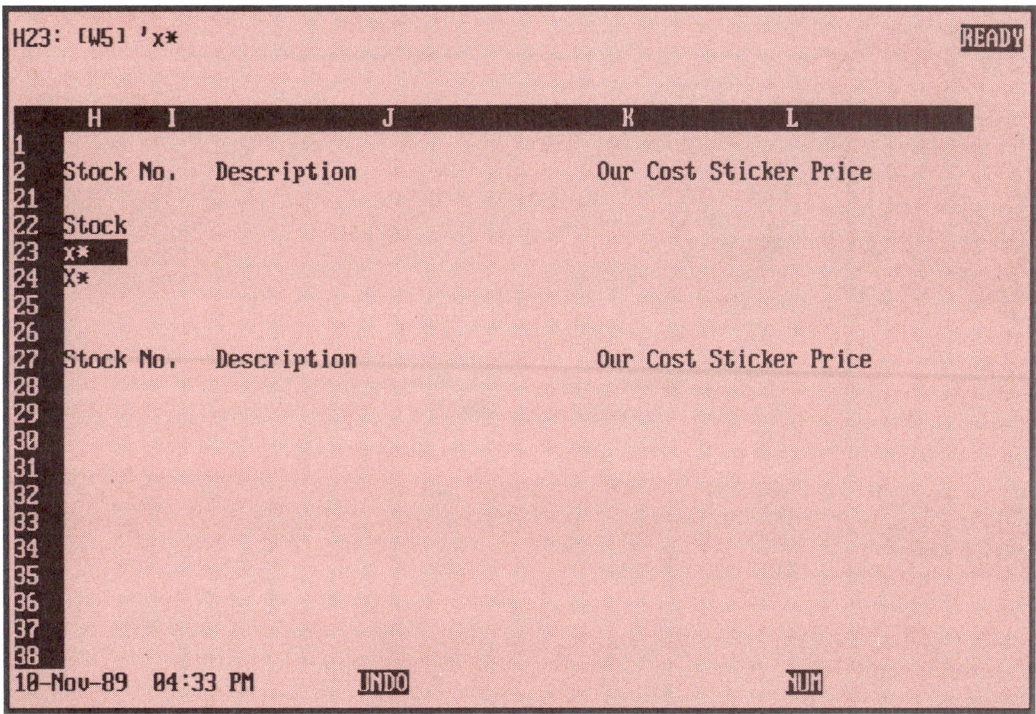

Figure G-4 The Query Section

17. The macro uses the /Data Query command in cell M16 to determine which automobile is marked. The input range is the inventory area. Both the criterion and the output ranges are illustrated in Figure G-4. Use the /Copy

command to copy the label in H2 to H22 and to copy the labels in H2..L2 to H27..L27. (Using the **/**Copy command ensures that the labels — field names — are exactly the same.) Enter **x*** in H23 and **X*** in H24.

18. Assign the following range names (you might have already created some of these):

CASE	C4
INPUT	A3..G18
INVENTORY	I3..L10
LOOP	M4
MENU	M8..O20
STOCK	H3..H10
STOCKCRIT	H22..H24
STOCKLIST	H2..L10
STOCKOUT	H27..L27
\0 *[zero]*	M3
\M	M3

19. Save your work.

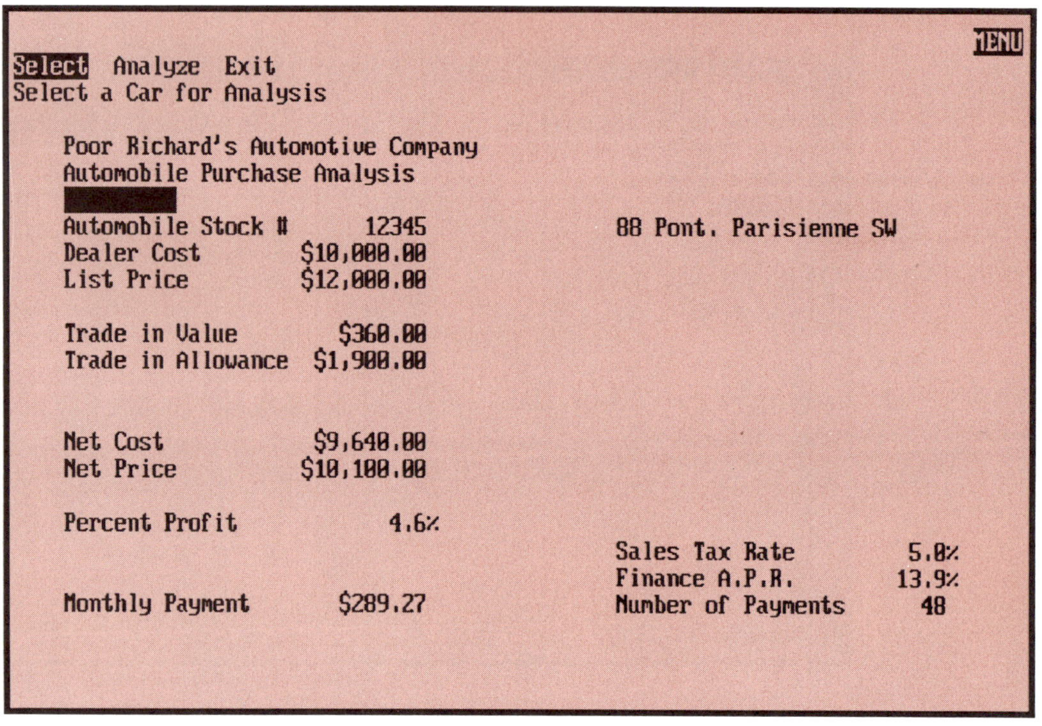

Figure G-5 The Macro Menu in Use

20. The spreadsheet should now be ready for the execution of the macro. Start the macro by pressing <Alt-M>. If you have entered everything properly, you should see a display like Figure G-5. Use the arrow keys to highlight each of the choices. The next several paragraphs discuss what should happen as you execute each of the choices, starting with the least complex. Read the descriptions and test your macro.

21. Consider what happens when **E**xit is selected. Lotus executes the commands starting on the second row below the choice row (i.e., row 10). First the cell pointer is sent home. Then global protection is turned off (making it easy for you to edit the worksheet). Finally, the macro is ended by the **{quit}** command. Simple. (After testing this option, remember that you can restart by pressing <Alt-M>.

22. Things are slightly more complex when **A**nalyze is selected. The **/R**ange **I**nput command takes us to the range named INPUT and allows us to make changes in the three unprotected cells in that range (see Step 12). We stay in range input until we press either <Esc> or <Enter> without first editing or entering something into a cell. Once range input has been terminated, the worksheet is recalculated and control jumps to LOOP (M4), which restarts the menu.

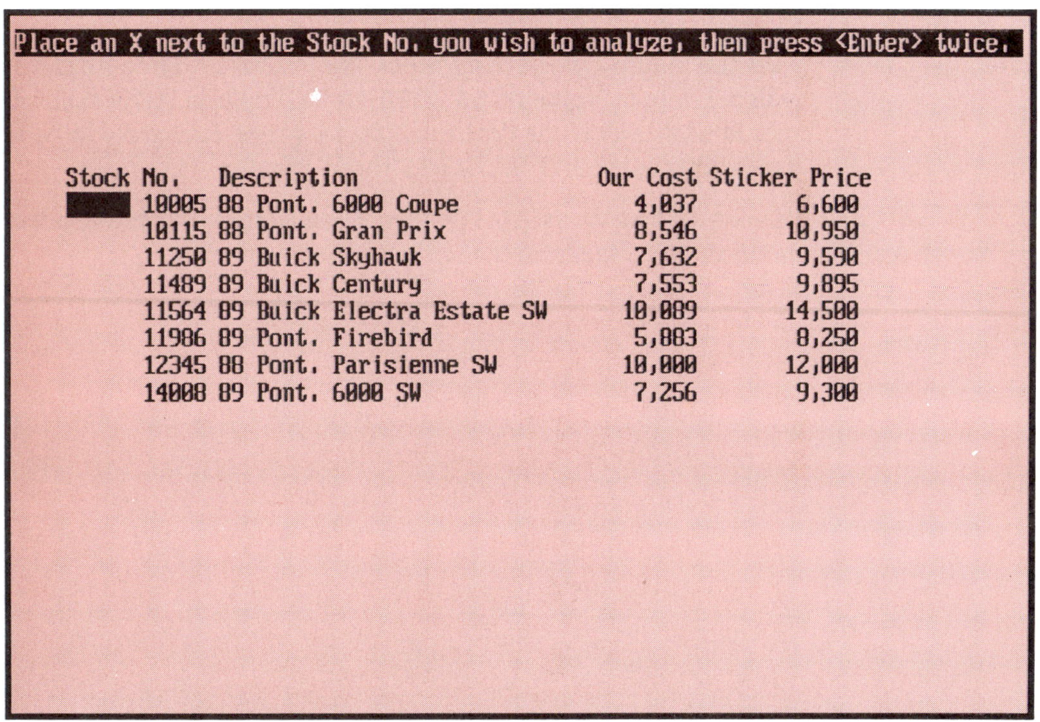

Figure G-6 Selecting a Car

23. The Select choice does a number of things. In M10, the worksheet is set to protection-off state, so we can fill in the selected stock number and car description. Cells M11..M13 take us to the STOCK range, so we can see what the choices are. (These could have been on one line, **`{goto}{name}STOCK~`**, but I spaced them like this so they would not run into the macros under the Analyze column.)

    Cell M14 prints the message `Place an X next to the Stock No. you wish to analyze, then press <Enter> twice` across the top of the screen (see Figure G-6). In M15, the range STOCK (the column under the word "Stock") is unprotected, erased, and opened for input. The **/R**ange **I**nput command is used to restrict the movement of the cell pointer to the desired column.

    After the user places an X in the Stock column and presses the <Enter> key twice (once to complete the entry, the second time to complete the range input operation), a **/D**ata **Q**uery **E**xtract is performed by the instructions in cell M16.

    In M17, the cell pointer is then positioned in the output range and further moved to the cell in the output range that contains the stock number. The contents of that cell are copied to the cell named CASE (which is C4, the "Stock #" cell on the analysis screen).

    In M18, the indicator is restored to its default and the range STOCK is re-protected. In M19, the loop is restarted.

24. Test the macro by selecting Stock No. **`11564`**. Then analyze the transaction with a Trade in Value of **`$1,000`** and a Trade in Allowance of **`$1,500`**. You should show a Percent Profit of `30.1%` (Poor Richard will be *very* pleased) and a monthly payment of `$372.32` for 48 months.

25. Finally, save again as AUTO, then **/F**ile **R**etrieve to see if it works. The macro menu should appear after the data are sorted.

UNIT 18

THE ALLWAYS SPREADSHEET PUBLISHING ADD-IN

This unit describes the use of the add-in program named *Allways*. This program is furnished with Lotus 1-2-3 Release 2.2, but you or the person who installs the program must accomplish certain steps to make it available for use. Once the program is installed, it is quite easy to use to achieve special effects.

LEARNING OBJECTIVES

1. At the conclusion of this unit you should know how add-in programs differ from built-in features of Lotus 1-2-3.
2. At the conclusion of this unit you should be able to
   a. attach the Allways add-in program,
   b. use Allways to change the format of various portions of the worksheet,
   c. print a spreadsheet using Allways,
   d. include graphs in the output.

IMPORTANT COMMANDS

/Add-In Attach
/Add-In Invoke

ADD-IN PROGRAMS

Although Lotus is a very sophisticated and versatile program, there are times when you might like to expand the applications of the program. To supplement the features of Lotus such as calculation, graphing, printing, and so on, you can obtain and use **Add-In** programs. Lotus supplies two add-in programs, and other companies (called **third-party vendors**) supply many more. The two add-in programs supplied with Lotus 1-2-3 Release 2.2 are called *Allways* and the *Macro Manager*. In this book we discuss the use of Allways; the use of the Macro Manager is beyond the scope of this text. The discussion in the remainder of this section applies to the use of all add-in programs.

ATTACHING AN ADD-IN PROGRAM

Before an add-in program can be used, it must be **attached**. To attach an add-in program means to load it into the computer's memory and to tell Lotus how to invoke (run) the program. There are two ways to attach an add-in:

- Attach the add-in automatically whenever Lotus is started.
- Attach the add-in on an as-needed basis after Lotus is started.

Whoever owns or is responsible for the software can decide whether to set it up for automatic attachment of the add-in program. If that has been done for your organization, your instructor or lab supervisor should be able to provide information as to how the add-in is set up and unique procedures necessary to invoke the program.[1]

To attach an add-in on an as-needed basis, you must know which disk drive or directory contains the add-in program, and the program must have been installed (again by the person who owns or is responsible for the software). Ask your instructor or lab supervisor which disk drive or directory contains Allways, and write the answer here:

Add-in programs are attached, *after* entry into the spreadsheet mode, with the /Add-In Attach command. When you are ready to attach the add-in, use the following sequence of instructions:

1. Enter the command **/AA**.
2. Lotus will present a list of add-in programs in the current directory:

```
A1:                                                   EDIT
Enter add-in to attach: C:\L022_INS\
```

3. If the current directory is not the directory containing the add-in programs (in instructional settings, you will usually have to change the directory), use the <Backspace> key to erase the current directory and then enter the correct directory (which you listed above). For instance, on my PC, Allways is contained in the C:\123\ directory, so I had to make that entry (*including the second backslash*). Press <Enter> after typing the directory name, and Lotus will display all add-in programs in that directory:

4. Highlight ALLWAYS.ADN, then press <Enter>. Lotus will then ask if you want the add-in assigned to a key:

---

1. If you own your own copy of Lotus, the automatic attachment feature is initiated with the /Worksheet Global Default OtherAdd-In Set command, and saved for future work with /Worksheet Global Default Update. Most of the necessary steps are covered in the discussion of "as-needed" attachment that follows.

```
A1:                                                        MENU
No-Key  7  8  9  10
Do not assign add-in to a key
```

5. I recommend that you assign Allways to key 7 — do so by pressing **7**. Then you will be able to invoke Allways by pressing <Alt-F7> (discussed in the next section).

6. Lotus will load the add-in, sometimes displaying an informational screen, and then return to the **/A**dd-In menu. Choose **Q**uit to return to the spreadsheet.

Once the add-in is attached, it remains in memory but does not (necessarily) do anything until it is invoked, as discussed in the next section. Add-in programs take up memory, and you might decide to remove one or more of them to free more memory for your work. To remove a specific add-in program, use **/A**dd-In **D**etach. To remove all add-in programs, use **/A**dd-In **C**lear.

INVOKING AN ADD-IN PROGRAM

Once the add-in program has been attached, you continue to work in spreadsheet mode until you need to use the features of the add-in program.[1] There are two ways to invoke an add-in program:

- Use the **/A**dd-In **I**nvoke command.
- If the add-in was assigned to a key number (7, 8, 9, or 10), press an <Alt> key combination (<Alt-F7>, <Alt-F8>, <Alt-F9>, or <Alt-F10>, respectively).

If you followed the advice to assign Allways to key number 7, then you can invoke it by pressing <Alt-F7>. Once the add-in program is invoked, the next steps are dependent on the program. The remainder of this unit discusses how to use the most popular features of Allways.

THE ALLWAYS ADD-IN PROGRAM (I)

Allways is called a **spreadsheet publishing add-in** program. The primary reason for using Allways is to create a more elegant printout of spreadsheet data. Allways allows you to use different styles and sizes of type (called **fonts**), to add type enhancements such as boldface and underlining, to draw lines and boxes, to add shading, and to include graphs in spreadsheet output. The quality of output depends on the sophistication of the printer. In this unit, we describe how to achieve some simple but very useful effects. To learn more about Allways, consult the Lotus *Reference*.

In this unit, we discuss the use of Allways to enhance the RB90PROJ worksheet developed in Units 6, 7, and 8. That spreadsheet was retrieved before Allways was invoked. We will make use of different fonts, add lines, boxes, and shading, and

1. Some add-in programs are working all the time, in the background. Others, like Allways, must be invoked before you can use their features.

include a graph. If you did not complete all the Guided Activities in those units, you might have to go back and do some of the work you skipped.

FONT(1) Triumvirate 10 pt ALLWAYS
A1:

	A	B	C	D	E	F	G
1			RB Company				
2			1990 Projections				
3							
4		Qtr	Qtr	Qtr	Qtr	Year	Projected Growth
5	REVENUE						5.0%
6	Sales	36000	37800	39690	41675	155165	
7	Service	45000	47250	49613	52093	193956	
8	Total	81000	85050	89303	93768	349120	
9							
10	EXPENSES						3.0%
11	Wages	52000	53560	55167	56822	217549	
12	Supplies	12500	12875	13261	13659	52295	
13	Total	64500	66435	68428	70481	269844	
14							

14-Nov-89 02:51 PM

Figure 18-1 The Initial Allways Display

INVOKING ALLWAYS

When you invoke Allways using one of the methods discussed earlier in this unit, you see a graphical representation of the screen (see Figure 18-1).[1] Note that the control panel indicates the font currently in effect and the current cell. Although you can move around the spreadsheet just as if you were in spreadsheet mode, you cannot change cell *contents* while in Allways. You use Allways to change the cell *display* characteristics, such as font, bold, underline, and others discussed below.

THE ALLWAYS MENU

Once Allways is invoked, call the Allways menu by pressing the / (slash) key, just as in Lotus. The following menu appears:

---

1. The display varies from one computer system to another. The figures in this unit were captured from a low-resolution portable computer screen. If you are using a different type of screen, your display might vary somewhat from the illustrations in this unit.

```
FONT(1) Triumvirate 10 pt                                             MENU
Worksheet Format Graph Layout Print Display Special Quit
Column Row Page
```

The operation of this menu is the same as in Lotus: either press the initial letter of the command or highlight the command and press <Enter>. Press the <Esc> key to back up in a menu. Most of our work with Allways will deal with the Format menu option. (We describe the use of the rest of the menu selections at the end of this unit.)

FONTS

One of the main uses you will make of Allways is to change the font in which a particular cell or range is printed. A **font** is a **typeface** of a particular size. The typefaces available in Allways are the following:

- Triumvirate — Is similar to the Helvetica font at left.
- Times — Is similar to the Times Roman font at left.
- Courier — Is similar to the Courier font at left.

Other typefaces may be available depending on the printer you are using. In addition to a normal upright typeface, some typefaces are available in *italic* or **bold** styles. A typeface might be available in different heights (the various heights of a typeface are different fonts). Font height is measured in **points**, with each point being 1/72 of an inch. (The type used in this paragraph is 11 point type.) If you change the height of the type, Allways changes the height of the row automatically. The size of fonts originally furnished with Allways varies from 5 points (less than 1/14 inch) to 24 points (1/3 inch).

To change the font of a section of the spreadsheet, start by moving the cell pointer to the upper left cell of the data to be affected (for instance, C1). Enter /Format Font, and Allways will present a list of available fonts:

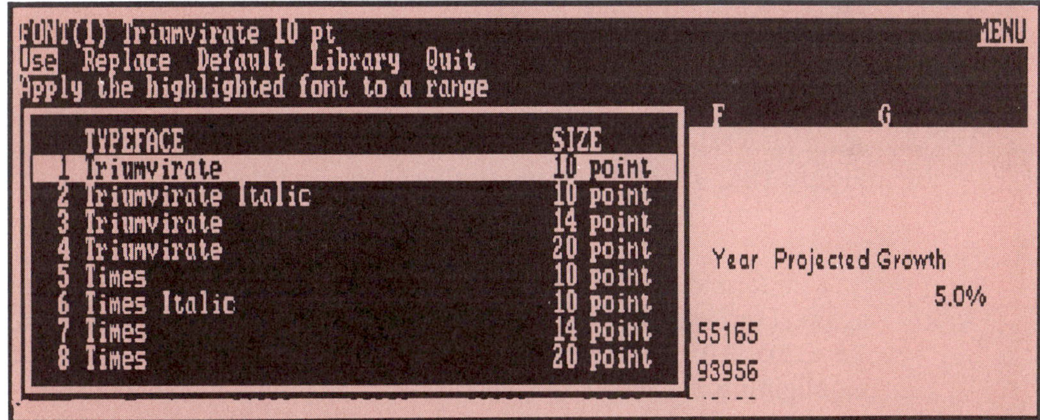

Highlight the desired font by pressing the <Down> and <Up> arrow keys, then highlight the desired action (usually Use) by pressing the <Right> and <Left> arrow keys. If the font style and height you want is not available, you might be able to change to the one you want by selecting Replace. In this example, we highlight

`Triumvirate 20 point`, then select **U**se. Allways responds by asking for the range to be formatted with the font:

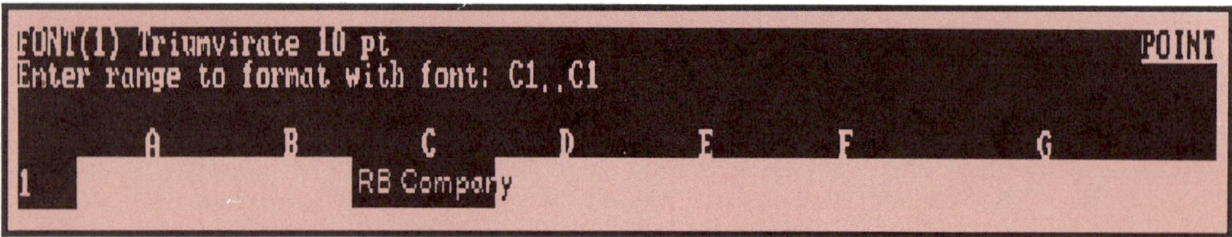

Here, we select only cell C1 by pressing <Enter>. The display changes to show the effect of the newly selected font (see Figure 18-2).

FONT(4) Triumvirate 20 pt ALLWAYS
C1: 'RB Company

	A	B	C	D	E	F	G
1			RB Company				
2			1990 Projections				
3							
4		Qtr	Qtr	Qtr	Qtr	Year	Projected Growth
5	REVENUE						5.0%
6	Sales	36000	37800	39690	41675	155165	
7	Service	45000	47250	49613	52093	193956	
8	Total	81000	85050	89303	93768	349120	
9							
10	EXPENSES						3.0%
11	Wages	52000	53560	55167	56822	217549	
12	Supplies	12500	12875	13261	13659	52295	
13	Total	64500	66435	68428	70481	269844	

14-Nov-89 03:19 PM

Figure 18-2 After Changing the Font for Cell C1

To format another cell, move to that cell and give the /**F**ormat **F**ont command again. For instance, I moved to C2 and formatted that cell with the `Triumvirate Italic 10 point` font. Changing the font of a larger area is just as easy. After highlighting the font and selecting **U**se, highlight the range to be affected. For instance, I formatted the range B6..F18 (the dollar amounts) with the `Times 10 point` font. Depending on the quality of your screen display, you might be able to see the difference between the Triumvirate and Times fonts and between normal and italic fonts.

Avoid the use of too many fonts in a document; you will confuse the person who reads it. Also, observe the effect on the screen after each font change. If you select a large font, there might not be enough room across the column to display the data. In such a case, use the /Worksheet Column Set-Width command (in either spreadsheet or Allways modes) to alter column width.

LINES

To draw lines around a range (including a box), use the /Format Lines command. You will be given the following choices:

- Outline draws a line around the entire range.
- Left draws a line to the left of each cell in the range.
- Right draws a line to the right of each cell in the range.
- Top draws a line above each cell in the range.
- Bottom draws a line below each cell in the range.
- All draws a line around every cell in the range.
- Clear removes all lines.

For example, I moved the cell pointer to G5 and gave the command /Format Lines Outline. I also added an outline around G10. (These cells contain the percent growth estimates.)

To obtain a single or double underline, use the /Format Underline command. For instance, you could use double underlining for cells in the range B18..F18 (the "bottom line" in the RB90PROJ worksheet).

SHADING

To use shading to highlight or decorate the output, use the /Format Shade command. Allways offers the options of Light, Dark, Solid, or Clear. Light shading is usually the best if you are shading a cell or range that contains text or data. (On many dot matrix printers, even light shading is too dark and you cannot shade data effectively.) To add a distinctive heading to the output, I used light shading in A1..B2 and F1..G2. If you have a laser printer available (or if your instructor directs you to), add light shading to F18 (the yearly net income).

GRAPHS

Graph picture files (.PIC extension; created by the /Graph Save command) can be incorporated into Allways output. Move the cell pointer to the cell where you want the graph to print. Enter the command /Graph Add. Allways will list all the graph picture files in the default directory; highlight the name you want (I selected the pie graph that I had named RB_PIE) and press <Enter>. Then you will be asked to indicate the range for the graph (I highlighted B21..F34). Allways will either display the graph or it will display a cross-hatch pattern in the graph area.

To achieve a display of the actual graph on your screen, you might have to do one or both of the following:

- Use **/Display Graphs Yes** [*Shortcut*: Press <GRAPH (F10)>].
- If Allways says that it cannot find the graph font files, use **/Graph Fonts-Directory** to tell Always where the fonts for PrintGraph are located. Then use **/Graph Settings Default Update** to save this information. (This is normally done by the person who owns or is responsible for the software.)

The graph will be displayed on the screen. What you see will be similar to what will print, but there will probably be some variation in the ratio of height to width (which is most noticeable in pie graphs — they become ovals instead of circles).

You can change the scale (size) of the text labels that accompany the graph. Enter the command **/Graph Settings**, highlight the name of the graph to be affected from the list presented, then choose **Scale**. Choose either font **1** (which affects only the first title) or font **2** (which is all other text: legends, x-range, data-labels, etc.). Then enter a scaling factor from 0.50 (makes the text ½ its current size) to 3.00 (triples the size of the text). After the scaling factor is entered, choose **Quit** to return to Allways mode. You will see the effect of changing the font size on the screen. For this example, I changed the scale of font 2 to 1.80 (after several experiments that resulted in the font being too large and losing part of the text).

You might have to experiment to get the effect you want with graphics. To remove a "mistake," use **/Graph Remove**.

EXITING ALLWAYS AND SAVING YOUR WORK

Periodically you should exit Allways and save your work. When in Allways, use **/Quit** to move back to spreadsheet mode. (Pressing the <Esc> key when no menu is displayed will also move you back to spreadsheet mode.) The cell pointer will be in the same cell you were in when in Allways.

Use the **/File Save** command to save your worksheet. Normally, you will continue to use the same name. The Allways settings will be saved in a separate file, with the same file name as the worksheet but with an .ALL extension. When you back up your data, ensure that you copy both files.

To return to Allways to continue to work, use either **/Add-In Invoke** or the appropriate <Alt>-key combination.

GUIDED ACTIVITY: FUNDAMENTAL ALLWAYS OPERATIONS

In this activity you begin to prepare a spreadsheet for Allways output. The final result will look like Figure 18-3, but you must complete this Guided Activity and the one that follows before you achieve that end result.

1. Before attempting this activity, check with your instructor or lab supervisor to ensure that Allways is available for your use. Ask about any special procedures necessary to attach Allways, especially whether or not it is automatically attached and, if not, what directory the Allways program is on.

2. Start Lotus and enter 1-2-3 spreadsheet mode.

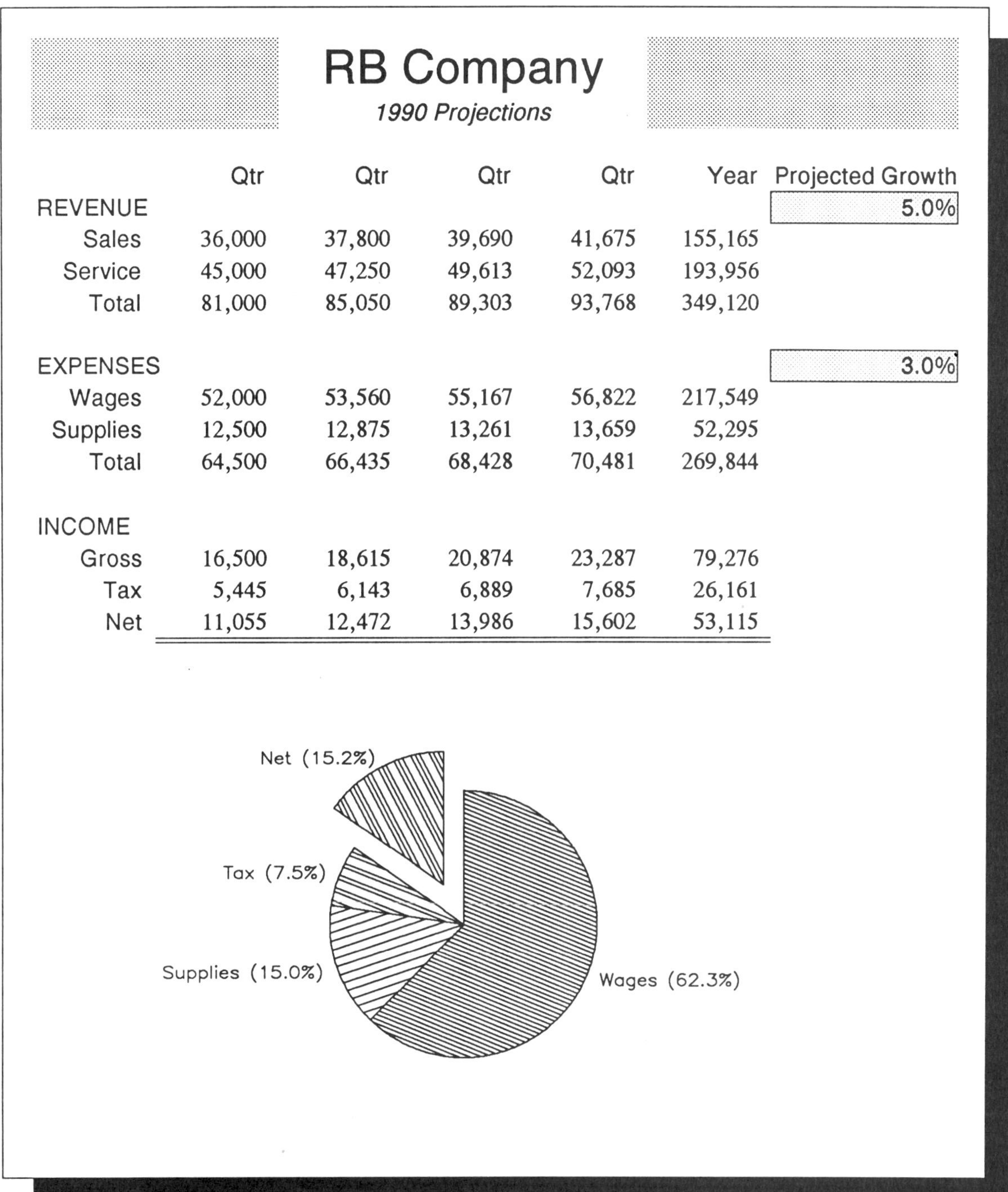

RB Company

1990 Projections

	Qtr	Qtr	Qtr	Qtr	Year	Projected Growth
REVENUE						5.0%
Sales	36,000	37,800	39,690	41,675	155,165	
Service	45,000	47,250	49,613	52,093	193,956	
Total	81,000	85,050	89,303	93,768	349,120	
EXPENSES						3.0%
Wages	52,000	53,560	55,167	56,822	217,549	
Supplies	12,500	12,875	13,261	13,659	52,295	
Total	64,500	66,435	68,428	70,481	269,844	
INCOME						
Gross	16,500	18,615	20,874	23,287	79,276	
Tax	5,445	6,143	6,889	7,685	26,161	
Net	11,055	12,472	13,986	15,602	53,115	

Figure 18-3 Sample Allways Output

3. Retrieve the RB90PROJ worksheet. Press <Home> to move the cell pointer to cell A1. You should have completed the Guided Activities in Units 6, 7, and 8 in order for you to obtain results like those illustrated in this unit. If your spreadsheet is different from the one illustrated in this unit, you might have to make a few adjustments to the row, column, and cell addresses discussed in this activity.

4. Attach Allways. Start with the command **/AA**. If the directory containing Allways is not displayed, use the <Backspace> key to erase what is displayed and type the correct directory (the most common directory is `C:\123\`). Press the <Enter> key after the directory is typed. Highlight `ALLWAYS.ADN` and press <Enter>. Assign the program to key number 7. After the program is loaded, select **Q**uit.

5. Invoke Allways. If you attached it to key number 7, press <Alt-F7>. Otherwise, use the /**A**dd-In **I**nvoke command.

6. Your display should look like Figure 18-1. Many of the following steps are discussed and illustrated earlier in this unit. You might find it useful to refer to that discussion as you complete the following.

7. Use the /**F**ormat **F**ont command to change the format of the entry in C1 to `Triumvirate 20 point`:

   a. Move the cell pointer to C1.

   b. Enter the command **/FF**.

   c. Press the <Down> and <Up> arrows to highlight `Triumvirate 20 point`.

   d. Press the <Left> and <Right> arrows to highlight **U**se in the menu area.

   e. Press the <Enter> key.

   f. Allways will respond by asking for the range to format, with C1..C1 being suggested. Press <Enter> to accept the suggested range.

   g. The screen display should look similar to Figure 18-2.

8. Format C2 to `Triumvirate Italic 10 point`.

9. Format the range B6..F18 to `Times 10 point`.

10. Move the cell pointer to G5. Use the /**F**ormat **L**ines **O**utline command to draw a box around that cell. Then draw a line around G10.

11. Move the cell pointer to B18. Use /**F**ormat **U**nderline command to draw a double underline under the range B18..F18.

12. This would be a good time to save your work. Use the /**Q**uit command to move from Allways back to spreadsheet mode. (*Do not* /**Q**uit *from Lotus!*) Then use the /**F**ile **S**ave command to save your work. The Allways formatting will also be saved (in a file named RB90PROJ.ALL).

13. Return to Allways by pressing <Alt-F7> or using /**A**dd-In **I**nvoke.

14. Use the command /Format Shade command to add Dark shading to the ranges A1..B2 and F1..G2 (requires that you give the command twice). If you have a laser or other high-quality printer available, add Light shading to the cells G5 and G10.

15. Move the cell pointer to B21. Give the /Graph Add command. Allways should display a list of all .PIC files on your default drive/directory. Highlight the name of the pie chart you created for this worksheet and press <Enter>. (If you get the wrong graph, you will be able to use /Graph Remove to get rid of it.) Allways will next ask for the range to be occupied by the graph. Highlight B21..F34, then press <Enter>. Allways will either display the graph or a cross-hatched pattern. If the latter, press <GRAPH (F10)> to see the effect.

16. Change the scale of font 2 to 1.80. (Specific instructions are given earlier in this unit.)

17. Again, exit Allways and save your work. Read the next several sections before proceeding.

THE ALLWAYS ADD-IN PROGRAM (II)

This section discusses how to print the Allways output, describes the interaction between Allways and Lotus formatting, and provides an example of how to create a fairly fancy "shadow" for the output.

PRINTING ALLWAYS OUTPUT

To transfer the effect to paper (or a disk file), you must use the /Print menu *contained within Allways*. If you print from Lotus, you will obtain the usual output. The operation of the Allways print menu is similar to that of Lotus, but there are some differences in the sequence of commands.

You must set the Range the first time you print. The command is /Print Range Set. Then highlight the range as usual. Allways surrounds the print range with a dashed line that is always visible.

After the range is set, you would normally choose Go to print the output. Depending on the nature of fonts and graphics and your specific printer system, printing can be fairly quick or it might take quite a bit of time.

If necessary, you can change the Configuration (the printer to be used) or Settings (first and last pages to print, number of copies, and so on). You can also send the print output to a file.

INTERACTION BETWEEN ALLWAYS AND LOTUS FORMATTING

Most of the formatting that you accomplish in Lotus affects the format of the spreadsheet in Allways. Conversely, little if any of the work you do in Allways affects the Lotus format.

For instance, if you change the global numeric format in Lotus, that will affect both Lotus and Allways displays. If you insert a column or row in Lotus, that will affect the columns and rows in Allways. If Allways has been attached, changes you make in the worksheet (for instance, inserting a row in the middle of the Allways print range) are automatically accommodated (i.e., the Allways print range would expand by one row).

On the other hand, if you change column widths in Allways, you do not affect the width of the columns on the spreadsheet in Lotus mode. None of the font changes, shading, lines, or any other formatting will be noticeable when you are in spreadsheet mode.

Because both Triumvirate and Times fonts are proportionally spaced (i.e., characters are different widths), you might decide to adjust columns widths. You should do so in Allways mode, not in spreadsheet (Lotus) mode. Also, label alignment in Allways is slightly different in Allways than in Lotus. In Lotus, a label that is preceded by the ^ character is centered within the cell *only when the width of the column is greater than the width of the label.* In Allways, a label preceded by the ^ character is centered *even if the label is wider than the cell.* In other words, the label will extend both left and right of the cell so that the center of the label is in the center of the column. You will see a demonstration of this effect as we complete the enhancements to RB90PROJ in the next Guided Activity.

GUIDED ACTIVITY: ADDITIONAL ALLWAYS OPERATIONS

In this Guided Activity we add additional enhancements to the RB90PROJ worksheet. The goal is to produce output that looks like Figure 18-3.

1. If you are not continuing from the previous Guided Activity, load Lotus, enter spreadsheet mode, retrieve RB90PROJ, and attach (but do not invoke) ALLWAYS.
2. Make the following changes to the spreadsheet while in Lotus spreadsheet mode:
   a. Move the contents of C1..C2 to D1..D2.
   b. Use the /**R**ange **L**abel command to change the label prefix of D1..D2 to centered.
   c. Move the cell pointer to A1. Use the /**W**orksheet **I**nsert command to insert a new row 1. Then use the command to insert a new column A.
   d. Move the cell pointer to column A. Use the /**W**orksheet **C**olumn **S**et-Width command to change the width of column A to 2. Also, set the widths of columns I and J to 2.
   e. Set the global format to comma, zero decimals. All numbers except the two percentages should be in this format. (If some cells are not in the global format, use /**R**ange **F**ormat **R**eset to remove whatever formats have been set.)
3. Invoke Allways.
4. Make the following changes while in Allways mode:
   a. Move the cell pointer to column H. Use the /**W**orksheet **C**olumn **S**et-Width command to set the width of this column to 14.00.

   b. Move the cell pointer to A1. Use the **/F**ormat **L**ines **O**utline command to draw an outline around A1..I36.

   c. Move the cell pointer to B37. Use the **/F**ormat **S**hade **S**olid command to shade the range B37..J37. Use the same command to shade J2..J36.

5. Exit from Allways and save the file. Then re-enter Allways.

6. Use the **/P**rint **R**ange **S**et command to set the print range to A1..J37.

7. While still in the **/P**rint menu, select **G**o.

8. Your output should look something like Figure 18-3. If your output differs substantially from Figure 18-3, you probably skipped a step. Go back through all steps in this and the previous Guided Activity, ensuring that you have accomplished each.

9. Exit from Allways and save your work. To better understand why each of the preceding commands was given, answer the checkpoint questions that follow. (Remember that the answers are in Appendix B.)

CHECKPOINT

Compare your output to the steps accomplished in *this* Guided Activity. Determine why each of the following was done:

18a. Why was the heading information moved from C1..C2 to D1..D2?

18b. Why were the labels centered in D1..D2, even though they are wider than the column?

18c. Why were a new row 1 and column A added?

18d. After adding the new row and column, what happened to the address of the heading information that was in D1..D2?

18e. Why was the width of columns A, I, and J set to 2?

18f. Why was the width of column H changed to 14, and what effect did that have on the spreadsheet?

18g. What was the effect of the **/F**ormat **L**ines **O**utline command?

18h. What was the effect of the two **/F**ormat **S**hade commands?

OTHER ALLWAYS MENU OPTIONS

This section contains a brief description of most of the Allways commands not already discussed. Read this section to get ideas, then try the commands. You can get help in Allways by pressing <HELP (F1)>. For more information and examples, refer to Chapter 18 of the Lotus 1-2-3 Release 2.2 *Reference*.

ALLWAYS WORKSHEET COMMANDS

There are only three /Worksheet commands in Allways. We used /Worksheet Column to adjust the width of a column in Allways mode, leaving the column width unchanged in worksheet mode. Use /Worksheet Row to specify the height of a row; zthis command is usually used to make a row narrower than the default format for that row. Use /Worksheet Page to direct Allways where to divide large output. In Allways, you can require a page break at a certain row (as in Lotus) and also at a certain column (in Lotus, the right margin determines where the column break occurs).

ALLWAYS FORMAT COMMANDS

Most of the /Format commands have already been discussed. /Format Bold prints a range in **bold** type. /Format Color allows you to print a range in color (if your printer will print in color). /Format Reset removes all formatting from a range and restores the default font (Font 1). Many of the formatting commands can be given with **accelerator** keys, which are discussed later in this unit.

ALLWAYS GRAPH COMMANDS

We have already used the /Graph commands to add (and perhaps remove) a graph. You can use /Graph Goto to move quickly to a specific graph. /Graph Settings allows you to change some of the appearance of the graph, such as font name and scaling and the colors of ranges. Also, you might have to use /Graph Fonts-Directory to inform Allways which disk/directory contains the PrintGraph font files.

ALLWAYS LAYOUT COMMANDS

The /Layout commands are used to specify the nature of the printed output. Many of these are similar to Lotus /Print . . . Options, such as page size, margins, headers, and so on. /Layout Library allows you to save your settings for easy recall for use with a different spreadsheet.

ALLWAYS PRINT COMMANDS

The /Print commands are used to specify the range to be printed and to start printing. They are also used for selecting which printer to use (if you have installed more than one printer) and for specifying which pages are to be printed.

ALLWAYS DISPLAY COMMANDS

The /Display commands affect how the worksheet is displayed on the screen; they do not affect the printed result. /Display Mode switches between the graphics dis play that we have used in this unit and a text mode, which is (usually) easier to read but does not illustrate the special effects. /Display Zoom allows you to reduce the size of displayed items so you can see more of the spreadsheet on the screen, or to enlarge the size of displayed items so you can see finer details. /Display Graphs controls whether graphs are displayed in picture form or as a cross-hatched area. /Display Colors allows you to change the colors Allways displays on your screen. Four function keys provide shortcuts for /Display commands: see the descriptions of <REDUCE (F4)>, <ENLARGE (Alt-F4)>, <DISPLAY (F6)>, and <GRAPH

(F10)> in Table 18-1.

ALLWAYS SPECIAL COMMANDS

The /Special commands are used for large-scale changes. /Special Copy copies the format of one range to another range (note: this command copies formats, not data). /Special Move transfers a format from one range to another. /Special Import brings the format of one worksheet into the current worksheet. You would use this command if you have several worksheets with the same layout (for instance, if you had several years of projections for RB Company, each in its own worksheet). /Special Justify allows you to adjust the placement of a series of formatted label entries so they fit in the width of a range of cells.

FUNCTION AND ACCELERATOR KEYS IN ALLWAYS

Allways uses some of the function keys and several <Alt>-key combinations to provide shortcuts for many menu operations. These are listed in Table 18-1. If you intend to use Allways a lot, you should become familiar with these. The occasional Allways user will probably find it easier to continue to use the menu system.

Table 18-1. Allways Function and Accelerator Key Assignments

HELP (F1)	Displays a help screen.
NAME (F3)	Displays a list of named ranges or file names.
REDUCE (F4)	Reduces the size of displayed items so you can see more of the spreadsheet on the screen.
ENLARGE (Alt-F4)	Enlarges the size of displayed items so you can see finer details.
GOTO (F5)	Moves the cell pointer directly to a specific cell or named range.
DISPLAY (F6)	Switches between graphic mode and text mode display.
GRAPH (F10)	Turns the display of graphs on or off.
Alt-B	Boldface: Set/Clear
Alt-G	Grid lines: On/Off
Alt-L	Lines: Outline/All/None
Alt-S	Shading: Light/Dark/Solid/None
Alt-U	Underline: Single/Double/None
Alt-1	Set Font 1
Alt-2	Set Font 2
Alt-3	Set Font 3
Alt-4	Set Font 4
Alt-5	Set Font 5
Alt-6	Set Font 6
Alt-7	Set Font 7
Alt-8	Set Font 8

To use one of the accelerator keys to format a single cell, move the cell pointer to that cell and then press the accelerator key combination (as usual, hold down the <Alt> key while you press the second key). To format a range, move the cell pointer to one corner of the range, press a period, move to highlight the entire range, and *then* press the accelerator key combination. Some of the accelerator keys cycle through several choices (e.g., shading light, dark, solid, and none). Continue to press the accelerator key until the desired effect is achieved.

EXERCISE: PUBLISHING THE SALES BY STATE DATA

In the Exercises for Units 7 and 8 you developed a spreadsheet (WESTREG) that compares the sales in various states of the Western Region. Use Allways to enhance the display of that spreadsheet and to incorporate the bar and pie graphs in the output.

REVIEW QUESTIONS

1. How does an add-in program such as Allways differ from a built-in feature such as /**D**ata **R**egression?
2.* What is the difference between attaching an add-in program and invoking it?
3. What are the largest and smallest fonts furnished with Allways?
4.* What is the difference between /**F**ormat **L**ines **O**utline and /**F**ormat **L**ines **A**ll?
5. Can you save your work while in Allways mode?

DOCUMENTATION RESEARCH

Using the reference manual, find and record the page number for each of the Allways commands discussed in this unit.

1. /**W**orksheet **C**olumn — how can you use the <Ctrl> and arrow keys with this command?
2. /**P**rint **F**ile — what type of file is created by this command?
3. /**L**ayout **O**ptions — what is the difference between grid lines created with this command and the lines created by /**F**ormat **L**ines?
4. /**G**raph **S**ettings — what is the difference between the **F**onts and **S**cale options?
5. /**D**isplay **Z**oom — what are the various sizes available?
6. /**F**ormat **F**ont — how can you change the set of eight default fonts?

APPLICATION H

DEMOGRAPHICS

This exercise contains a real world problem that I was asked to analyze. An organization of which I am a member was concerned about whether or not its membership was representative of the community in which it resides. The organization compiled data about its members and also obtained census data, and wanted to know whether or not there were groups in the community that were not adequately represented in the organization. This exercise challenges your analytical as well as spreadsheet skills.

1. Retrieve the file named DEMOGRAF. The first screen you see has instructions, which are repeated here.

   The marital status of organization members is contained in range A1..B10, which is named MEMBERS. The marital status of the area population is contained in range A16..M36, which is named MARITAL. A profile of the age of the area population is contained in range A41..N59, which is named AGE. Before you start, take time to look at each of these ranges to see what data are contained therein.

2. In cells B46..B59, compute the total population for each census tract and the total area. The total population is the sum of persons of all ages (under 5 to 75 and over) in that tract.

3. In cells C3..C8, compute the relative percentage of organization members in each category. Relative percentage is computed by dividing the number in a given category by the total membership. Format the cells to *Percent - 2 decimal places*.

4. Create a bar graph named MAR_COMP, which compares the marital status of organization members with the area population on a percentage basis. Because there are only four categories for organizational members' marital status, you must combine some of the census data before computing the percentages. (Hint: Put the aggregated data in column D and the percentages in column E, next to the members figures.) For instance, males and females in a given cate-

gory must be combined into one total for that category. Also, separated males and females should be considered "single." For this graph, ignore "Married Families w/Children" and "Female Family Head w/Children" categories.

A minimal graph will have A and B ranges. You deserve extra points for X Range, Titles, Y Scale in % format, and Legend. Make sure you use the /Graph Name command when you are satisfied with the graph.

5. Determine the answer to the following question and support your answer with calculations and notes in cells H1..M10. Do the "Married Families w/Children" and "Female Family Head w/Children" categories duplicate the information found in the other categories, or are these additional persons?

6. Remember to save the file.

APPLICATION I

COMPOUND INTEREST (II)

In this exercise you automate the calculation of compounded returns. Your instructor will either provide a version of the COMPOUND file or direct you to use your earlier version.

Your boss was so impressed with your work on the COMPOUND worksheet that she has asked for enhancements. She wants you to calculate and display interest on a quarterly basis, to use the data table commands, and to have a macro command that prompts for the interest rate, recalculates the table, and prints the result. Since your salary review is imminent, you are happy to accede.

After retrieving COMPOUND, make the following changes:

1. Set the global format to *Currency, 2 decimal places*.
2. Erase the range B3..F12, which is to be filled in by the table.
3. Use **/D**ata **F**ill to replace the numbers in row 2 with values from 1 to 20 (the number of quarters in 5 years). Format this range to *Fixed, 0 decimal places*.
4. Put a generic formula in A2 that computes the balance based on the principal, time, and rate. This formula is similar to the formulas originally in COMPOUND, but uses input cells such as X1 and Y1 instead of cells in column A and row 2. Also, you must adjust the interest rate, dividing by 4, to reflect the quarterly compounding.
5. Compute the data table and print the result before writing the macros (next step).
6. Write a series of macro commands that
   a. Prompt for the interest rate and store the input number in cell A1.
   b. Recalculate the data table (using the <TABLE (F8)> key).
   c. Print the worksheet.

7. Name the macro \I (for Input, Interest, or whatever).
8. Save the file as COMPO2.

APPENDIX A

GETTING STARTED ON YOUR MICROCOMPUTER

This appendix covers the knowledge necessary to use applications software and the Disk Operating System (DOS) with the IBM PC or compatible microcomputers. It is not intended to make you an expert in DOS, but to "Get You Started" by discussing necessary operations external to the software discussed in this manual.

THE KEYBOARD

The IBM and other personal computers have over eighty keys, about forty more than most typewriters. We describe typical personal computer keyboards, illustrated in the back of this manual. Other keyboards are similar, although placement and color of specific keys and the text or characters used to identify the key might vary slightly. Many of the "extra" keys have symbols or mnemonics rather than characters. To minimize confusion, we use the following conventions in this manual to refer to specific keys.

The names of keys with multiple character names or symbols[1] are enclosed in < > (less-than and greater-than signs)and spelled out, usually followed by the word *key* (e.g., <F1> key, <Home> key, <Shift> key). The following keys are identified only by symbols on some keyboards — make sure you know where they are on *your* keyboard.

<Tab>	A gray key, usually to the left of the Q key, with two arrows on it.
<Shift>	Two gray keys, usually to the left and right of the bottom row of letter keys, with open arrows that point up.
<Backspace>	A gray key at the top of the keyboard, with an arrow pointing left.

1. On some keyboards, the <Tab>, <Shift>, <Backspace>, and <Enter> keys have words and symbols; on other keyboards they contain only symbols.

<Enter>	A gray key with a "bent" arrow pointing down and left. This key is sometimes called "the Return key."
<Arrow> keys	A set of white keys on the right of the keyboard, also called <Up>, <Left>, <Down>, and <Right>. Note that <Left> and <Backspace> are two different keys and that they do different things. Some keyboards have a separate keypad containing only the <Arrow> keys.

We assume that you know how to use the <Shift> key to obtain an uppercase letter or a symbol character, and we do not explicitly mention the <Shift> in most cases.

FUNCTION KEYS

These keys are located in two columns of five along the left edge of the keyboard, or as a row of twelve keys across the top of the keyboard. Most application software packages make special use of these keys. Although these keys also have special meanings when used by DOS, we ignore those uses here to avoid confusion with the application program that is the subject of this manual.

MULTIPLE KEY COMBINATIONS

On a typewriter, <Shift> is used in conjunction with a letter key to produce a capital letter. The same is true on a computer. On a computer, the <Ctrl> and <Alt> keys also act as modifying keys: if either of these is used in conjunction with another key, the original meaning of the letter key is modified. These keys are manipulated in the same manner as <Shift>. For example, to enter <Alt->M, hold down the <Alt> key, then press M.

TOGGLE KEY FUNCTIONS

Toggle keys act as on-off switches. Press a toggle key once and the function is activated, press it a second time and the function is deactivated. The toggle keys are the <Num Lock> key (which activates the numeric keypad), the <Scroll Lock> key (used in only a few software packages), the <Ctrl-PrtSc> combination (which directs screen display to the printer as well), and the <Caps Lock> key.

CAPS LOCK KEY

The <Caps Lock> key shifts all alphabetic (A . . . Z) characters to uppercase, but has no effect on any other key. (This is unlike a typewriter, where the Shift Lock key changes numeric character keys to symbols.) The <Caps Lock> key is a toggle key. If you are typing in capital letters and need one or two lowercase letters (such as in the word *McCLELLAN*), pressing <Shift> plus the letter you wish in lowercase will yield the desired effect.

NUMERIC KEYPAD KEYS

These are the keys on the right side of the keyboard arranged as a 10-key pad. The keys with arrows on them are referred to as <Arrow> keys, or as <Up>, <Left>, <Right>, and <Down>. The other keys in this group are referred to by the text that appears on them: <Home>, <PgUp>, <PgDn>, <End>, <Del>, and <Ins>. The numeric function of the keys can be activated by using the <Num Lock> key (a toggle). Most of these keys have no effect when in DOS, but are used by many application programs to control movement on the screen.

STARTUP AND SHUTDOWN PROCEDURES

LOADING DOS

Loading DOS means transferring some of the programs in the Disk Operating System from a **system disk** into the computer's memory. You must load DOS before you can use any application software or any of the system's utilities.

Some application software requires you to use the DOS disk to load the system before using the application program disk. Other application software gives you instructions on how to install DOS onto the software program disk in order to make the software self-loading and provide some system functions without having to switch disks.

THE DOS PROMPT

The DOS or system prompt (A>_ with most floppy disk systems and C>_ with most hard disk and network systems) tells you that it is your turn to type information; that is, you must tell DOS what to do next by entering a command. The DOS prompt will appear on the screen after you have successfully loaded DOS. *Many of the command examples in this appendix show the DOS prompt, but you should not type the* A> *or* C>*; it has already been supplied by DOS.*

STARTUP PROCEDURES IF THE MICROCOMPUTER SYSTEM IS TURNED OFF

Floppy Disk Systems

1. Insert the DOS disk or a program disk on which DOS has been installed into Disk Drive A. (This is the left-hand drive on IBM PCs. Your instructor or lab supervisor will tell you if otherwise on the equipment you are using.)
2. When the disk is fully inserted, close the drive door. You should not have to force the door closed; if the door is not closing easily, remove the disk and insert the disk again.
3. With a dual-disk system, insert the disk you will use for your data files into Disk Drive B.
4. When the disk is fully inserted, close the drive door.
5. If a printer is attached to your computer, make sure that it is turned on and that the POWER, READY, and ON LINE lights (or their equivalent) are on.
6. Turn on the power switch. On IBM PCs, this is at the rear of the right side of the computer. On some other PCs, the power switch is on the rear of the computer. On some systems, you must also turn on the monitor (display screen) power switch.

7. When the red disk-in-use light goes off, DOS should be loaded. You may need to adjust the contrast and brightness controls on the monitor. In some cases, you will be asked to enter the date and time.
8. The next step is dependent on specific software. For the DOS commands discussed in this appendix, leave the DOS disk in Drive A. For the software discussed in this manual, appropriate instructions are presented in Part 1 of the manual.

Hard Disk and Network Systems

1. If a printer is attached to your computer, make sure that it is turned on and that the POWER, READY, and ON LINE lights (or their equivalent) are on.
2. Turn on the power switch. On IBM PC/XTs, this is at the rear of the right side of the computer. On some other PCs, the power switch is on the rear of the computer. On some systems, you must also turn on the monitor (display screen) power switch.
3. When the red disk-in-use light goes off, DOS should be loaded. You may need to adjust the contrast and brightness controls on the monitor. In some cases, you will be asked to enter the date and time.
4. The next step is dependent on specific software. For the DOS commands discussed in this appendix, you can place the disk you will use for your data files in the disk drive. For the software discussed in this manual, appropriate instructions are presented in Part 1 of the manual.

STARTUP PROCEDURES IF THE MICROCOMPUTER SYSTEM IS TURNED ON

Floppy Disk Systems

1. Insert the DOS disk or a program disk on which DOS has been installed into Disk Drive A. (This is the left-hand drive on IBM PCs. Your instructor or lab supervisor will tell you if otherwise on the equipment you are using.) You may need to adjust the contrast and brightness controls on the monitor.
2. When the disk is fully inserted, close the drive door. You should not have to force the door closed; if the door is not closing easily, remove and reinsert the disk.
3. With a dual-disk system, insert the disk you will use for your data files into Disk Drive B.
4. When the disk is fully inserted, close the drive door.
5. If a printer is attached to your computer, make sure that it is turned on and that the POWER, READY, and ON LINE lights (or their equivalent) are on.
6. Load (or re-load) DOS by pressing and holding, in order, the <Ctrl>, the <Alt>, and the <Del> keys. After pressing <Del>, *release all three keys*.
7. When the red disk-in-use light goes off, DOS should be loaded. In some cases,

you will be asked to enter the date and time.

8. The next step is dependent on specific software. For the DOS commands discussed in this appendix, leave the DOS disk in Drive A. For the software discussed in this manual, appropriate instructions are presented in Part 1 of the manual.

Hard Disk and Network Systems

1. If a printer is attached to your computer, make sure that it is turned on and that the POWER, READY, and ON LINE lights (or their equivalent) are on. You may need to adjust the contrast and brightness controls on the monitor.
2. Load (or reload) DOS by pressing and holding, in order, the <Ctrl>, the <Alt>, and the <Del> keys. After pressing <Del>, *release all three keys*.
3. When the red disk-in-use light goes off, DOS should be loaded. In some cases, you will be asked to enter the date and time.
4. The next step is dependent on specific software. For the DOS commands discussed in this appendix, you can place the disk you will use for your data files in the disk drive. For the software discussed in this manual, appropriate instructions are presented in Part 1 of the manual.

```
Current date is Tue  1-01-1980
Enter new date: 3-22-86
Current time is  0:00:51.41
Enter new time: 12:40


The IBM Personal Computer DOS
Version 2.10 (C)Copyright IBM Corp 1981, 1982, 1983

A>_
```

Figure App-1 Setting the Date and Time at Startup

SETTING THE DATE AND TIME

We strongly recommend that you set the date and time in the computer each time you begin a work session. This will allow the computer to **time stamp** your files so you will know when you last edited a file and, if you have the same file on many disks, which version of the file is most current. (Some microcomputers have a built-in clock that will automatically set the time. If your system has this feature, the operating system disk will normally bypass the date and time queries and you can skip these procedures unless you have some reason to change the date or time.)

When Loading DOS. The setting of the date and time at startup is illustrated in Figure App-1.

1. When DOS asks for the current date, type today's date using the following format: mm/dd/yy *or* mm-dd-yy, replacing *mm* with the number of the month (e.g., 03 for March), and so on. Press the <Enter> key after entering the year number. *Do not type the name of the day, even though DOS will show you the name of the day.* If you make an entry that DOS does not recognize, an *invalid date* message will be displayed and you will be asked to reenter.
2. When DOS asks for the time, type the current time using the format hh:mm:ss.hs. (In most cases, hours and minutes — hh:mm — are sufficient; any number not entered is set to 0 [zero].) You must use the 24-hour clock, that is, 10 A.M. is entered as **10**, while 1:25 P.M. is **13:25**. If you make an entry that DOS does not recognize, an *invalid time* message will be displayed and you will be asked to reenter.

Resetting the Date. If you entered the wrong date or forgot to set the date when you started the system, you can reset the date with the DATE command:

1. Type **DATE** followed by the <Enter> key.
2. Enter the appropriate date as discussed above.

Resetting the Time. If you entered the wrong time or forgot to set the time when you started the system, you can reset the time with the TIME command:

1. Type **TIME** followed by the <Enter> key.
2. Enter the appropriate time as discussed above.

SHUTDOWN PROCEDURES

1. Make sure you have followed the proper escape or exit procedures for the software program you are using. Failure to follow such precautions can result in lost data.
2. When you have successfully exited the applications software or completed the last DOS command, you should see the command (A>_ or C>_) prompt.
3. Remove the disk(s) from the disk drive(s). Place the disk(s) in their protective jackets or other holders. *Do not shut the disk drive doors.*
4. Follow your organization's policy concerning turning the power off or leaving the system on. In general, it is advisable to leave the system on if someone else will be using it within a short amount of time; otherwise turn everything off. If you leave the system on, turn down the contrast control or type the DOS command **CLS** to protect the display screen.

DOS COMMANDS

TO ISSUE COMMANDS

1. The command must be typed exactly as described in this appendix, including any spaces within the command.
2. Commands can be entered in uppercase or lowercase. DOS will convert them to uppercase.
3. Terminate all commands by pressing the <Enter> key.
4. If the command contains a typographical error, a missing space, or a space where there should be none, the message *Bad command or file name* will appear after you press <Enter>. If this happens, simply retype the command correctly. Many commands are disk files and require that the DOS disk be present. If you get this message when you have not made a typographical error, check to see if the command is on the disk (using the DIR command discussed below).

TO CORRECT A TYPING MISTAKE BEFORE YOU PRESS <ENTER>

1. The <Backspace> key can be used to correct errors made while in DOS. Characters will be erased as you backspace. The <Left> arrow key has the same effect (in DOS). Once the mistaken character has been erased, type the proper character. If the remainder of the line (to the right of the error) was correct, press the <Right> arrow key to reinstate the characters. Otherwise, retype from the point of the correction.
2. If a line has many errors, you may prefer to press the <Esc> key, which will eliminate the line. A backslash (\ ) will appear and the cursor will move down one line. The line with errors may still appear on the screen, but it will not affect the command. You can now enter the corrected command.

TO STOP A COMMAND IN PROGRESS

1. Press and hold the <Ctrl> key, then the <Scroll Lock/Break> key.
2. Release both keys; execution of the command will halt.
3. The system prompt (A>_ or C>_) will appear and the next command can be entered.

COMMAND AND FILE NAME PARAMETERS

Command and file names must be carefully entered into the system. Since most commands are special types of files, we can discuss parameters that apply to both **command names** and **file names**. Some parameters are required and others are optional. If a parameter is omitted, the system will supply a default value. Upper- and lowercase letters are equivalent. The parameters you will see in this manual and some applications software manuals are explained in detail in Table App-1.

Table App-1 File Specification Parameters

[filespec] The **file specification** is the complete description of the file and might appear as *[filespec]* or as *[d:][filename][.ext]*.

Examples: b:myfile.doc
a:yourfile
anyfile.bas
thisfile

An explanation of each part of the *[filespec]* follows.

[d:] This parameter is the drive indicator. Enter the drive letter followed by a colon to indicate the intended drive.

For example, to obtain a directory of the disk in Drive B (when B is not the default drive), type **DIR B:** followed by the <Enter> key. The system displays the directory of the disk in Drive B.

If you do not specify a drive in the command, the system assumes that the default drive is intended. For example, if the default drive is Drive A and you type **DIR** followed by the <Enter> key, the system displays the directory of the disk in the A drive.

[filename] You can assign any name to a file as long as it meets the following criteria: The name assigned to the file can be from one to eight characters long; the only valid characters are A to Z 0 to 9 $ & @ % / \ _ - ( ) ’ ‘ { } # !

Some versions of DOS and some applications software programs will not accept all of these characters. We recommend the use of the letters, numbers, and the _ (underscore) character for greatest compatibility.

[.ext] The extension is optional for many situations and preassigned by the applications software in other instances. The extension is from one to three characters long, preceded by a period, and follows immediately (no space) after the file name.

The characters listed for *filename* above are the only valid characters for the extension. If an extension is assigned to the file (by you or by the software), it must be included as part of the *[filespec]* whenever you wish the system to locate the file.

THE DEFAULT DRIVE

The letter in the DOS prompt indicates the default drive. The default drive is the disk drive to which DOS will go automatically if you do not type a drive specification as part of a command or file name. On floppy disk systems, the default drive is usually A; on hard disk and network systems the default drive is usually C. Entering another drive letter will override the default. If you intend to perform a number of operations (copy, erase, rename, etc.) on the files in the drive that is not the default, you may wish to change the default disk drive.

Changing the Default Drive. To change the default drive to B, type

A>**b:** <Enter> *The colon is required!*

To change the default drive to A, type

B>**a:** <Enter>

To change the default drive to C, type

A>**c:** <Enter>

The last command will not work unless you have a hard disk drive or a specially configured PC. Remember that the A> illustrated in the commands is supplied by the system, not typed by you.

PREPARING A DISK FOR USE

The FORMAT command is used to prepare a blank disk for use (a disk cannot be used to store programs or data until it is formatted) or to erase an entire disk that contains data you no longer need. The disk can then be reused. Unless you wish to use the FORMAT command to erase a disk, you need format each disk only once.

CAUTION: The FORMAT *command will effectively erase the entire contents of the disk.* If you have any doubts about the contents of the disk you are going to format, obtain a directory of the disk to ensure that it does not contain any files you wish to keep (see the DIR command discussion in this appendix).

To Format a Disk

1. DOS should be loaded and the DOS disk should be in the default drive.
2. Type either

A>**format b:** <Enter>	*Floppy disk system; DOS disk in Drive A, disk to be formatted in Drive B.*
C>**format a:** <Enter>	*Hard disk system; DOS on hard disk, which is Drive C, disk to be formatted in Drive A.*

3. When the system prompts you to insert a new disk in the designated drive, make sure that the disk you wish to format is in the drive and the drive door is closed (5¼" systems).
4. Press any key to begin the formatting process (some versions of DOS do not require this step).
5. When the formatting process is complete, you will be asked if you wish to format another disk. If so, press the letter **Y** and follow the screen prompts to insert another disk. If you are finished formatting, press the letter **N**. Your data disk is now ready for use with the system. (With some versions of DOS, you must press the <Enter> key after Y or N.)

```
A>format b:/v
Insert new diskette for drive B:
and strike any key when ready

Formatting...Format complete

Volume label (11 characters, ENTER for none)? steve ross


   362496 bytes total disk space
   362496 bytes available on disk

Format another (Y/N)?n
A>_
```

Figure App-2 Formatting a Disk with Volume Label

Format with Volume Label. By using the **/v** option, you put an electronic label on your disk. When the DIR or CHKDSK commands are used, this electronic volume label will be displayed. The operation of the FORMAT/V command is illustrated in Figure App-2.

1. DOS should be loaded and the DOS disk should be in the default drive.
2. Type either

   A>**format b:/v**<Enter> *Floppy disk system; DOS disk in Drive A, disk to be formatted in Drive B.*

   C>**format a:/v**<Enter> *Hard disk system; DOS on hard disk, which is Drive C, disk to be formatted in Drive A.*

3. When the system prompts you to insert a new disk in the designated drive, make sure that the disk you wish to format is in the drive and the drive door is closed (5¼" systems).
4. Press any key to begin the formatting process (some versions of DOS do not require this step).
5. When the system asks for the volume label, enter any meaningful label, such as your name, identification number, or the contents of the disk. Use only legal file name characters. Press the <Enter> key when the label is complete.
6. After the label is entered, you will be asked if you wish to format another disk. If so, press the letter **Y** and follow the screen prompts to insert another disk. If you are finished formatting, press the letter **N**. Your data disk is now ready for use with the system.

Bad Sectors. On occasion, the format process will report a number of bytes in **bad sectors**, which means that the system was unable to format a portion of the disk.

Often the problem is a speck of dirt, which will be dislodged if you try the format process once or twice more. If you receive a *bytes in bad sectors* message, answer **Y** to the *format another* prompt and leave the same disk in the drive. If the bad sectors persist after several tries, you should return the disk to where it was purchased and ask for a replacement. If you cannot get a replacement for the disk, you can still use it because DOS marks the sectors that are bad and does not store data in those areas. You can copy files to and from the disk using the COPY command (discussed below), but you cannot copy the entire disk using the DISKCOPY command (also discussed below).

THE DISK DIRECTORY

The directory, obtained by entering the DIR command, is a listing of the files on a specific disk. It is possible to display the directory of any disk on the system, and there are many variations of the command.

The Complete Directory. The DIR command, by itself, will display all files on the disk in the default disk drive. The [*d:*] parameter will yield the directory of the disk in a different drive. Examples:

A>**dir**<Enter>	*The directory of disk in Drive A (the default).*
A>**dir b:**<Enter>	*The directory of disk in Drive B.*
C>**dir a:**<Enter>	*The directory of disk in Drive A (hard disk system).*

An illustration of the use and result of the DIR command appears in Figure App-3. This command will tell you the disk volume label, how many files are on the disk, the size and date and time last modified of each, and the amount of space remaining on the disk.

Paused Directory. Once you have more than 20 files on a disk, you will not be able to see the entire directory on the screen at once. Use the **/p** option as illustrated in the following examples to cause the directory listing to pause after each screen full of information:

A>**dir/p**<Enter>
A>**dir b:/p**<Enter>
C>**dir a:/p**<Enter>

```
A>dir b:

 Volume in drive B is STEVE ROSS
 Directory of  B:\

KEYDOC11 DOC      3072   9-12-85    8:32a
KEYDOC2  DOC      2048   9-12-85    9:46a
FORMAT0  WKS      1536  10-20-85    9:27p
FORMAT1  WKS      1536  10-20-85    9:29p
EX1A     FW       1360   7-08-85    1:34p
EX1B     FW       7168   1-01-80   12:10a
SAMPLE_F FW      21952   9-16-85    1:21p
   7 File(s)    321536 bytes free

A>_
```

Figure App-3 Illustration of the DIR Command

Wide Directory. This form of the command produces a wide display of the directory, which lists only the file names and extensions, five across. Examples:

A>**dir/w**<Enter>
A>**dir b:/w**<Enter>
C>**dir a:/w**<Enter>

Printed Directory. The directory listing can be sent directly to the printer instead of to the screen by adding **>prn** after the command. Examples:

A>**dir>prn**<Enter>
A>**dir b:>prn**<Enter>
C>**dir a:>prn**<Enter>

DISK AND MEMORY STATUS REPORT

The CHKDSK command produces a disk and memory status report. The report will tell you how much space your files are using on the disk, how much space is available on the disk, and whether the disk has any bad sectors. This command will also indicate how much memory is installed and available in the computer system that you are using.

1. The DOS disk should be in the default disk drive (normally Drive A on a floppy disk system and normally Drive C on a hard disk system). If you want to check a disk *other* than the DOS disk, that disk must be in the other drive.

2. Type either

   A>**chkdsk**<Enter> *To check the DOS disk.*

   A>**chkdsk b:**<Enter> *To check the disk in the other disk drive.*

The result of the CHKDSK command is illustrated in Figure App-4. The *hidden file* is the volume label. The *bytes available on disk* refers to disk capacity. The *bytes free* refers to computer system capacity.

```
A>chkdsk b:
Volume STEVE ROSS  created Mar 22, 1986 12:43p


   362496 bytes total disk space
        0 bytes in 1 hidden files
    40960 bytes in 7 user files
   321536 bytes available on disk

   655360 bytes total memory
   453744 bytes free


A>_
```

Figure App-4 Illustration of the CHKDSK Command

COPYING FILES

The COPY command allows you to transfer a copy of one or more files from one disk to another without erasing any of the data located on the disk to which you are copying, *except that a file from the source disk will overwrite a file with the same name on the target disk*. This is one method that can be used to back up data disks.

The disk that contains the files you wish to copy is called the **source disk**. The disk to which you are copying the files is called the **target** or **destination disk**.

In order to use this command, the target disk must be formatted and have sufficient bytes free (available) to hold the files being copied. The name of the file to be copied must be spelled correctly and include the complete *filespec*, in other words, include the drive designation (unless you are copying from the default drive), the file name, and the extension (if any).

1. Place the source disk in one drive and the target disk in the other drive.
2. Type **COPY**, a <Space>, enter the source drive, file name, and extension next, another <Space>, then the target drive. Terminate the command with the <Enter> key. Consider the following examples.
    a. If the file you wish to copy is in Drive A and the target disk is in Drive B, you would type the command as follows:

        A>**copy a:filename.ext b:** <Enter>

        Since a file name is not specified for the target (B), the file on the target disk will have the same name and extension on both disks.

b. If the file you wish to copy is in Drive B and the target disk is in A, the command would be

   A>**copy b:filename.ext a:newname.ext**<Enter>

   In this case, the file on the disk in A will have a different name and extension.

c. To copy from the hard disk (C) on a hard disk computer, the command would be

   C>**copy c:filename.ext a:**<Enter>

   As in case a., the file name does not change.

With each of these forms of the command you are specifying that you want to copy the named file from the disk in the first drive to the disk located in the second drive. Although you do not need to name the default drive, we recommend that you always name *both* drives to ensure that the copy goes in the proper direction.

3. If the system cannot find the file, it will indicate *File not found* and *0 file(s) copied*. Check the spelling of the file name. Be sure you have included an extension if the source file contained an extension. If you have made a mistake, you can reenter the command.

Copy Using the Global Match Character. When you wish to copy several files that have file names or extensions in common, use the global match character (*) to expedite the process.

1. Place the source disk in one drive and the target disk in the other drive.
2. Type **COPY**, a <Space>, enter the source drive and file name next, another <Space>, then the target drive. Terminate the command with the <Enter> key. Consider the following examples.

   a. If the files you wish to copy are in Drive A and the target disk is in Drive B, and the files to be copied have the same extension, you would type the command as follows:

      A>**copy a:*.ext b:**<Enter>

      All files on the disk in the A drive with the extension *.ext* will be copied to the disk in the B drive. Neither file names nor extensions will be changed.

   b. If the files you wish to copy are in Drive B and the target disk is in A, and the files all have the same file name, the command would be

      A>**copy b:filename.* a:**<Enter>

      All files on the disk in the B drive with the name *filename* will be copied to the disk in A. Neither file names nor extensions will be changed.

   c. To copy to the hard disk (C) on a hard disk computer, the command would be

C>**copy a:filename.* c:**<Enter>

All files on the disk in the A drive with the name *filename* will be copied to the hard disk (C). Neither file names nor extensions will be changed.

With each of these forms of the command you are specifying that you want to copy the named file from the disk in the first drive to the disk located in the second drive. Although you do not need to name the default drive, we recommend that you always name *both* drives to ensure that the copy goes in the proper direction. There are many additional uses of the global replacement character that are not illustrated here.

3. If the system cannot find any files that match, it will indicate *File not found* and *0 file(s) copied.* Check the spelling of the file name or extension. If you have made a mistake, you can reenter the command.

Copy All Files. With this version of the COPY command, you can copy all files from the source disk to the target disk. The target disk must be formatted and must have sufficient room for all the files. Files already on the target disk will not be erased, *except that a file from the source disk will overwrite a file with the same name on the target disk.*

1. Place the source disk in one drive and the target disk in the other drive.
2. Type **COPY**, a <Space>, enter the source drive and ***.*** next, another <Space>, then the target drive. Terminate the command with the <Enter> key. Consider the following examples.
   a. If the files you wish to copy are in Drive A and the target disk is in Drive B, you would type the command as follows:

      A>**copy a:*.* b:**<Enter>

      The files will have the same name and extension on both disks.
   b. If the files you wish to copy are in Drive B and the target disk is in A, the command would be

      A>**copy b:*.* a:**<Enter>
   c. To copy to the hard disk (C) on a hard disk computer, the command would be

      C>**copy a:*.* c:**<Enter>

   With each of these forms of the command you are specifying that you want to copy all the files from the disk in the first drive to the disk located in the second drive. Although you do not need to name the default drive, we recommend that you always name *both* drives to insure that the copy goes in the proper direction.
3. If the system cannot find any files, it will indicate *File not found* and *0 file(s) copied.* If you have made a mistake, you can reenter the command.

COPYING AN ENTIRE DISK

The DISKCOPY command is used to copy the entire contents of one disk to another. The target disk will be formatted if necessary. Be careful when you use this command, because anything on the target disk will be erased and unrecoverable.

1. The DOS disk or another disk with the DISKCOPY.COM program file must be in the default drive (or on the hard disk or network system path).

2. Enter one of the following commands:

   A>**diskcopy a: b:**<Enter> *To copy from A to B.*
   C>**diskcopy a: b:**<Enter> *To copy from A to B on a hard disk system.*
   A>**diskcopy b: a:**<Enter> *To copy from B to A.*

   depending on which drive will hold the source diskette and which will hold the target diskette. Note: This command cannot be used to copy to or from a hard disk, but can be used on a hard disk system to copy from one floppy disk to another.

3. When the program has been loaded from the DOS diskette, you will be told to insert the source and target diskettes, and press any key when ready. Make sure you put the proper disk in each drive, then press any key to commence the disk copy process. You can make multiple disk copies if you wish.

DELETING OR ERASING FILES

Two commands, DEL and ERASE, are used to delete a specified file or files from the disk. The two commands are equivalent.

1. The disk with the file to be deleted must be in one of the drives (and you must know which drive).

2. Use the appropriate form of the command. Examples:

A>**del a:filename.ext**<Enter> A>**erase a:filename.ext**<Enter>
A>**del b:filename.ext**<Enter> A>**erase b:filename.ext**<Enter>
C>**del a:filename.ext**<Enter> C>**erase a:filename.ext**<Enter>

3. If the file is found and erased, there is no message. You can use the global character with these commands, just as with the COPY command, but be careful. Multiple file erasures are somewhat risky, it is easy to erase more than you intended.

4. If the system cannot find the file, an error message appears. Check the spelling of the file name and extension and retype the command if you have made an error.

PAUSE DISPLAY

If information is moving on the screen or scrolling "off the top" of the screen too fast for you to read it, you can cause the display to pause until you are ready to continue.

1. Press and hold the <Ctrl> key, then the <Num Lock> key, then release both. Output to the screen is suspended until you press any other character key.

2. Press any character key (including <Enter> and <Space>) to resume display. You can use the <Ctrl-Num Lock> combination as often as you wish.

PRINT SCREEN FUNCTION

The print screen function is available through DOS and remains active in most applications programs. This capability is especially useful when you are having problems and no one is available to help you. Use the following procedure to make a screen print and take that print to your instructor or a friend for help.

1. Make sure the printer is turned on (usually there is a light indicating POWER) and on-line (look for an ON LINE indicator).
2. Press and hold <Shift>, press the <PrtSc> key, then release both keys.
3. The cursor traces the entire screen as the text is sent to the printer, then returns to its previous position when the system is ready for the next operation.

PRINTER ECHO FUNCTION

The print screen function is a snapshot: a view of the entire screen at a point in time. The printer echo function is more like a movie: once activated, everything typed or sent to the screen also appears on the printer until the echo is deactivated. Printer echo *does not* work with most applications software, and is generally used in DOS operations.

To Activate Printer Echo

1. Make sure the printer is turned on (usually there is a light indicating POWER) and on-line (look for an ON LINE indicator).
2. Press and hold the <Ctrl> key, press the <PrtSc> key, then release both keys.
3. Nothing will seem to have happened. Test the echo status by pressing the <Enter> key once or twice. You should hear (and see) activity on the printer. The command prompt (A> or C>) is printed and the paper advances each time you press <Enter>.
4. If you get no response in Step 3, repeat Step 2. You may have held the <PrtSc> key down too long, effectively activating and immediately deactivating the printer echo function.

To Deactivate Printer Echo

1. Press the <Enter> key once to clear any text that has been sent to the printer.
2. Press and hold the <Ctrl> key, press the <PrtSc> key, then release both keys.
3. Nothing will seem to have happened. Test the echo status by pressing the <Enter> key once or twice. You should not hear (nor see) activity on the printer.

4. If you get a response in Step 3, repeat Step 2. You may have held the <PrtSc> key down too long, effectively deactivating and immediately reactivating the printer echo function.

APPENDIX B

ANSWERS

ANSWERS TO CHECKPOINTS

1a.	Press the <Home> key to move quickly to cell A1.
3a.	/File Save FUNCTION
4a.	The date entries are different because the date entry reflects the date each of us did the work.
5a.	No, Lotus remembers the range from the previous /Print.
6a.	The formula refers to different cells, but in both cases the formulas refer to the cells immediately above them.
6b.	The formulas refer to different cells, but in all cases the formulas refer to the cell immediately to the right.
7a.	The formula in E7 should be `+D7*(1+$G$5)`.
7b.	A3 is a function of A4, and A4 is a function of A3.
8a.	You must Quit from the Graph Settings sheet, then use the /File Save command.
9a.	You must enter 1-2-3, change the graph, and /Graph Save again.
10a.	The dates are different because the @NOW entry reflects the date each of us did the work.
10b.	Use the /Range Format command to format the dates.
10c.	`125*X1        200*X1`
10d.	`@PMT(X1,Y1/12,60)`

11a. `A2..D39`
11b. `+D2>35000`

13a. <Right> and <Down> can be done, but not <Up> or <Left>.
13b. The cell pointer moves to C6 because that is the upper left cell of the nontitle area.
13c. /**W**orksheet **G**lobal **P**rotection **E**nable
13d. Give the /**W**orksheet **G**lobal **P**rotection **D**isable command.

14a. The formulas adjusted.
14b. No, the logic is intact.
14c. The width was set in RECALC and retrieved with that worksheet.

ANSWERS TO REVIEW QUESTIONS

1-2a. <HELP (F1)> is the Help key; it starts through a series of help screens.
1-2d. Pressing the <Home> key moves cursor to upper left of spreadsheet, usually cell A1.
1-2f. The <Esc> key is used to back up through menus and range definition.
1-2h. Pressing the <Backspace> key deletes character to left of the cursor.
1-5. To enter 1-2-3, select `1-2-3` and press the <Enter> key.

2-1. A cell is the building block of a spreadsheet.
2-4. The Lotus 1-2-3 worksheet is 8192 rows by 256 columns.
2-5. The control panel area is the three rows at the top of the screen where cell contents and menus are displayed.
2-7. No, no lock keys are indicated in the lower right corner of the screen.
2-9. Move to the cell, type **`98.6`**<Enter>.

3-2a. `+D5+D6` or `@SUM(D5,D6)`
3-2b. `@ABS(D5-D6)`
3-2c. `@INT(D5/D6)`
3-2d. `@MOD(D5,D6)`
3-2e. `@ROUND(D5/D6,2)`
3-3. `@PMT(F8,F9/12,60)`
3-4. `@DATE(87,1,14)`

4-3. /**W**orksheet **G**lobal **F**ormat
4-5. /**W**orksheet **I**nsert **R**ow
4-7. /**R**ange **E**rase
4-9. /**R**ange **F**ormat

5-1. A sticky menu is a menu that must be exited by choosing the **Q**uit option.
5-2. /**P**rint . . . **R**ange is used to indicate the area of the worksheet to be printed.

6-6. Use /**C**opy to duplicate a formula, number, or label.
6-7. Use /**M**ove to rearrange the entries on a spreadsheet.

7-2. Use mixed or absolute addresses when row, column, or cell reference must not change.
7-3. Relative cell addresses change to reflect the new position.
7-4. Absolute cell addresses do not change.
7-5. The part of the mixed cell address that is fixed by $ does not change, the other part does.
7-6. Use manual recalculation to speed up construction of a large worksheet.
7-9a. + down-1 + left-1
7-9b. +D9+C8
7-12. /**W**orksheet **G**lobal **R**ecalculation

8-2a. The pie chart is best for relative proportions.
8-2b. The line graph is usually used to show trends.
8-2c. The bar graph might be best to compare the three at each year.
8-2d. Use stacked bar graphs for totals.
8-2e. Use XY graphs to show relationship between two numeric scales.
8-3. /**F**ile **S**ave saves the worksheet, /**G**raph **S**ave saves an graph for printing.
8-5. Yes because the files have different extensions (.WK1 and .PIC).

10-1a. 40000+69.95*X1
10-1b. @PMT(X1,Y1/12,36)
10-2a. 0
10-2b. .1
10-2c. 1
10-2d. A1..A11 *or* A1 to any cell A11 or below
10-3a. K1..K7
10-3b. K1 14, K2 24, K3 34, K4 44, K5 54, K6 64, K7 74, K8 through K10 *blank*

11-2a. K1: Name K2: Ross
11-2b. K1: Name K2: ~Ross
11-2c. K1: Phone K2: 3883
11-2d. K1: Dept K2: Personnel
11-2e. K1: Salary K2: +D2<20000
11-3a. A2..D39
11-3b. D2, or any other cell in column D.
11-3c. D, for descending, which will put the highest salary first.
11-4a. @DMIN(A1..D39,2,F1..F2)
11-4b. F1: Dept F2: Production

12-1. Currency format precedes all numbers with $ signs.
12-2. Those columns whose width has been previously set by the /**W**orksheet **C**olumn **S**et-Width command are not affected by /**W**orksheet **G**lobal **C**olumn-Width.
12-3. row 4

13-1. You can make changes to a protected cell whenever the worksheet is in the protection-off state.
13-2. The normal (default) state of all worksheet cells is protected.
13-4. <NAME (F3)>

15-1a. ASCII files are in plain text, program-specific are specially coded. Many program-specific file formats can be translated by the Translate program. ASCII-generic file formats need editing or require **/D**ata **P**arse.

16-1. `@IF(H19<=J19,-1,1)`
16-2. `@IF(K9>0,100,@IF(K9=0,@NA,@ERR))`

17-2. `/FSmacro~R`

18-2. Attaching an add-in program loads it into memory but does not cause the program to do anything. Invoking an add-in program executes it.
18-4. **/F**ormat **L**ines **O**utline draws a line around the entire range. **/F**ormat **L**ines **A**ll draws a line around every cell in the range.

APPENDIX C

LOTUS 1-2-3 RELEASE 2.2 FUNCTIONS

This Appendix contains a reference to all Lotus 1-2-3 Release 2.2 functions. The functions are arranged according to their primary use: mathematical, financial, logical, and so on. Some of the functions are illustrated in the units of this book; for others you will need to refer to the *Reference* manual that is part of the Lotus 1-2-3 package for more information.

MATHEMATICAL FUNCTIONS

@ABS(x) *absolute value of x.*

@ACOS(x) *arc cosine of x*, the angle in radians whose cosine is *x*. If *x* is not between -1 and +1, the value is ERR. To convert radians to degrees, multiply [radians]*180/π: for example, if cell H8 contains a cosine, then the angle in degrees is determined by the function **@ACOS(H8)*180/@PI**.

@ASIN(x) *arc sine of x*, the angle in radians whose sine is *x*. If *x* is not between -1 and +1, the value is ERR.

@ATAN(x) *arc tangent of x*, the angle in radians whose tangent is *x*.

@ATAN2(x,y) *arc tangent of y/x*, the angle in radians whose tangent is *y/x*.

@COS(x) *cosine of x in radians*. To convert degrees to radians, multiply [degrees]*π/180: for example, if cell G12 has a number in degrees, then the function is **@COS(G12*@PI/180)**.

@EXP(x) *exponential*: e^x.

@INT(x) *integer part of x.*

@LN(x) log_e *of x.*

@LOG(x) log_{10} *of x.*

@MOD(x,y) *x mod y: modular part* (remainder) of x/y.

@PI π is 3.141592653589794

@RAND *random number* between 0 and 1.

@ROUND(x,n) *round number x to n decimal places.*

@SIN(x) *sine of x in radians.*

@SQRT(x) *square root of x.*

@TAN(x) *tangent of x in radians.*

FINANCIAL FUNCTIONS

@CTERM(int,fv,pv) *Compounding periods*, number of periods required for present value *pv* to increase to desired future value *fv* at stated interest rate *int*.

@DDB(cost,salvage,life,period) *Double declining balance depreciation*, the depreciation amount in a specific *period*, given the initial *cost*, *salvage* value, and *life* of the item.

@FV(pmt,int,term) *Future value of an ordinary annuity* with payments of *pmt* at the end of each period, at a per-period interest rate of *int*, for *term* periods.

@IRR(guess,range) *Internal rate of return* of the series of cash flows in the *range*. The *guess* is necessary because some income streams have more than one IRR. It is generally safe to use 0.10 as the guess.

@NPV(x,range) *Net present value* of the series of cash flows in the *range*, discounted at *x* interest rate.

@PMT(prn,int,term) *Payment* on a loan of principal *prn* at a per-period interest rate of *int*, for *term* periods.

@PV(pmt,int,term) *Present value of an ordinary annuity* with payments of *pmt* at the end of each period, at a per-period interest rate of *int*, for *term* periods.

@RATE(fv,pv,term) *Periodic interest*, the rate necessary for the present value *pv* to grow into the future value *fv* over the number of periods in the *term*.

@SLN(cost,salvage,life) *Straight-line depreciation*, which is the same amount for each period, given the initial *cost*, *salvage* value, and *life* of the item.

@SYD(cost,salvage,life,period) *Sum-of-the-years' digits depreciation*, for a specified *period*, given the initial *cost*, *salvage* value, and *life* of the item.

@TERM(pmt,int,fv) *Number of periods*, the number of end-of-period payments necessary to achieve the future value *fv*, given the payment *pmt* and interest *int*.

DATE AND TIME FUNCTIONS

@DATE(year,month,day) *Serial number of a given date*, where **@DATE(00,01,01)** [January 1, 1900] is number 1 and **@DATE(199,12,31)** [December 31, 2099] is number 73050. *Note*: Do not enter the year 1990 as 1990, enter it as 90; enter 2001 as 101.

@DATEVALUE(date string) *String to date*, converts a string to a serial date number, for example **@DATEVALUE("16-Feb-87")** yields 31824.

@DAY(date) *Day of the month* of the given date.

@HOUR(time number) *Hour value of time number.*

@MINUTE(time number) *Minute value of time number.*

@MONTH(date) *Month number* of the given date.

@NOW *Current date and time*, assuming you set the proper date when you started or reset the system. This returns both date (integer) and time (fractional) components. To see both current date and time, have two **@NOW** entries; one formatted as date and the other as time. @NOW is updated whenever the worksheet is recalculated.

@SECOND(time number) *Second value of time number.*

@TIME(hr,min,sec) *Serial time number*, computes the time number of the arguments.

@TIMEVALUE(time string) *String to time*, converts a string to a serial time number, for example **@TIMEVALUE("6:06 PM")** yields 0.754166.

@YEAR(date) *Year number* of the given date.

STATISTICAL FUNCTIONS

@AVG(list) The *average value* of the items in the list.

@COUNT(list) The *number of items* in the list. Every non-blank cell in a range counts, whether it contains a value or a label.

@MAX(list) The *maximum value* in the list.

@MIN(list) The *minimum value* in the list.

@STD(list) The *standard deviation* of the items in the list (N weighted).

@SUM(list) The *sum* of the items in the list.

@VAR(list) The *variance* of the items in the list (N weighted).

DATABASE STATISTICAL FUNCTIONS

@DAVG(input,offset,criterion) *the average value* of the items in *offset* column of *input* range that meet the *criterion.*

@DCOUNT(input,offset,criterion) *the number of items* in the *offset* column of *input* range that meet the *criterion.*

@DMAX(input,offset,criterion) *the maximum value* in the *offset* column of *input* range that meets the *criterion.*

@DMIN(input,offset,criterion) *the minimum value* in the *offset* column of *input* range that meets the *criterion.*

@DSTD(input,offset,criterion) *the standard deviation* of the items in the *offset* column of *input* range that meet the *criterion* (N weighted).

@DSUM(input,offset,criterion) *the sum* of the items in the *offset* column of *input* range that meet the *criterion.*

@DVAR(input,offset,criterion) *the variance* of the items in the *offset* column of *input* range that meet the *criterion* (N weighted).

CHOICE FUNCTIONS

@CHOOSE(x,v0,v1, . . . vn) *select value*: if $x = 0$, then the cell containing this function displays value *v0*; if $x = 1$, then the cell displays value *v1*; and so forth. *x* and *v0 . . . vn* can be constants, other cell addresses, or functions.

@HLOOKUP(x,range,offset) *table lookup with index row.*

@INDEX(range,col,row) *value of cell at intersection*: this yields the value of the cell in *range*, *row* rows from the top and *col* columns from the left.

@VLOOKUP(x,range,offset) *table lookup with index column.*

SPECIAL FUNCTIONS

@ERR *error*; sets the value of the cell to ERR. Any cell that depends on this cell via a formula also has the value ERR.

@NA *not available*; sets the value of the cell to NA.

LOGICAL FUNCTIONS

@FALSE *false*, 0 (zero).

@IF(cond,x,y) *if the condition is true or nonzero, then x; if the condition is false or zero, then y.*

@ISAAF(name) *1 (TRUE) if name is the name of an add-in function.*

@ISAPP(name) *1 (TRUE) if name is the name of an add-in program.*

@ISERR(x) *1 (TRUE) if content of x is ERR.*

@ISNA(x) *1 (TRUE) if content of x is NA.*

@ISNUMBER(x) *1 (TRUE) if content of x is a value.* Values are generated by numeric entries, formulas, most functions (including @NA and @ERR), and blank cells which are considered a numeric 0 (zero).

@ISSTRING(x) *1 (TRUE) if content of x is a string (label).* Strings are generated by label entries and the string functions discussed below.

@TRUE *true*, 1 (one).

STRING FUNCTIONS

@CHAR(x) *character whose ASCII value is x.* This is often used to create characters that are not directly accessible on the keyboard.

@CLEAN(string) *removes control characters from string.*

@CODE(string) *ASCII value of first character in string.*

@EXACT(string1,string2) *exact equivalence of two strings*, where exact equivalence includes capitalization.

@FIND(search string,string,start number) *location of search string in another string.* This is used to determine position of the *search string* in the *string*, starting with character at *start number.*

@LEFT(string,n) *first n characters of string.*

@LENGTH(string) *number of characters in string.*

@LOWER(string) *lowercase conversion.* This converts all characters in *string* to lowercase and displays the result.

@MID(string,start number,length) *middle characters from string*, starting at *start number*, proceeding for *length* characters.

@N(range) *label to value conversion.* This converts label in upper left corner of range to numeric type, with value of 0 (zero), allowing numeric formulas to reference cells that might or might not contain labels.

@PROPER(string) *proper capitalization.* This capitalizes the first letter of each word in *string.*

@REPEAT(string,n) *repeat string.* This repeats the *string n* times.

@REPLACE(original string,start number,n,new string) *replace text in string with new string.* This replaces *text* in original string, beginning at character *start number*, for *n* characters, with *new string.*

@RIGHT(string,n) *last n characters in string.*

@S(range) *value to label conversion.* This turns values into empty labels so they can be used in string functions.

@STRING(value,n) *value to label conversion*. This creates a string out of a number, allowing specification of *n* decimal places.

@TRIM(string) *remove excess spaces*. This removes leading and trailing space characters and converts multiple embedded spaces to single spaces.

@UPPER(string) *uppercase conversion*. This converts all characters in string to uppercase and displays the result.

@VALUE(string) *label to value conversion*. This converts any of the following to values that can be used in numeric computations: **@VALUE("13 3/5")** yields 13.6; **@VALUE(K9)** yields 10 if cell K9 contains **'10**; **@VALUE("TV")** yields ERR (error).

CELL AND RANGE REFERENCE FUNCTIONS

@@(cell address) *value of cell referenced by cell at cell address*. This allows one cell to reference another cell that contains a value.

@CELL(attribute,range) *attribute of range*, where range attributes include type of data, contents of cell, numeric format, protection status, and several others.

@CELLPOINTER(attribute) *attribute of current cell*, i.e., the attribute (such as address) of the cell where the cell pointer was at the time of the last recalculation.

@COLS(range) *number of columns in a range*: most useful when used with named ranges.

@ROWS(range) *number of rows in a range*: again, most useful when analyzing named ranges.

APPENDIX D

LOTUS 1-2-3 RELEASE 2.2 COMMANDS

This Appendix contains a list of the commands of Lotus 1-2-3 Release 2.2 through three levels where appropriate. The commands are listed in the order they appear on the Lotus menus. Prompts for ranges and values are not listed. For more information, consult the body of this manual and the Lotus *Reference Manual*.

/WORKSHEET COMMANDS

/**W**orksheet **G**lobal **F**ormat is used to establish a default format for all numeric values in the worksheet. This setting affects numbers and formulas already entered as well as subsequent entries, but does not affect values in cells that have been formatted with the /**R**ange **F**ormat command.

/**W**orksheet **G**lobal **L**abel-Prefix is used to establish a default alignment for all labels subsequently entered in the worksheet. This setting does not affect labels already entered.

/**W**orksheet **G**lobal **C**olumn-Width is used to change the width of all columns except those that have been set by the /**W**orksheet **C**olumn command.

/**W**orksheet **G**lobal **R**ecalculation is used to determine the order and method of formula evaluation.

/**W**orksheet **G**lobal **P**rotection is used to enable or disable the protected status of cells.

/**W**orksheet **G**lobal **D**efault is used to tell Lotus which **P**rinter, disk **D**irectory, and other settings to use.

/**W**orksheet **G**lobal **Z**ero is used to suppress the display of cells that have values of zero.

/**W**orksheet **I**nsert is used to add a row or column to the worksheet.

/**W**orksheet **D**elete is used to remove a row or column from the worksheet.

/Worksheet Column is used to set the width of a column, also to hide (remove from view) a column.

/Worksheet Erase is used to clear the worksheet from memory.

/Worksheet Titles is used to freeze rows or columns on the screen.

/Worksheet Window is used to split the screen so you can see two different parts of the worksheet at once.

/Worksheet Status is used to determine the condition of various /Worksheet - Global and other settings.

/Worksheet Page is used to force a page break when Lotus prints the worksheet.

/Worksheet Learn is used to record a series of keystrokes in a range as an aid to macro command writing.

/RANGE COMMANDS

/Range Format is used to change the display format of numeric values in a range of cells.

/Range Label is used to change the alignment of labels already entered into the worksheet. It has no effect on labels entered subsequently.

/Range Erase is used to remove the contents of a series of cells.

/Range Name is used to assign a name to a cell or range.

/Range Justify is used to realign labels within a range.

/Range Prot is used to set a range to protected status.

/Range Unprot is used to remove protected status from a range.

/Range Input is used to limit data entry to unprotected cells in a range.

/Range Value is used to convert a series of formulas to constant values.

/Range Trans is used to transpose a matrix of values.

/Range Search is used to locate and replace cell contents.

/COPY COMMAND

/Copy is used to replicate a formula in one or more other cells.

/MOVE COMMAND

/Move is used to change the location of cell entries.

/FILE COMMANDS

/File **Retrieve** is used to move a file from disk storage to active memory.

/File **Save** is used to move a worksheet from active memory to disk storage.

/File **Combine** is used to consolidate the values of two worksheets, one already in active memory and the other in a disk file.

/File **Xtract** is used to take a portion of a worksheet and save it in a disk file.

/File **Erase** is used to remove a file from the disk directory.

/File **List** is used to display the disk directory.

/File **Import** is used to bring non-worksheet file data into a worksheet.

/File **Directory** is used to change the default directory.

/File **Admin** is used to lock files in a network system, to create a listing of files on the worksheet, and to update all values from linked files.

/PRINT COMMANDS

/Print **Printer** sends a copy of the worksheet to a printer.

/Print **File** sends a copy of the worksheet to a disk file.

/Print . . . **Range** is used to designate the area of the worksheet to be printed.

/Print . . . **Line** is used to advance the paper in the printer one line.

/Print . . . **Page** is used to advance the paper to the next page.

/Print . . . **Options** is used to alter the effect of the printout. Options include **Header**, **Footer**, **Margins**, **Borders**, printer **Setup** codes, **Pg-Length**, and others.

/Print . . . **Clear** is used to reset various settings.

/Print . . . **Align** is used to inform Lotus that you have manually set the paper to the top of the page.

/Print . . . **Go** is used to produce the printout or disk file.

/Print . . . **Quit** is used to return to READY mode.

/GRAPH COMMANDS

/Graph **Type** is used to designate the type of graph to be drawn.

/Graph **X**, /Graph **A**, /Graph **B**, /Graph **C**, /Graph **D**, /Graph **E**, and /Graph **F** are used to designate the ranges that contain the data to be graphed.

/Graph **Reset** is used to remove range settings from the graph.

/Graph **View** is used to display the graph.

/Graph **Save** is used to store the graph image in a .PIC file that can be printed.

/Graph **O**ptions is used to enhance the graph display. Among the options are **L**egend, **F**ormat (lines and/or symbols) for line and XY graphs, **T**itles, **G**rid, **S**cale sizing and format, **C**olor or **B**&W display, and **D**ata-Labels.

/Graph **N**ame is used to assign names to different sets of graph settings so you can have more than one graph with a worksheet.

/Graph **G**roup is used to assign multiple graph ranges in one step.

/Graph **Q**uit is used to return to READY mode.

/DATA COMMANDS

/Data **F**ill is used to enter a series of numbers into a range.

/Data **T**able is used to compute tables with the results of equations with one or two variable values.

/Data **S**ort is used to arrange data in a particular order.

/Data **Q**uery is used to select records for further analysis based on a criterion.

/Data **D**istribution is used to compute a distribution table.

/Data **M**atrix is used to **I**nvert a matrix or **M**ultiply two matrices.

/Data **R**egression is used to compute regression statistics.

/Data **P**arse is used to divide imported text data into label and value entries.

/SYSTEM COMMAND

/System is used to call the operating system while retaining the worksheet in memory.

/ADD-IN COMMANDS

/Add-In **A**ttach is used to load an add-in program into memory.

/Add-In **D**etach is used to remove a specific add-in program from memory.

/Add-In **I**nvoke is used to activate a specific add-in program.

/Add-In **C**lear is used to remove all add-in programs from memory.

/Add-In **Q**uit returns control to the READY mode.

/QUIT COMMAND

/Quit is used to exit from Lotus to the operating system.

INDEX

TOPICAL INDEX

E

S

SYMBOLS INDEX

COMMANDS INDEX

/ COMMANDS

MACRO PROGRAMMING COMMANDS

FUNCTIONS INDEX

KEYBOARD INDEX

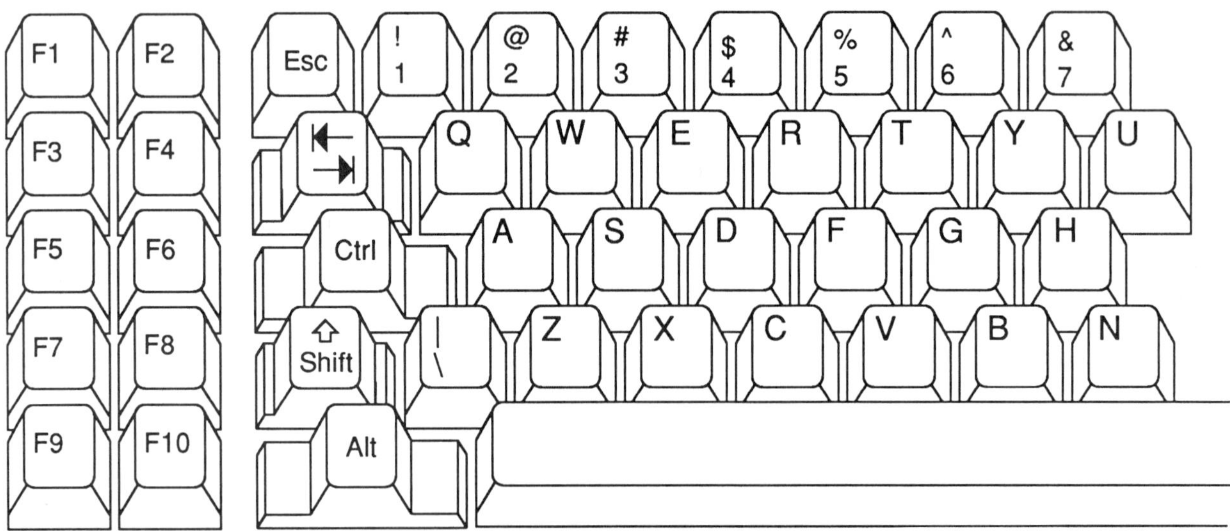

Standard Keyboard

DOS Keyboard

The last command entered at the DOS prompt is stored in a template buffer.

DEL	Does not copy the current template position to the command line
ESC	Voids the new command line and leaves template unchanged
F1	Plays back one character at a time from the template
F2	Plays back all characters from the template up to a specified character
F3	Plays back the remaining characters in the template
F4	Skips over all characters in the template up to a specified character
F5	Causes the current line to be the new template
F6	Inserts an End-of-file mark at the cursor location
Ins	Causes command line to toggle between insert mode (from keyboard) and insert mode (from the template)

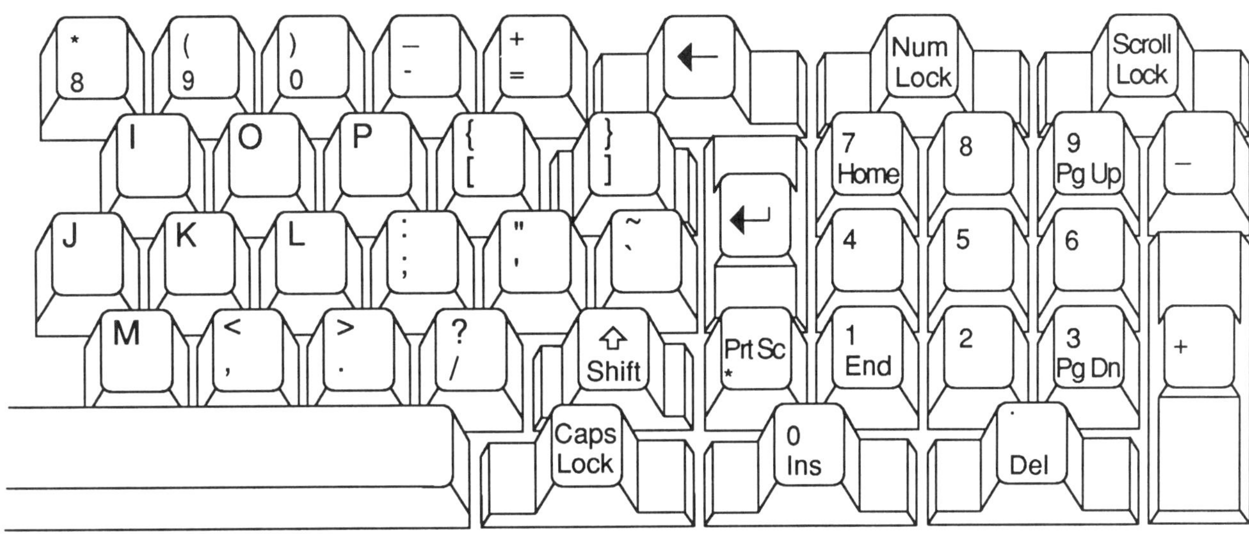

IBM PC Abbreviations

Alt--Alternate Key
Caps Lock--Capital Letter Lock Key
Crtl--Control Key
Del--Delete Key
End--End Key
Esc--Escape Key
Home--Home Key
Ins--Insert Key
Num Lock--Number Lock Key
PgDn--Page Down Key
PgUp--Page Up Key
PrtSc--Print Screen Key
Return--Enter Command Key

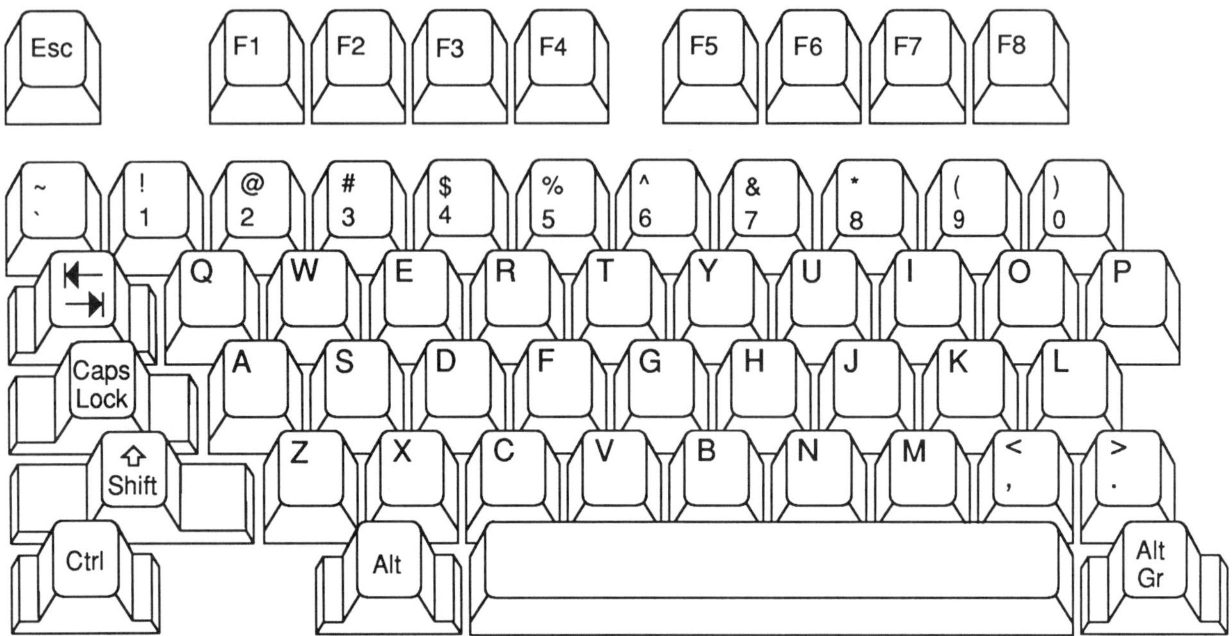

Enhanced Keyboard

DOS Keyboard

The last command entered at the DOS prompt is stored in a template buffer.

DEL Does not copy the current template position to the command line
ESC Voids the new command line and leaves template unchanged
F1 Plays back one character at a time from the template
F2 Plays back all characters from the template up to a specified character
F3 Plays back the remaining characters in the template
F4 Skips over all characters in the template up to a specified character
F5 Causes the current line to be the new template
F6 Inserts an End-of-file mark at the cursor location
Ins Causes command line to toggle between insert mode (from keyboard) and insert mode (from the template)

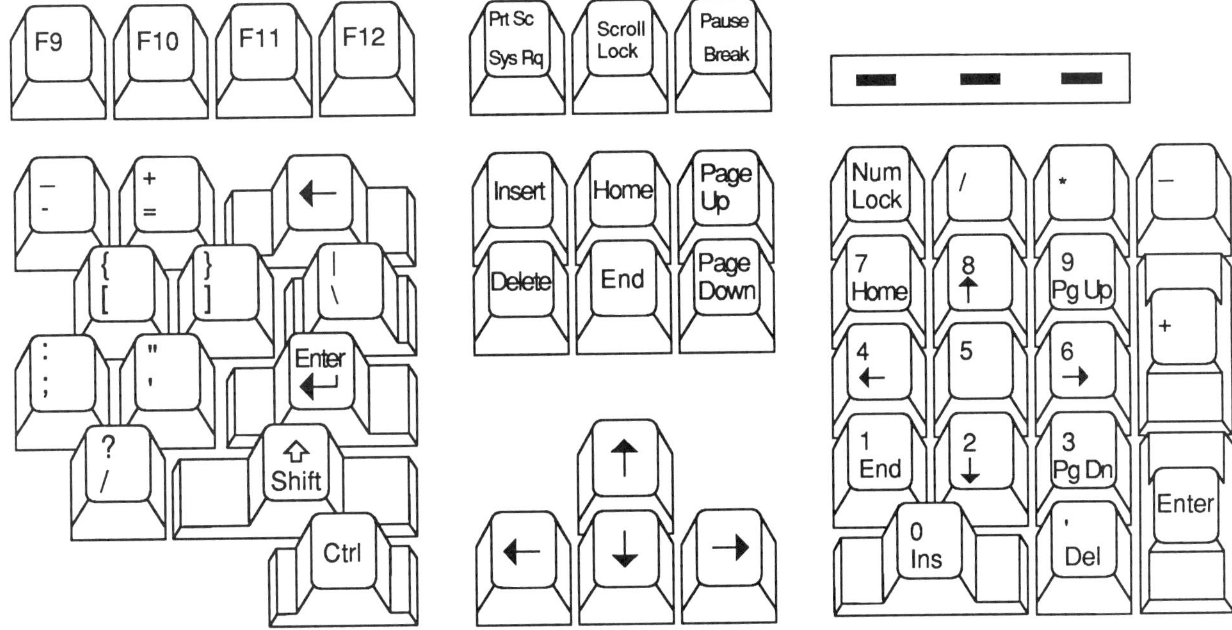

IBM PC Abbreviations

Alt--Alternate Key
Caps Lock--Capital Letter Lock Key
Crtl--Control Key
Del--Delete Key
End--End Key
Esc--Escape Key
Home--Home Key
Ins--Insert Key
Num Lock--Number Lock Key
PgDn--Page Down Key
PgUp--Page Up Key
PrtSc--Print Screen Key
Enter--Enter Command Key

NOTES

NOTES

NOTES

NOTES

NOTES

NOTES

NOTES

IMPORTANT:PLEASE READ BEFORE OPENING DISKETTE PACKAGE.
THIS TEXT IS NOT RETURNABLE IF SEAL IS BROKEN.

STUDENT DATA DISK
LIMITED USE LICENSE

By accepting this license, you have the right to use the Software and the accompanying documentation, but you do not become the owner of these materials.

1. PERMITTED USES
You are granted a non-exclusive limited license to use the Software under the terms and conditions stated in this License. You may:

a. Use the Software on a single computer.
b. Make a single copy of the Software in machine readable form solely for backup purposes in support of your use of the Software on a single machine. You must reproduce and include the copyright notice on any copy you make.
c. Transfer this copy of the Software and the License to another user if the other user agrees to accept the terms and conditions of this License. Transfer of this license may only be within education. If you transfer this copy of the Software you must also destroy the backup copy you made. Transfer of this copy of the Software and the License automatically terminates this License as to you.

2. PROHIBITED USES
You may not use, copy, modify, distribute or transfer the Software or any copy, in whole or in part, except as expressly permitted in this License.

3. TERMS
This License is effective when you open the diskette package and remains in effect until terminated. You may terminate this License at any time by ceasing all use of the Software and destroying this copy and any copy you have made. It will also terminate automatically if you fail to comply with the terms of this License. Upon termination, you agree to cease all use of the Software and destroy all copies.

4. DISCLAIMER OF WARRANTY
Except as stated herein, the Software is licensed "as is" without warranty of any kind, express or implied, including warranties of merchantability or fitness for a particular purpose. You assume the entire risk as to the quality and performance of the Software. You are responsible for the selection of the Software to achieve your intended results and for the installation, use, and results obtained from it. West Publishing and West Services do not warrant the performance of nor results that may be obtained with the Software. West Services does warrant that the diskette(s) upon which the Software is provided will be free from defects in materials and workmanship under normal use for a period of thirty days from the date of delivery to you as evidenced by a receipt. Some states do not allow the exclusion of implied warranties so the above exclusion may not apply to you. This warranty gives you specific legal rights. You may also have other rights which vary from state to state.

5. LIMITATION OF LIABILITY
Your exclusive remedy for breach by West Services of its limited warranty shall be replacement of any defective diskette upon its return to West at the above address, together with a copy of the receipt, within the warranty period. If West Services is unable to provide you with a replacement diskette which is free of defects in material and workmanship, you may terminate this License by returning the Software and the license fee paid hereunder will be refunded to you. In no event will West be liable for any lost profits or other damages including direct, indirect, incidental, special, consequential or any other type of damages arising out of the use or inability to use the Software even if West Services has been advised of the possibility of such damages.

6. GOVERNING LAW
This Agreement will be governed by the laws of the State of Minnesota.

You acknowledge that you have read this license and agree to its terms and conditions. You also agree that this license is the entire and exclusive agreement between you and West and supersedes any prior understanding or agreement, oral or written, relating to the subject matter of this agreement.

West Publishing Company

QUICK REFERENCE

Lotus 1-2-3

File Commands	Purpose
/FileCombine	to consolidate files
/FileImport	to retrieve a non-Lotus file
/FileRetrieve	to retrieve a file from disk
/FileSave	to place a file on disk
/FileXtract	to place a portion of a file on disk
/PrintFile	to print to a file
Translate (Lotus Access System)	to change file format

Enter/Edit Commands	Purpose
/Copy	to duplicate cell entries
/Move	to rearrange cell entries
/Quit	to exit Lotus to operating system
/RangeErase	to clear an area of the spreadsheet
/RangeFormat	to change display of values
/RangeName	to assign a name to a cell or range of cells
/RangeProtect	to prevent alteration of cell contents
/RangeUnprotect	to permit alteration of cell contents
/System	to exit to operating system, leaving Lotus and worksheet in memory
/WorksheetColumnSet-width	to change width of columns
/WorksheetDelete	to remove entire row or column from spreadsheet
/WorksheetErase	to clear entire spreadsheet
/WorksheetGlobal	to change various modes of operation and settings
/WorksheetGlobalColumn-width	to change width of all columns
/WorksheetGlobalFormat	to change display of values
/WorksheetGlobalLabel-prefix	to establish default placement of labels
/WorksheetGlobalRecalculation	to affect method of calculation
/WorksheetInsert	to insert a row or column into spreadsheet
/WorksheetStatus	to display available space and other items
/WorksheetTitle	to prevent columns or rows from scrolling
/WorksheetWindow	to split spreadsheet into two parts

Printer Commands	Purpose
/PrintPrinter	to print to printer
PrintGraph (Lotus Access System)	to print a graph

Graphics and Database Commands	Purpose
/DataSort	to sort rows or columns of data
/DataQuery	to query database
/Graph	to draw a graph on the screen